Y0-BCB-322

Class, Ideology, and the Rights of Nobles During the French Revolution

SECTION POISSONNIÈRE. 55.

LE COMITÉ DE SURVEILLANCE RÉVOLUTIONNAIRE,

AUX AUTORITÉS CIVILES ET MILITAIRES.

Le 5 floréal de, l'an 2e de la République Française, une et indivisible.

En vertu du Décret du 27 Germinal, *concernant les ex-nobles et les étrangers des pays avec lesquels la République est en guerre;*

Laissez passer la nommée Marie Louise Martin femme de françois pierre alexandre taboureau de Montigny Exnoble

native de Paris

Département de Paris

~~District d~~

âgé de 41 ans taille de 5 p. 2 p.

cheveux et sourcils chatain front ordinaire

nez ordinaire yeux bleus bouche petite

menton pointu visage oval

allant à la Commune de Passy

Département de Paris

Les Membres du Comité révolutionnaire.

Pour copie conforme

A pass directing a noblewoman to leave Paris for Passy in 1794. See page 205. (Archives nationales F7 4779)

CLASS, IDEOLOGY, AND THE RIGHTS OF NOBLES DURING THE FRENCH REVOLUTION

BY

PATRICE HIGONNET

CLARENDON PRESS · OXFORD
1981

Oxford University Press, Walton Street, Oxford OX2 6DP

London Glasgow New York Toronto
Delhi Bombay Calcutta Madras Karachi
Kuala Lumpur Singapore Hong Kong Tokyo
Nairobi Dar es Salaam Cape Town
Melbourne Auckland

and associate companies in
Beirut Berlin Ibadan Mexico City

Published in the United States by
Oxford University Press, New York

British Library Cataloguing in Publication Data

Higonnet, Patrice
Class, ideology, and the rights of nobles during the French Revolution.
1. Nobility—France—History
I. Title
305.5'2'0944 HT647

ISBN 0–19–822583–0

Typeset by Latimer Trend and Co. Ltd, Plymouth
Printed in Great Britain at the University Press, Oxford
by Eric Buckley, Printer to the University

For †Ethel and Margaret

Facies non omnibus una,
Nec diversa tamen; qualem decet esse sororum.

Ovid, *Metamorphoses*, ii. 13–14

Acknowledgements

Many people have helped me to write this book, and I am grateful to all of them. I cannot mention by name all the students, friends, and colleagues who have patiently allowed me to discuss my ideas with them, but they will, I hope, find here and there problems and solutions which I could not have grasped without their help.

Even the list of those who have read this manuscript in part or in whole is too long. Dina Keller, Frederick Martin, and Jonathan Zeitlin helped to edit a text which Sarah Stewart typed with skill enhanced by fortitude. Stanley Hoffmann, Stephen Holmes, Julian Jacobs, Wesley Johnson, and Chuck Sabel also read these pages. I wish that I could have pleased them more by making my text at once more readable, personal, general, specific, and sociological.

Heartfelt thanks go to my former colleagues, H. Stuart Hughes and David Landes, both of them old friends whose judicious comments were of particular use to a former and devoted pupil. I wish to thank also my office-mates and friends at 5 Bryant Street, and Molly Nolan especially, many of them Marxists and none of them much interested in nobles.

I owe a great deal to the insights of Roberto Unger. It is a privilege to live in the company of so powerful a mind, and it is rare indeed to find such lucidity allied to unfailing optimism and generosity of spirit.

The Chinese have a custom that I much admire: guests at a banquet will sometimes place an unusually pleasing morsel on the plate of their neighbour. The gesture is self-contained and requires no counterpart. I hope that this is the way that my parents feel about the help they have given me. I am grateful for their advice on the structure and style of this book. I was touched also by the solicitude of my parents-in-law, and I now understand, as I did not before, that former chairmen of English departments have especial insights into the genius of the English language which ordinary mortals cannot hope to gain. Their help went far beyond the call of duty. My gratitude to them is matched only by my feelings for them, as it is also for their daughter, Margaret.

Her untiring friendship and boundless patience did not blunt her judgement; my affection for her thrives on the respect I have of her many talents. *Ilusión*.

Contents

Chronological Table of some events relating to the Revolution and to legislation or decisions concerning nobles and émigrés

1774–1776	Turgot's ministry
1787, 22 February	Assembly of the Notables
1788, 8 August	Convocation of the Estates General
1789, 24 January	Royal decision on the organization of the Estates General
1789, 5 May	First meeting of the Estates General
1789, 17 June	Third Estate styles itself the National Assembly
1789, 14 July	Storming of the Bastille
1789, 20 July	Beginning of the Great Fear
1789, 4–11 August	*Abolition of the feudal system 'in its entirety'*
1789, 5–6 October	Crowd marches to Versailles; King returns to Paris
1790, 28 February	*Abolition of the nobility's monopoly on promotion to the Officer corps*
1790, 19–23 June	*Abolition of the nobility*
1790, 12 July	Civil Constitution of the Clergy
1790, 14 July	Fête de la Fédération
1790, 16 August	*Abolition of the Parlements*
1790, September	*Regulation of promotions in the army*
1791, 14 June	Le Chapelier Law
1791, 20 June	Flight of the King to Varennes
1791, 25 June	Émigrés' right to collect pensions abolished
1791, 17 July	Massacre of the Champs de Mars
1791, 27 September 16 October	*Further decrees on the illegality of using titles of nobility*
1791, 1 October	First meeting of the Legislative Assembly

1791, 9 November	*Assembly passes legislation against émigrés*
1791, 11–12 November	*Royal vetoes on decrees relating to titles of nobility and émigrés*
1791, 12 December	Robespierre's speech against war. Split between Girondins and Montagnards appears
1792, 9 February	*Émigré property placed 'sous la main de la nation'*
1792, 15 March	Formation of a Girondin Ministry
1792, 30 March 8 April	*Legislation against émigrés*
1792, 20 April	War declared against the King of Bohemia and Hungary
1792, 12–16 May	*Archives relating to orders of chivalry are ordered burnt*
1792, 19–24 May	*Genealogical titles in public archives are ordered to be burnt*
1792, 13 June	Girondin Ministry dismissed by Louis XVI
1792, 19 June	*Assembly orders genealogical titles to be burnt*
1792, 20 June	Tuileries palace invaded by a mob
1792, 25 July	*Section du Louvre denounces 'l'aristocratie nobiliaire'*
1792, late July	Girondins draw closer to the monarchy
1792, 10 August	Monarchy overthrown
1792, mid-August to mid-September	*Laws passed against émigrés; parents of émigrés to be held as hostages; confiscation of émigré property*
1792, 2–16 September	September Massacres
1792, 19 September	*Suppression of the Order of Malta*
1792, 21 September	Abolition of the monarchy; Convention meets
1792, 23 October	*Death penalty for captured émigrés in military units and for émigrés who have returned to France*
1792, 26 November	*Émigrés who had returned to France since the outbreak of the Revolution*

	are ordered to leave Paris within a day, France within eight days
1793, 21 January	Execution of Louis XVI
1793, 14 February	*Reward for information leading to the arrest of émigrés*
1793, 26 March	*Disarming of all nobles and ci-devants seigneurs*
1793, 28 March–9 April	*Variety of anti-émigré legislation enacted. Émigrés banished forever*
1793, 27 March–5 April	General Dumouriez betrays the Republic
1793, 1 April	*Marat asks that noble generals be relieved of their army commands*
1793, 31 May 2 June	Fall of the Girondins
1793, 24 June	Adoption by the Convention of the Constitution of 1793
1793, 17 July	*Feudal documents ordered to be burnt*
1793, 5 September	Second arrest of the enragé Roux
1793, 29 September	Maximum adopted for a large number of commodities
1793, October	Terror begins
1793, 19 October	*Decree on the destruction of chateaux-forts*
1793, October	Dechristianization begins
1793, 31 October	Execution of the Girondins
1793, 17 November (27 brumaire an II)	*Further codification of anti-émigré legislation*
1793, November–December	War turns to the advantage of the Republicans
1794, February–March	Crisis of ventôse; bourgeois and popular revolutions diverge in earnest
1794, early March (3, 8, and 13 ventôse an II)	Decrees of ventôse on the sequestration of the property of suspects
1794, 24 March (4 germinal an II)	Execution of the Hébertists
1794, 5 April (16 germinal an II)	Execution of Danton and Desmoulins

1794, 16 April (27 germinal an II)	*Law barring nobles from public office and exiling them from Paris and from fortified cities*
1794, 20 April (1 floréal an II)	*Law on the division of émigré property*
1794, 10 June (22 prairial an II)	Great Terror begins
1794, 27 July (9 thermidor an II)	Fall of Robespierre
1794, 3 August (16 thermidor an II)	*Prohibition of nobles in public office repealed*
1794, 21 September	Prorogation of the Maximum (temporary suspension of price controls)
1794, 26 October (5 brumaire an III)	*Individuals cleared of the charge of emigration have a right to their property*
1794, 12 November (22 brumaire an III)	Jacobin Club is closed
1794, 24 December (4 nivôse an III)	Maximum abolished
1795, 20–23 May (1–4 prairial an III)	Sans-culotte insurrection of prairial
1795, 21 July (3 thermidor an III)	Victory of Hoche at Quiberon
1795, 19 September (3e journée complémentaire)	*Confirmation of laws against émigrés*
1795, 23 September (1 vendémiaire an IV)	Constitution of the Directory is proclaimed
1795, 5 October (13 vendémiaire an IV)	'Royalist' insurrection in Paris
1795, 25 October (3 brumaire an IV)	*Law forbidding access to public office for émigrés*
1795, 26 October (4 brumaire an IV)	*General amnesty decreed for everyone except émigrés*
1796, 10 May (21 floréal an IV)	Babeuf's conspiracy is quashed
1796, 4 December (14 frimaire an V)	*Law of 3 brumaire an IV is upheld though émigrés recover some civil rights*
1797, 20–31 March (germinal an V)	Conservative victory at the election for the Corps Legislatif
1797, 4 May	*Repeal of the law of 3 brumaire an IV*

(15 floréal an V)	*disbarring émigrés from civil office and other civil rights*
1797, 4 September (18 fructidor an V)	*Republican coup against the newly elected conservative deputies. The law of 3 brumaire an IV is revived and extended to the relatives of émigrés*
1797, 29 November (9 frimaire an VI)	*Nobles deprived of French citizenship*
1798, 11 May (22 floréal an VI)	Purge of left wing deputies
1799, 12 July (24 messidor an VII)	*Law on Hostages*
1799, 9 November (18 brumaire an VIII)	Napoleon's coup against the Directory
1799, 9 December	*The émigrés shipwrecked at Calais are ordered to be released and deported*
1799, 27 December	*The 1797 laws against nobles are held to have lapsed*
1800, 26 February	*The requests of émigrés who wish to have their names removed from the émigré listings to be considered within four months*
1800, 1 March (10 vendémiaire an VIII)	*Rehabilitation of all émigré nobles who had voted for the abolition of feudal dues on 4 August, 1789*
1800, 3 March (12 vendémiaire an VIII)	*Émigré lists are declared closed*
1802, 26 April (6 floréal an X)	*General amnesty for émigrés; their unsold properties are to be restored to them*

Chapter One

Introduction

i. The rights of nobles during the French Revolution

The privileges of nobility were abolished in France on the night of 4 August, 1789, as was nobility itself one year later. Nobles then became private citizens, equal to others before the law. But in November 1797, well after the fall of Robespierre, the rights of the noble-born fell to a new low: all nobles, including babes in arms, were deprived of French citizenship. For some Frenchmen, at least, birth had proved a liability stronger than the claims of liberty, equality, and fraternity. The vicissitudes of the rights of nobles during the French Revolution were far-reaching indeed. But historians have shown little interest in examining this subject, which they have always considered to be a 'non-problem'. One might as well worry, in their view, about the rights of bankers during the Russian Revolution.

This lack of concern is puzzling. The role of nobles in France before and after the Revolution is recognized to be a critical aspect of the social, political, and even economic history of that country. Moreover, the intervening years of the French Revolution have been more diligently scrutinized than any other period of modern history, as well they might, since the Revolution is the central world-historical event of recent times. To be sure, it is perhaps still impossible to write the total history of the French nobility during these years because the archival work on which such a study must be based is still incomplete. But the documentary evidence for the changing rights of nobles, which is a critical aspect of that larger whole, is plentiful and unexploited. The subject deserves attention and the state of the art allows an adequate discussion of that aspect of the question at least.

There is no doubt that the question of the rights of nobles has wide-ranging implications for the history of the entire French Revolution. The different and contradictory restrictions that were imposed on nobles from 1789 to 1799 are a barometer that helps to gauge the extent of the Revolutionary bourgeoisie's ideological devotion to the principles of popular sovereignty. They also express the bourgeoisie's shifting appreciation of the relationship of public good and virtue to the rights of individuals and especially to individualism in property. The fluctuating scope of the rights of nobles is an indirect but telling indication of the bourgeoisie's varying commitment to the central values of equality and community: eager to proclaim in 1789 that all men are equal, bourgeois Revolutionaries after 1794 were convinced that some are more equal and virtuous than others.

Two groups were pushed out, at the top and at the bottom. In late 1793/4, the sans-culottes were repressed; in 1794, and again in 1797, nobles were denied the rights of citizenship. One of my aims will be to show that the exclusion of these two very different groups had a common cause in the interplay of ideology and class during the years of Revolution. Finally, of course, the shrinkage during the French Revolution of the rights of men born noble holds our attention because the persecution of any group defined by birth has a lively and horrid interest for our generation.

The general social context in which the 'nobles question' will be considered here relates to interpretations of caste and class in French society on the eve of the Revolution. Most historians now agree that France in the latter decades of the eighteenth century was increasingly a class society, characterized by the breakdown of traditional corporatist entities such as guilds, professions, estates, and status groups. Classically Marxist historians have gone on to argue that the older divisions of estates between noble and burgher had after 1750 taken on a new meaning because the aristocracy was still committed to the defence of 'feudalism' while the bourgeoisie was now eager to create new social and political forms with the help, if need be, of the 'people'. Revisionist historians, on the other hand, have suggested that this Marxist (or, as they would have it, vulgar Marxist) view is off the mark. They admit that France in 1789 was no longer a society of estates, but their claim is that the renewed social structure did not revolve around the conflict of modern bourgeoisie and of a traditionalist nobility. In their minds, the basic social conflict was now of the poor against the rich, that is, of the unpropertied mass of landless peasants and future sans-culottes versus a propertied and composite élite. For the revisionists, the gap between bourgeois and nobles is far less important than it is for the Marxists.

The distinction is fundamental. To side with the Marxists is to say that the growing radicalism of the Revolution was the realization of the bourgeoisie's unrelenting desire as a coherent class to destroy feudalism, a goal which implies a series of bourgeois concessions in both town and country to the popular masses without whose support the bourgeoisie could never have destroyed the monarchy and the nobility, the two bulwarks of the traditional feudal social order. To side with the revisionists, however, is to suggest that the unfolding of the Revolution after the summer of 1789 was a mistake. True, in June and July of that year, historical logic required that the new propertied élite should topple the discredited divine-right monarchy of the Bourbons who had abandoned the task of institutional modernization. But the revisionists also insist on the uselessness of insurrectionary steps after 1789, steps whose ultimate effect was to divide and weaken the varying segments of the propertied élite.

For the Marxists, the elimination of the traditionalist monarchy is relatively unimportant. What really matters for them is the creation of a historical alliance of the bourgeoisie and the people against feudalism. For the revisionists, however, the Revolutionary bourgeoisie in 1791, and perhaps even in late 1789, lost track of its basic goal, which was the defence of property. The Revolution broke down. What happened in Britain in 1688, that is to say, the forging of an alliance between enterprising gentry landlords and the commercial bourgeoisie within the political context of a parliamentary, non-bureaucratic monarchy, 'ought' to have happened in France and would indeed have taken place if fortuitous events and circumstances, such as the obtuseness of the King, had not intervened. Because of this political breakdown, claim the revisionists, it was only in 1814 that the French propertied élite finally achieved what it had consciously desired in 1789—equality before the law, a modernized institutional system, and the rule of an integrated élite in a parliamentary monarchy.

The view presented here borrows from both the Marxists and the revisionists, but it emphasizes that the Revolutionary bourgeoisie was more divided in its opinions than has been allowed. The central argument of this book (derived ironically from Marx himself)* is that the bourgeoisie's drift towards anti-nobilism† was neither inevitable nor accidental. Had circumstances been more propitious, the bourgeoisie might have

* See Appendix 1.

† 'Anti-nobilism' is a neologism. (Anti-aristocratism is the more proper term.) But the use of this barbarism can perhaps be justified by the confusion surrounding the meaning of the term aristocrat during the French Revolution (see pp. 152–3).

right away established a working agreement with the more liberal nobles. But this did not take place. Though basically intent on maintaining the domination of property over non-property, the bourgeoisie, as I see it, none the less drifted towards an egalitarian commitment to the sans-culottes which implied abhorrent economic and social levelling. Driven to the left by the ensuing *dérapage* or deviation of the Revolution, the bourgeoisie found itself in a hopeless situation which it attempted to resolve by giving a moralistic and communitarian definition of the state and, in turn, by persecuting nobles as proof of its commitment to that universalist view.

My interpretation, then, is in many ways similar to those of historians like Furet and Chaussinand-Nogaret, without whose work this book would make little sense.

At the same time, though dependent on the work of the revisionists, this book also has many points of contact with the classical Marxist interpretation, that of Mazauric and Soboul especially. The French bourgeoisie, though quite close to the aristocracy (itself in 1789 far more modern than it had been), was also hostile to nobles and theoretically sympathetic to the poor. The bourgeoisie did not realize how contradictory its views were and how dangerous its egalitarian yearnings would be to the defence of property, which, in the end, was its first social goal; that ambiguity often described by Marxists, is the essence of the ideological context in which the description of the rights of nobles will be set in these pages.

Though adamantly committed to the particularist cause of the absolute rights of private property, the bourgeoisie was also convinced that different social groups could naturally and harmoniously co-exist within the compass of a virtuous, all powerful, but limited state at once organic and liberal. Though clearly a social class, with interests antithetical to those of other classes, the bourgeoisie blithely assumed that if caste were destroyed, social harmony would then effortlessly prevail. Thus, it interpreted 'public opinion' as the expression of society's common sense rather than of the particular needs of those bourgeois writers and readers who determined what public opinion was. In 1789, the French bourgeoisie misread the message on the wall, and took up an egalitarian, anti-noble rhetoric as its ideological mode. It identified with 'le peuple', most of whom owned no property, rather than with other owners of property, many of whom were nobles.

The composite view defended here is that the bourgeoisie after 1789 could follow one of two antithetical policies. It could unite with the nobles to create a state which would recognize the passive equality of citizens before the law but emphasize the rights of the propertied interest; or it could choose to ignore nobles in order to pursue an active alliance with 'le peuple'. The latter position made no sense in terms of the defence of property, but it did make ideological sense, because, as it happens, the ideology which expressed the French bourgeoisie's drive for political power as a Revolutionary class was still the universalist, classically humanist idea that *all* men are created equal and that all men, regardless of property, might live harmoniously in a casteless, classless, and virtuous polis.

The two policies were obviously exclusive, but both prevailed, if at different times. In 1789–91, the Revolutionary bourgeoisie tried to find a place in its new system both for nobles as citizens and for noble forms of property, i.e. seigneurial rights. In 1791–3, on the other hand, as the tempo of the Revolution quickened and the poor became more vociferous, nobles were sacrificed for demagogic reasons. The gods were athirst and concessions had to be made. But gradually, the bourgeoisie itself took fright. The contradictions between its universalist politics and its aims as a class could not be indefinitely sustained. In 1799, the problem was finally resolved: universalist politics were suspended and the rule of property in civil society, law, and business was firmly established. The state, which in 1794 had been defined as the incarnation of virtue and the scourge of vice, was now openly recognized as having for its first purpose to guarantee the supremacy of the propertied *honnêtes gens*. The state was now the incarnation of a sum of interests rather than the expression of transcendental moral values.

Most historians of the French Revolution have presented the history of the period in ineluctable terms. For the Marxist, the bourgeoisie was from the outset intent on the destruction of feudalism. For the revisionist historians, the bourgeoisie and the liberal nobles were in basic accord; they knew from the beginning what it was that they wanted and would have secured their ends if they had not been betrayed by the events of the times (e.g. losing the war, financial crisis, or counter-revolution). There was, according to the revisionists, a fortuitous *dérapage*, or slide, of the Revolution away from its understood, normative purpose—the union of élites—which had been reached in 1789–91 and would not have broken down had it not been for the fact that History sometimes depends on the likes of Cleopatra's nose.

Much is to be said for both of these interpretations. In accord with the revisionists, my thesis holds that a new composite class of notables was indeed coming into being; but I emphasize also the ideological incompleteness of the new social arrangements and the continued hostility of bourgeois to nobles. My own view is that the material basis of a 'one-class society' dominated by a single propertied élite may have been taking shape, but that the bourgeoisie's awareness of its new situation was in many ways circumscribed. Hence the ambivalence and volatility of its relationship with both nobles on the right and sans-culottes on the left. Hence also the variety of political possibilities which existed in 1789. That some were realized does not by any means imply that other solutions did not exist. As the revisionists suggest, an 'English' solution to the French problem was materially possible and could perhaps have been found. Many Frenchmen, such as Necker or the conservative liberal Monarchiens, wanted it.

Politically, therefore, the situation in 1789 was highly ambiguous. There were powerful factors which drove the bourgeoisie towards the left and the people, just as other factors might drive it to the right and the nobles. What took place was in my view neither inevitable nor fortuitous. An unbroken thread links the bourgeoisie's acceptance of nobles as individuals in 1789 to its rejection of nobles as citizens in 1794–7 to the final acceptance of nobles as fellow notables after 1799.

It will by now be clear that this book deals primarily with bourgeois attitudes to the rights of nobles rather than with these rights as such. The actual fate of nobles or other tangential matters, such as the size and purpose of aristocratic emigration, are introduced only in so far as they relate to the more central problem of bourgeois politics. More archival work needs to be done on the subjects that are peripheral to my topic, but the need for this work ought not, in my opinion, to be exaggerated. Much is known about nobles during the Revolution: aristocrats were very visible people, members before 1789 and after 1794 of legally distinct groups. Many nobles were highly literate, liked to complain, and, after 1815, had a vested interest in making the most of whatever misfortunes may have befallen them in preceding years. The archival work that I have done for this book (mostly on the fate of nobles in 1793–4) makes me think that the study of additional and as yet unpublished documents will confirm what is said here. I think it most unlikely that new archival research could dramatically reverse the understanding that is now possible of the behaviour of nobles during the Revolution. Nor would a more detailed examination of the activities of individual nobles seem likely to invalidate my argument, which is that the behaviour of nobles was in a sense irrelevant to their fate. What is chiefly relevant here is the amply documented evolution of bourgeois politics. My subject though focused on nobles is in truth the nature of Revolutionary politics.

I shall follow the changing bourgeois definitions of 'noble rights' through three periods, each of which answers to a basic phase of the first part of the Revolution. Though overlapping in no small degree, the three periods run from the summer of 1789 to the winter of 1791/2 and the failure of the Feuillants' policy of constitutional monarchy; then, from the decline and fall of monarchy to the rise of the Terror in the autumn of 1793; and, finally, through the Terror. From 1795 to 1799, a second, more feeble cycle reproduces the earlier turn.

The first period shows the determination of the 'reformist' bourgeois majority to accommodate nobles within the compass of bourgeois universalism, then in full if evanescent bloom. The second reveals a tactical and opportunistic persecution of nobles. Only the third, terroristic, phase involves the universalist ideology functioning in the void. Its culmination came on 29 November, 1797 (9 frimaire an VI) when two assemblies, devoted to the principle of equality for all regardless of birth, passed a decree which read that

> Les ci-devant*nobles et annoblis, c'est-à-dire, tous ceux qui avaient reçu la noblesse de leurs pères, ou qui l'avaient acquise transmissible héréditairement à leurs enfants, ne pourront exercer les droits de citoyen français dans les assemblées primaires, communales et électorales, ni être nommés à aucune fonction publique qu'après avoir rempli les conditions et les délais prescrits à l'égard des étrangers par l'article 10 de la Constitution (sur la naturalisation).

A unique decision: no state that had disallowed the importance of birth and established the equality of citizens before the law

* In French, the word 'ci-devant', which will often be used here, should be inflected only in its adjectival form. Thus, two 'ci-devants Marquis' but two 'ci-devant'. To follow this usage in English would be confusing, and I have arbitrarily chosed to inflect all plural forms of the word.

would again take such a backward step until the rise of Hitlerism and the passing of the Nuremberg laws of 1935.

ii. Bourgeois universalism: individualism and community

Like some figures out of Dante's inferno, the histories of France in the eighteenth century and of the French Revolution are at once inseparable and locked in unending combat. The second is the culmination of the first; the first is an anticipation of the second. Neither at this point can really be grasped in its own terms; nor can the constituent parts. The 'nobles problem' is no exception to the larger rule. Its unfolding after 1789 was, obviously, a response to the often fortuitous political upheavals of the decade of Revolution, but the range of Revolutionary possibilities was constrained by the shape of French culture before 1789. Of particular relevance, though this could hardly have been grasped before the Revolution, was the relationship of individualism and community in the world view of the Enlightened French public, two values that were thought complementary at the time but which appear antithetical in our own historically conditioned and post-Revolutionary perspective. For a variety of reasons, as shall be seen, the relative weight that was ascribed by literate opinion in France to these values proved to be of critical importance in determining the political choices that were to set the limits of the nobles problem. The Enlightened bourgeoisie's reluctance to place individualism (including individualism in property) at the centre of their social concerns went hand in hand with an illusory belief in their ability to conciliate individualism and community. That illusion in turn implied a denigration of nobles as the symbol of anti-communitarian selfishness and a slighting of their importance as potential defenders of private property.

It is to be doubted that most contemporaries would, at the time, have recognized individualism and community as the central concerns of their world view. Indeed, the conscious thrust of Enlightened social thought was decidedly elsewhere. What mattered was the struggle of mankind against the powers of darkness, against ignorance, superstition, and folly. 'Sapere aude!' For Immanuel Kant, this was the heart of the Enlightenment. The *Aufklärung*, in his words, was

> man's emergence from his self-imposed minority. This minority is the inability to use one's own understanding without the guidance of another.

It is self-imposed if its cause lies not in a lack of understanding, but in the lack of courage and determination to rely on one's own understanding and not another's guidance.[1]

Voltaire's *Écrasez l'Infâme* was an elliptical way of expressing the same idea. The enemies of man were fear and foolishness. By girding his loins against these foes which were outside himself, Enlightened man could triumph over prejudice and error.

This was the apparent message of the Enlightenment and most historians have described the period in these same terms. Peter Gay's treatment, for example, is cast in that mould. For him, the Enlightenment was a culmination of the Renaissance, and the grandest assertion of man's ability to know. The philosophes were 'The Party of Humanity'.

A different and much less positive view, however, may be maintained. With typical bombast, Malraux once declared that, although the ostensible motif of nineteenth-century politics had been that of republic versus monarchy, the real conflict of the period had been that between worker and capitalist. The remark is not as shallow as it first appears and by analogy can be applied to the eighteenth century. Then, the ostensible thrust of the Enlightenment was of Enlightened man against political tyranny and superstition, but the deeper problem was that of man against himself and society. Where did the rights of man stop and those of society begin? Or, in Rousseau's terms, what were the limits of the 'moi humain' and the 'moi commun'? These were questions *internal* to man's nature, and the resolution of their limits can now be shown to have been *sub specie aeternitatis* the central problem of Enlightened social thought. The socialist theoretician Mably (1709–85) stated the problem with great clarity: 'Tout Législateur est insensé, qui en voulant faire le bien public, ignore que je ne puis être remué que par mon avantage particulier.'[2]

Indeed, it may well be that eighteenth-century social theory has an especial meaning for us today because of this particular emphasis on man and society taken as a whole (a position which we still face) as against the social thought of the nineteenth century, which focused instead on the question of class against class (a conflict which is perhaps less sharply drawn today than it has ever been since the onset of the Industrial Revolution).

The social and political implications of individualism before 1789 were opaque, and in fact it is because the French Revolution dispelled much of this opacity that it, more than the American

Revolution, for example, was a truly world-historical event.

On the one hand, the Enlightenment, in nearly all of its myriad forms, was resolute in its assertion that the individual self, rather than the organic whole, should become the first concern of man. For Rousseau, self-love and an awareness of his own existence were the first concerns of man. For Montesquieu, 'self-interest was the strongest monarch in the world'. Diderot went further yet and at times drifted towards extreme individualism:

> Toute philosophie contraire à la nature de l'homme est absurde, ainsi que toute législation où le citoyen est forcé continuellement de sacrifier son goût et son bonheur pour le bien de la société. Je veux que la société soit heureuse; mais je veux l'être aussi; et il y a autant de manières d'être heureux qu'il y a d'individus. Notre propre bonheur est la base de tous nos vrais devoirs.[3]

In the debate that *Moi*, ostensibly the selfless and bourgeois paterfamilias, has with *Lui* in Diderot's dialogue, *Moi* is faced time and again with an objection that he cannot overcome: 'We must be whatever self-interest requires us to be.' That individualism should be the bedrock of social organization was commonly assumed in society at large as well, and Mme d'Épinay was perhaps speaking for her age when she wrote to the Abbé Galiani in 1769, 'la première loi est d'avoir soin de soi: n'est-ce pas?'[4]

The point was nicely made, but its specific implications, social or political, were not clear. At all levels the Enlightenment found it unusually difficult to sort out the overlapping spheres of individualism and community.

At the highest level of abstraction, the very essence of human nature was in question. Lockean psychology started from man as a *tabula rasa* who became himself through the exclusive working of his own sense perceptions; at the same time, however, man's sense of himself was widely understood to be a reflection of his place in the world around him; hence, for example, the intense Enlightened speculation on the nature of language. Speech was essentially a collective form, but without language each man's sense of himself would shrink, because it was through language that the concepts basic to our view of ourselves crystallized in our minds. In the same way, altruism was held to be an essential aspect of reflected egoism; but how could Robinson Crusoe be altruistic? Man's need to live in a community with other men was self-evident. 'Morality is private, but the stage is public.'[5] Enlightened thinkers felt the attraction of anarchic individualism, but they never yielded to it.

At a similarly abstract level, no trenchant dictate on the limits of individualism arose from the Enlightenment's reliance on natural law. All truths were imbedded in nature, but what indeed were these truths? Unlike Aquinas and the medieval schoolmen, Enlightened thinkers did not base natural law on God's will; natural law, as Montesquieu explained, was embedded in a more opaque *natura naturans*: 'Laws in their broadest sense are the necessary relations which are derived from the nature of things.' In addition, because natural law referred to the 'ordering order' (*ordo ordinans*),[6] natural law was not the mere sum of what had been arbitrarily decreed or enacted historically. Necessarily, the implications of such laws were unclear. Although Voltaire might swiftly cut the Gordian knot and peremptorily announce that 'a day suffices for a sage to know the duties of man', others found this same task more difficult. 'La Nature', wrote the physiocrat Mercier de la Rivière, 'est le premier instituteur de l'homme social . . . parce que c'est elle qui a voulu la réunion des hommes en société',[7] but the paradoxical limits which this partisan of economic individualism then proceeded to impose on the rights of community appeared downright unnatural to most of his contemporaries.

The extent here of what could safely be assumed was that, in nature, no man was an island. On that score, wide agreement did prevail. For Condillac (1715–80), the social contract was less the abrogation of an anarchic state of nature than the direct fulfilment of man's natural needs.[8] Mercier de la Rivière extended this view to encompass not just city-states or nation-states, but the human race as a whole:

Sans autre loi que celle de la propriété, sans autres connaissances que celle de la *raison essentielle et primitive*, de toutes les lois, sans autre philosophie que celle qui est enseignée par la nature à tous les hommes, nous voyons qu'il vient de se former une société qui jouit au dehors de la plus grande consistance politique et, au dedans, de la plus grande prospérité; nous voyons qu'il vient de s'établir parmi nous une réciprocité de devoirs et de droits, une *fraternité* qui nous intéresse tous à la conservation les uns des autres et dont les liens sacrés embrassent et tiennent unis tous les peuples étrangers.[9]

In fact, most enlightened philosophers, throughout the eighteenth century, were united on this crucial point. 'L'amour de la patrie', wrote Montesquieu, 'conduit à la liberté des mœurs, et la liberté des mœurs mène à l'amour de la patrie.' Morelly thought that benevolence and self-love were mirror images; and Holbach, a precursor of utilitarianism, flatly asserted that a vicious man would necessarily be a bad calculator.

Rousseau's awareness of the central duality of man and society was therefore hardly novel. What differed, of course, was the depth of understanding which he brought to this much-debated issue. Man, for Rousseau, was enmeshed in the life of the community. He might ignore politics but he could not ignore his fellow man. His *moi humain*, though distinct from his *moi commun*, also overlapped with it.

Rousseau's solution had two facets. First, society had to be made moral, or rather, be made moral again, a difficult thing to do since Rousseau believed that the progress of corruption, once it had begun, was nearly irresistible.[10] Indeed, where social mores were irreversibly corrupt, the citizen had no choice but to withdraw, a most cruel alternative for Rousseau, who thought that exile was, in truth, no solution at all. Man's sense of his *moi commun* was based on the habits and instincts of a lifetime. A moral man living in a moral society which was not his homeland would in all likelihood be miserably unhappy. *Ubi patria, ibi bene.*

Second, man should become more independent, less demanding, and, in a word, more virtuous, where, as Judith Shklar explains, 'virtue was self-love utterly transformed'.[11] Only then would each man be able to bring about within himself that 'reconciliation of duty and inclination' which was the central moral strategy of Rousseau's thought.[12] In this perspective, it may be added, education was crucial, as the author of *Émile* laid out in overwhelming detail. Everything that threatened man's sense of his *moi commun* was bad. All that supported it was good.[13] Man had to search within his soul to distinguish between an *amour propre*, a positive and integrative form of self-love, and an *amour de soi* which was selfish and exclusive.[14]

At a lower level of abstraction, in pragmatic social or political theory, for example, the Enlightenment's path to a reconciliation of selfishness and selflessness was no less hard to find. The praxis of 'civic humanism', the useful term that Pocock has assigned to the traditional political belief that individualism and community could be brought together, remained elusive.[15]

Property and luxury were two issues which illustrated the difficulty of resolving the rights of the one and the many. Was property a desirable political goal? Should the state attack or defend private wealth? Sound reasons could be marshalled on either side. On behalf of private property, it was said that a material independence enabled men to be free citizens. The preamble of the act of 1711, which made high landed qualification compulsory for all members of Parliament, claimed that it was 'securing the liberty of Parliament'. Similarly, Bolingbroke in the middle decades of the eighteenth century vigorously defended the propertied autonomy of the country gentry as the guarantee of its political freedom, and in some measure every philosophe before 1770, including Rousseau, concluded that some private property was undeniably desirable. Voltaire was positively enthusiastic about the whole matter, and wrote in the *Philosophical Dictionary*, 'Liberty and property. C'est le cri anglais. Il vaut mieux que "Saint Georges et mon Droit", "Saint Denis et Mont-joie". C'est le cri de la nature'.[16]

At the same time, of course, natural law and community reminded men that society taken as a whole also had rights over property, and that the great discrepancies of wealth were not only undesirable but positively evil since they gave to the few power over the many. Property, like individualism itself, was both desirable and undesirable, and the philosophes shuttled uneasily from condemnation to admiration of that institution.

Rousseau in his *Discours sur l'inégalité* explained that mankind had progressed and the arts had been founded only when the existence of the fruits of labour had enabled men to conceive of property. But what he granted here he soon withdrew, going on to say that the existence of property had also led to the creation of vast inequalities and insoluble conflicts: 'la société naissante fit place au plus horrible état de guerre'.[17] For Diderot, 'l'esprit de propriété' and 'l'esprit de communauté' may have diverged in theory, but *laissez-faire* was in practice unavoidable. Diderot at once deplored the inhumanity of life in coal mines and thought that to close the mines would ruin both state and society.[18] Helvetius, though convinced that modern nations were divided into oppressed and oppressors, none the less maintained that property was 'le droit le plus sacré . . . dieu moral des empires'.[19] Individuals had rights, but so did the community; private property was good, but it was also bad. The theme of luxury brought in focus similar, contradictory interpretations. In some respects, luxury was obviously undesirable. Why should one man have more while another man starved? And was it not true that the luxury trades catered to the useless classes, that is, essentially, to nobles who were the parasitic class *par excellence*? To encourage luxury was obviously to make a mockery of community. But, on the other hand, luxury gave pleasure, and the pursuit of pleasure gave meaning to individual sensibility. Its enjoyment provided a goal to life in a society which was extremely sensitive to the problems of individual happiness. Moreover, the claims of luxury gave employment to the poor and were an incentive to progress since the fruits of luxury were a proof of man's ingenuity and skill.

For those who craved both economic growth and virtue, the question of luxury was basically irresolvable. After the Revolution, in 1797, the conservative Republican Edouard Lefebvre, in his *Considérations politiques et morales sur la France constitutée en république*, did defend luxury on practical grounds: self-interest was indeed impure, but, practically speaking, experience had shown that the toleration of luxury was unavoidable.[20] E. G. Lenglet, a more radical Republican, came to the same conclusion at the same time: to be sure, the fruits of one's work, he explained, were the only ones to which man was really entitled, but was it not true that 'pour que tous aient le nécessaire, il faut que quelques uns aient du superflu'?[21] After 1799, the French bourgeoisie concluded that aristocrats did after all have a place in French life. But before 1789, the problems of property, luxury, or for that matter nobility were theoretically insoluble. Only the experience of the Revolution would enable the bourgeoisie to resolve these difficulties by making much more clear the incompatibility of individualism and community. Once that had been done, it then became far easier to accept private property, as well as the need for luxury, and with both of these, the presence of nobles also.

At a yet more pragmatic level, the Enlightenment was unable to describe the actual institutions of government which might best guarantee the varying rights of either individual or community. Should men rule themselves directly, as they did in the Swiss cantons? Should they instead, as Burke suggested, delegate their powers to representatives who would be able to rise above themselves and espouse the common good? Or should they rule themselves at all? Was not the rule of one Enlightened despot preferable to that of a hundred lawyers?

In a way, it is true, the problem as a whole did not matter then as much as might now be supposed: if it had, the range of acceptable political solutions would surely have been more narrow, as happened after 1789 when the overlap between institutions acceptable to both left and right vanished nearly overnight. Before 1789, however, it was widely assumed that politics or the nature of the state were not crucial because the very functions of the state did not matter very much. Once the natural order of society had been allowed to come into its own, the state would naturally atrophy. In this context, there was little to choose between bureaucratic reform or parliamentary rule. For the French, Prussia and Britain were both modern Enlightened states. For this reason, the philosophes, even when of a liberal frame of mind, did not hesitate to sing the virtues of Enlightened Despotism. If the prerogatives of the state were few, the power of even an unchecked monarch would necessarily be circumscribed. Diderot might, therefore, and with a straight face, simultaneously hail Catherine of Russia as the Semiramis of the North and proclaim that 'La vraie et légitime puissance a donc nécessairement des bornes'.[22] So could Rousseau assert simultaneously that the modern state must be all powerful and that Hobbes had been the apologist of 'an atrocious despotism'.

In any event, a desire to balance individualism and community did not *per se* lead the philosophes to any simple conclusions about political institutions. A convinced espousal of community and popular sovereignty in theory did not by any means lead to an acceptance of democracy in practice. In one sense, of course, natural law could be interpreted as justifying men's self-evident right to be free and self-governing. In practice, however, men, collectively taken, were thought to constitute an illiterate and savage mob. This was a problem which the tradition of civic humanism had faced by asserting that the rights of all were best defended by the preponderance of the few, of a wise, experienced, leisured, and, as it happens, propertied élite. It is striking to see with what eagerness this particular lesson was taken up by the most radical of the philosophes.

Theoretical or practical apologists of popular sovereignty, from Rousseau to Turgot, all rushed forward to say that the best institution of government was aristocracy; that is, rule by the few, not of course by an élite of birth but by an élite none the less. Though everyone agreed that the people were in theory admirable, an equal consensus prevailed about their contemporary frailty. Hume thought that the 'bulk of mankind' was governed by authority, not reason, and he did not think that men would become reasonable in the foreseeable future. Rousseau in *Émile* rejected not only life in the beau monde of the French capital but the mores of the uneducated poor as well. Condillac thought the people to be a ferocious animal. The Legislator, he wrote, 'se propose moins de conduire des êtres raisonnables, que de forcer des animaux qui n'ont que des passions'.[23] Democracy would culminate only in anarchy or slavery. Voltaire was no less harsh: 'A l'égard de la canaille?' he wrote to d'Alembert, 'je ne m'en mêle pas; elle restera toujours canaille. Je cultive mon jardin, mais il faut bien qu'il y ait des crapauds; ils n'empêchent pas mes rossignols de chanter.'[24] There was little point in trying to do much about it: 'on a jamais prétendu éclairer les cordonniers et les servantes; c'est le partage des apôtres'.[25]

There is no denying, then, the inconclusive nature of much of French social and political thought in the middle decades of the eighteenth century. It is with justice that Lucien Goldmann, a Marxist, has written that the social thought of these French philosophes rested on a fundamental contradiction, implicit in the simultaneous and unlimited defence of the 'essential mental categories of the French Enlightenment, freedom and equality'.[26] The point is not hard to prove, and it is developed also by the violently anti-Marxist historian, Talmon, who writes of these late eighteenth-century thinkers that they 'spoke the language of individualism while their preoccupations led to collectivism'.[27] That Talmon and Goldmann disagree radically on how this contradiction should have been resolved is not at issue. What matters is that the contradiction, latent in the works of men like Montesquieu or Rousseau, widened as the century went on. After 1789, most of these writers who had survived finally understood what had happened, and nearly to a man, rallied to the cause of property. But before 1789, in France, an apprehension of these contradictions in bourgeois universalism was beyond the reach of the *bourgeois moyen sensuel*.

* * *

Epistemologically and politically, then, the contradictory claims of community and individualism, or of democracy and élitism, had never been satisfactorily reconciled. In the 1770s and 1780s, rapid economic and social change made the problem even more complex. Commercial wealth, a newer and more unstable form, overshadowed the older and hence more tolerable landed wealth. Society, more concerned with money, appeared more 'corrupt'. The economic and cultural claims of individualism grew apace. The compromise of civic humanism, which had always been difficult to keep in balance, became ever more precarious.

As one would expect, Rousseau had a lively sense of living in such a changing age: 'The crisis is approaching,' he wrote, 'and we are on the edge of revolution.' Like King Carol of Romania, who insisted that his son, who was in fact later deposed, should learn a manual skill—in this instance that of a locomotive engineer—Rousseau had Émile master the trade of a carpenter so that he might be protected against the 'inscrutable changes' which were about to destroy society.[28] Indeed, Rousseau counted as his single greatest insight that the progress of the arts, like the development of urban life, was not a force for good as everyone had assumed, but a force for evil. Society was changing, but it was changing for the worse. Men as individuals were certainly no better than they had been.[29] The lust for power and possession, like the claims of ambition and vanity, were more than ever the dominant force of the age. A great crash was in the offing.

What Rousseau understood in moral terms can, of course, be interpreted economically and socially as the effect of the rise of capitalism, that is, of the growing importance in human affairs of the laws of the market, coupled with the acceptance of rationality as the individual's best mode of defence and self-aggrandizement. It is hardly necessary to belabour the fact that capitalism and individualism progressed by leaps and bounds in north-western Europe and in America during the eighteenth century. The decline of corporatism in both France and Britain, the enclosure movement in Britain, the development of banks and credit are so many hallmarks of capitalistic development. Manifestations of a growing sense of individualism are equally well known: the legal rights of individuals were everywhere proclaimed in property, law, and religion. The pursuit of individual happiness in this society, like fears of death or boredom and the fascination of suicide has been the subject of elaborate study.[30]

This new vigour of individualism and of capitalism placed intolerable strains on the ethic of civic humanism and community. By shattering the vision of a virtuous society, the development of individualistic capitalism forced a drastic rethinking of the central problem of eighteenth-century social thought, that is, of the balance between individual and community. Only two durable solutions were possible.

The first, capitalist, solution accepted the new claims of individualism and accordingly redefined the ancient concepts of 'community' and 'the people' which would now have to be adapted to the needs of economic individualists, that is to say, of private property, unfettered and triumphant. The second solution was the opposite of the first. The claims of community were reasserted and even strengthened. Private property, which had been tolerated, was now condemned. The distribution of wealth was now said to be a collective responsibility.

Between these two poles lay, however, a third but unstable solution that endeavoured to reconcile recent capitalism with the ancient tradition of civic humanism. It claimed that individualism, now become capitalist and more demanding, might none the less be fitted into the framework of a classically virtuous society. This third and unstable solution, I have called bourgeois universalism.

As was to be expected, the most developed restatement of civic humanism along capitalist lines took place in Britain and in America, which were the two societies of the European world where traditional and corporatist economic modes had been most completely undermined by the inroads of market forces. Civic humanism had defined man as a virtuous citizen; but Englishmen and Scots, such as Mandeville, Davenant, and Adam Smith, redefined him as a culture-bound being, where culture was a protean form which varied as did economic change. They saw, in J. G. A. Pocock's words, that 'as the goods produced, and the techniques of producing and distributing them grew . . . more complex, human culture, imagination, and personality correspondingly increased in complexity'.[31]

In the past, the ideal state had embodied immortal principles of virtue, defined in terms of immutable natural law. But increasingly, the public good, in the new perspective, was presented in terms of consensus and changing interests. The business of statecraft was to accommodate the fluid needs of the different interests that made up society at any given time. Virtue had become, so to speak, a side-effect of other, more critical concerns.

In this context, to be a good citizen was to be industrious and productive. The virtue or wholeness of man was no longer at issue. What mattered above all was the individual's ability to produce. There was, for example, a shift on the question of the division of labour. Rousseau had railed against it, since this method of organizing work weakened man's ability to stand alone and placed men in a state of forced dependence on one another. Adam Smith, to the contrary, saw in the division of labour the great vehicle of technical progress. So did the abbé Sieyes, perhaps the most explicit apologist of private property in France before and during the Revolution. For Sieyes, work was *the* basic social value and the Third Estate had rights that nobles did not have because it was the Third that produced the goods which the nobles merely consumed. All labour was good, as was its division. In Sieyes's view:

La nature nous a soumis à la loi du travail; elle nous a fait les premières avances, ensuite elle nous a dit: veux tu jouir? travaille. C'est pour une consommation plus assurée, plus abondante, plus choisie, et par conséquent pour une plus grande énergie de production, et par conséquent pour garantir et perfectionner de plus en plus son travail, que l'homme est censé s'unir avec ses semblables. La raison, ou du moins l'expérience, dit encore à l'homme: tu réussiras d'autant mieux dans tes occupations, que tu sauras les borner. En portant toutes les facultés de ton esprit sur une partie seulement de l'ensemble des travaux utiles, tu obtiendras un plus grand produit avec de moindres peines et de moindres frais. De là vient la séparation des travaux, effet et cause de l'accroissement des richesses et du perfectionnement de l'industrie humaine.[32]

In Britain, virtue gave way to utility as the criterion of social effectiveness; and this new view of society and of the individual was first given explicit political expression in America.

As Gordon Wood has said in his magisterial book, *The Creation of the American Republic*, American conceptions of politics and citizenship underwent a major change between the radical Revolution of 1776 and the conservative Revision of the late 1780s. The essence of American Republicanism in 1776, as would still be true of French Republicanism in 1793–4, was the fusion of the individual and of the community. Similarly, the purpose of the state, in this Franco-American perspective, was not to be the simple expression of a random collection of divergent interests but, as Samuel Adams said in 1776, to be a 'moral person' with an interest and a will of its own.[33] Long traditions of Whig and Puritan thought justified the Americans' view of themselves as a chosen people, and in 1776, Wood concludes, 'the solution of the problems of American politics seemed to rest not so much in emphasizing the private rights of the individual against the general will as it did in stressing the public rights of the collective people against the supposed privileged interest of their rulers'.[34]

By 1789, however, all had changed, or, at least, all was changing. The rights of individuals and of society were now understood to be distinct. The purpose of government was no longer thought to be the promotion of the collective happiness of a single and harmonious society; it was instead to protect different citizens in their different liberties and properties. 'Justice', said Madison, 'is the end of government. It is the end of civil society,' and justice implied the protection of the citizen against the state as well as of the state against the selfish particularism of isolated individuals.[35]

As Wood explains, this was the end of 'classical politics'. In America, the term 'people' now took on a new meaning, and in 1792, Joel Barlow, who had lived in Europe since 1788, wrote that this word no longer meant in the United States what it still meant in France. In America, it referred not only to the whole community but also to every individual within that community. In Europe, he added, it meant 'something else more difficult to define'.[36] Americans, in the words of a prominent Federalist, had united liberty with luxury and had proved 'the consistency of the social nature with the political happiness of man'.[37]

The nature of government in such a society was far different from what it had been. Direct representation, the conquest that had been made in 1776, was not abrogated, but the limits of the state were more sharply drawn. In 1792, Jefferson wrote to Monroe that it would be ridiculous to think that a man should surrender himself to the state: 'This would be slavery, and not that liberty which the bill of rights has made inviolable, and for the preservation of which our government has been changed.'[38] Classical Republicanism had detested factions, as it had detested luxury, but American Republicanism made room for both. Faction was no doubt undesirable, but it was, as Madison laid out in the *Federalist*, 'sown into the nature of man'.[39] Man was selfish; factions were inevitable because man was by nature bad as well as good. Indeed, it was because of his selfish nature, Madison explained, that men needed to be governed at all: 'If men were angels, no government would be necessary. . . . In framing a government which is to be administered by men over men, the great difficulty lies in this: You must first enable the government to control the governed; and in the next place, oblige it to control itself.'[40]

The secular traditions of civic humanism in both America and Britain had been deeply entrenched; but given the pace of change there, the birth of modern liberal economics in the one and the end of 'classical' politics in the other were irresistible developments. Long before the 1780s, England had become a bourgeois society where land was enclosed and where jurisprudence had made room for modern contract theory. And America, regardless of the intentions of its founders, may have been a bourgeois society from the first: its population was mobile and differences of inherited rank and status were far less pronounced there than in Europe. It was in the nature of things, then, that traditional social and political forms in these two countries should soon adapt themselves to those exigencies of individualistic capitalism that had exploded the concepts of man virtuous and society harmonious.

In the 1770s and 1780s, French writings reflected the changes that had been taking place in America and Britain, but French thoughts on the fading theme of civic humanism and traditional community were more ambiguous. Publicists in the last decades before the Revolution were more likely to side for either capitalist individualism or socialist community than they had been before. At the same time, however, because economic and social change in France was less profound than in Britain or America, French public opinion continued to temporize. The more typical French reaction was to go on with a compromise solution, the contradictory solution of bourgeois universalism.

Counterparts to the doctrine of Adam Smith did exist in France, of course. The doctrine of the Physiocrats, which presented individual property as the foundation of economic and political life, was well articulated. Indeed, it was to Quesnay, the father of Physiocracy, that Adam Smith had intended to dedicate his *Wealth of Nations*. Between 1756 and 1778, Physiocrats such as Quesnay, Mercier de la Rivière, Mirabeau *père*, Dupont de Nemours, and Turgot published a number of important works which secured a large audience for 'the sect'. The claims of property were upheld by these men. Economic progress was linked by them to the greater profit of the landlord, and it was Turgot who discovered and welcomed the iron law of wages which forced labour costs down and guaranteed the advance of social progress by raising land rents. The height of wisdom in economic affairs was, in this view, to combine investment with the maximum amount of enjoyment and the greatest diminution of expense. At the same time, however, and as might be expected in the less congenial atmosphere of eighteenth-century France, physiocratic doctrine was less developed economically and politically than were the theories of Smith or the Federalists. The Physiocrats were agrarians who were not interested in industrial development.

For them, only land could yield true profits, a theory which paradoxically led them to advocate a land-tax and to ignore industrial profits.

Unlike the American Federalists, the Physiocrats persisted in the universal assumption that society was a naturally harmonious whole. Even after the Revolutionary attack on property, Jean-Baptiste Say, the heir of the Physiocrats and the popularizer in France of the works of Adam Smith, a man who might, therefore, have been expected to be truculent in the defence of the rights of property, took up as the theme of his book *Othie, ou les moyens de transformer les mœures d'une nation*, written in 1800, the construction of a social paradise. Like the civic humanists, the Physiocrats continued to assume that a natural and harmonious order could be discerned beneath the debris of the political and social errors that had accumulated over time.[41] The Physiocrats, in short, did extol individual rights, without a doubt, but they did not for all that abandon a traditional view of the public good: 'Il est de l'essence de l'ordre,' explained Quesnay, 'que l'intérêt particulier d'un seul ne puisse jamais être séparé de l'intérêt commun de tous, et c'est ce qui arrive sous le régime de la liberté. *Le monde va alors de lui-même*. Le désir de jouir imprime à la Société un mouvement qui devient une tendance perpétuelle vers le meilleur état possible.[42]

The capitalist revision of civic humanism, then, did have some impact on French life through the writings of the Physiocrats, though not in the crystalline form that it took on in the writings of Smith and the Federalists. A remarkably pure socialist revision of civic humanism, by contrast, can be found in the French 'utopian' thinkers, who reacted to the increased claims of individualism by reinforcing the rights of community and by drastically suspending the rights of private property.

French 'utopian' socialists did not point-blank deny the rights of the individual. Morelly, for example, was something of an epicurean who favoured the enjoyment of life to the full and condemned Rousseau's strictures on the progress of the arts. But both Mably and Morelly though private property detestable: 'Ôtez la propriété aveugle et l'impitoyable intérêt qui l'accompagne,' wrote Morelly, and the result would be 'plus de passions furieuses, plus d'actions féroces, plus de notions, plus d'idées de mal moral'.[43] These were strong words, but they were overshadowed by the strictures of Mably, who condemned not only property but its psychological mainsprings as well: 'si notre avarice, notre vanité et notre ambition sont des obstacles insurmontables à un bien parfait, subissons sans murmurer la peine que nous méritons'.[44] Indeed, Mably fell over himself in his eagerness to destroy everything which had made man more selfish, such as mechanical inventions, foreign trade, and the Academy of Fine Arts.

For the bulk of the French reformist bourgeoisie, the doctrines of both the Physiocrats and the socialists were too bold. In Britain and in America, the new capitalist ethos had made quick gains in theory and practice. As we know from the work of E. P. Thompson, the new ethic was hardly accepted uniformly, but in both countries the propertied élites quickly rallied to a new, more consistent, and to them more sensible world view. The French bourgeoisie could not take so bold a step. Though France was being transformed by market forces and was for that reason far more 'modern' than any other continental nation, the forces of traditionalism in that country were still quite strong, and the typical theoretical stance of the French political class reflected the hybrid nature of their society. The Physiocrats and the socialists made a decisive break, but the more typical bourgeois response was to straddle the issue and to pretend, desperately, that the universalist principle of commonwealth was still relevant in what we would now describe as an increasingly capitalist society. Bourgeois individualism was certainly extolled, but universalism, the communitarian legacy of tradition and civic humanism, was not abandoned.

So complete was the French bourgeoisie's naïve belief in the possibility of universal harmony that it is now almost uncharitable to expose the inconsistencies of pre-Revolutionary bourgeois thought on any number of issues. Property, for example, elicited in the 1770s and 1780s the most contradictory opinions, next to which the confused expectations of the 1750s and 1760s had been models of clarity.

The abbé de Raynal, an immensely popular writer, is particularly vulnerable in this respect. In his best-selling *Histoire philosophique des deux Indes*, published in 1772, Raynal, though he did recognize that some forms of property were justifiable, railed at length against its abuses: everywhere, he wrote, the rich exploit the poor. 'Combien de fois a-t-on entendu l'homme du peuple demander au ciel quel était son crime, pour naître sur terre dans un état d'indignité et de dépendance extrême!'[45] He may have had occasion to reflect on this passage in 1791, by which time he had already so changed his opinions as to lambast the National Assembly for having destroyed corporate bodies like Parlements and Estates.

Restif de la Bretonne, the 'Rousseau du ruisseau', a novelist and pornographer of considerable talent, dealt with the issue of property in the same way. To want to suppress property, he maintained in his *Dangers de la ville* (1775) and in his *Découverte australe par un homme volant ou le Dédale français* (1782), was unrealistic. But the ownership of property should none the less have as wide a base as possible. Revealingly, Restif, who idealized country life, was like Voltaire particularly impressed by the familial and agrarian communities of the Auvergne as he was also by those of the Moravian brothers.[46]

Mably, as Talmon has pointed out, was perhaps the most confused. Ultimately, Mably would have abolished property altogether, since mankind could never otherwise reach 'the highest state of perfection'.[47] But Mably also thought that in mankind's present 'state of sin' attacks on property were simply one more anti-social manifestation of man's cupidity. 'Property is the source of all evil,' writes Professor Talmon, 'and yet he would protect it.'[48]

The future Conventionnel Mercier neatly summed up the contradictory thought of the 1780s on property. For him also, the rights of property could not be abrogated, but his utopian project, entitled *L'An 2240*, written in 1780, was a long attack against the prerogatives of property which he defended elsewhere:

> Un Lapon en naissant a du moins en apanage un renne; on lui assigne un second renne quand les dents lui percent. Mais je vois des enfants qui viennent au monde sans pouvoir dire avoir une pomme en propriété. Les êtres sauvages ont leur tannière; et tel malheureux pressé tyraniquement par les lois mêmes qui ont fait les propriétés exclusives du moindre pouce de terre ou d'un misérable plancher, n'a pas de quoi reposer sa tête. Tout est pris, tout est envahi. L'homme dans nos gouvernements modernes, en recevant son corps de la nature, n'obtient point des lois civiles une place en propre pour y respirer. On lui accorde l'espace d'un tombeau, celle d'un berceau lui est interdit.[49]

Mercier's conclusion was prophetic: 'il y aurait un terrible livre à faire sur le mot propriété'.

The cult or fetish of ancient Rome and Greece, with its varied implications about the state and the citizen, was, in the 1780s, another expression of bourgeois universalist expectation (or confusion, as one would have it).[50]

Greece and Rome were popular themes throughout the North Atlantic world at the end of the eighteenth century, in Britain and America especially, where the colonists liked to think of themselves as close approximations of ancient simplicity. For the French, however, references to the ancient world had an even greater political resonance because it was commonly assumed in France that the balance between individualism and community had been most successfully achieved in antiquity. Helvetius explained in *De l'esprit*, 'Si l'histoire grecque et romaine est pleine de ces traits héroïques, et si l'on parcourt presque inutilement l'histoire du despotisme pour en trouver de pareils, c'est que dans ces gouvernements l'intérêt particulier n'est jamais lié à l'intérêt public. . . .[51] The ancient hero had also been a model citizen, and the terms 'Greece' and 'Rome' were in the 1780s an Aesopian code in the contemporary debate on civil rights and obligations.

This cypher was understood by all concerned, including the apologists of private property and of egocentric bourgeois individualism who realized that it was incumbent on them to deny the relevance of ancient mores. Sieyes, for example, pointed out that 'les peuples européens modernes resemblent bien peu aux peuples anciens. Il ne s'agit parmi nous que de commerce, d'agriculture, de fabriques, etc. . . . Aussi, les systèmes politiques, aujourd'hui, sont exclusivement fondés sur le travail; les facultés productives de l'homme sont tout.'[52]

After 1789, the difference between the 'liberties of the ancients' and the 'liberties of the moderns' would become a classic theme of bourgeois liberal polemics, in the works of Mme de Staël and of Benjamin Constant, for example. But by the same token, the praise of the classical polis in literature, painting, or architecture before 1789 was an indirect theoretical statement about the continued applicability of civic humanism. The most famous text on Greece was that of Montesquieu: 'Les politiques grecs qui vivaient dans le gouvernement populaire, ne reconnaissaient d'autre force qui put les soutenir que celle de la vertu.'[53] The theme of classical virtue, i.e. restrained individualism, hardly waned as the century progressed. Grimm, walking through the gardens of the Palais Royal, was moved to think of the gap between the moderns, who were corrupt, and the ancients: 'Anciennes républiques: Vos débris attestent ce que vous fûtes. . . . Que nous sommes petits!' Condorcet, in his *Considérations* of 1793, would be even more categorical: 'On trouveroit à peine dans les républiques modernes . . . une institution dont les républiques grecques n'ayent offert le modèle.'[54]

For those who regretted Greece and Rome, civic humanism had lost none of its applicability, and it was assumed in France that America was a modern proof of the doctrine's continued relevance. Although, as has been seen, Americans by the late 1780s had begun to shift their view of the public good, this was not perceived in Paris. Most thoughtful Frenchmen in the 1780s persisted in thinking that America was for them a valid example precisely because the rebellious colonists, they assumed, had somehow managed to conciliate private gain and public good.[55]

For Rousseau, the choice had been between virtue and the progress of the arts, but Americans, as was explained by a contestant for a literary prize sponsored by Raynal, had managed to reconcile these divergent goals. Settlers there had discovered liberty and ease:

> les campagnes ont retracé les siècles des patriarches avec toutes les jouissances des nôtres. Les villes ont rassemblé des citoyens de toutes les nations; tous les arts de l'Europe y ont été cultivés; toutes les sciences y ont trouvé des amateurs, une urbanité simple & bienfaisante est venue par sa douceur embellir toutes les vertus.[56]

Lacretelle made the same point: in America, where virtue and progress went hand in hand, the thirteen 'peuples législateurs' held the fate of the world in their hands

> Puisez un noble orgueil, un saint enthousiasme dans la vaste influence de vos destinées. Vous tenez l'Univers dans une grande attente; dans cinquante ans, il saura, par vous, si les peuples modernes peuvent encore conserver des Constitutions républicaines, s'il est de bonnes mœurs compatible avec les grands progrès de la civilisation, si l'Amérique doit rendre meilleur ou pire le sort de l'humanité![57]

Translated *en clair*, this meant that in America civic equality and private property had somehow been fused. Though property in France was deleterious, in America it had retained its classic defensive role, as civic humanism had defined it. In the Old World property had become the means of oppression; in the New World, as Condorcet explained in his *De l'influence de la Révolution de l'Amérique sur les opinions et la législation de l'Europe* of 1786, private wealth was still a bulwark of the citizen's independence: 'l'homme, qui n'a jamais craint d'outrage pour sa personne, acquiert une âme plus élevée et plus douce; . . . celui dont la propriété est toujours assurée, trouve la probité facile. . . .'[58] In America, differences of wealth seemed not to matter, and in 1776, Lafayette commented naïvely on this surprising fact. Americans, he wrote to his wife in France, were as amiable as one could hope:

La simplicité des manières, le désir d'obliger, l'amour de la patrie et de la liberté, une douce égalité règnent ici parmi tout le monde. L'homme le plus riche et le plus pauvre sont de niveau; et, quoiqu'il y ait des fortunes immenses dans ce pays, je défie de trouver la moindre différence entre leurs manières respectives les uns pour les autres.[59]

For the French, America was a promised land where politics were a model that all might follow. It is suggestive that the newly drafted state constitutions of the early 1780s aroused great interest in France, but very little in England. After the War of Independence, Burke paid no attention to American constitutional development,[60] but the state constitution of Massachusetts, drafted by John Adams, was translated into French by Mably.

Characteristically, also, when Americans appeared in their new constitutions to lean too far away from a unified concept of virtue, French observers became critical and were at a loss to understand what was going on. Those American state and federal constitutions which divided power in order to neutralize or balance conflicting interests were a puzzle to French observers. Turgot opined that 'all authorities should be brought into one, that of the nation,' and Morellet in his *Observations sur la Virginie* 'forgot' to mention Jefferson's proposed constitution, which provided not only for a divided legislature but for indirect elections as well.[61]

The myth of America, the critique of luxury, the reconciliation of individualism and community, however different they may appear, were so many aspects of the same bourgeois universalism. For that reason, they could be shown by contemporaries to dovetail nicely, and many philosophes expressed their fears for the future of America in conventional and interlocking terms. Diderot, for example, who died in 1784, warned the Americans that greater wealth might bring corruption, luxury, and the decline of equality. Mably concurred. In Philadelphia, the rot had already set in since the effect of the restricted Pennsylvanian franchise had been to create 'une noblesse héréditaire que les loix Américaines proscrivent.' A corrupt urban bourgeoisie would soon oppress a moral, rural, minority: 'Dès que les bourgeois de vos villes, corrompus par leur fortune, ne regarderont qu'avec mépris les habitans de la campagne & les artisans, n'est il pas vrai que vos loix auront inutilement établi la plus parfaite égalité? Ces favoris de la fortune aspireront à former des familles d'un ordre supérieur'.[62]

Yet most believed Americans had re-created the ancient polis, and Chastellux thought the United States to be not a new civilization, as Rome had been to Greece, but a second and fragile Syracuse. This was the theme also of the abbé Brizard's *Fragment de Xénophon*, which described America allegorically as an ancient Greek colony where complete liberty coincided with the unprecedented progress of the arts. America, concluded Mercier in his *De la littêrature* on 1778, was the asylum of liberty, 'les âmes de la Grèce les âmes fortes & généreuses y croîtront ou s'y rendront, & ce grand exemple donné à l'Univers, prouvera ce que peut l'homme, quand il met en dépot commun son courage & ses lumières'.[63]

America was a screen on which the minor philosophes of the 1780s projected their unsubstantial hope for what France itself might become. It was widely supposed in Paris that divisions of property would be transcended in France as they were said to have been in America already. The rich bathed in a warm glow of artificial good feelings. They welcomed the invention by Count Rumford, an American, as it happens, who lived in Paris, of Rumford soup, at once nutritious and cheap to cook since made largely of water. They approved warmly of the endowment of the hospital *Des Enfants Malades* by Necker, the most prominent banker of his day. A vast, and to our eyes, mawkish iconography of charity dispensed to the deserving poor suddenly appeared. Drawing on Rousseau and Marivaux, writers like Delille and Lemierre elaborated Arcadian fantasies. At Versailles, Louis was a locksmith and Marie Antoinette tended sheep. Misconceptions grew worse, and the shock to the bourgeois universalists in 1793 was all the greater for the theoretical illusions of the 1770s and 1780s.

* * *

From the Enlightened, theoretical perception of the overlap between individualism and community emerged a vision of future social relations. The social problem lay in opening up men's minds rather than in economic redistribution: an egalitarian 'loi agraire' as it would later be called, appeared unnecessary, since it would complicate matters and would resolve nothing. Schemes of social insurance, the likes of which were popular in the 1780s, might be enough. Individualism and community would be easily reconciled.

On the one hand, Enlightened opinion rejected anti-individualist, corporatist survivals. Hierarchic feudalism was particularly detested. On the other, the disciples of the philosophes assumed that the gift of citizenship would transform potentially selfish individuals and make them good. Human beings would be freer than they had ever been, and society would also be more harmonious than before.

In this new system, social extremes would easily be reconciled. It was assumed that the poor, at the bottom, and nobles, at the top, would willingly agree to become free citizens of a free state. At the bottom, the poor did seem tractable. They had, it appeared, given up on the older corporatist arrangements, and neither peasants nor artisans appeared to expect very much from the new ones. The halting efforts of the monarchy to restore corporatist guilds after Turgot's dismissal in 1776 had not aroused much popular support, and in 1791, even Marat would accept the dissolution of these corporatist guilds which had afforded the 'plebs' a manner of protection.

Similarly, though popular religious feeling was not exhausted as was once supposed, there was no popular religious revival in eighteenth-century France comparable to Methodism in England, revivalism in America, or Pietism in Germany. This was an important 'non-event' because, as some historians like E. P. Thompson would have it, the newer forms of religious belief that emerged at the end of the eighteenth century were expressions of the malaise that gripped popular masses which were no longer enclosed by a sustaining traditional order but were not yet class conscious. By comparison with England, riots and strikes in France were infrequent and tepid. 'Une émeute', wrote the writer and future Conventionnel Mercier in 1783, 'qui dégénèrerait en sédition est devenu moralement impossible.'[64] The offer of social promotion through diligent hard work would perhaps be enough, or so it seemed to the bourgeoisie in the 1780s. As some Marseillais *sectionnaires* were to put it shortly after the outbreak of Revolution, now that 'la carrière de la fortune' was open to all, 'chacun peut y parvenir sans devenir criminel, le talent n'a plus d'entraves et le soleil ne refuse sa lumière à personne'.[65]

Bourgeois expectations on the peaceful integration of nobles as individuals into a harmonious, bourgeois social order were even more explicit. Individualism had given to the bourgeoisie a new sense of self. It had enabled individual non-nobles to ignore the 'cascade de mépris' which was now thought to be the *leitmotiv* of social life under the *Ancien Régime*. Could it not be supposed that aristocrats would also sense that they too could gain power and prestige by placing their talents in the competition of a free market? Gains might outweigh losses for nobles also. Individual conversions like that of Lafayette, 'le héros des deux mondes', gave credibility to such beliefs.

Nobles would surely understand that they too might find as bourgeois citizens new opportunity for fame and fortune. As individuals of talent and as property owners, aristocrats might do very well. Camille Desmoulins would later describe with grace the *modus operandi* of this social metempsychosis:

généreux patriciens, en qui la voix de la raison a été plus forte que celle de l'intérêt et que les préjugés germaniques, vous qui, en nous reconnaissant pour vos frères, en vous empressant de vous réunir avec nous, pour coopérer à rendre le nom de citoyen français plus honorable que celui de gentilhomme, venez de vous ennoblir bien plus que n'avaient fait vos pères par un sacrifice pénible; ne craignez pas que nous l'oublions jamais.

The French bourgeoisie would be grateful to nobles; and historical precedent was there as a guarantee that nobles would do well in the new system:

A Rome, lorsque le peuple eut forcé toutes les barrières qui lui fermaient l'entrée des charges et obtenu de pouvoir parvenir au consulat, il n'en abusa point et continua d'élever les patriciens aux premières dignités. Il en est aussi une foule parmi vous que nous saurons toujours distinguer, et dont nous pourrons placer à la tête des armées les noms redoutables à l'ennemi; et nul n'aura plus illustré ces noms que ceux d'entre vous qui ont voulu généreusement renoncer à toutes les prérogatives qu'ils connaissent, et recommencer leur noblesse.[66]

Even the future Montagnard Romme, the uncompromising *martyr de prairial*, thought that nobles would become model, and honoured, citizens. Of course, he explained in April 1789, all merit should be recognized regardless of its origins, but at the same time, co-operative nobles should be particularly rewarded. What Romme wanted to see, he wrote to a friend, was that 'à parité de mérite, le noble fût préféré, afin d'honorer un homme vertueux jusque dans sa descendance'.[67]

Bourgeois writers were quite serious about integrating nobles and naturally assumed that many nobles would respond, since the stakes were so high. In early 1789 again, Murat de Monferrand, a commoner, apostrophized the descendants of the '*preux chevaliers*' in just these terms. The sacrifice that nobles might make for the common cause would be amply rewarded: 'Soyez nos chefs, & non pas nos oppresseurs: présidez dans les fonctions paisibles de l'administration, & nous vous y porterons le tribut mérité du respect & de la reconnoissance publique.'[68]

Bourgeois absorption of the nobility was possible and even inevitable, as Rabaut-Saint-Étienne pointed out. To be sure, the nobility as a collective entity might for a while try to resist the dictates of public opinion, 'the queen of the world', but nobles, taken singly, would soon be engulfed for fear of being ridiculous and from a desire to please.

In retrospect, of course, it is all too clear that the bourgeoisie's expectations that rich and poor, noble and non-noble, might alike be fitted into a renewed community were hopelessly unrealistic. The course of politics after 1789 showed that individual aspirations and communal responsibility did not completely overlap by any means. 'Dans une République sagement constituée', wrote Daunou in 1793, 'l'intérêt personnel est indissolublement lié à l'intérêt commun.'[69] But after 1792, it had become painfully obvious to most that such was not the case, and for that very reason, the Revolutionaries' rich vocabulary for civic virtue and values (*peuple*, *nation*, *patrie*, *humanité*, *unité*, *indivisibilité*, *cité*, *commune*, *vertu*, *fraternité*, *justice*, *sacrifice*, *héroisme*) was something of a fraud, though perhaps a fraud that was, so to speak, perpetrated in good faith by an inexperienced and relatively inchoate bourgeoisie at the expense of an inexperienced and inchoate population of unpropertied rural and urban manual workers. In any case, one can easily claim, as J.-Y. Guiomar has done, that the use of the word 'nation' in 1793–4 was something of a mystification, a red herring which distracted the attention of the poor from concrete problems of social and economic inequality.[70]

In fact, it can even be said that indications of the inadequacy of bourgeois universalism had already surfaced before 1789. In addition to the theoretical statements of utopian socialists like Mably, many ordinary men and women began to think, even before the Revolution, that existing arrangements on property could not really be made compatible with a sense of community and with genuine freedom for all.

Admittedly, extreme statements similar to those of Mably and Morelly were still quite rare before the Revolution. None the less, in the 1780s, a growing number of intellectuals were inching towards that collectivist position. From the defence of individualism and the rejection of traditional bonds of dependence and hierarchy, it was a short step to demand not just freedom from oppression, but freedom for fulfilment of the self as well. After 1789, under the pressure of events, the sans-culottes were quick to make this leap which simple logic had required before 1789 already, or so it had increasingly seemed to some. A few intellectuals began to suggest that there should be more equality for the poor, for women, and even for blacks, that is to say, for all human beings whose condition was such as to make implausible the bourgeois argument that the claims of equality could be realized politically and morally in a society where the distribution of wealth and power was as it had always been. From time to time, heretics like Linguet and Dufourny in his *Cahier of the Fourth Estate* reminded their bourgeois audience that the richer members of the Third Estate were themselves privileged men: 'Je demande à tous les Ordres,' wrote Dufourny in 1789, 'et particulièrement à celui de Tiers, s'ils ne sont pas éminemment privilégiés en comparaison du quatrième Ordre?'[71]

Bourgeois universalism as a doctrine had begun to creak even before 1789. Convinced liberals found it too narrow; and from the other shore, parsimonious bourgeois with an eye to economy found it much too broad. The problem of the poor was a suggestive test case. The need to cope with nation-wide poverty in some massive and positive manner was widely understood. But at the same time, many bourgeois bristled at the prospect of the cost of such massive relief. Although benevolence remained, in theory, the mode in which poverty was to be resolved, the actual handling of this particular problem told a different story and historians of poverty during the last decades of the *Ancien Régime* have pointed to a pre-Revolutionary stiffening of bourgeois attitudes on this score. Although convinced that the Catholic system of poor relief was inadequate, many bourgeois philanthropists also began to think that self-help alone could eradicate poverty, a view of the question that led some observers to think that the idle poor might after all be abandoned to a fate that they somehow deserved: 'Partout on parle du pauvre,' wrote a philanthropist in a particularly backward part of France, 'partout on vante et on exalte les soins ou secours immenses que lui distribuent en secret les âmes les plus renommés en charité. Ces soins, ces attentions si exaltées me paraissent l'écueil et l'abus de la charité . . . l'entretien de la paresse, de l'hypocrisie et du vice.'[72]

This was an attitude which is commonly associated with the nineteenth-century mentality of 'classes laborieuses, classes dangereuses', and it is revealing that it was voiced before 1789. It would none the less be mistaken to suppose that bourgeois universalism was in its essence a conscious mystification. Frenchmen in 1793 did gain a new sense of their communal self by destroying corporatism (of which feudalism was only a part). It may well have been the illusion of the reality of bourgeois universalism that enabled the Revolutionary bourgeoisie to galvanize itself and the nation at large, first against the *Ancien Régime* in 1789, and then against Europe in 1793–4. It must likewise be said that the French Revolution was in some respects a genuinely universalist movement in that the equality of rich and poor before the law was not an empty promise. The inclusion in civil society in 1789–91 of Protestants and Jews, a religious and a 'racial' minority, was of great importance and is still today symbolic of the relevance of liberalism to modern life.

Bourgeois universalism possessed a genuine if ephemeral credibility at the end of the eighteenth century and has a limited relevance for the nineteenth and twentieth centuries as well. The same claim holds for the constituent parts of the Revolutionary, bourgeois, and universalist message. It is true, of course, that nationalism has been used by the right (in Wilhelminian Germany, let us say) or by the left (in Stalinist Russia) as a surrogate for durable liberal solutions to domestic problems. But it is anachronistic to read a similar function into the French bourgeois nationalism of 1789–94, which was in many respects a genuinely civic and libertarian force.

In fact, it is altogether impossible to understand the zeal of bourgeois Revolutionaries in 1789–99 if the genuineness of their ideological convictions is brought into question. The reformist bourgeoisie in the 1780s earnestly believed that the social circle could be squared, and their belief in the capacity of their doctrine to transform France, or the world, can even be seen as a form of religious fervour. Such was the view of Tocqueville, Mathiez in his younger days, and Lefebvre, who wrote that Frenchmen in 1789 had been swept up by the 'message', by an unspecified hope of something better. 'Social revolutions', he concluded, 'like religious ones, at least in the West, are annunciations of a radical transformation of life. . . . In every revolution of this sort, some millenarianism is to be found; in other words, each one of them is what Georges Sorel called a myth, the intelligible formulation of an irrational hope.'[73]

The French bourgeoisie in 1789 was indeed moved by a myth, a myth which held that the present and the past might be reconciled, and that the new aspirations of individualism might easily be blended with the secular Western nostalgia for community.

* * *

An understanding of the bourgeoisie's universalist myth and of its concurrent belief in the virtues of individualism is a fundamental step to the solution of the nobles problem, which it affected in three critical ways.

Bourgeois universalists were, before all else, bourgeois individualists. They may have craved community, but they by no means denied the importance of unfettered private property with all that this implied for their dealings with other owners of property who happened to be nobles. However communitarian it may have been, the National Assembly in 1789 did decree the free trade of grain which the poor opposed above all else; and it was with the utmost reluctance that the Conventionnels, even at the height of their dependence on the urban poor in 1793, agreed to control wages and prices. Ultimately, therefore, a concern for property would rule. Should the ambiguities of bourgeois universalism be called into question, the ultimate solution was a foregone conclusion. Bourgeois individualism would come first, universalism, second. In that respect, some room would eventually have to be found for nobles once it had become possible to consider them as being first and foremost fellow members of the possessing class.

At the same time, however, the legacy of civic humanism and traditional community was still very strong in France. The idea that the state should be virtuous was deeply entrenched. For that reason, though property would eventually triumph, it could only do so after a prolonged struggle. Owners of property, however Enlightened, did abandon their universalist dreams once it was proven to them that libertarian fantasies were dangerous; but only the most dismal series of failures would convince them that they had, after all, been hopelessly confused. Until the bourgeoisie could come to this realization, the fate of nobles might well become unpleasant. Nobles, it was well known, had no place in a virtuous society. They were idle parasites, incapable of becoming citizens.

Finally, it is important to see that, in 1789, the conflict of these two themes, the one universal and the other particularist, was hardly superficial. Because it was so widely and earnestly believed that a way could be found to reconcile men of different wealth and backgrounds as citizens of a 'moral' and virtuous state, bourgeois social and political thought was structurally imperfect. The chastening of the bourgeoisie, and with it the salvation of nobles, was long in coming. If the appeal of bourgeois universalism had been less strong in 1789 and the communitarian myth less convincing, it would have been possible to create from the first a durable alliance of nobles and bourgeois on the basis of a common defence of property. Each of these basic aspects of bourgeois universalism had an immediate bearing on the handling of the nobles problem.

First, the sincerity of the Revolutionaries' belief in the power of benevolent individualism led them to suppose that nobles could be transformed. Nobility would have to be struck down because it was a divisive and therefore immoral social institution. But nobles as individual citizens could be redeemed. They too would become virtuous members of a virtuous state. Their immorality, it was thought, had been a function of their situation rather than of their innate character as men. In 1789, therefore, the bourgeoisie made a genuine effort to encompass individual nobles into the new order of things.

But the bourgeois universalist vision was flawed and frail. It was intellectually contradictory, and in the confusion entailed by institutional and economic adjustments after 1789, it soon began to collapse. It is in this second phase that the bourgeoisie began its drift to the left. In 1791, when the universalist vision proved thoroughly impractical, the initial tendency of the bourgeoisie was to pursue the virtuous millennium. Gradually, parliamentary majorities lost their hold on political legitimacy, which was seized by those small groups, in and out of the Assemblies, that could claim to be the incarnation of the spirit and will of the Revolution.[74] Bourgeois perceptions of nobles moved accordingly. Nobles who in 1789–91 had been thought redeemable as citizens 'métamorphosés par la liberté' were seen between 1792 and 1794 as incarnations of divisiveness, idleness, immorality, and treason. There was no room for them in the new Republic. Indeed, the bourgeoisie was eager to exclude nobles; to do so was a proof of devotion to equality and fraternity. Property might then remain sacrosanct. To call the nobles corrupt and treacherous had the convenient effect of countering the sans-culottes' increasingly vociferous demands for a reordering of the property settlement.

Finally, in the last phase, after 1799, when virtue had become irrelevant and when the bourgeoisie had abandoned its efforts to placate the poor by appearing to be egalitarian, nobles were once again readmitted to the family circle, by General Bonaparte, not as virtuous citizens, of course, but as owners of property.

Because it was so contradictory and so volatile, bourgeois universalism probably ought not to be described as a theory at all. But though doctrinally unsound, it was none the less emotionally quite powerful. It ought perhaps to be described as a faith, somewhat as Peter Brown describes in *The World of Late Antiquity* the way that the governing classes felt about the Roman Empire in AD 400. The principal strength of the empire, Brown says, was the 'elusive glow of shared sentiments, of unquestioned loyalties, [and of] half-sensed images of security' that it evoked—feelings, he thinks, that are best expressed by the term that Spaniards use for the bonds of affection that unite a married couple, *ilusión*.[75]

Alas, of course, the marriage in France of 'plebs' and bourgeoisie was a union that could not last. The two partners soon fell out, with a rancour and bitterness—clearly stated by both Babeuf and Sieyes—that had much to do with disappointed hope. Bourgeois universalism was soon revealed to have been illusory indeed. But before the Revolution, it had been deeply felt. The serious and sickly sweet, *petit-bourgeois* moralism of Greuze, much admired by Diderot, replaced the baroque frivolity of Fragonard as the dominant aesthetic mode of the 1780s. The contours of the new feelings were vague, as are those of *ilusión*, but we should not for that refuse to see their critical importance as a determinant of politics.

iii. On the supposed existence of a single noble-bourgeois élite in pre-Revolutionary France

Bourgeois universalism provides the conceptual setting of the nobles question: ideologically, the prospect of a bourgeois-noble alliance in 1789, based on a common defence of property, was both desirable and distasteful. We can now turn to the social and cultural aspects of the problem. Granted that the bourgeoisie was (precariously) committed to follow a certain line of action on nobles, can it also be said that such a tactic was practically feasible? Were nobles and bourgeois so far apart that a reconciliation of the two groups in 1789 was in fact unthinkable? Two types of issues must be considered here: first, the actual positions in the 1780s of nobles and bourgeois on issues like property, political influence, or social relations; and, second, the contemporary perception of what these material and social relations were.

The background of the relationship of nobles to non-nobles after 1789 lies in the disintegration during the second half of the eighteenth century of the French *Ständestaat*. Gradually, the interlocking orders of the *Ancien Régime* came apart. Corporative regulations were increasingly evaded. The older social units (extended families, trades, corporations, villages, towns, *pays*, provinces, or the like) ceased to encompass the aspirations of ordinary Frenchmen.

How and why the decline of this corporate social structure occurred is not yet clear: the extent of material change was slight in France—at least in comparison with England—and French economic growth was decidedly 'schizophrenic' for the period which runs from the end of the 'seventeenth-century crisis' to the time of the French Revolution. Some commercial and 'proto-industrial' development took place, but much of it was concentrated in a narrow band of seaports. Cities like Nantes or Marseilles had economic connections with the world economy rather than with their own hinterland; their political connections were with government finance and the court, as might be expected in a country which had a strong mercantilist tradition.[76]

In 1789, the larger part of France remained materially as it had been four or five decades before. Its agriculture, though made gradually more efficient, remained traditional in its structure: techniques were not greatly improved; land was not enclosed; commons were not divided; communal customs were on the whole respected. Feudalism, represented materially by the lord's judicial prerogative and by the payment of certain dues derived from the original political and seigneurial domination of the land, was no longer a meaningful political and cultural framework. But seigneurialism, represented by another set of payments made in deference to the lord's vestigial rights as the owner of the soil, was, though unwell, very much alive.

In this context of only partial economic change, it is hard to see why traditional French social forms should have decayed as completely as they did, and the problem of the transition of French society to capitalism in the eighteenth century can still be best apprehended at the more abstract level of social rather than of purely economic change, and presumably, as Marx described it, with an emphasis not on technology *per se* or on the extent of the 'naturalistic' change, but on the spread of the division and sale of labour, the mobility of population, the growing volume of exchange, and especially the adoption of individualism and rationality as modes of economic behaviour.[77]

Why French society was transformed, then, is hardly obvious, but the lineaments of the new social structure are somewhat clearer: personal ties and corporate loyalties gave way to a sharper sense of self and to a greater respect for merit. Market relations became more important. The definition of property was more closely drawn and eighteenth-century jurists succeeded in translating medieval concepts such as *domaine utile* and *domaine direct* into the more modern terms of absolute property and lien. Lines of status gave way to the exigencies of class. By 1789, France was a place where the overt violence that is characteristic of a more spacious age was becoming more rare. French society was more ordered and more 'bourgeois'.

To be sure, France cannot be said to have become bourgeois in the sense that 'modes of production' were radically altered in a material way. But a large segment of its land-owning population, including nobles, came to accept the basic cultural assumptions of bourgeois life, such as individualism, a sense of measured order, and the desirability of thrift.

The checkered inception in eighteenth-century France of new economic and social modes has been variously interpreted. Alfred Cobban, for example, has seized on the survival of traditional problems to argue that the French Revolution was not made by a modern-minded bourgeoisie at all. It was the work instead, he thinks, of a declining *officier* class whose sinecures were falling in value and who were often in straitened circumstances.[78]

Such an argument, however, is more ingenious than revealing, for it does not really matter too much that the destruction of corporatism (symbolized by the Le Chapelier law) was accomplished by lawyers who as individuals may not have liked bankers or manufacturers. In the same way, it is also beside the point that many French businessmen did not care much about the rationalization of economic institutions, as had earlier been shown by their indifference to the crown's efforts to abolish domestic tariffs.[79] It is indeed true that less emphasis was placed in France than in Britain on the economic aspects of bourgeois life: though obsessed by desire to achieve that moderate, but serious, level of wealth without which a family would soon become *déclassée*, typical French bourgeois were not economically adventurous. They were more interested in cultural than in economic change. There is no doubt that the respectable *grand-bourgeois* gentlemen of the 1780s would have been appalled to realize that high capitalism would soon emerge from their enthusiastic demolition of rural traditionalism and their defence of economic individualism. But this only means that capitalism differs from the bourgeois structures of thought and action that are its necessary and organic preconditions.

In my view, liberal nobles and notable bourgeois alike, including the declining *officier* class, can be said to have been the spearhead of the new bourgeois, individualist, and capitalist world order, regardless of their personal material circumstances or institutional status. The ostensible distaste of these people for money, like their inability to acquire it, is not at issue. What matters is that, ultimately, neither cultural nor economic forms can be reified or sundered. Involvement with bourgeois life in one sphere (e.g. an acceptance of individualism) implies the eventual acceptance of bourgeois mores in other spheres as well (e.g. careers open to talent). Isolated individuals did of course successfully distinguish in their private lives between a distasteful economic individualism and a more attractive cultural individualism. But such distinctions could not be definitively achieved at a collective level. The *officier* class did provide the cadres of the Revolutionary bourgeoisie, as Cobban has argued, but it is also true that such men were the unwitting apostles of new cultural and economic forms whose legalization during the Revolution was to have far-reaching consequences for the capitalistic development of the French nation.[80]

From tracing the decline of traditionalism in eighteenth-century France, historians have gone on to draw different conclusions about the changes in French social structure during the last decades of the *Ancien Régime*.

Most historians are prepared to grant that traditional society provided for its members at least a semblance of protection and community: as Mirabeau *père* explained, nobles in olden days had truly cared for their peasants. They may have vexed them, but they did so directly and paternally rather than by proxy as in recent times.[81] In the same way, Marmontel, in his memoirs, said of life in his home town in the backward province of Auvergne that nobles and bourgeois there had got along quite well:

> J'ai eu l'avantage de naître dans un lieu où l'inégalité de condition et de fortune ne se faisait presque pas sentir. Un peu de bien, quelque industrie et un petit commerce formaient l'état de presque tous les habitants . . .; la médiocrité y tenait lieu de la richesse; chacun était libre et utilement occupé. Ainsi la fierté, la franchise, la noblesse du naturel n'y étaient altérées par aucune sorte d'humiliation.[82]

Opinions, however, differ on the nature of social relations that came into being *after* the decline of this 'traditional' model.

The claim of orthodox Marxist historians is that social divisions widened after 1750. They admit that the prestige of the older distinctions of birth may have waned, but they counter that this decline was more than balanced by the appearance of newer sources of friction. Nobles, they say, withdrew from modern life; aristocrats, as they were now called, became insecure and aggressive, eager to recover forgotten feudal dues. The bourgeoisie, meanwhile, was itself more established, self-confident, and aggressive. In this view, the older waning distinctions of *Gemeinschaft* gradually became the equally divisive distinctions of *Gesellschaft*. The bourgeoisie, which in 1689 had been a distinct caste of non-nobles, had become by 1789 a distinct class of owners of property, much of it commercial, financial, and industrial.

In Marxist perspective, the French bourgeoisie, a modern class, was determined to overthrow the existing legal and political system because it wanted the State to make the laws of the market the laws of the land. By contrast, the nobility, a backward class, remained sullen and retrograde. 'The mass of the provincial and court nobility', writes Albert Soboul, 'thought that it could only be saved by an ever clearer affirmation of its privileges.'[83]

The aristocracy, feudal and obscurantist, was on one side. On the other was the bourgeoisie, involved in trade, banking, and manufacturing. 'The spectacle of this economic activity', writes Soboul, 'gave to the men of the bourgeoisie a consciousness of their class and made them understand that their class was irremediably opposed to the aristocracy.'[84]

The evidence on which the Marxist interpretation rests is considerable, a fact, incidentally, which did not impress Alfred Cobban, who quipped that historians, like others, are apt to find those things for which they seek. The Marxist evidence focuses on two issues. On the one hand, the dependence of the aristocracy on 'feudal modes of production' is emphasized. Thus, the continuing importance of traditional feudal dues is stressed, as is the dependence of the court aristocracy on royal favours, pensions, and government employment.

On the other hand, Marxist historiography also emphasizes the fact that the bourgeoisie's possibilities of social mobility were being cut off, a particularly telling development because the bourgeoisie was at the very time becoming richer, better educated, and culturally more secure. As Barnave put it, 'les chemins sont fermés de toutes parts'.[85]

The Marxists rely on different types of evidence to support their view that French professional and institutional structures were stultified. In some instances, they point to geographical regions taken *in toto*, like Brittany, where older nobles were so exclusive that even recently ennobled nobles could be radicalized.[86] More commonly, however, they point to particular professions where an esconced aristocracy now blocked the paths which *arriviste* bourgeois had in the past taken to find high office. In the army, for example, access to the officer corps was gradually denied to non-nobles. In 1758, the Minister of War, Belle Isle, though himself born of a recently ennobled family, ordered that nobles be advantaged for further promotion. Then, in 1763, it was decided that commissions in the infantry would no longer be sold, a decision which was a disadvantage for the *nouveau riche* bourgeoisie. Noble birth was given a greater edge in 1751, when four quarters of nobility were required for entry to the new military school in Paris, a provision extended to artillery schools in 1772 and to military engineering schools in 1776. Henceforth, the only non-nobles who might be promoted to officer rank were former soldiers of lines. A grand total of forty-six troopers, it may be added, were so promoted, all of whom rose to the rank of general in the armies of the Revolution.

Roughly similar statements could be made about the law courts. In the seventeenth century, through the Parlements, the bourgeoisie had gained a political voice. Moreover, thanks to the venality of offices, this social-political promotion connected the new forms of wealth to the traditional 'feudal' state, which in consequence became a semi-modern, relatively efficient, bureaucratic machine. Louis XIV's apocryphal 'l'État, c'est moi' was true in the sense that the King was indeed more powerful than he had ever been, but it was true only because the monarch had consented to associate the bourgeoisie with his rule.

In the eighteenth century, however, the venality of offices dried up. Old offices declined in value, and few new ones were created. The older *parlementaire* families became thoroughly aristocratic. They blended with the older nobles, and denied advancement to the *nouveaux riches* of the day. In Besançon, for example, lawyers as a profession fell into two groups: the more successful ones who 'stiffened in their defence of privilege', and the less successful ones who, to their chagrin, found themselves forced to take up sides with a Third Estate from which they had been trying to escape.[87] The administrative bourgeoisie also failed to renew itself and *intendants* in the 1780s were more and more often the ennobled sons of former bourgeois *intendants*.[88] Even the financiers, once disreputable, became more respectable and moved away from the newer commercial bourgeoisie.[89]

In the seventeenth century, runs the Marxist argument, the feudal, aristocratic, and monarchic 'complex' had been rejuvenated; but in the eighteenth century, no such renewal took place, despite the fact that the economic boom of the 1760s and 1770s had greatly increased the number of postulants to social promotion: merchants, lawyers, doctors, publicists, and the like. Cut off from political power, and increasingly aware of its dignity and professionalism, this new bourgeoisie was, we are told, dramatically set apart from the older aristocracy. This was the class that directed the Revolution.

In the last fifteen years or so, historians have begun to develop a new interpretation of French social structure and politics on the eve of the Revolution. To the older and by now well-worn Marxist view, which holds that a great chasm separated the reformist bourgeoisie from the traditionalist nobility, revisionist historians have opposed another interpretation, best summarized by Guy Chaussinand-Nogaret, who suggests that because of the 'absence of prejudice of the great nobles' a 'composite class' had by 1789 come into being. This new class of 'bourgeois-nobles' dominated, he thinks, the financial and economic life of France; its existence corroded the old *Ständestaat* and sapped the older division of orders. On the eve of the Revolution, concludes Chaussinand-Nogaret, the nobility, now close to the bourgeoisie, no longer depended on traditional sources of income, like feudal rents or royal grants: 'This was the most profound social revolution that France underwent until the belated coming of democracy in the nineteenth century.'[90]

The revisionists have relied on a variety of arguments, many of them the opposites of the Marxist ones. Thus, it is their claim that, in France, the older categories of bourgeois and noble had by 1789 lost their substance. Nobles were heavily involved in capitalism, such as it was, and conversely, many bourgeois were still set in older ways. It is the claim of the revisionists also that the supposedly *Ancien Régime* governmental machine was run by men who fully understood the new power of money.

Much impressive evidence has been produced to support these anti-Marxist views. The revisionists have argued, for example, that the Marxists were not justified in assuming that the French bourgeoisie of the 1780s was a modern class distinct from the aristocracy and impatient of traditional restraints on economic or industrial growth. In 1789, the French bourgeoisie was still, in many ways, a traditionalist estate, more interested in small but safe returns from land than on more profitable but risky commercial and industrial ventures.[91] It is well known that in the eighteenth century, the families of successful merchants continued to drift away from urban towards rural investments in a quest for stability and respectability. Revisionists have pointed to the bourgeoisie's lack of interest in the campaign for the removal of internal tariffs, a classical first step towards the creation of a national market society. This goal did not elicit much support in France and was more often supported by royal bureaucrats than by prominent merchants. It is likewise of consequence that the bourgeoisie, by 1789, had ensconced itself in the seigneurial system by purchasing seigneuries which often brought to their owners some of the social advantages of nobility. It is critical that bourgeois land-owners in France were uninterested in enclosing land, as had been done in England for more than a century.[92]

On the one hand, then, the revisionists have argued that the bourgeoisie in some ways remained traditionalist. On the other, they have insisted on the fact that many nobles were heavily involved in overseas (and especially Caribbean) commerce, like the Lameth brothers, the comte de Ségur, or Joséphine de Beauharnais. It may be added that the protection of this colonial commerce had become the first strategic concern of the monarchy: unlike its late nineteenth-century counterpart, eighteenth-century French imperialism was neither geopolitical nor racist nor ideological in its inspiration, but straightforwardly mercantilistic. This was understood by all, including aristocratic naval officers who, unlike their British colleagues, automatically assumed that their first strategic task was to protect trade rather than to destroy the enemy battle fleet.

Nobles were heavily involved in the most advanced industries, like chemicals, and aristocratic capital was important in the development of coal mining and of minerals. In the district of Rennes, 86 per cent of all foundries belonged to nobles, as did more than half of such establishments in places as widely removed as Strasbourg, Besançon, and Alençon.[93] Not all nobles were so engaged, of course, but as Robert Foster has shown in his *Nobility of Toulouse*,[94] even those who led uneventful rural lives were by now more orderly, account-keeping, budget-balancing, landed proprietors.

In short, neither the Second nor the Third Estate retained much of its older economic coherence. Merchants in Bordeaux had little to say to the rural bourgeois seigneurs of the Auvergne, and noble steel magnates had little in common with Breton *hoberaux*, with petty squires. The older estates had never been particularly homogeneous in the first place: the legal nobility had never completely fused with the *noblesse d'épée*; as Carnot put it, there was a difference between the 'noblesse de robe' and the 'noblesse de garde-robe'.[95] Nor was there much love lost between provincial nobles and court nobles, and in 1789, Ferrières, a provincial gentleman, then a deputy at Versailles, interpreted the rise of the Third Estate as the humbling of the great nobles: 'Que la Noblesse fasse un pas, le Tiers en fera dix; et à tout prendre, j'aime encore mieux que Coucaud se croie mon égal, que de voir un Grand me croire son inférieur, et m'assimiler presque aux gens qu'il gage, et qu'il nourrit.'[96]

With the breakdown of the older economic and social distinctions, came also, or so the revisionists assume, a breakdown of the older ideological categories. Many nobles, they suggest, had developed world views which corresponded fully to their newer economic and social situations. Most nobles, for example, probably accepted the validity of some modern principles (like freedom of conscience) and some nobles, it appears, accepted all and any modern principle whatsoever, including that of social equality. The running war of nobles against absolutism in the 1770s and 1780s is well known, and a sizeable minority of nobles remained at the cutting edge of radicalism through both the Terror and the Directory. In a celebrated passage, the comte de Ségur described the ideas of the aristocratic *jeunesse dorée* in the 1780s:

Voltaire entrainaît nos esprits, Rousseau touchait nos cœurs, nous sentions un secret plaisir à voir attaquer le viel édifice qui nous semblait gothique et ridicule. . . . Nous applaudissions les scènes républicaines de nos théâtres. . . . La liberté, quel que fût son langage, nous plaisait par son courage, l'égalité par sa commodité. On trouve du plaisir à descendre, tant qu'on croit pouvoir remonter dès que l'on veut. Et, sans prévoyance, nous goûtions à la fois les avantages du patriciat et les douceurs d'une philosophie plébéienne.[97]

Some nobles were positively radical about the rights of men, like the comtesse d'Harville, the benefactress of the Conventionnel Romme, who described this lady as 'Une amie vraiment noble, vraiment sage, ayant trouvé nécessaire de combattre ma fierté naturelle, effet des premières habitudes de mon enfance, [qui] parla à mon cœur, fonda en moi les lois de l'humanité, [et] fit de l'antiquité d'origine un devoir de supériorité en bonté, bienfaisance, générosité.'[98]

Most of the members of the provincial *sociétés de pensée* were nobles, as had been many of the leading theoreticians of the Enlightenment. It is indeed one of the ironies of modern European history that the first cultural statement of bourgeois life (the Enlightenment), like the first general critique of that cultural form (Romanticism), was in large part elaborated not by bourgeois or workers, but by aristocrats: philosophes like Buffon, Montesquieu, Mably, and Condillac; and later, by poets and writers like Lamartine, Vigny, Musset, Shelley, Byron, Alfieri, and Kleist.

Like the bourgeoisie, nobles in eighteenth-century France evolved new ways of thinking about topics as varied as happiness and death or economic growth and the relative merits of urban and rural life. These were not random innovations; they were instead different aspects of a more individualistic and rational perception of social life. A new world view was coming into being, of which the works of the philosophes can be seen as the most sophisticated statement, and which appealed to different social milieus. Moreover, to the Marxists who see culture as an expression of more fundamental forces, the revisionists retort that this new culture was in and of itself an important factor in bringing together individuals of different social milieus but of similar cultural orientation. This theoretical orientation is by no means revolutionary: it has been taken up in other national historical traditions by historians like E. P. Thompson, in Britain, and Eugene Genovese, in America, who are ordinarily thought to be Marxists; but in the more rigid context of French Marxism, the revisionist's approach seems particularly novel.

The efforts of the French state to modernize itself are also grist for the revisionist mill. Heretofore, Marxists insisted on the importance in pre-Revolutionary France of feudalism and of the *Ancien Régime* state as the guarantor of this outmoded system, but it has now been pointed out that the monarchy, in the 1760s, 1770s, and 1780s was not really hostile to the new ethos of individualism and economic growth. While all the ministers of Louis XVI but one were nobles, those ministers who really counted—Turgot, Necker, or Malesherbes—had bourgeois affinities. In many ways, the *Ancien Régime* state was more modern than its critics: it encouraged domestic as well as international free trade; it supported revolutionaries in America and in Holland; it attacked corporatism. The leading servants of the state, though themselves nobles, understood in which direction the monarchy had to move. Malesherbes in 1788 wrote to Louis that 'un Roi placé à la fin du xviiie; siècle, ne convoque pas les trois Ordres du xive; qu'il appelle les propriétaires d'une grande Nation renouvelée par sa civilisation.'[99]

The political importance of private property was understood by high government officials, as was also the need to give social and political promotion to those people who owned it. Ennoblements by the state, as against ennoblement by purchase, though infrequent, became more numerous, and twice as many people were granted noble status in the twenty years after 1760 as in the forty-eight years before that date. Moreover, a comparison of the two periods shows that though the number of administrators and artists who were made nobles rose four times, the number of ennobled '*négociants*' or prosperous businessmen rose by a factor of twelve.[100]

After 1760, the attitude of the state to commerce and nobility shifted significantly: in the past, the state had enforced the rules of *dérogeance* which deprived aristocratic would-be merchants of their noble status. Now, in a complete turnabout, the King ennobled merchants precisely because they were merchants. In the letters of nobility given to Jean and Barthélémy Lecoulteux of Rouen in 1756, for example, it was stated that

Le commerce a toujours été regardé comme une des sources les plus sûres et les plus fécondes de la force et de la puissance des États. . . . Nous remarquons que la plupart des familles qui s'adonnent au commerce ne l'envisagent que comme un moyen de passer à des emplois décorés de titres et de prérogatives leur paraissant communiquer un état plus honorable . . . préjugé, si nuisible au progrès du commerce. [Il importait de] faire connaître à la nation qu'elle pouvait trouver dans le commerce l'honorable comme l'utile.[101]

Birth may have remained critical as a determinant of social status, but money was ever more important. 'De l'or, de l'or', says Rameau's nephew. 'L'or est tout, et le reste, sans or n'est rien. . . . Je veux que mon fils soit heureux, ou, ce qui revient au même, honoré, riche, et puissant.' By 1789, rich versus poor was a more meaningful distinction than noble versus *roturier*. Turgot explained in 1776, 'il n'est aucun homme riche qui, sur-le-champ, ne devienne noble; en sorte que le corps des nobles comprend tout le corps des riches, et que la cause du privilégié n'est plus la cause des familles distinguées contre les roturiers, mais la cause du riche contre le pauvre'.[102]

In 1787, Sénac de Meilhan went one step further in his *Considérations sur les richesses et la luxe*: money, he said, was everywhere, and wealth placed those who possessed it, like those who did not have it, on the same level: 'neither rank nor privilege can resist its sovereign power . . . it divides society into classes in accordance with their degree of opulence'.[103]

What these new 'classes' were is, however, the focus of wide and raging debate. The Marxists are of a mind that nobles and bourgeois were still like night and day. The revisionists discern a newer and more blended palette of pastel shades.

The first step of the revisionist argument, as has been seen, was to deny that one could still find in 1789 a traditionalist aristocracy separate from a modernizing bourgeoisie. The second step is to suggest that a new social structure had replaced the older ones.

Agreement on that score is, however, incomplete. Chaussinand-Nogaret argues that ownership of property pure and simple was the key. In a thorough and stimulating article entitled 'Nobles,

Bourgeois, and the Origins of the French Revolution', Colin Lucas has suggested instead that the operative principle of social distinction was whether one was engaged in trade or not: 'In the upper reaches of French society', he writes, 'the great articulation was not between noble and commoner, which as I have tried to show, is an almost impossible division to demonstrate. It was between those who traded and those who did not.'[104] Leonard Berlanstein, in his book on men of law in Toulouse in the 1780s and 1790s, is even more categorical in his denial of the relevance of caste: 'The cleavage at the Toulouse bar did not cut neatly across the barrier that motivated so much revolutionary rhetoric, the noble commoner divide.' Many noble barristers had advanced opinions, so that 'the percentage of noble barristers who supported the Revolution was slightly higher than the percentage of pro-Revolutionary men at the bar as a whole.' Political opinions in Toulouse were hard to sort out: they did not correspond to caste, wealth, or, for that matter, intellectual background. Looking forward to the Revolution, Berlanstein concludes that 'the revolutionary barristers had supported the same reforms, read the same books, and joined the same associations as had their counter-Revolutionary colleagues'.[105]

* * *

It cannot be denied that a survey of the evidence that bears on the concrete situation of nobles and bourgeois before 1789 justifies much of the revisionist critique of Marxist themes. The revisionist statement, however, appears less strong if attention is focused on *perceptions* of what existed rather than on the supposed realities of the situation. Granted that bourgeois and nobles may have been increasingly alike, is it also true that contemporaries understood this to be so at the time? Reality, to some degree at least, is what people think it is. If it is assumed that nobles and bourgeois were increasingly alike in their material circumstances, just as they had become more alike in their manners, culture, dress, and speech, can it also be assumed that propertied Frenchmen in 1789 understood what their situation was? Did nobles accept the idea that the bourgeoisie would acquire equal civil status? Did ordinary bourgeois accept the idea that hereditary aristocracy was a socially useful institution? The problem has been stated with clarity by Jean-Marie Goulemot: 'the notion of concurrent élites now being brought forward by contemporary historiography seems more pertinent than the traditional, Marxist explanations but it has yet to be tested in the realm of ideology'.[106]

The matter is an important one. It involves the bourgeoisie's and noble's views of themselves and each other, as well as bourgeois appreciation of nobility as a social concept. It is reflected also in the types of *apologia pro vita sua* which different social groups presented at different times. Revisionist historians have useful things to say about these varied issues.

In the earlier decades of the century, for example, nobles had justified their prerogatives much as Bossuet had done in the seventeenth century: the superiority of nobles in society was self-evident. It was more to be mentioned than to be justified. De la Rocque, in his *Traité de la noblesse* (1735), similarly explained that nobles were inherently superior: 'Il y a dans les semences je ne sais quelle force et je ne sais quel principe qui transmet aux enfants la vertu de leurs parents.'

Significantly, however, later references were made instead to the virtue and achievement of existing nobles rather than to those of their forebears. In 1751, the well-known advocate of a revitalized military nobility, the Chevalier d'Arcq, made his case in these terms:

L'État nourrit ses membres, il faut que tous les membres servent l'État. Le citoyen oisif, par conséquent inutile, est criminel envers se patrie et lui dérobe tout ce qu'il consomme. Le Gentilhomme est citoyen avant d'être Noble, et le seul privilège que lui donne la Noblesse, c'est le choix parmi les services importants que l'État peut et doit en attendre. L'instant où il cesse de penser ainsi est celui où il cesse d'être Noble.[107]

Though nobles were often judged by non-nobles to be idle and corrupt, noble apologists insisted that aristocratic privileges were justified by the nobility's greater sense of virtue and devotion to the public good. Utility also was invoked on their behalf, by l'abbé Coyer for example, with his notion of a *noblesse commerçante*, a concept which, as has been seen, was tentatively endorsed by the state after 1760. Similarly, the reassertion of an aristocratic monopoly of promotions in the army can be interpreted as a defence of professional military men against the frivolous pretensions of *nouveaux-riches* would-be officers, more interested in the prestige of soldiering than its technique.

Many nobles understood that the justification of nobility needed to be revised, and at the same time, many bourgeois understood that the idea of nobility was by no means incompatible with an individualist view of social life. Although nobles in the flesh might be unattractive, the concept of nobility in the abstract appealed to the bourgeoisie because it could be seen as the culmination of a successful bourgeois 'carrière ouverte aux talents'. The names of commoners like Roland de la Platière, Creuzé de la Touche, Brissot de Warville, de la Revellière de Lépaux (all of them Girondins of sorts), or of Montagnards like Barère de Vieuzac, d'Anton, de Robespierre, and de Saint-Just, or even of future *enragés* and feminists like Leclerc d'Oze, Taboureau de Montigny, Théoroigne de Méricourt, and Etta Palm d'Aelders speak for themselves. Those who would acquire privilege were bound, in logic, to accept privilege as legitimate, at least until their own careers had been aborted. A Burgundian lawyer made this point with forthrightness in the last days of 1788:

> Les privilèges de la Noblesse sont de véritables propriétés qui seront d'autant plus respectées que nous n'en sommes point exclus et que nous pouvons les acquérir: les grandes actions, le valeur, le courage, le mérite personnel, les charges, la fortune même sont autant de chemins pour nous y conduire; et pourquoi donc supposer que nous pensions à détruire les germes d'émulation, qui sont la boussole de nos travaux?[108]

It was often stated that although the fiscal exemptions of the nobles were bad, nobility itself was good. The author of a pamphlet of 1789 entitled *Réflexions d'un citoyen de Besançon sur les privilèges et immunités de la noblesse*, presented this case with naïve confidence:

> La noblesse comme grâce du prince, comme prix d'un devoir accompli, comme distinction honorifique, est un bienfait; sous un autre aspect, elle n'est qu'un titre oppressif, une hypothèque illégale, un crime de lèse-nation, une atteinte à la propriété universelle, puisque le peuple n'a été ni consulté, ni entendu, et qu'il n'a point sanctionné, par un consentement libre, le privilège qui doit l'écraser. C'est surtout la noblesse fiscale que la nation ne peut trop se hâter de réprimer.[109]

Rabaut-Saint-Étienne was equally explicit. The presence of a nobility justified emulation, he thought, and, in addition, only emulation would make possible that continuity of social conditions without which King and Nation would drift apart. 'C'est donc à la noblesse, soit héréditaire, soit personnelle', he explained in 1788, 'qu'appartiennent les illustrations, les décorations, les titres & privilèges honorifiques; avantage que le public ne sauroit lui envier, qui excitent l'émulation, & qui servent à remplir graduellement les distances entre le peuple et le Roi.'[110]

A justification of nobility on such principles made a great deal of bourgeois universalist sense; the public good would necessarily arise from the individual's drive for distinction, very much as the wealth of nations emerged from the manufacturer's pursuit of private profit. Distinctions were good. Virtuous men and talented literateurs deserved praise and prizes, like Montyon's prix de vertu, awarded yearly by the French Academy after 1782. To be sure, the concept of nobility would only momentarily incarnate this meritocratic dogma, but it is worth noting that the principle of distinction itself remained intact throughout the Revolution, and was emphatically reasserted by the Constituant Assembly after the abolition of titles: 'L'état doit récompenser les services rendus au corps social quand leur importance et leur durée méritent ce témoignage de reconnaissance.'[111]

As a concept, nobility had a place in the bourgeois cultural pantheon, and the royalist publicist Rivarol observed even after the Revolution had broken out, that the French bourgeoisie was not fundamentally anti-noble: 'la noblesse est, aux yeux du peuple, une espèce de religion dont les gentilshommes sont les prêtres; et, parmi les bourgeois il y a bien plus d'impies que d'incrédules.[112]

In some ways, the desirability of creating a new élite based on merit was understood by both bourgeois and nobles. Many nobles accepted the equality of men at birth, just as many bourgeois accepted the idea that nobility might become the just reward of bourgeois merit. As has often been observed, nobles had a relatively good bourgeois press in the eighteenth century. Gresset in his play, *Le Marchand*, and Saurin in *Les mœurs du temps*, did unfavourably compare the morality of the nobility to that of the bourgeoisie; but the more frequent stance was represented, for example, by Beaumarchais's Aurelly and Sedaine's Vanderk, two merchants who prove to be nobles of ancient or modern lineage.[113]

None the less, and regardless of the considerable evidence that can be marshalled to support the idea that nobles and bourgeois were much alike and understood that to be the case, the revisionist statement is not altogether convincing. The traditional Marxist argument has considerable merit. Many dissonant voices could be heard, of traditionalist nobles on one side, and of radical bourgeois on the other. Nobles were far from unanimous in their tolerance of civic equality. Many still justified their social and political privileges as God-given prerogatives. For every Lafayette, there was, it seemed, a Prince de Condé. The reactionary holding action of the Parlementaires and the monarchy's inability to overawe them were understood to be the critical political events of the 1770s and early 1780s. There was no denying that access to top-level jobs had been essentially cut off. It was obvious also that many aristocrats had a lively and insolent sense of their distinct identity, as became evident when *annoblis* were excluded from the drafting of noble *cahiers* in 1789. A feudal spirit did survive as did also a longing for feudal utopias. It was in 1771, for example, that the first historical paintings of the feudal prowesses of medieval knights appeared. And contemporaries were not unaware of the wholly spurious biological and racialist defence which some nobles like Boulainvilliers, or for that matter, Montesquieu, had made of their vanishing privilege.

The fact seems to be that some nobles were for some change, some against, some alternated, and some were either ambivalent or undecided. Many nobles alternatively subscribed to the liberal integrationist, élitist argument as well as to the unreformed aristocratic message. After 1815, a blend of this kind, when advocated by Chateaubriand, for example, was essentially a pose; but before 1789, the confusion of aristocratism and liberalism was perfectly acceptable and stands in fact at the heart of Montesquieu's social and political message.

In the same way, just as many nobles remained obdurate obscurantists, so were many bourgeois adamantly anti-noble. It can hardly be denied that the bourgeoisie in the 1770s and 1780s developed a new ethic, which emphasized the values of work, discipline, professionalism, and, as Mauzi has observed, of happy mediocrity. Bourgeois were much more self-confident about being non-nobles. The *roturier* heroes of Mercier's *La Brouette du vinaigrier*, like Beaumarchais's *Figaro* and Sedaine's *Le Philosophe sans le savoir*, were very assertive about the dignity of their condition and profession. Moreover, it is clear that this bourgeois view of life was carefully elaborated as a conscious alternative to supposedly aristocratic values. The revolutionary oaths of eternal loyalty were a reply to the ephemeral quality of aristocratic fireworks.

Every noble argument had a bourgeois parry. If some asserted that nobles would effortlessly become citizens if given a chance to do so, others denied it, like Helvetius, a man close to the court and whose wife was born a countess, who wrote: 'Nos prêtres sont trop fanatiques et nos nobles trop ignorants pour devenir citoyens, et sentir les avantages qu'ils gagneraient à l'être, à former une nation. Chacun sait qu'il est esclave, mais vit dans l'espérance d'être sous-despote à son tour.'[114] Boulainvilliers might make a case for feudalism on the grounds of the nobility's conquering and Germanic origins, but so could bourgeois pamphleteers ridicule today's nobles as the heirs of yesterday's parvenus. Many bourgeois writers, like Roederer and Dulaure, a future Conventionnel, laid emphasis on the spuriousness of the nobles' ethnic claims; and in the same way, one lawyer from Dijon who was later arrested as a noble in 1793 emphatically denied that he was a noble or could ever have wished to be one even before 1789 because the nobility, he argued, was less respectable than was the bourgeoisie. His family had been lawyers for three centuries, he explained, 'sans avoir ambitionné de sortir de cette antique, vertueuse et *peu commune* roture pour entrer dans l'ordre d'une noblesse achetée à prix d'argent, que mes principes ont toujours su apprécier à leur juste valeur'.[115]

The aristocratic pretensions of newly ennobled bourgeois could appear particularly odious, as they did to Dubois-Crancé. He did not deny that from time to time the aristocracy had had the good sense to draw some non-noble inside its magic circle, but the results were not to his liking: 'alors, ce nouveau parvenu, tout fier de ses alliés qui le méprisaient en vidant son coffre-fort, reportait avec une impudence éhontée, sur ses vassaux de nouvelle acquisition, toutes les humiliations dont il était abreuvé au milieu de ses enfants adoptifs'. Promotions into the nobility, he concluded, sapped the bourgeoisie's 'motif d'émulation'.[116]

Nobility might in theory be acceptable, but its expressions were nearly always decried. Corporate distinctions in particular were thoroughly detested: 'DÉFIEZ-VOUS DES CORPS,' warned Rabaut-Saint-Étienne.[117] Individual emulation and distinction might be acceptable; but institutionalized distinctions were not, and as has been said, the existing advantages of being noble were, of course, widely and almost universally attacked. Particularly galling in this respect were the undeserved privileges and tax exemptions of the aristocracy: it was irrelevant that most nobles were not rich, that all of them paid some tax, and that some of them bore a relatively greater burden than, let us say, bourgeois Parisian rentier holders of government bonds. It was *thought* that nobles did not pay; and their supposed exemptions ran against the grain. Why should idle individuals secure favour and privilege? Nobles were doubly offensive: as a caste, they vitiated the concept of a harmonious, equal society; and as individuals, they also gave offence, because individualism means achievement

—but what had nobles achieved? It is revealing that the principal complaint which was raised against aristocrats at the end of the *Ancien Régime* was precisely that they were mere parasites, useless and uncreative leeches stuck on to the body social.

On the meritocratic grounds of achievement, nobility was praiseworthy; as obstacles to equality and the reign of virtue, nobles were offensive, and in the late 1780s bourgeois writers comically oscillated from the acceptance of nobles as owners of property and future citizens to their rejection as arrogant reactionaries. In November 1788, Rabaut-Saint-Étienne advocated a two-chamber parliamentary system since nobles had a social purpose and 'stimulated zeal';[118] but in January 1789, he was pushing with equal warmth for the dilution of the nobility in a single parliament. The arguments he used then, writes his biographer, Martin Göhring, were every bit as powerful as those he had brought forward two months before—as well they might be, since the debate on the usefulness of nobility could not be resolved.[119] And Romme, who was genuinely grateful to the nobles who had befriended him, could also be very harsh about court nobles, for example, 'ces idoles livides et dorés'.[120] Nobles, in short, were both good and bad.

Although the revisionists may well have made the Marxist view untenable, they have not completely proved their point. It is too strong to conclude, as did Guy Chaussinand-Nogaret, that in their grievances, 'the French bourgeoisie and nobility appear to be accomplices, determined to destroy a discredited regime and to substitute for it a new order'.[121] However, it is also true that the older Marxist interpretation must be amended. Marcel Reinhard, the wisest historian of the French Revolution in modern times, was right to conclude that in 1789, 'the problem of the relations between élite and nobility was still unresolved. The resolution of this capital question was left to those who wanted to regenerate the kingdom.'[122]

At the same time, the point, it must be emphasized, is *not* that the truth lies somewhere in the middle, half-way between the Marxist and revisionist stances. Both analyses are correct in that the varying views on caste and class of nobles and bourgeois in pre-Revolutionary France can be simultaneously apprehended in terms of both the Marxist and revisionist constructs. 'A first-rate intelligence', wrote Scott Fitzgerald, can be defined as 'the ability to hold two opposed ideas in the mind at the same time, and still retain the ability to function.' The deputies who met at

Versailles and their constituents were not all, by any means, first-rate minds. But they did function, for a short time in any case.

To summarize this introduction, it can be concluded that the Marxist and the revisionist historians of eighteenth-century France all have extremely useful things to say. Their differing views must be subsumed rather than cancelled out. The fact is that relations of bourgeois and nobles in 1789 were still open-ended; in certain circumstances, unity was possible. An élite did exist, potentially at least. But at other times, latent divisions of class could resurface. Social relations were intensely volatile, and very sensitive to the vagaries of political events.

The vicissitudes of the changing rights of nobles during the French Revolution emerged directly from this ambivalent setting. If the bourgeoisie in 1789 had been ideologically committed to the exclusive defence of property, the nobles problem would never have arisen as it did. If the bourgeois had been adamantly anti-noble in 1789, the rights of nobles, in politics or property, would have been dramatically and immediately curtailed. But no simple solution could emerge in 1789, when the bourgeoisie's ideological and practical goals were still confused. Only the course of Revolutionary politics made possible the emergence of a definitive solution to the nobles problem on the basis in practice of the defence of property and in theory of bourgeois individualism.

The *leitmotiv* of this essay as a whole is that the actions of nobles had little to do with their fate. What mattered instead was the evolution of bourgeois attitudes to nobles which went through a number of stages. Initially, in 1789–91, nobles were accepted as the individual citizens of a state which respected existing propertied arrangements, now transcended by the existence of citizenship. It was assumed at that time that the nobility as an institution should be utterly destroyed but that nobles, as propertied citizens, should have complete equality. For a variety of reasons, as shall be seen, this optimism vanished in the summer and autumn of 1791.

From late 1791–2 to late 1793–4, the Revolutionary bourgeoisie, unwilling to abandon its communitarian hopes and committed to the idea of a virtuous state, steadily drifted leftwards. Unable to deny popular aspirations and unable to meet them as well, bourgeois politicians were driven to accentuate the nature of the Revolution as a war of vice versus virtue. They reaffirmed the egalitarian spirit of their enterprise by sacrificing to the 'plebs' individual nobles who were now held up to public scorn as the embodiment of selfish corruption and as the enemies of a moralized and virtuous Republican state.

After 1795, the bourgeoisie desperately tried to undo the mess that it had made. In practice, this meant a break with the 'people' and the institutions that represented them, like the Paris Sections. Ideological disentanglement, however, was more painful. Though the practice of Revolutionary idealism was quickly abandoned, the ideology (or rhetoric) of Enlightened universalism was more enduring. Only in 1799 did the bourgeoisie finally understand that all property owners should make common cause. 'Les nègres de nos colonies', wrote Rivarol in August 1789, 'et les domestiques dans nos maisons peuvent, la Déclaration des Droits à la main, nous chasser de nos héritages. Comment une assemblée de législateurs a-t-elle feint d'ignorer que le droit de nature ne peut exister un instant à côté de la propriété?'[123]

But so they did, though not for long. In 1789, the need for the constituent parts of the élite to band together was only faintly understood by men whose gaze was then still directed towards the decaying *Ancien Régime*. After 1794, and especially after 1799, when politics were set against the backdrop of the popular complaint that had arisen during the Terror, the need for unity was grasped by nearly everyone as was also the danger of assuming that the State should be virtuous or do more than represent the interests of the possessing class. These were conclusions that had been inconceivable in 1789 but appeared self-evident by 1799. By then, the French bourgeoisie was indeed in a position to make its mind up about nobles, but the process by which it got there was, to say the least, arduous.

Chapter Two

The integration of nobles in a bourgeois universalist state in 1789–1791

i. Nobles for and against the Revolution

The dominant Marxist historiographical interpretation of the French Revolution has accepted as a given the natural hostility of bourgeois and nobles *after* 1789, just as it has assumed the existence *before* 1789 of a decided split between a traditionalist aristocracy and a modernizing bourgeoisie. In this view, the gradual decay of noble rights is held to be self-evident and self-inflicted. There is no intellectual issue to consider, and *a fortiori* no interplay of noble rights and bourgeois universalism. The problem vanishes: it has not been and is not to be considered. Nobles were indeed pushed out, but, in the words of Georges Lefebvre, for the obvious reason that they themselves desired it: 'the majority of the French nobility refused to accept civic equality, although such a step would not have affected either its wealth or its influence'.[1]

It may seem bold to question such a central concept, endorsed by so great a historian as Georges Lefebvre. None the less, it can, I think, be argued that nobles were politically ambivalent after 1789, just as their social and ideological situation had been ambiguous before the Revolution. Lefebvre's judgement is too schematic. As Alfred Cobban showed, much of the theorizing on the French Revolution is a form of self-fulfilling prophecy: if the French Revolution is conceived from the outset as a bourgeois, anti-feudal, anti-noble movement, much evidence can then be found to prove it. Statements of 1789 which throw doubt on this view are deemed idiosyncratic, and those of 1793 which sustain it are considered *ipso facto* normative.

This intellectual perception, it may be added, is reinforced by the revolutionaries' own view of their political trajectory: guilt in 1793 implied that guilt had existed in 1789, even if not then perceived. Although the Mountain's own opinion on all specific issues had varied wildly from moment to moment, its prosecution of the Gironde took as evidence of royalism in 1793 statements made in 1792 or even 1791, notwithstanding the Gironde's defence that others had also changed their minds. So did the accusation levelled against the King reach back to a pre-constitutional period, as even he had the sense to point out. In a world where men were either virtuous *or* immoral, it was unthinkable that men should have been in succession both good *and* bad. 'La Révolution est un bloc' said Clemenceau; many contemporaries concurred, and so have, more or less consciously, many historians: since some nobles were shown to have become anti-Revolutionary later, they must have been anti-Revolutionary before. What nobles thought in 1789 is deduced from what was said about them in 1793–4. Such preconceptions ought to be put aside.

To be sure, many nobles in 1789 already had decided not to co-operate with the bourgeoisie. In the autumn of 1789, mournful complaints were drawn up here and there to protest against the destruction of the Parlements and of corporate orders.[2] Resigned lamentations of this kind were soon followed by conspiracy. But from the first, counter-Revolution in France transcended the division of estates. We do not need to consider the plots in Britanny of La Rouerie in 1792 or in Paris of the Marquis de Favras in 1790 and of the supposed *Chevaliers du Poignard*, all of them frivolous enterprises of no general significance; but more popular disturbances like those which took place in the south in May and June 1790, and were led at Nîmes by the lawyer Froment, are important.[3] What they reveal, however, is not so much the hostility of nobles *per se* as the continued existence within French society of a broad, traditional, Catholic 'subculture' resistant to modernizing change. Geography was the critical factor here, and what is really significant may well be that these early rebellions occurred in the most backward parts of France, untouched by the commercial revolution of the eighteenth century, that is to say, in those parts of France where religion could still serve to express the political passions of the day. South Central France was *sui generis*, and it does not make too much sense to infer from the presence of Auvergnat nobles at the counter-Revolutionary assembly at Jalès the supposed opinions of worldly nobles in Paris or Bordeaux.

Although some nobles opposed the Revolution from the first, others were enthusiastic supporters of the New Order, and thousands of them remained in the army, not only in 1789–91, but through 1793 and 1794 also. Only 7 or 8 per cent of them left the country, and it is quite unwarranted to suppose that the opinions of even this small minority were homogeneously reactionary.* More (the precise number is unknown) resurfaced after 1789 as local officials. Many of them bought *biens nationaux*, fifty of them in the department of the Sarthe alone.[4] Later, many nobles claimed to have done so under duress, but their actions speak more loudly than their words.

Many nobles may well have understood that they could do better for themselves under the new regime, just as bourgeois pamphleteers had promised that they might. This was precisely the argument that was presented some years later by one Picot de Lapeyrousse, an imprisoned Girondin, required to justify his allegiance to the Revolution: 'Je suis noble,' he explained, 'mais on chassait mes enfants de tous les états. . . . Peut-on se persuader qu'un homme organisé qui n'a trouvé que des entraves dans un régime de fer n'adore pas une révolution qui le met à sa place?'[5]

Such cases may be isolated, but this type of argument appeared plausible to contemporaries, and Brissot himself offered the prospect of bourgeois achievement as an enticement to the country gentry, the one group which might have been thought to be least sympathetic to the Revolution.[6]

The pattern of noble co-operation, discernible in the country at large, is visible also in the National Assembly, where about one hundred noble deputies supported progressive opinion. Some of these men sat for the nobility, others had been elected to the Third Estate.

On the whole, nearly all noble deputies eventually accepted the creation of a National Assembly without too much fuss. Almost none of them emigrated in the summer of 1789 and the role of nobles during the night of the fourth of August and the abolition of the feudal system is well known.

Ironically, nobles also played a crucial role in the abolition of nobility in June 1790. La Rochefoucauld's unofficial committee of liberal nobles worked for the suppression of titles behind the scenes, and Lafayette officially spoke on behalf of such an abolition. This radical posture earned Lafayette the plaudits of the journalists of *L'Ami du Roi*, who remarked that in order to be the object of the admiration of the 'universe', the *héros des deux mondes* did not need 'the splendor of his ancestors'.[7] Mention should also be made of Menou, a noble who was President of the Assembly on the day that titles were abolished. This law, he later explained, had 'forever' destroyed the nobility, a privileged class

* See Appendixes 3 and 4.

'que j'ai appris en même temps à . . . connoître et à . . . mépriser'.[8] The marquis de Ferrières wrote to his wife that nobles ought not to be aroused by the abolition of their titles. The monarchy, he explained, might be restored to its previous glory; and even if that did not happen, the situation of nobles would still be quite tolerable, and no worse, certainly, than in England:

l'ancienne forme de gouvernement entièrement changée, il se formera, après de violentes secousses, un gouvernement à peu près semblable à celui de l'Angleterre. Alors la Noblesse sera ce qu'elle est dans cette île, une distinction purement honoraire, bornée à la société particulière des nobles. Mais dans toute supposition, la seule conduite que doivent tenir les nobles, est d'attendre les événements, et surtout d'éviter qu'on les suppose un obstacle qu'il faille écarter par la force: car dans la fermentation actuelle des esprits, il y a une foule de gens qui ne cherchent qu'un prétexte.[9]

It was suggested then[10] and has been since[11] that Revolutionary nobles were acting from private interest: Noailles was an impoverished *cadet de famille* and Lafayette a calculating opportunist. But this approach to the nobles in 1789 is no more fruitful than similar *ad hominem* arguments about leftists in 1793 (i.e. Marat was a thief; Babeuf, a forger; and Robespierre, a paranoiac). Individuals have private motives, but their personal vices must find an echo in order to become the law of a great nation.

It would of course be absurd to argue that the French nobility as a group was enthusiastic about the Revolution. There was opposition in some provinces, and there were many die-hard noble deputies in Versailles as well. Yet a closer look at aristocratic 'anti-revolutionism' in the National Assembly shows that the stance of nobles there does not have the rigid quality which a number of historians have taken for granted. Conservative deputies certainly opposed a wide range of bourgeois measures, but often with surprising feebleness. Though left and right in the Assembly fell into many knock-down fights over the constitution, the veto, and the new religious arrangements, some anti-aristocratic acts passed nearly unnoticed. On 15–20 March, 1790, for example, when primogeniture was abolished 'sans égard à l'ancienne qualité des biens et des personnes', Merlin remarked that the use of the loaded term '*ancien*' 'n'excita pas une seule réclamation, même dans la partie de l'Assemblée Constituante qui semblait avoir juré de défendre toutes les erreurs et tous les abus'.[12] The King himself appeared to have quietly assumed that the nobility as an order was defunct, and Chérin, the court genealogist, was told by Saint-Priest: 'Le roi me charge, Monsieur, de vous prévenir que Sa Majesté ne veut plus que vous receviez les titres généalogiques qu'il était d'usage de vous remettre, pour avoir l'honneur de lui être présenté. Vous voudrez bien vous conformer à cet ordre de Sa Majesté.'[13]

The debate on the abolition of titles was, it is true, much more lively. In the country at large, the law of 19 June 1790, which the King did not veto,[14] certainly caused a number of ripples. In the Cotentin, the local nobility formally protested, comparing its titles with the flags of regiments; the nobility of Poitou thought the law to be contrary to the Declaration of the Rights of Man;[15] in Paris, the duc de Brissac caused a scandal by attempting forcibly to resist the removal of his escutcheon from the portal of his *hotel particulier*. Near Vire, in Normandy, a noble, Thoury de Corderie, achieved local notoriety first by refusing to pay any tax bill addressed to him as Monsieur Thoury, and, second, by taking pot-shots at the local national guard. His castle was sacked and burnt at once.[16] More seriously, at Versailles, Ferrières said that the law that abolished nobility was met 'non pas par des cris, mais par d'horribles hurlements'. A petition of protest against the suppression of titles asserted that the legislation ran 'contrary . . . to the interests of the Monarchy [and] the will of the Nation', and was signed by nearly one hundred nobles.[17]

It must be added, however, that many dissenting nobles were careful to place their objections in the context of accepted bourgeois thinking. Just as the defence of noble privilege before 1789 had insisted on the professionalism and merits of the aristocracy, so did many nobles in 1790 defend their titles as a form of property: all property was sacred, including the right to call oneself a marquess or a prince.

Many nobles like Faucigny took a different but related tack: nobles did not have a God-given right to their status, but some social distinctions were inevitable, and to destroy the nobility of birth was to signal the legitimacy of the even less attractive nobility of wealth. In Burkean tones, Faucigny announced the end of the glory of Europe: moral worth, he said, would now yield to the power of the 'propriétaires de cent mille écus de rente'.[18] Faucigny's complaint, as it happens, was well taken, and very close to Marat's thinking on the problem. Faucigny may have been a conservative, but his was no unthinking reactionary obduracy.

Historians have perhaps been too quick in their categorization of noble opinion. It is by no means obvious that most nobles rushed into the opposition or that most of the bourgeois revolutionaries thought that this had happened. In fact, even the opinions of the more conservative nobles bear looking into, and some mention at least should be made of the very 'bourgeois' principles which were tacitly and at times even explicitly assumed by leaders of the aristocratic right in the Constituent Assembly.

No troglodytes by any means, these men were inching towards what would be the programme of the bourgeoisie itself after 1814, a doctrinally unsound but practically useful fusion of popular sovereignty with equality before the law and of a parliament, under the thumb of the propertied interest, working in tandem with a strong and independent monarch. Mounier, Lally-Tollendal, Bergasse, and Calonne (in his 1790 manner), accepted the idea of a British system of government with a two-chamber parliament. At a more conceptual level, Montlosier explicitly urged the acceptance of popular sovereignty and the domination of society by the men of property. So did Cazalès, who has none the less been described by a learned and sensitive historian, Michel Vovelle, as the most adept defender of 'l'esprit aristocrate', as a man bitterly intent on the 'défense des prérogatives royales et des privilèges'.[19] Yet, in October 1789, Cazalès stated that although merchants were rootless cosmopolites, all men of landed property could be relied upon: 'le capitaliste, le banquier, l'homme qui possède l'argent, sont des cosmopolites; le propriétaire seul est le vrai citoyen . . . c'est à lui de délibérer de l'impôt'.[20] Indeed, one and a half years later, Cazalès was still arguing this same point, at a time, it may be added, when the Girondin bourgeoisie was beginning to waver in its defence of property. It was not birth but wealth which should be the foundation of political life, Cazalès explained:

Je ne crois pas qu'il soit nécessaire d'apprendre à l'Assemblée nationale que les propriétaires sont la société elle-même; que c'est par la propriété que la société a été fondée; et que s'il est juste que tous soient soumis à la loi, que tous doivent être égaux en droits devant elle, il n'en est pas moins vrai que toutes les fonctions publiques doivent être remises aux propriétaires pour l'avantage même de ceux qui sont soumis à ces fonctions, pour l'avantage des justiciables et pour l'avantage des administrés.[21]

All Tories and most Whigs could have said the same.

The revisionists are reasonable in arguing that most nobles and most bourgeois in 1789 roughly agreed in practice on what was to be done, just as they would finally agree in both practice and theory in 1799 and 1814. What separated them in 1789 was sensibility as much as substance. Ferrières expressed this mood in a letter to his wife, who had to deal with Revolutionary upstarts: 'je sens, ma bonne amie, l'ennui de ta position. Rien n'est plus triste que de vivre avec des gens qui n'ont ni nos goûts, ni notre manière de voir et de sentir; mais je t'en conjure, ne t'abandonne point à cette triste mélancolie.'[22]

Men like Cazalès would have accepted modernization in practice, if it had been set in a monarchical and traditional setting, as it had in Britain. But at this time, the Revolutionary bourgeoisie, though intent above all on the defence of property, also insisted on using a rhetoric of civic egalitarianism. In actual fact, the distance between most nobles and most bourgeois was probably not great in 1789. It was the gap of style that was immense.

A parallel of sorts can be drawn between the evolution of rightist politics in 1789–91, and those of the Revolutionary bourgeoisie in late 1791–3. A true understanding of the bourgeoisie's social and economic interests would have precluded in the autumn of 1791 a policy of no-enemies-to-the-left which was ideologically consistent but practically disastrous. And yet the left did follow such a course. In the same manner, the aristocratic right in 1789–91 drifted for largely sentimental and rhetorical reasons away from what it basically understood to be its true interests towards the handful of unrepentant court traditionalists who had gathered around d'Artois and Condé. For the nobles in 1789, like the bourgeoisie in late 1791, idea had more substance than fact.

Although most nobles probably could have accepted what had happened in 1789–91, many of them also found it hard to admit this to themselves or to each other. Most of the deputies who had voted against the suppression of the nobility, wrote Ferrières again, had done so 'à l'imitation les uns des autres; le gentilhomme français croit que l'honneur consiste à se hâter de faire toutes les sottises qui supposent du courage'.[23] Many nobles who were at once modern in their political and cultural outlook, and reluctant to accept the social consequences, repeatedly faltered. Some hurtled forward into the Revolutionary party; others yielded to the temptation of emigration, which some of them thought to be a lark. Many withdrew from public life. Chateaubriand spoke for his milieu when he later wrote of his feelings at the time: 'Je n'avais . . . ni adopté ni rejeté les nouvelles opinions; aussi peu disposé à les attaquer qu'à les servir, je ne voulus ni émigrer ni continuer la carrière militaire: je me retirai.'[24]

Visible at a personal level, the disarray of nobles can also be grasped in a more abstract way. Before 1789, when politics were directed to the destruction of arbitrary 'absolutism', or again, after 1799, after the Terror and the anti-noble Directory, nobles were able to make common cause with non-noble owners of property. During the intervening years, however, nobles were out of step. No longer a caste, they were powerless without the bourgeoisie. Not yet perceived as inherent members of the propertied class, they could not act within it. For ten years, nobles received the worst of two worlds. Attacked by their enemies as members of a caste, they could not defend themselves as one and were in consequence politically rudderless. Socially neither fish nor fowl, the nobility in 1789 could present neither a united front of conservative opposition nor an anchor for the politically liberal but socially conservative bourgeoisie. In short, it was incapable of sustained political action.

Taken literally, the behaviour of nobles in 1789–91 often appears to have been contradictory and sometimes even incoherent. Thus, historians of varying persuasions have been able to interpret the actions of nobles as they wished, for much evidence can be gathered to support any of a variety of points of view. Here, every man is truly his own historian.

For early nineteenth-century bourgeois authors of an anti-aristocratic frame of mind, nobles could easily be shown to have been guilty on all scores. So was it, for example, that J. A. Dulaure could suggest in his *Esquisses historiques sur la Révolution française* of 1825 that the Second Estate was to be blamed for an active opposition that caused the breakdown of the bourgeois Revolution, a theme that was to be shortly thereafter developed by Mignet. But bourgeois authors of a later period, much disturbed by the inability of the right to contain the left, came to argue the reverse. For Taine, the nobles' sin was not to have acted at all:

> Like all other Frenchmen, nobles had also experienced the enduring pressure of monarchic centralization. They had no 'esprit de corps' and had lost their associative instinct. They no longer knew how to act on

their own. They waited for a stimulus from the centre, and at the centre, the King, their hereditary general, now a captive of the people, had ordered them to be resigned and not to do anything.[25]

Forty years later, Madelin presented a similar picture. 'Strange to say,' he wrote, 'those who seemed to be the least upset were those whom, on the face of things, the Revolution was hurting most: the nobles. These amiable people were admirably lackadaisical. They had been ruined by the abolition of feudal dues. They were persecuted in the provinces and insulted in Paris. But most of them by far were still smiling, as we can see in the hundreds of *lettres d'aristocrates* which Vaissière has published.'[26]

All history is contemporary history, at times for better, at times for worse, and it is striking that historians' explanations of the conduct of nobles during the Revolution have so often dovetailed neatly with their overriding interests in other fields. A parallel can be drawn here with the debate on the origins of the Vendée rebellion: historians of a royalist persuasion were eager to show that Vendéen peasants had willingly followed the lead of their natural betters: King, nobles, and clergy. So, paradoxically, were leftist historians, who had to explain somehow the delusions of anti-Republican peasants.

The same thinking applies to an appreciation of noble politics in 1789–91. From a conservative point of view, the thought of a 'collaborationist' noble is every bit as unwelcome as it is from the more progressive point of view, which portrays the Revolution as a class war of the unprivileged against intolerable aristocratic abuse.

Many of the historians who have considered the nobility's initial reaction to the French Revolution have had a vested interest in presenting it as a clear-cut thing, and it is worth mentioning that most contemporary observers were less categorical about this. In 1789–92, even the most advanced revolutionaries did not conclude that nobles had refused to accept civic equality. No less a personage than Marat, in fact, said that they had accepted it. For *L'Ami du peuple*, nobles could most definitely not be blamed for wanting to revive feudalism: 'leur orgueil a eu beau se soulever contre ces réformes indispensables que prescrivait le bien public, la conscience leur criait qu'elles étaient justes, ils les ont approuvées au fond du cœur, et ils ont fini par souscrire eux- mêmes à ces douloureux sacrifices'.[27]

By implication at least, Robespierre agreed on this score with Marat, as appears from his speech of 2 January 1792:

> C'est ainsi que parmi vous ce sont les parlements, les nobles, le clergé, les riches, qui ont donné le branle à la révolution; ensuite le peuple a paru. Ils s'en sont repentis, ou du moins ils ont voulu arrêter la révolution, lorsqu'ils ont vu que le peuple pouvoit recouvrer sa souveraineté; mais ce sont eux qui l'ont commencée; et sans leur résistance et leurs faux calculs, la nation seroit encore sous le joug du despotisme.[28]

Robespierre's assumption is reasonably clear: the privileged order had accepted civic equality and the collapse of the *Ancien Régime*, but had refused to accept popular sovereignty, a compromise which would of course prove to be the French bourgeoisie's own position from 1795 to the mid-1860s. And even Brissot, the émigrés' fiercest foe, did not argue that France's enemies were eager to restore the *Ancien Régime* plain and simple. In 1791, he said that the powers of Europe were intent on a 'résurrection de la noblesse et cette imitation de constitution anglaise à laquelle s'attachent maintenant les rebelles'.[29] In fact, since Danton at that same time was accusing Lafayette of yearning to give to France that same 'constitution anglaise avec l'espérance de lui donner bientôt celle de Constantinople', it follows that in late 1791 some of the most advanced revolutionaries could not clearly distinguish between the political goals of émigrés and those of undoubted constitutionalists.

ii. Anti-corporatism versus anti-nobilism

To speak of the nobles' acceptance of civic equality and of a common bourgeois-noble stake in the maintenance of order naturally leads to re-examination of the seemingly anti-noble legislation of 1789. Sieyes's immensely popular and anti-aristocratic *What is the Third Estate* needs to be explained as does a rash of apparently anti-noble acts.

First, in June 1789, came the creation of a single and National Assembly, a step followed in early August by the supposed destruction of the 'entire' feudal system. Taxes would fall equally on all; civil, ecclesiastical, and military careers were to be opened to talent. Then came the *arrêté* of 15 October 1789, abolishing distinctions of dress among the deputies of the three Orders, now all members of a single National Assembly. The further convocation of assemblies of Orders was declared illegal, as were the

Orders themselves in early November 1789. On 28 February 1790, restrictions of birth as a requirement for military promotions were set aside, as was primogeniture in March. Then, as has been said, in June 1790, titles were abolished.[30] Other measures directly or indirectly eroded the influence of nobles in the country at large: the creation of elected municipalities reduced their influence in local politics; and the suppression of patronage was obviously a financial blow.[31] Most crucial, however, was the abolition on 6 September 1790, of the Parlements and of every privilege of jurisdiction. Henceforth all citizens would plead 'sans distinctions . . . en la même forme et devant les mêmes juges, dans les mêmes cas'.

But it must none the less be remembered that these various steps were by no means the expression of some specific bourgeois animosity for ci-devants as private persons. Nobility, as a caste, was anathema; but nobles as individuals did not suffer. By birth, none, of course, would have special rights, but none was disenfranchised as a citizen, and it was in this spirit that Romme in April 1790 preached moderation and reconciliation regardless of what some nobles might want:

Tachez mes bons compatriotes de porter à la paix toute notre milice nationale. Qu'elle surveille sans cesse, que le service soit une suite de son courage, de sa persévérance, de son dévouement au bien général, mais qu'elle n'oublie pas que nos ennemis sont ici nos frères et que si nous devons les mettre dans l'impossibilité de nous faire du mal, nous devons aussi éviter de leur en faire. Travaillons pour eux quoique malgré eux. Le temps pourra mettre les personnes et les sentimens à leur place naturelle.

Individual nobles who publicly sided with the Revolution were warmly acclaimed. When Joseph de Talhouët became mayor of Rennes the *Journal des Départements* wrote on 17 November 1790: 'Ce choix prouve bien,' 'que nous savons également estimer et distinguer les ci-devant privilégiés, sans considérer une caste qui n'existe plus, lorsqu'ils annoncent des vues conformes au bien public.'[32]

In the eyes of the leaders of the Third Estate, many of whom were themselves nobles, like Mirabeau, Lafayette, and Lameth, aristocrats might be anathema as members of corporations but were, when taken one by one, citizens whose rights could not be denied. Even the pathologically anti-noble J.-A. Dulaure concurred in 1790 in the conclusion of his book, the *Histoire critique de l'aristocratie jusqu'à nos jours; où l'on expose ses préjugés, ses brigandages, ses crimes, où l'on prouve qu'elle a été le fléau de la liberté, de la raison, des connoissances humaines, et constamment l'ennemi du peuple et des rois.* To be sure, argued Dulaure, the nobility as a social entity was hateful, 'mais ce n'est point les individus, mais le seul régime de la noblesse que j'ai prétendu peindre avec les couleurs qui lui conviennent'. Nobles were vicious, their reason was perverted, but their corruption 'n'était pas plus dans leur cœur, que dans celui des autres hommes'. It was the 'régime' of the nobility which was vicious and not its members.[33]

Even Sieyes at this point had agreeable things to say about nobles taken one by one:

Je ne suis point étonné que les deux premiers Ordres aient fourni les premiers défenseurs de la justice et de l'humanité. Les *talents* tiennent à l'emploi exclusif de l'intelligence et aux longues habitudes: les membres de l'Ordre du Tiers doivent, par mille raisons, y exceller; mais les *lumières* de la morale publique doivent paraître d'abord chez les hommes bien mieux placés pour saisir les grands rapports sociaux et chez qui le ressort originel est moins communément brisé; car il est des sciences qui tiennent autant à l'âme qu'à l'esprit.[34]

Like Tocqueville, most historians have assumed that Sieyes genuinely wanted to see French nobles return to Franconia, but, in his *Projet d'un décret provisoire sur le clergé*, published in the second half of 1789, Sieyes insisted that the unity of all owners of property came first: 'Puisque c'est avec des prêtres, avec des nobles, que vous avez à faire votre constitution, n'ayez pas l'imprudence de les attaquer, de les braver d'avance. Tout le monde sent aujourd'hui la nécessité d'établir l'unité sociale sur la destruction des ordres et de toutes les grandes corporations.'[35]

To be sure, nobility as a caste could not go on. For Sieyes, it was imperative that 'le noble et le prêtre n'ayent d'autre intérêt que l'intérêt commun et qu'ils ne jouissent, par la force de la loi, que des droits de simples citoyens'[36] but there was no question of despoiling either the nobles or, for that matter, the Church, whose right to keep its property Sieyes vigorously defended.

Nobles and Jews were here in the same juridical situation, and one might well say of nobles what a liberal noble said of the Jews: 'Il faut tout refuser aux juifs comme nation, il faut tout leur accorder comme individus, il faut qu'ils soient citoyens. . . . On prétend qu'ils ne veulent pas l'être: qu'ils le disent et qu'on les bannisse; il ne peut y avoir une nation dans la nation.'[37]

A distinction should be made between anti-corporatism, which was at the heart of the bourgeois Revolutionary message, and anti-nobilism, which the deputies of the Third Estate were eager to avoid. As Cerrutti explained in February 1789, a civil war had broken out between 'privilège' and 'le droit naturel',[38] and in June 1789, Mirabeau railed against the 'delirious claims' of the estates or orders: 'leurs intérêts privés sont en contradiction ouverte avec [l]'intérêt général'.

But this public concern did not spill over into private affairs. For Mirabeau orders had to be abolished, but only because they had themselves become a threat to order and property. The existence of estates had caused 'la division entre les intérêts' and had brought 'la corruption dans toutes les classes dont se compose la grande famille'. Once the nobility became a patriciate, he thought, all would be well.[39]

The Constituents were undeniably intent on destroying corporatism root and branch in order to set up the individual citizen and the national state as the only poles of French social and political life. *Arrière pensées* may also have incited the legislators to excessive zeal. As Tocqueville pointed out, envy is the quintessentially bourgeois vice, and many noble observers explained the abolition of nobility precisely in those terms. At the same time, it is also true that anti-corporatist legislation was intensely positive in its purpose. The covert motive of the deputies who voted for the Allarde and Le Chapelier laws may well have been to hobble the labour force, but their ostensible goal was not ignoble: 'Il n'y a plus de corporations dans l'État,' explained Le Chapelier; 'il n'y a plus que l'intérêt particulier de chaque individu et l'intérêt général. Il n'est permis à personne d'inspirer aux citoyens un intérêt intermédiaire, de les séparer de la chose publique par un esprit de corporation.'[40] All Frenchmen would henceforth be the completely free citizens of a completely sovereign state. A generous nation-state would embrace all her children, including nobles.

Far from being methodically hostile to the interest of nobles—now to be considered as a mere sub-group of the larger category of property-owning citizens—the anti-corporatist policies of the National Assembly were, at their harshest, erratic in nature and, at times, positively advantageous to nobles. Nowhere was this more clearly brought out than in the Constituants' legislation on feudal dues.

As a social and political system, feudalism was of course annihilated, but the forms of property on which its rickety structure had rested were, in the main, preserved. The bourgeoisie's efforts to salvage property rights of French seigneurs (the majority of whom were nobles) have often been described.[41] Merlin's elaborate subtleties may have been inspired either by a respect for property in general or by a desire to placate nobles; but they are in either case proof that nobles as individuals were neither ignored nor slighted.

Conciliatory anti-corporatism, rather than aggressive anti-nobilism, also explains what would at first glance appear to be the most gratuitously anti-noble act of all: the suppression of titles. The issue was not at all simple, as can be seen at once, since Necker and Marat both opposed a measure which Lafayette and Sieyes had endorsed.

Paradoxically, advanced leftist opinion did not favour the abolition of either titles or nobility. *Les Révolutions de France* was decidedly unenthusiastic. The night of the fourth of August had been a real benefit to the poor, but what was the use of abolishing titles?

Les sacrifices du 4 août avaient tourné en apparence, au profit de la classe la plus pauvre et la plus opprimée. On ne vit, le 19 juin, que l'acharnement d'un parti victorieux contre un parti vaincu; ne pouvant plus ravir (aux nobles) de droits utiles, les 'patriotes' leur enlevèrent jusqu'à leur chimères et leurs hochets; à peu près comme des enfants méchants qui brisent les joujoux de leurs camarades, afin de les priver d'amusements dont ils ne peuvent jouir eux-mêmes.[42]

Significantly, Marat himself was against the law. The abolition of titles, as he saw it, would throw the nobility into the opposition and disrupt the course of the Revolution. And to what end, since the abolition of titles was of no relevance? The material privileges of noble status had already been abolished; where then was the necessity 'd'abolir en même temps toute distinction purement honorifique, toute dignité sans puissance'? This could only be the work of some 'petits ambitieux, lâches hypocrites et fourbes adroits'. The 'Pères conscrits', it seemed, were a hundred times more contemptible than their predecessors; as for the 'pauvre peuple . . . puisqu'il est né pour l'humiliation, mieux valait s'abaisser devant un maréchal de France, qui a reçu de l'éducation, que devant un manant de grippe sou, paré de son écharpe tricolore'.[43]

At the other end of the political spectrum, Necker concurred, if for very different reasons. An excessive concern for civic equality would confuse the people: 'en poursuivant dans les plus petits détails tous les signes de distinction, on court le risque d'égarer le peuple sur le sens du mot égalité qui, chez une nation civilisée, ne peut jamais signifier l'égalité de rang ou de priorité'. Inequality was in the nature of things, and it made sense for the state to recognize the hierarchy of wealth and talent that was embedded in social life: 'la diversité des travaux et des fonctions, les différences de fortune et d'éducation, l'industrie, la gradation des talents et des connaissances, toutes ces disparates productrices du mouvement social entraînent inévitablement des inégalités extérieures; or le seul but du législateur doit être de les réunir toutes vers un bonheur égal quoique différent dans ses formes et ses développements.'[44]

In short, for social conservatives or social radicals, the suppression of titles was undesirable. For Marat, the real distinction was between rich and poor: titles were irrelevant and might as well be retained. Their suppression could be no more than a snare and a delusion. For Necker, bourgeois society would necessarily be hierarchical, and it was wise to recognize this explicitly. Social levelling was unthinkable, and titles were useful as bulwarks of those social rankings without which social life would make no sense.

By a similar but inverse reasoning, the elimination of titles was crucial to those who denied the importance of economic hierarchies and who yearned for the creation of a moral egalitarianism that would transcend material differences. For them, the abolition of titles mattered a great deal. Predictably, the future Girondin leader, Brissot, was prominent in that camp. For him the abolition of titles was a moral necessity. It had less to do with nobles than with the very purpose of the French Revolution. Abolishing material inequality was an impossible task, and, as it happens, an unnecessary one: 'L'inégalité de richesse et de talents', Brissot went on, 'ne révolte personne parce qu'elle n'est point le fruit d'un privilège.'[45] Titles were something else. 'Où est l'égalité des droits,' asked Anthoine of Necker, 'si votre voisin a le droit de s'appeler marquis de . . ., tandis que vous devez vous nommer Necker tout court? Où est l'utilité générale dans les effets des titres de la noblesse?'[46]

This had been Sieyes's point as well when he had railed against honorific privilege as a vice, 'le plus grand de tous'.[47] It was also this same principle that was invoked by liberal nobles like Noailles ('Plus de distinctions que celle des vertus') and Mathieu de

Montmorency: '[Les titres sont] l'une des marques qui rappellent le plus le système féodal et l'esprit chevaleresque.'[48]

The issue was an important one, and, it may be added, much ink had been spilt about it even before the Revolution began, albeit in a different context, that of the American Cincinnati. When this society of French and American officers was created in the newly founded United States in 1784, the complaints of American democrats had even then found an echo in France, where Lafayette had sided against the new order, as had Mirabeau;[49] and Benjamin Franklin's tirade against the American Cincinnati was appropriately cited by Grouvelle in the *Journal de la Société de 1789*,[50] an ironic twist since Franklin shortly before his death had agreed to become an honorary member of the Pennsylvania Cincinnati.[51] In a sense, therefore, the debate on nobility in France in 1790 was not specific to nobles at all, but was part of an ongoing debate about the place of hereditary élites in democratic states. The arguments of 1790 were the same as those of 1784, though some of the actors had taken on new roles, like Mirabeau, who now opposed the abolition of titles in France and who had little use for his family cognomen, Riquetti.

To be sure, the issue was not clear cut.[52] Titles were perhaps a form of property; Lafayette could not decide. In 1787, he had thought that the monarchic system could not be 'uniquement populaire . . . la première Nation du monde qui subsiste si glorieusement depuis tant de siècles, ne doit pas attenter légèrement aux principes de sa constitution'.[53] But on 19 June 1790, he was pushing very hard for the suppression of titles: 'La motion . . . est tellement nécessaire que je ne pense pas qu'elle ait besoin d'être appuyée: mais si elle en a besoin, j'annonce que je m'y joins de tout mon cœur.'[54] Five days later, he had changed his mind again.

A persistent and 'canine craving for publicity'[55] may explain these pirouettes, but the limit that separated privilege from property was genuinely hard to find. Where was the one true line that separated bourgeois universalism from universalism *sans phrases*? How was equality to be defined? For those who wanted moral equality, the abolition of titles mattered a great deal. For those (leftists and rightists) who rejected moral equality, the suppression of titles was irrelevant or dangerous. In either case, however, the heart of the issue was not nobles *per se* but a particular conception of the social good.

iii. The moderate tone of anti-émigré legislation

The Third Estate continued deferential to the rights of individual nobles in 1789–91, and this appears also from its handling of the central issue of bourgeois-noble friction in these years, emigration.

On the face of it, emigration was a political problem, and laws that dealt with it were framed as general measures. Legal niceties of this kind, however, did not obscure the fact that the laws which penalized emigration were at that time aimed at one part of a particular social group, the nobles, as is perhaps perversely indicated by the unusual frequency of the ritual opening 'tout français' in the relevant legislation.*

The moderate tone of the debate on the rights and wrongs of sanctions against run-away nobles was revealing. For the conservative revolutionaries, the issue was very plain. Nobles as citizens enjoyed that right to come and go which is common to all men. The constitution guaranteed this right. The deputy Henri de Jessé, for example, stated his case with some eloquence:

[la nation] ne peut rien contre les droits naturels, contre les droits sacrés et imprescriptibles des hommes; c'est ici que l'adage, tant cité, *salus populi suprema lex* est manque absolument d'application. Si, dans l'espèce présente, vous blessiez ces droits naturels, antérieurs à la société, et qu'elle ne fait que protéger de toute la force publique; si dans la rénovation du pacte social, vous enfreigniez cette liberté d'aller et de venir, de se choisir ses dieux et ses amis, vous seriez coupables d'un délit social.

It did not make any difference that emigration was something of a collective movement. Each individual émigré had inalienable rights.

Non, Messieurs, et je ne crains pas d'avancer devant vous, que si comme on l'a vu chez des nations barbares, le sacrifice d'une tête innocente était cru nécessaire à la prospérité éternelle de la Nation française; si le salut de vingt-cinq millions d'hommes dépendait de la perte illégale d'un seul, ils n'auraient pas le droit d'exister à ce prix. Le patriotisme, cette religion que vos lois propageront sur la surface de la France: cette religion qui a aussi ses martyrs, lui ferait sans doute ce sacrifice; mais elle en serait indigne si elle osait l'exiger.[56]

Now, it is true that in some instances the progressive and punitive leftist minority (which in the autumn of 1791 gradually

* For a more detailed discussion of the social content of emigration, see Appendix 2.

became a majority) simply ignored this defence of individual rights which Jessé and others had invoked. The future Director Reubell, for example, ever a practical man, thought that émigrés had forfeited their right to property because reciprocity was the key to social relations: no man can expect his property to be defended by those whom he has abandoned. But as a rule, the left bourgeois revolutionaries in 1790–1 also started from a defence of individual freedom, which, admittedly, they then proceeded to narrow and interpret. Barère, for example, on 3 July 1791, did grant that a law forbidding emigration would ordinarily be 'une loi d'esclave indigne du dix-huitième siècle', but went on to suggest that the suppression of disorder was also essential and that this could only be done by thwarting emigration which, from abroad, fed unrest at home: 'Vous nous parlez sans cesse des droits du citoyen: ils sont grands, sans doute: mais ne nous parlerez-vous jamais des droits de la cité? Ils sont plus grands encore.' 'La liberté', he warned, 'a aussi son fanatisme, et le salut de la patrie nous ordonne de l'éviter.'[57]

Characteristically, therefore, the leftist arguments began with an acceptance of the nobles' right to leave and concluded with ingeniously involuted schemes which limited that right in practice without, however, ever denying the nobles' underlying right in principle. Brissot, for example, opened with a ringing proclamation of everyone's right to leave, without which 'la liberté n'est qu'un mot'. But the nation, he thought, must be defended. To reconcile these divergent claims, he then proposed that ordinary nobles should be allowed to come and go but that restraints should be imposed on the princes of the blood and on other public functionaries, that is, soldiers and priests: 'de cette manière, vous concilierez la justice, les droits de l'homme et des citoyens, la dignité de la Nation française, et le maintien de la Révolution'.[58]

Condorcet's *Opinion sur les émigrants* of 23 October 1791 was even more ingenious. In his view, universalist principles and common sense overlapped, for laws that were just were useful, while laws that were unjust only appeared to be useful. Dissident nobles must be forced to return, but this was not so hard a task as it might seem because many of them had emigrated 'par la crainte des troubles trop réels sans doute, mais qu'une exagération coupable a rendu plus effrayants. . . . Offrons-leur encore une fois le moyen de cesser d'être nos ennemis.' If émigrés were confronted with loss of property, they would overcome their fears and return to France where they would be better off: 'Ils sentiront qu'il est doux d'être libre.'

This was a practical argument. Condorcet also presented its theoretical justification. He did not deny the individual noble's right to leave and the Assembly, if it adopted his plan, he explained, would not be moving away from an 'équité rigoureuse . . . même à l'égard de ses ennemis les plus perfides'.[59] And in truth Condorcet more or less successfully squared this circle: in his scheme, émigrés who agreed to take an oath of loyalty to the constitution might stay abroad and retain their rights as French citizens; émigrés who refused the oath but agreed not to act against the constitution for a period of two years would for that period be given the status of foreigners residing in France. Necessarily, the remaining émigrés could be supposed to harbour the design forcibly to oppose the constitution; their rights could be equitably rescinded and their property sequestered.[60]

Condorcet's concerns were transparent: something must be done, but the natural rights of all men must be respected. Like other French citizens, émigré nobles had the right to be judged on the basis of their individual actions alone. Punishment could not be collective: 'les fautes sont personnelles'. As citizens, nobles had rights that could not be denied.

Gentle about emigration in theory, the bourgeois reformists in this first universalist phase of the Revolution were in practice also mindful of the rights of émigrés. The laws on emigration before August 1792 were mild despite the verbal truculence of their makers. The Brissotins spoke very loudly but did very little: basically conservative, they were appealing to the mob, but for show only.

Parisian districts began in October 1789 to ask for punitive legislation against émigrés, but the Assembly did not even discuss the problem at any length until February 1791, when Le Chapelier in the name of the Constitutional Committee presented the Draft of a proposal, only to speak against it. Any infringement of the citizen's right to come and go, he warned, would be 'hors des principes . . . une véritable dictature'.[61]

The National Assembly also showed its reluctance to act against noble susceptibilities by dragging its feet about purging the officer corps. On 11 June 1791, before the King's flight to Varennes, Robespierre had spoken with unusual sharpness about this question: 'Vous avez détruit la noblesse, et la noblesse subsiste au centre de votre armée! . . . Je le dis avec franchise, peut-être même avec rudesse, quiconque ne veut pas, ne conseille pas le licenciement est un traître. . . . Donnez aux soldats des chefs auxquels ils puissent obéir.'[62]

Robespierre also asked that officers who insisted on taking an 'engagement d'honneur' in lieu of oath be dismissed, but he was followed neither by the Assembly nor by most leaders of the patriotic left, who did not speak up.

The King's flight interrupted this era of good feeling, but only momentarily. On 21 June 1791, one day after Louis's departure, the National Assembly did finally make it illegal to leave the kingdom or to send out of it weapons or specie. In the same vein, during the following days, various modifications were added to make it more difficult for absentees to collect pensions or salaries: punitive taxes were imposed on 9 July 1791, on 'tout Français' presently out of the kingdom and especially on the King's relatives abroad, who were singled out by name.

But paradoxically the King's flight, which marked the definitive break between the rightist, Catholic traditionalists, and the moderate constitutional monarchists, soon led to an improvement of the nobles' over-all situation. Moderate Feuillant leaders of the patriot party, like Barnave, Duport, and Lameth, decided at this point to stop the Revolution in order to find some common cause with the right and especially with the King. Narbonne, the King's Minister of War, pointed out to his master that he could not afford to reject such an overture. The 'bourgeois propriétaires', he wrote, were doctrinally agnostic. 'La forme du gouvernement leur est assez indifférente; ce qu'ils veulent, c'est la conservation de ce qu'ils possèdent. Ils se rallient à ceux qui la leur garantissent.'[63] In fact, Narbonne, a friend of Mme de Staël, was six or seven years ahead of his time. The 'bourgeois propriétaires' of 1791–2 were not ideologically indifferent, and the majority of them fell in behind the Gironde and the Mountain, at that time working in rough unison. Nor did the King seriously heed Narbonne's advice to become a constitutional monarch.

The Feuillant solution was precarious, but it appeared to have achieved some measure of stability in the autumn of 1791. The King benefited from this new state of affairs, as did the nobles. When the first of the Revolution's parliamentary commissioners were sent to report on the army after the return of the King from Varennes, each of the five commissions included a noble deputy, among them Custine, Dillon, and Latour-Maubourg. Many of the Feuillants toyed with the idea of restoring titles to the nobility; in keeping with the new mood, in August an anonymous pamphlet appeared in Paris entitled '*Le Rétablissement des titres purement honorifiques de la noblesse*', which developed the idea that no demand for the abolition of titles had been made in any *Cahiers de doléances*. The law on the abolition of titles should be repealed because all the misfortunes of the past year were to be traced to that 'fameux décret'.

The popular agitation which Bailly and Lafayette brutally suppressed with the Massacre of the Champs de Mars in mid-July 1791 reinforced the moderate constitutional revolutionaries' belief in the wisdom of their pro-monarchy and pro-noble tactic. The laws on emigration were revised. Provisions were still made for the punitive taxation of returning émigrés, but the operative message of the law was to be found in the preamble, which held that the present circumstances of the French nation 'lui [faisait] un devoir de rappeler dans son sein tous les enfants de la patrie absents'. On 14 and 15 September, when a new constitution was drawn up and accepted by the King, the Assembly abrogated all previous legislation: the obligation to have a passport in order to travel was rescinded, and local authorities were forbidden to harass returning émigrés for any reason whatever.

The all-important disintegration of the Feuillant programme in the winter of 1791–2 did mark the beginning of the end of these halcyon days, but only the beginning. Betrayed once more by the King, who still had no intention of becoming a constitutional monarch, the Feuillants lost their political grip. Though genuinely eager to establish civil equality before the law, they were also socially conservative and now fell between two stools, being at once unable to contain the traditionalists on the right, who rejected civil equality, or the more progressive revolutionaries on the left, who hoped to stabilize the Revolution by mobilizing popular allegiance through a quick, little, successful war.

In consequence, the Legislative Assembly hesitated from the winter of 1791 to the early summer of 1792, for the deputies were now torn between a conservative solution which would respect the individual rights of nobles and a nationalistic and demagogic policy which curried popular favour by showing a growing indifference to the rights of nobles as citizens.

In theory, therefore, drastic penalties were imposed on all émigrés as a group regardless of individual motivation. Yielding to Girondin pressure, the Assembly ignored the prudent recommendations of its legislative committee. A decree, vetoed by the King, placed a death warrant on those émigrés who did not return by 1 January 1792, as well as on those inside France who urged military desertion. In December 1791, émigrés were once again deprived of their right to collect salaries abroad; and on 1 February 1792, passports were once more required for foreign travel. In February, March, and April 1792, the goods of émigrés were ordered to be sequestered, a procedure hallowed by precedent—Louis XIV had done this to Protestants, as had the English Parliament to Irish and Jacobite rebels, and Catherine the Great to the Poles. Indeed, the law of 30 March–8 April 1792 was disquieting by its extreme vagueness, since it affected the property not only of recognized émigrés but of all persons not certified by the relevant municipalities as being at the time domiciled in the department where they were landlords. Nor was it clear whether the ensuing confusion between the merely absent and the genuinely emigrated should be resolved by those who held jurisdiction over the property or over the proprietor. Finally, it was also disturbing that the act presumed guilt rather than innocence as had become the principle of French law.[64]

But in spite of it all, émigré-nobles in the spring of 1792 were neither immediately deprived of their civil rights nor excluded forever from the bosom of the nation. On the contrary, the law of 28–29 July 1792, which forbade the issuance of new passports to leave the country, gave as its inclusive motive the need to keep any citizen from refusing the 'devoir sacré de marcher au secours de la patrie'. The law of 8 April likewise promised again to those émigrés who would return within a month that all would be forgiven: they could reclaim their property, though admittedly their taxes for 1792 might be doubled. In addition, the relatives of unregenerate émigrés were guaranteed protection; they were allowed to reside in the houses of recognized absentees whose property was theoretically forfeited; it was also agreed that they would continue to enjoy one-half of their relatives' income.

As the élitist or 'fayettiste' compromise disintegrated, anti-émigré legislation did become more serious. None the less, the campaign against departed nobles remained sporadic in the spring of 1792. Even then, on the verge of the monarchy's collapse, the Revolutionary bourgeoisie was still reluctant to give nobles irremediable offence.

iv. The contrasting truculence of popular anti-nobilism

In the first months of 1792, émigrés were still for the bourgeoisie a figure of fun. Ever-fascinating, the yo-yo has been reinvented from time to time; in 1791–2, it was known as 'le coblentz' or 'l'émigrette': a single shop manufactured twenty-five thousand such toys whose use Beaumarchais described as 'un noble jeu qui dispense de la fatigue de penser'.[65] Bourgeois notables and liberal nobles could still find a middle ground which precluded any serious persecution of nobles or émigrés. This entente at the top, however, is all the more striking for its contrast with popular rural anti-nobilism, which was no laughing matter.

The question of the peasantry's feelings about nobles is difficult to handle, and for a simple reason. In some measure, all peasants did form one social group and shared a common goal: peasants, it is safe to assume, all disliked both taxes and feudal dues. In that respect, attitudes on either nobles or the state were roughly similar in the whole of France. The problem is, of course, that taxes and dues were not everywhere the same. They varied, as did patterns of landholding and the cohesiveness of peasant communities. Peasant attitudes towards nobles fluctuated accordingly.

Structures of property differed widely from one end of France to the other. The clergy's share of land ranged from 1 per cent to 20 per cent, as did that of nobles from 2 per cent to 44 per cent, and of peasants from 22 per cent to 98 per cent.[66] The weight of feudal dues was also not the same, a fact which was particularly significant, because feudalism was widely identified with nobility. Near Toulouse and Bordeaux, dues represented between 5 per cent and 8 per cent of noble income as against 63 per cent in Aunis and Saintonge. Dues in Brittany mattered ten times more to nobles than they did in Burgundy, where they figured as only 5 per cent of the noble landlord's budget.[67]

This issue is further complicated by the fact that dues, regardless of their size, were varyingly perceived from place to place. Some nobles did care about them deeply: one deputy from Auvergne, for example, insisted in 1790 on the desirability of seigneurial payments, which were 'plus solide, plus assuré, que celui des rentes; il n'est pas exposé à aucun danger, il ne coûte aucune dépense. . . . Les rentes ont d'autres advantages qui leur donnent une valeur beaucoup au-dessus du setier que recueille le propriétaire, elles sont portables et solidaires; elles emportent un droit casuel.'[68]

But two years before the Revolution, in the neighbourhood of Lyon, one Rieussac, the author of a *Discours sur les causes morales de la dégradation de l'agriculture, et les moyens d'y remédier*, wrote that 'dans cette généralité où toutes les directes sont mêlées, presque tous les seigneurs sont eux-mêmes emphytéotes; par conséquent, ils sont presque tous intéressés, à raison de leurs biens ruraux à l'affranchissement des servitudes féodales, au rétablissement de la plénitude de la propriété'.[69]

If local nobles themselves favoured the abolition of seigneurialism pure and simple, it hardly makes much sense to suppose that the presence of these dues could have separated nobles and peasants across the board. Nor is it clear why it was that some peasants tolerated dues less well than the more burdensome weight of taxes. The weight of dues was in any case relative and might seem heavier in those places where the tax burden was already high, an important variable in a country with an irrational tax system.

Other arguments are of relevance. Can it be said that the peasants' hostility to dues (and nobles) was based on the newer grounds of civic dignity, so that any dues, however light, had come to appear intolerable, as appears to have been the case in one small southern village where they were held to represent 'une captivité qui dégrade en quelque sorte l'humanité et sont d'ailleurs trop humiliants pour un peuple naturellement libre'?[70] Another aspect of the question was that peasants who might detest feudal or seigneurial dues may not have detested nobles for owning them as much as they did the bailiffs for collecting them. Such in any case was the point made in 1789 by the liberal duc d'Aiguillon in his simultaneous apologia for nobles and for anti-noble terrorism. Insurrections had been frequent and justifiable:

> dans plusieurs provinces, le peuple tout entier forme une espèce de ligue pour détruire les chateaux, pour ravager les terres, et surtout pour s'emparer des chartriers, où les titres des propriétés féodales sont en dépôt. Il cherche à secouer enfin un joug qui depuis tant de siècles pèse sur sa tête; et il faut l'avouer, Messieurs, cette insurrection, quoique coupable (car toute agression violente l'est), peut trouver son excuse dans les vexations dont il est la victime.

But the landlords were not to blame:

Les propriétaires des fiefs, des terres seigneuriales, ne sont, il faut l'avouer, que bien rarement coupables des excès dont se plaignent leurs vassaux; mais leurs gens d'affaires sont souvent sans pitié, et le malheureux cultivateur, soumis au reste barbare des lois féodales qui subsistent encore en France, gémit de la contrainte dont il est la victime. Ces droits, on ne peut se le dissimuler, sont une propriété, et toute propriété est sacrée; mais ils sont onéreux aux peuples, et tout le monde convient de la gêne continuelle qu'ils leur imposent.[71]

In addition, it is all too clear that tenants, sharecroppers, and small landlords could hardly consider the question of feudal dues from the same point of view.

Finally, the peasants' ability to do anything about their complaint would also depend on the strength of peasant association. Here also, great variety prevailed: in the Basse Auvergne, the peasant community in 1789 was still 'une réalité vivante',[72] but it was much less vigorous in Burgundy.[73] The issue is unclear since authors also disagree on the political effect of this same community, such as it may have been. For Paul Bois, it was the more individualistic peasants of the western Sarthe who resisted the Revolution;[74] Roland Marx also raises the issue, but without taking sides;[75] and Robert Foster concludes as I would that 'the Revolution in Burgundy witnessed the last counter-offensive of the village community against the seigneurie'.[76]

Manifestly, then, the condition of French peasants was highly heterogeneous, and it can hardly be supposed that all of them shared a single view of what was to be done about nobles. For nearly a century, peasants would in fact be the great political unknown of French life. To speak, therefore, of a single popular anti-nobilism is to simplify a vast problem, but it does still make sense to speak of a nation-wide, popular anti-nobilism which can be seen to have gone through three distinct phases.

In the first months of the Revolution, the discrepancy between the views of the 'plebs' and of the bourgeoisie on nobles was very wide. The bourgeoisie, as has been seen, was eager to work with nobles, but that was hardly true of the urban masses, and even less so of the peasantry. In a second phase, however, from the spring of 1792 to the autumn of 1793, the bourgeoisie and the peasants moved into closer accord. Bourgeois parties were then looking for popular support, and if the people disliked the nobles, the bourgeoisie would follow suit. Then, in a third phase, as shall be seen, the bourgeois and popular views of nobles diverged once again and punitive legislation was passed by the Convention just as popular feelings waned.

At the outset of the Revolution, popular hatred of nobles was widespread, or so it seemed to many. The variety of conditions in the countryside was itself a source of confusion and insecurity. If contemporaries had had a clearer view of what it was that peasants wanted and of what nobles would have had to concede, less credence might then have been given to terrifying rumours of impending peasant insurrection.

The moral imperatives of universalism, though they might be obvious to the Constituants and Législateurs alike, were, to say the least, more opaque for artisans and peasants. Deputies might distinguish between nobility and nobles, and they did make year-long efforts to distinguish between feudal and seigneurial dues. But peasants after the summer of 1789 were no more willing to take unto their bosom a supposedly reformed aristocracy than they were to pay any dues whatsoever. In February 1791, when the King's aunts left for Rome (a decision which caused anxiety in both Paris and the provinces, since it was taken to be a dry run for the departure of the whole royal family), Robespierre remarked in a spirit of virile condescension that 'les femmes de la maison royale peuvent aller et venir où leur piété ou leurs caprices pourraient les conduire',[77] but when they arrived at Arnay-le-Duc the princesses were told instead that 'la liberté est faite pour le peuple, et non pas pour les princes'.[78]

Some peasants continued to be deferential, like the punning inhabitants of Vougecourt, near Besançon, who are reported to have told the Baron de Tricornot upon his installation as mayor that 'Il y a longtemps que vous êtes notre père, il faut aussi que vous soyez notre maire'.[79]

More to the point both as a barometer of peasant opinion and as an indication of what nobles thought they had to fear, was a wide variety of disorders. When the grain riots of May 1789 gave way to the *Grande Peur*, anti-noble rural rioting seemed fearsome. In the Rennes-Redon-Ploermel triangle alone, one of many such areas, thirty chateaux were invaded, fifteen of them sacked, and two burnt[80]—or as Choderlos de Laclos would later put it, 'éclairés par le patriotisme'.[81] The disappearance of the authorities and of the maréchaussée, never too numerous in any case, gave rioters a free hand.

In July 1789, many castles were destroyed in the Maconnais,

the Beaujolais, and in Normandy, where the marquis de Saint Vast was chased about by peasants armed with pitchforks.[82] In many instances, noble women were whipped or humiliated.

Few people were killed, but in the confusion of the day many old scores were settled. Relations between peasants and nobles were immediate and intensely personal, quite different, obviously, from what was true in the cities, and agitation was most widespread in regions where feudal dues had been unusually burdensome and nobles oppressive. In Normandy, for example, at Falaise, François d'Arouges, seigneur de la Coulonche, was a local tyrant of whom the regional *sub-délégué* had written in the early 1780s that 'il vexe et ruine les paroissiens. Il prétend être si despotique que les huissiers royaux n'oseraient y aller pour faire sortir les deniers royaux, étant menacé d'être pris et emprisonnés dans son chateau: il y a eu déjà plusieurs exemples'. In 1789, his castle and records went up in flames.[83] And in 1791, Gracchus Babeuf published a defence of rural rioters in the Somme which was essentially an indictment of the countess de la Myre, another local tyrant, who had squeezed her peasants in the 1780s by reviving forgotten feudal dues.[84]

In a circular which dealt with the use of patois, l'abbé Grégoire asked his correspondents if nobles and priests had been mishandled in their districts. Most replied that they had not: as one of them put it, 'quant aux nobles, si on ne leur connaît point d'aristocratie, ils n'ont aucune persécution à endurer'. But others did say that there had been disorders and usually cited two causes, bad behaviour by nobles before 1789, and continued aristocratic efforts to collect dues.[85]

Popular disorders spilled over from the country to the city. In Besançon, on 27 July 1789, bands of young men formed a confederation 'pour assommer les nobles' who had protested against the course of events; and at Vesoul, an aristocrat was accused of poisoning a well.[86] At Dijon, Basire, a future Conventionnel, took the lead of a patriotic group and placed priests and nobles under a form of house arrest.[87] In mid-July, nobles were threatened in Paris and were given special protection or placed in protective custody, sometimes at their own request.[88] At Manosque and Riez, bishops were stoned. M. de Montesson was shot at Le Mans. At Aups, a noble was cut up in little pieces, as was in August M. de Barras for the edification of his assembled family. At Troyes the Parlementaire mayor, Huez, was strung up and while still alive repeatedly stabbed in the eyes.

Taken to task in their own right, nobles in the cities were also attacked *qua* officials of the old order: when the noble deputy d'André reported to the Assembly that the populace and national guard of Marseilles had inflicted on the body of the Chevalier de Beausset 'les plus affreuses atrocitiés', it was difficult to distinguish between Beausset as a noble and Beausset as a military commander.[89] Necessarily, municipal revolts were directed against officers who were also nobles as were most anti-seigneurial riots aimed at seigneurs who were also nobles.

Popular pressure did not die out in the summer of 1789. On the contrary, nobles continued to be blamed for a variety of ills. In July, they were attacked as *accapareurs* of grain, and from the winter of 1789 onwards it was standard fare in *L'Ami du peuple* and elsewhere to blame the émigrés and their removal of specie for what were in fact the first consequences of economic dislocation and, eventually, of a depreciating paper currency. On 5 October 1789, the district of Saint Philippe du Roule urged the Assembly to take steps against any citizens who might want to leave Paris, a call repeated a few days later in the district of l'Abbaye de Saint-Germain des Prés.[90] In the summer of 1790, the Assembly's repeated endorsements of military discipline (and with it *ipso facto* of the presence of noble officers) was widely resented.[91] Court nobles, who were alone entitled to attend court functions, were extremely unpopular, and on the eve of the Fête de la Fédération in July 1790, it was rumoured in Paris that all nobles would soon be massacred.[92] It was widely assumed in the country at large that new revolutionary administrative institutions ought to be *adelrein*, and at Besançon, for example, former noble judicial officers were excluded from the National Guard.

Similarly, the Assembly's abolition of titles was thought to be justly punitive by the 'menu peuple' and especially by its would-be representatives like the Père Duchesne, who hailed the suppression of 'toutes ces foutues misères, qui alimentaient un orgueil méprisant et méprisable, [et qui] doivent être éffacées dans un pays ou les vertus seules vont servir d'armoiries . . . plus belles et plus éclatantes que celle de vos vieux bougres qui radotaient et qui, dans le principe, étaient roturiers'.[93]

A great rash of prints, it may be added, bore witness to the extent of popular anti-noble feelings, such as the punning Fesse Mathieu, which represented a Garde-Française whipping Anne-Mathieu de Montmorency; and 'le Pied de Nez ou l'Aristocratie écrasée', or the 'Naissance des aristocrates', where a winged devil, holding a syringe and hovering over a chamber pot, produced from the relevant orifice a mitred bishop and an armed noble, sword in hand.[94]

Lines of battle were not, of course, completely clear. Some bourgeois were punitively anti-noble from the beginning, and popular attitudes were also mixed in 1789–91. A large number of popular pamphlets developed the theme of the reconciliation of all. Good curés, for example, could be accommodated: 'les hommes vertueux les respecteront, de même que les ci-devant gentilshommes qui n'auront pas besoin de disputer aux rats leurs titres de grandeurs et de considération pour valoir quelque chose'.[95] But popular acceptance of the ci-devants was at best ambiguous, rather like a print circulated in July 1790 that showed priests and nobles labouring on the Champs de Mars with two legends, one at the top: 'aristocrates vous voilà donc F. . . . Nous baiserons vos femmes. Et vous nous baiserez le C. . . .'; and at the bottom a compliment to all the 'bons citoyens [qui] ont mis la main à l'œuvre' to ensure the success of the Fête de la Fédération.[96] By snipping off the class-specific language of one caption or the other, retailers would be sure to reach their market.

Important in its own right, popular anti-noble feeling is none the less of greatest relevance here as a foil to the bourgeoisie's conciliatory attitude towards nobles as individuals. When need be, however, the bourgeoisie could make undifferentiated anti-noble noises to please its popular audience. One of Bailly's feints during the difficulties of July 1791, which led to the 'Massacre of the Champs de Mars', was to assure the would-be rioters that he too realized that nobles and priests were behind the disorders of the day.[97] But in practice the more common pattern during 1789–91 was of bourgeois-noble co-operation against popular attacks on property. The rural upheaval of the summer of 1789 may have enabled the bourgeoisie at Versailles to push for the end of feudalism on the night of the fourth of August, but, at the same time, it caused many a bourgeois-noble alliance in the field.

In the Dauphiné, a quickly forged social entente echoed the political accord of 1789, when bourgeois and nobles had united against monarchic absolutism. In the Maconnais, a bourgeois militia actually fired on the peasants; at Rennes, a self-styled *comité provisoire* urged the sénéchaussée to prosecute marauders who in August 1789 had attacked seigneurial dovecotes. In the

Franche-Comté the Great Fear of 1789 had a decidedly anti-noble ring, but the municipality of Lons-le-Saulnier was not amused. And on 19 July, it lambasted as 'worse than brigands' those who would separate 'le titre de citoyen [de] celui de noble'.[98] There were clear limits to what the rural masses would be allowed to do.

The reverse would have been surprising, for once rioting began, it was difficult to channel it in the right direction, as some seigneurial officers 'entièrement dévoués à la chose publique' explained to the municipality of Rennes in January 1790:

> Messieurs, vous avez connaissance de ce qui s'est passé aux paroisses d'Augan, Guer et autres limitrophes, où des gens attroupés se sont portés vers les châteaux pour retirer des propriétaires des déclarations de renoncer à leurs droits féodaux.
>
> Aujourd'hui ils se sont tournés vers les procureurs fiscaux et autres particuliers, notamment contre les habits bleus. . . .
>
> Dïmanche 24, il fut répandu à la sortie des grandes messes de Beignon et Plélan que les têtes des officiers nationaux de cette dernière paroisse étaient à prix.
>
> Le même jour encore, un homme se dressant à l'un de ces officiers et lui faisant voir une tombe, lui dit: 'Bourgeois, je vous mettrons là.'
>
> Le même jour il fut dit à un autre: 'Bourgeois je vous grillerons.'[99]

As defenders of law and order, regardless of political implications, the new bourgeois authorities now suddenly found themselves the butt of that same endemic rural criminality which before 1789 had been directed against the royal authorities. Many peasants who had been anti-noble before became anti-bourgeois after the municipal revolution of 1789.[100] When they switched sides, so in a sense did the rural bourgeoisie.

Nobles like the memorialist Ferrières counted on just such a reversal. The bourgeoisie and the lawyers, he thought, were ultimately responsible for popular disorders, but they were gradually coming to the realization that anti-noble disorders were potentially dangerous: 'Ils commencent de le sentir, mais il est bien tard. Ce sont les insurrections continuelles, le délire fanatique qu'ils ont montré, la haine, la persécution contre la Noblesse et le Clergé. Comment la gent robinocratique et bourgeoise pouvait-elle s'imaginer qu'elle ruinerait, dégraderait la Noblesse et le Clergé, sans que les suites d'un tel bouleversement s'étendissent jusqu'à eux.'[101]

It would not be accurate to depict a nobility pining as a whole for

Revolutionary change, and it would also be incorrect to make a case for a bourgeoisie eager to embrace the ci-devant nobles. None the less, it is true that in 1787–91, although peasants were very anti-noble, bourgeois exhibited a spectrum of attitudes towards the Second Estate. Their view of the ci-devants varied as did the politics of the aristocracy. In May 1788, non-noble reformists stood squarely behind the noble Parlementaires, then a bulwark of liberty against the 'tyranny' of the monarchy. In December 1788, however, Mallet du Pan was quite right in saying that the nature of the debate had entirely changed: King versus Constitution had become far less important than bourgeois versus noble,[102] a change of heart that came when the 'neo-noble' Parlementaires sided with the monarchy on behalf of tradition and against liberal change. Politics were a key, but for that reason also, anti-noble bourgeois feeling diminished in the late summer of 1789, when feudalism had been abolished 'in its entirety'.

Later, of course, in 1792, the entente at the top between bourgeois and nobles became a liability for the bourgeoisie. When the more democratic (and demagogic) wing of the reformist party took the helm of the Revolution and decided to shoot Niagara, then the participation of nobles in politics became less important than did the support of the 'people'. When the Gironde decided to stabilize the Revolution by mobilizing popular energies in a war against Europe, pacificist Girondin universalists suddenly became bellicose noble-haters. But in the first phase of the Revolution, from the summer of 1789 to the spring of 1791, for both practical and theoretical reasons, the Revolutionary bourgeois reformists, in striking contrast to the people, gave as wide a definition of the rights of nobles as was compatible with their own universalist goals.

The existence of an entente in 1787–91 of bourgeois and liberal nobles, all of them future 'notables', has often been described. The real problem lies in the analysis of its meaning. In his *Histoire de la Révolution française*, Albert Soboul takes note, for example, of the 'fayettiste' policy of conciliation of bourgeois and nobles, a description that somewhat prejudices the case by associating this political strategy with the ambitions of a single man. Albert Soboul discounts Lafayette's calculations on the grounds that the pursuit of a compromise between the liberal aristocracy and the upper bourgeoisie in 1789–91 was 'chimerical' because the last vestiges of feudalism had not been destroyed. As long as it could be supposed that monarchy or privilege might be restored, the nobility, he writes, necessarily continued to offer great resistance to the bourgeoisie, 'that is to say to the triumph of the capitalist relations of production which were injurious to the nobility's interest'.[103]

In his long and thoughtful reply to François Furet's *Catechisme révolutionnaire*,[104] Claude Mazauric takes up a similar argument. He criticizes with vigour and elegance the arguments of those (I am among them) who have insisted on the reconciliation of the propertied élites in 1789–91. He concludes that all such attempts are essentially irrelevant because they are not set in a dynamic context, which he defines as the bourgeoisie's gradual realization in 1789–91 of its historical purpose, the destruction of feudalism.[105] The existence of a 'fayettiste' policy of reconciliation is not denied, but it is characterized as the first step of a process which ended with the emphatic negation of reconciliation in 1793–4.

The Revolution *was* a dynamic whole, and the unity of views between Revolutionary bourgeois and liberal nobles did indeed disintegrate during the middle phase of the Revolutionary decade. But this estrangement cannot be described as a nearly automatic reaction triggered by the bourgeoisie's detestation of the feudal system. Such reasoning may perhaps explain the peasantry's relationship to the aristocracy, although even that is not obvious; but it cannot fully explain the anti-nobilism of either the urban masses or the bourgeoisie.

How close nobles and bourgeois really were in their material goals was made clear in the summer of 1789, when both groups rallied to the defence of rural property, which was after all the economic foundation of both noble and bourgeois wealth. Bourgeois-peasant relations were ambiguous: it may well be that without the peasant revolution, the bourgeoisie would not have been able to overthrow the monarchy. But it is no less true that the bourgeoisie would soon have given up all thought of revolution if the French peasant movement had become a *jacquerie*, comparable to what later took place in Galicia in 1846 or in Russia in 1905.

For Mazauric, the bourgeoisie's class interests required that it make common cause with the peasantry and the 'plebs' against nobles as well as nobility. This may have been true, but only up to a point, a point that was quickly reached. Economic concerns, had they been as critical as Mazauric supposes, would on the contrary have united the aristocracy (many of them liberals) to the bourgeoisie (most of them landlords and many of them seigneurs as well). Indeed, the essence of the bourgeoisie's problem after 1791 (and in consequence, of the nobility's also) was precisely its incomplete understanding of its commitment to individualism and private property. In 1792, virtue and community were primary concerns still and would remain so until 1794 certainly, perhaps even to 1799.

Mazauric is right in part; but for the wrong reason. The entente of noble and bourgeois did break down after the critical threshold of the autumn of 1791; but two points must be made: first, that such an agreement was in the logic of history despite its initial failure; and second, that this accord failed in 1791 for ideological reasons that had little to do with the bourgeoisie's supposed hatred of feudalism.

If the bourgeoisie in 1789 had intended merely to create a political system which conformed to its positivistic social and economic needs, bourgeois politicians would hardly have gone as far as they did beyond the normative élitist alliance of 1789, renewed in 1799, confirmed in 1814, and certified in 1830 at the outset of the July Monarchy. Since bourgeois and nobles had in the second half of the eighteenth century become to a large extent partners in the gradual modernization of French society, a straightforward translation of their social situation into political terms after 1789 would not have led them very far beyond the hybrid system of 1814–48.

In the long run, the prospect of a durable reconciliation of bourgeois and nobles as the leaders of a half-modern and half-traditional society, very ably described by Theodore Zeldin, was implicit in the fabric of French social life. Such an alliance did in fact develop after 1799, when it was resolutely set in the ideological context of the solidarity of a nakedly particularist class of notables. But in 1789–91, élitist solidarity remained extremely fragile because it had to bear the consequences of two basic bourgeois assumptions: that the economic cleavage between rich and poor would not find political expression since society was basically harmonious; and that Revolutionary sensibility and rhetoric could be given a free rein because the trappings of the *Ancien Régime* were without substance and could be easily destroyed. In this ideological setting, every popular complaint, like every betrayal of the Revolutionary cause by the King or by the fates, convinced the Revolutionary leaders in 1792–3 that they should move further to the left, where more reliable allies might be found to defend virtue and community. Under these circumstances, the élitist compromise of 1789 could not be sustained.

The bourgeoisie itself would pay for these mistakes. Like Saturn, the Revolution devoured its own children, and liberal nobles were its first victims.

Chapter Three

Two years of opportunistic anti-nobilism: 1792–1793

i. The new and radical course of the reformist party in the autumn of 1791

In 1789, popular anti-noble feelings ran high, but tactics as well as principles dictated that the bourgeois Revolutionaries should make ample room for nobles as individuals. In the late summer and autumn of 1791, however, this strategy was cast aside. A second phase of the Revolution began during which the rights of nobles gradually decayed. Opportunism became the key to bourgeois Revolutionary politics, where opportunism implied among other things concessions to the 'plebs' by the supposedly egalitarian bourgeoisie at the expense of supposedly reactionary nobles.

From the summer of 1789 to the spring of 1791, the reformist party had been more or less united in the belief that the Revolution could be painlessly achieved: politically liberal nobles and socially conservative bourgeois would work together with the King and with the 'people' but not with the mob. In the summer of 1791, that entente broke down. This was the decisive turning point in the progress of the French Revolution, more important even than the 'second revolution' of 10 August 1792, when the monarchy was finally overthrown. Though united in 1789–90, the propertied, privileged, and Enlightened elements of French society (i.e. Revolutionary bourgeois and liberal nobles) fell apart after the King's flight to Varennes. On the left, some advanced patriots began to think they might be able to do without King or nobles. On the right of the Revolutionary party, however, the more cautious patriots decided that 'the Revolution was over'. For them, the good will of King and nobles mattered more than ever.

The new caution of these conservative revolutionaries, of the Feuillants and the Triumvirate (Barnave, Duport, and Alexandre de Lameth) can be explained at two levels. On a concrete plane it can be suggested that these moderate conservatives were frightened by a growing number of specific socially and politically distrupting civil conflicts, by economic disorders, and also by the unexpected resistance of the King on various issues, such as the Civil Constitution of the Clergy.

But their anxiety can also be considered in a more general way as the first signs of the unravelling of the Revolutionary bourgeoisie's 'false consciousness'. Barnave and his friends were the first politicians to grasp what would eventually be understood by everyone, by Brissot in the autumn of 1792, Robespierre in the autumn of 1793, and by the great majority of the French bourgeoisie in 1799, namely, that the ideological defence of communitarian universalism was potentially explosive. The defence of property came first, and in 1791, it required some concessions to the traditionalist conservative right. In late 1793–4, Robespierre would make overtures to the Catholics and, inside the Convention, to the Plaine. In 1791, Barnave made overtures to the King and Queen. The issues are different, but the political logic is the same, and it was in the late summer of 1791 that the dilemma of the Revolutionary bourgeoisie first appeared.

In the perspective of traditional Marxist historiography, the Gironde in late 1791, and the Mountain later, are seen as the only valid interpreters of the bourgeoisie's profound aspirations as men determined to destroy feudalism by relying on the people. But the Gironde and the Mountain can also be seen as the varyingly inconsequent pursuers of that will-o'-the-wisp, reconciliation with 'le peuple'. Theirs was a pipe dream, and it was moderates such as Barnave who first understood that it was. The defence of the new bourgeois order in a society of classes required the selfish neutralization, and if need be the destruction, of those who would take popular sovereignty seriously. The reformist patriots would have to choose. *Hic Rhodus, hic salta.* Barnave followed this Marxist precept. Brissot did not.

In the summer of 1791, when the contradictions of the bourgeois Revolutionary programme first appeared, the problem of politics lay in finding an exit from the impasse made evident by the flight of the monarch. Optimistic constitutional monarchists like Barnave concluded that the only way out was to give up the alliance with 'le peuple' in order to strike a bargain with the King who had just fled. Less optimistic constitutional monarchists like Lafayette hoped to repair their system by declaring war on Europe, and in so doing pre-empt the right and neutralize the left, a fatal miscalculation on all counts. A third group of reformists, led by the future Girondins, took up a basically similar but far more demagogic position. Like the bellicose Fayettists, the Girondins were socially conservative; they too thought of war as the way to bind the 'plebs' to the regime. But unlike Lafayette, Brissot and his friends were far more vocal in their currying of popular favour and far less prepared to work with the King, although subsequent experience would show in July 1792 that they too were ready to accept Louis, should he agree to rule on their terms. The Girondins' devotion to popular sovereignty was ephemeral, but their lip service to this principle was widely advertised. In December 1791, Pétion's view, in the words of Gouverneur Morris, the American Minister in Paris, was that the Gironde 'would not fall out with the *Fous* and *Enragés* because it is they and not the reasonable People who support Revolutions, and for his own Part he does not chuse to be hanged for the Sake of giving Triumph to Reason'.[1] In more public form, this same programme was presented, by Pétion again, as a paean to a Popular Front of sorts: 'la bourgeoisie et le peuple réunis ont fait la révolution; leur réunion seule peut la conserver'.[2]

Various consequences flowed from Brissot's and Pétion's approach. The more innocuous were purely demagogic: in December 1791, the Girondin paper, the *Patriote Français*, ran a series on the usefulness of the *pique*, that archetypal symbol of sans-culotte virility. In early 1792, the Gironde also suddenly rediscovered the iniquity of the popular repression that had been staged by the Feuillants in the previous summer. Most grotesquely, in February 1792, Brissot began to wax prolix on the Englishman Pigott's apologia for the use of the *bonnet rouge*. Less entertaining was the stoking of popular anticlericalism: 'Frappez [les prêtres] pour les moindres fautes,' said Isnard (never too discreet a man), 'il faut un dénouement à la Révolution française, car le peuple commence à se détacher des intérêts publics'.[3] More practical were the concessions that were offered to the peasantry: in the summer of 1791, the conservative revolutionaries had done their best to disfranchise the poorer voters, the overwhelming majority of whom were peasants; but in April 1792, the Girondins and their leftist allies reversed the pattern and gave to the peasants what they wanted, concessions on the redemption of seigneurial dues. In 1790, it had been decided that peasants would pay such dues unless it could be shown that such rights were invalid. But in June 1792, the burden of proof was shifted to the other side; henceforth, it was the *seigneurs* who would have to show title, a very difficult thing for them to do since in some regions, such as

Provence, rioting peasants had destroyed most of the relevant medieval charters in 1789.[4]

The lynchpin of the Girondins' programme, however, was more simply war. A war of European liberation, they thought, would be doubly useful. Externally, it might bring to power those various exiles, Dutch, Belgian, Swiss, or even English, who were in Paris the friends of the Girondins, many of whom had extensively lived or travelled abroad. Internally, a war would be even more efficacious: it would unite the bourgeoisie and the people. Condorcet's paper, *La Chronique de Paris*, made this point very clearly in January 1792:

> Nous sommes en paix et notre commerce languit, notre change baisse tous les jours et nos assignats perdent de plus en plus. . . . La confiance diminue, les mécontents se multiplient. . . . Si les Français ne . . . décident pas [la guerre], l'état de désunion se prolongera, la perte des assignats augmentera, l'effervescence des esprits, qui eût été utilement dirigée contre l'ennemi commun et vers un grand but, se tournera contre nous-mêmes. . . . Tous les dangers disparaissent au premier coup de canon.[5]

Where Robespierre's and Marat's policy of crisis and catharsis through purge and civil war implied the violent destruction of the Revolution's enemies at home, the Brissotins expected domestic counter-Revolution to crumble from within when faced by the single front of an assembled and non-noble nation united in a warring cause. A quick, galvanizing, demagogic war was in the logic of their vision (as were in Robespierre's the domestic coups of 10 August 1792, and of 21 May 1793).

In this context, the émigré-noble 'threat' was a godsend for the Girondins. It enabled them to make a connection between war abroad and politics at home. By sliding back and forth from an encouragement of the popular suspicion of nobles to the menacing presence of émigrés at Coblenz, Brissot and his party gave plausibility to their warmongering scheme. Émigré nobles were now fair game, and in the autumn of 1791 they became, ostensibly at least, the *bêtes noires* of the Gironde.

ii. The Gironde's ambiguous hostility to émigrés and nobles before and after the fall of the monarchy

In keeping with this new line, Brissot's first speech to the Legislative Assembly was a philippic against these faithless aristocrats. In late December 1791, his Girondin colleague Guadet likewise proposed to outlaw as a crime of *lèse-nation* any discussion of a reconciliation between them and the nation. On 25 November 1791, the journalist Carra, from the forum of the Jacobin Club, denounced a vast aristocratic plot which involved the King's protection of refractory priests and émigrés, an ironic charge since the monarchy's relations with the émigrés were at the time quite poor.* Carra did not hesitate to threaten the monarchy with popular upheaval: 'Dites au pouvoir exécutif qu'il faut qu'il marche, qu'il obéisse, ou qu'il descende du trône.'[6] On 1 February, Grangeneuve, a Girondin sympathizer, attacked the War Minister's policy of 'protecting' the émigrés. He, too, threatened the monarchy with an 'appel au peuple':

> Si cette connivence entre les rebelles et l'un des agens du pouvoir exécutif reste impunie, alors la confiance de la nation dans ses représentans élus va disparaître, le peuple se liverera à l'abattement, ou peut-être, ce qui aurait des conséquences bien plus funestes, son ressentiment le portera à des mouvemens d'insurrection. . . . (Les tribunes applaudissent.)—Il s'élève de très-grandes rumeurs dans l'assemblée.—M. le président rappelle M. Grangeneuve à l'ordre.—Une partie de l'assemblée insiste pour qu'il soit noté au procès verbal—Elle est très agitée.—[7]

Vergniaud was even more extreme: not only should the Holy Roman Emperor forbid the display of the white cockade in his realm and deport the émigrés as fugitives from justice, but France should risk a war to achieve this goal.[8] The campaign against émigrés was carefully orchestrated, and the actor Orfeuil was delegated by the Paris Jacobin Club to the provinces, where he would spread the word.

Émigrés received a place of honour in the declaration of war of 20 April 1792, presented by another Girondin, Gensonné, who gave as the principal cause of conflict the Emperor's protection of the 'Français rebelles'. This line of attack was maintained during the last weeks of monarchic rule and beyond. Brissot harped on it at every opportunity and asked in his speech at the Jacobins on 25 July 1792, 'Eh! qui peut contester que le foyer de contre-révolution établi à Coblenz soit plus actif que jamais?' Two conspiracies at least were now afoot, he explained, that of the émigrés abroad and, at home, of those who would restore nobility, extend royal power, and create two chambers. 'Non,' he concluded, 'ces complôts ne peuvent être des chimères, ils sont vraisemblables, ils sont vrais.'

* See Appendix 6.

In the summer of 1792, the most common variant on these themes was the association which Brissot tried to create between the émigrés and the new Republicans, who might sabotage his last-ditch efforts to strike a bargain with the King. Brissot did not actually say that the Gironde's enemies on the left and the right were part of a single conspiracy, but he implied as much when he said that all these groups should be punished at once: 'Le glaive de la loi', he explained, 'doit frapper sur [les hommes qui travaillent à établir à présent la république sur les débris de la Constitution] comme sur les amis actifs des deux chambres, et sur les contre-révolutionnaires de Coblenz.'[9]

It can hardly be proved of course that the Girondins' persecution of émigré nobles was purely opportunistic. Some of them may have half-believed their lies, since the fear of the émigré menace was rampant in France in 1792. Indeed, the resulting mood has sometimes been interpreted as an extension of the tense moral climate of 1789 and the Great Fear: émigrés were seen under every bed, and rumours were rife in 1790 already of imminent invasions by Swedes, Russians, and their noble native allies.[10] In the spring of 1792, nobles were said to have infiltrated the columns of volunteers marching to the front. The number of émigrés was commonly distorted, and in October 1791, Marat had (without much comment) printed a report of some 50,000 émigrés in Flanders alone. So had the *Révolutions de Paris* talked of 60,000 passports, and the *Gazette de Leyde*, in November 1789, of 80,000 to 100,000 departures.*[11]

But informed observers knew all such figures were false. In September 1791, Gouverneur Morris very accurately wrote of '16,000 French refugees',[12] and in May 1792, of 20,000 'French emigrants'. In the Convention itself, the Girondin minister Roland, in his report of January 1793, spoke of 16,930 known émigrés and of a supposed 40,000 additional and unreported cases.[13] In view of this, the Girondin denunciations should have been obviously incredible to everyone including themselves.

This was precisely Robespierre's argument: opposed to war, he derided the threat of émigrés and labelled them 'une tourbe de fugitifs aussi ridicules qu'impuissans'.[14]

That the Girondins knew they were lying in claiming that émigrés were dangerous appears all the more likely for the paltriness of what was actually done: émigrés, after all, were already abroad. Robespierre's plan for a purge of noble officers

* See Appendix 3.

at home would have had much greater effect. Brissot's passivity on this issue was telling. When they chose, the Girondins could be savage, as they were to the non-juring Catholic clergy, whom they genuinely detested: those people were ordered to be deported. But the oratory against émigrés was largely for show, and harsh words, after all, break no bones.

The same contrast of Girondin words and actions also appeared in their handling of nobles as nobles rather than as émigrés. Gradually, Brissot and his friends developed a rhetoric which suggested that the Revolution had not been about principle in general but about nobles in particular. This was the gist of a speech by Pétion on 6 February 1792, which underlined the hatred of nobles common to both bourgeois and 'le peuple': 'Il semble à la bourgeoisie', he said,

> que la noblesse n'existe plus, qu'elle ne peut jamais exister; de sorte qu'elle n'en a aucun ombrage, qu'elle n'aperçoit pas même ses desseins. Le peuple est le seul objet de sa défiance. On lui a tant répété que c'était la guerre de ceux qui avaient contre ceux qui n'avaient pas, que cette idée-là la poursuit partout. Le peuple, de son côté, s'irrite contre la bourgeoisie; il s'indigne de son ingratitude; il se rappelle les services qu'il lui a rendus; il se rappelle qu'ils étaient tous frères, dans les beaux jours de la liberté. Les privilégiés fomentent sourdement cette guerre qui nous conduit insensiblement à notre ruine.[15]

More eloquent, Vergniaud was also more violent. For him, to speak of nobility was tantamount to dividing mankind into two classes, 'l'une pour la grandeur, l'autre pour la bassesse, l'une pour la tyrannie, l'autre pour la servitude. . . . La noblesse! Ah, ce mot seul est une injure pour l'espèce humaine. Quel autre d'ailleurs rappellera désormais à la France des parjures plus réfléchis, des défections plus honteuses, des trahisons plus perfides, des conspirations plus atroces?'

If the Revolution did not go forward, it would necessarily go backward towards 'la contre-révolution, c'est-à-dire la dîme, la féodalité, la gabelle, des bastilles, des fers, des bourreaux pour punir les élans sublimes de la liberté, les fureurs du fanatisme, celles de la vengeance, le pillage, l'incendie, enfin le despotisme et la mort. . . .'[16]

The Girondins were warming to their theme and they did not let the pressure up as the fall of the monarchy drew nearer. With the King, some compromise might be made, but nobles were seemingly beyond the pale. On 19 June 1792, Isnard and Guadet appeared at a banquet held to celebrate the anniversary of the abolition of nobility; and on that same day at the Jacobins, Condorcet welcomed the Assembly's order that publicly owned proofs of noble rank be destroyed. In mid-May, the records of chivalric and noble orders stored at the Augustins had been ordered to be burnt, and Condorcet thought that more should be done in this line of work: 'C'est aujourd'hui', he explained, 'que dans la capitale, la raison brûle aux pieds de la statue de Louis XIV, six cents volumes infolio, dépôt orgueilleux de la vanité d'une caste dont les chimères se dissipent en fumée',[17] an example which he thought the provinces should follow.

But again, Girondin declamations about the iniquity of nobility had no more practical effect than did their lamentations about the émigrés. The laws against emigration had, so to speak, bolted the door after the horse had fled, and the Gironde's anti-nobilism was no more efficacious.

The implication of opportunism is unavoidable because the critical issue was not dealt with: nobles who had become officers before 1789 because they were nobles were neither purged nor dismissed as Robespierre would have liked. The concern of Rouyer, a minor Girondin, on 12 April 1792, about the undeserved promotions of noble-born captains to the rank of lieutenant-colonel was most significant in its assumption that noble-born captains were there to stay.[18] It was therefore in the nature of things that Girondins like Brissot or Pétion should both rail against feudalism, and then, on 2 May 1792, join the rest of the Assembly in demanding the expulsion of the sans-culotte leaders, Vincent and Momoro, who had asked that the officer corps be purged.

The Gironde's policy towards nobles and émigrés in late 1791 and especially 1792 remained ambiguous. To be sure, the Girondins had resolutely embarked on a policy of no enemies to the left, a strategy that necessarily implied the eventual sacrifice of nobles' rights to the mob's anti-noble feelings. What the Gironde did not have, however, was the will to act out the drama that it had staged. Carrying out this role was something that would be left to the Dantonistes and the Montagnards.

Ostensibly, the fall of the monarchy on 10 August 1792 was indeed a 'second French Revolution'.[19] In many ways, however, it merely institutionalized the Revolutionary bourgeoisie's decision, taken in the autumn of 1791, to find a solution to the problem of

Revolutionary politics on the left rather than on the right as Barnave and Lafayette had hoped. Instead of opting for an alliance with the moderate conservatives and perhaps even the King, the Gironde in late 1791 had chosen to side with 'le peuple'. The consequences of this choice it was now unwillingly forced to bear. In actual fact, the Gironde had begun to turn to the right in June and July 1792, but, for some time, it continued to go through the motions of being a progressive party. Its policy had been hypocritical for some months; it now became duplicitous.

Correspondingly, for the émigrés, the insurrection of 10 August 1792 meant no more than a continuation, if in accentuated form, of the opportunistic policy of persecution that had been inaugurated by the Gironde in the early winter of 1791. Conceptually, the situation remained as it had been. Eventually, the Mountain would pick up the Gironde's policy of opportunistic populism; in the meantime, the Gironde itself tried to go on with its tactic of reliance on 'le peuple'. When faced, for example, with the murderousness of the Septembriseurs, whose work Danton and Robespierre had tacitly endorsed, the Gironde's first reaction was to cling to Revolutionary legitimacy as best it could. It still presented itself as *the* party of the left, and it continued to attack the foreign and domestic enemies of Revolutionary progress. Émigrés were every bit as useful to the Gironde in the autumn of 1792 as they had been in the autumn of 1791.

Anti-émigré legislation reflected this continued determination, and from 14 August to 23 November 1792, no fewer than twenty-six laws, decrees, and proclamations about émigrés were put on the statute books. Where émigrés in July 1792 had still been urged to return, a decree of 23 October 1792—one month after the débâcle of émigré hopes at Valmy—forbade them to do so under pain of death. On 15 November, émigrés who had already returned were given fifteen days to leave again.

The relatives at home of émigrés abroad were more closely watched, and on 15 August 1792, another legal threshold was passed when the Assembly voted a law of hostages, already proposed some months before by the Girondin Rouyer: henceforth the parents of émigrés were *ipso facto* consigned to their municipality regardless of their personal opinions, on the grounds that 'les maux qui affligent la France . . . ont pour cause les trahisons et les complôts des mauvais citoyens qui ont émigré'. On 9 September, the remaining fathers and mothers of émigrés were decreed by law to be 'mauvais citoyens' who had urged their children to leave and would themselves have left had they been able, an act which warranted a special imposition: each parent would equip two soldiers for every child of theirs abroad.

The implication of these laws was clear: some individuals were now less entitled to the protection of the constitution than other individuals, and Jaurès quite rightly thought that the law which considered the parents of émigrés responsible for the sins of others was a prolegomenon to the September massacres: 'It is clear', he wrote,

> that [Merlin's laws on émigré hostages] was the first signal of the [coming] Massacres. Who could hope for a legal solution to this lugubrious settlement of accounts when Revolutionary passion had risen to such a point that the women and the children of émigrés were made to pay for crimes of the émigrés themselves? . . . That day, and at that moment [the Legislative Assembly], in the depths of its conscience, consented to bloody reprisals, and it is not surprising that it had neither the strength nor the desire to intervene on the day of the massacre itself.[20]

Emigration became a very serious offence. Dissident nobles were now *the* enemies of the Revolution and the accusation of emigration was a brush which the Gironde used to tar all of its enemies in turn.

Before 10 August, Guadet had deplored the sad identity of views which was supposed to bind the monarch and his noble liege-men across the Rhine. 'Par quelle fatalité, Sire,' he asked, 'n'avons-nous pour ennemis que des hommes qui prétendent vous servir?'[21] But three weeks later, the Gironde had come to grips with the sad truth of royal duplicity, and on 15 August, Henry-Larivière presented to the Assembly a correspondence of Delessart which indubitably linked Louis with his brothers abroad and the Emperor. Royal ministers were also fair game: on 21 August and again on 31 August, Brissot, Fauchet, Gensonné, Lasource, and Guadet hounded Montmorin and secured his arrest on the grounds of his supposed tolerance of émigré machinations. When the Minister was able to show that some of the incriminating evidence related to another Montmorin who lived at Fontainebleau, the Girondins secured that man's arrest as well, and this at a time when imprisonment in Parisian jails was tantamount to death, as Brissot reproached Robespierre, who had tried to have the Girondins locked up.

Such machinations were banal. Little ingenuity was required after the fall of the monarchy to connect the right at home with the right abroad. Far more original in these same weeks was the Girondins' other gambit, which was to say that the sans-culotte Septembriseurs were themselves the tool of the émigré faction.

In September and October 1792, the Girondins' feelings about law and order remained ambivalent. After the September massacres, they now feared the mob, but for some weeks they continued to suppose that they might maintain their rule not as a party of the right but as a party of the left. Hence the need to disqualify, in leftist terms, the ultra-left, the men of the Mountain and their sans-culotte allies.

Here the existence of the émigrés once again answered the Gironde's most heartfelt need. Before 10 August, their line had been to return to power by claiming that the King was working with Coblenz. But now in order to keep power, they proclaimed that a different conspiracy was afoot. On 17 September 1792, the Girondin Lasource spelt this out to his fellow Legislators. The men of blood, in Paris, were only pawns. The brain was elsewhere. 'Coblenz et Brunswick', he explained, 'ont dans Paris cinq ou six cents brigands soudoyés qui préparent leur horrible triomphe.'[22] And that evening the same theme was taken up by Vergniaud, who had displaced Brissot as the spokesman of the Girondin faction: 'le peuple est juste et il abhorre le crime. Mais il y a ici des satellites de Coblenz, il y a des scélérats soudoyés pour semer la discorde, répandre la consternation, et nous précipiter dans l'anarchie.[23]

Girondin feelings about émigrés and nobles sometimes continued to be trivial, as they had been in late 1791. Roland, for example, was very concerned about the destruction of *chateaux-forts*: on 23 September 1792, he announced that 'les Français ont en horreur les crimes des nobles, l'hypocrisie des prêtres, et la tyrannie des rois; ils n'en veulent plus',[24] and a few weeks later he decided to give substance to this thought by reminding local officials that not enough had been done to wipe out the symbols of nobility: 'La plus absurde de toutes les distinctions, celle qui voulait que des hommes naquissent audessus des autres hommes, n'existe plus; mais ses ridicules vestiges subsistent encore en divers lieux.'[25]

And in late November, Roland considered the possible dismantling of ancient chateaux: What was to be done with the confiscated estates of émigrés? he asked the Convention. Who would want to buy these incommodious 'sumptuous and immense' buildings? Would it not be wise to destroy them and divide the land on which they stood in small lots so that the purchasers might rebuild? 'On aurait alors pour enchérisseurs tous les nouveaux acquéreurs qui, jaloux de se faire une habitation dans leurs nouvelles propriétés, joncheront ces campagnes de maisons utiles, riantes et commodes, nées des colosses qui ont si longtemps pesé sur la France.'[26]

At times, the Gironde's demagogic purpose had more serious effect. Propitiatory victims had to be found, and the Girondins had no choice but to persecute émigrés. It was their lot to be cruel, though by now they would have preferred to be kind.

Their viciousness emerged in the debate on what was to be done with some émigré soldiers captured after Valmy. On 1 October, Debry, an uncommitted Conventionnel who hounded émigrés during his entire political career, suggested that these men be tried by civil courts. But this was not enough for the Gironde, and on 8 October 1792, when the capture of some émigrés was announced to the Convention, which was asked for a ruling on them, Vergniaud reminded his colleagues that the matter had already been decided: 'Il existe une loi qui porte que tout émigré qui sera pris les armes à la main sera puni de mort. Il faut charger le ministre de la guerre de rendre compte de l'exécution de la loi.'[27] Guadet, the next day, also suggested that captured émigrés should be shot immediately and on the spot. On 16 October, Manuel similarly expressed surprise at the comings and goings of captured émigrés: 'je demande que le ministre de l'intérieur prenne des mesures pour faire exécuter cette loi, et que désormais les émigrés ne fassent plus le voyage de Paris qui ne servirait qu'à retarder l'exécution de la loi'.

Such calls for execution were not in vain, and a short notice in the *Moniteur* of 23 October reported laconically that nine of the thirteen émigré prisoners brought to Paris in the preceding weeks had indeed been put to death.[28] It appears that the generals who ordered that the émigrés be sent back to Paris were in this matter far more accommodating than the civilian Girondins, whose commitment to murderous opportunism was decidedly unbending.

In the autumn of 1792, however, Girondin feelings began to veer. The deaths of émigrés were, as such, an acceptable misfortune; but as an incitement to bloodshed which might some day reach even the Girondins, such deaths were troublesome. On 23 October 1792, with Guadet in the chair, the Convention approved Buzot's motion which confirmed that returning émigrés would be executed; but winds of change were blowing. On 25 September, when the leftist Montagnard Billaud-Varennes proposed the execution of all those who had helped in some way to bring the enemy on to French soil, a leading Girondin criticized his 'enthusiasm'. And the debate of 28 October 1792 was an even clearer landmark, since on that day another prominent Girondin, Gensonné, offered (in vain) to read to the Convention a letter sent to Biron, a noble, then commanding the army on the Rhine, by two émigré officers eager to return to France. And by 3 November, it was clear to the Englishwoman Helen Maria Williams, a close friend of many Girondins, that the execution of captured émigrés (many of whom, she now thought, had left against their will) was 'legal murder'.[29] The slackening of pressure against émigrés was clearly felt, and in the winter of 1792/3 Paris was rife with rumours that 10,000 or even 20,000 émigrés had returned.[30]

But here as elsewhere the Girondins were conspicuously incompetent, and in a characteristic way, for they chose to sacrifice their long-term chances for a short-term gain. In mid-December 1792, they suffered a relapse into their persecuting mood when they attempted to blacken their enemies, the Mountain, by associating that group with the disrepute of the most prominent noble still in France, Philippe Égalité, the Revolutionary cousin of Louis XVI and the father of the future Louis-Philippe, King of the French.

Between 4 and 15 December 1792, Buzot attacked Égalité directly and indirectly by proposing to exclude all nobles from office in the newly conquered Belgian provinces. Camille Desmoulins, the *enfant terrible* of the Mountain, then rose to the bait. In order to shield Égalité, sitting at the time as a Montagnard Conventionnel, Desmoulins—in accord with Marat but not with Robespierre, who held aloof—defended the rights of nobles: 'Ce sont les nobles qui ont fait la révolution des Belges et vous voudriez les exclure!'[31]

Buzot's manoeuvre backfired in every way: the Girondins now placed themselves on record as having favoured the lifting of parliamentary immunity, in this case Égalité's, but soon their own. The move also ran against the grain of the Girondins' policy of resistance to a further radicalization of the Revolution, which had in its true logic the defusing of the policy of revenge against nobles or émigrés.[32] A more consistent stand on nobles would perhaps have made more credible the other conservative steps which the erstwhile Revolutionary Gironde was taking in the autumn of 1792 to court the right, such as overtures to the Feuillants, the condemnation of the Revolutionary tribunal, demands for the release of prisoners, and most obviously the campaign to save the King.[33]

The Gironde had botched its disengagement on the question of the rights of nobles. It did not gain much from its equivocal moderation here, but it did lose the initiative in this sphere which now became the preserve of the least respectable members of the Convention—Dantonistes, *affairistes*, Hébertists of sorts, future Thermidorians most of them—that is, by men who were of the left or of the extreme left, but who were not wholly of the Mountain. The Gironde had begun to falter, the Mountain had not yet come fully into its own, and in late 1792 and early 1793, Danton and the men around him reached the pinnacle of their influence.

Relying on the 'people' as did, in some way, every political group from 1788 to the autumn of 1793, politicians had no choice but to show sympathy for anti-noble passions, which, especially in Paris, were running very high. There was, however, a difference between Danton and Brissot on this issue, not of tactics but of resolution: the Girondins had merely babbled, but Danton acted forcefully. As he told the future Louis-Philippe shortly after the September massacres, which he condoned and may well have encouraged, the loyalty of the Parisian volunteers would be assured only if the Revolution released a river of blood which would sever them from the émigrés.[34]

In Danton's wake followed other men of the same stamp, equally corrupt but less forceful, though often more bizarre. Debry and Charlier (both future Thermidorians, one of them deranged) were prominent on this issue, as were Garnier and Merlin de Thionville, all of them pushing for the immediate execution of captured émigrés. Close behind Danton was Thuriot, who on 10 August, with the approval of Gensonné proposed that local authorities be given the right to search all noble residences at any time:

Nous ne pouvons nous dissimuler que nous sommes depuis très longtemps en guerre avec une portion de l'Empire français, par conséquent cette portion doit être surveillée. Il faut donc que des autorités constituées puissent faire des perquisitions dans tous les châteaux et demeures où il est nécessaire de savoir s'il y a des armes et de la poudre.[35]

Also active in this business was Anacharsis Cloots, a Prussian baron by birth. On 29 October, he warned the Convention about the 'fer des nobles', the 'torches des prêtres', and recommended the despoliation of Belgian nobles. And in the rear came Basire, later executed with Danton, who told his colleagues on 4 November that recent disorders had been caused by royalists who had escaped the scrutiny of the *visites domiciliaires*. When on 22 November the noble-born General Biron petitioned the Convention on behalf of his émigré wife, one of Danton's closest friends, Legendre, leapt to his feet: 'L'on emploie tous les moyens possibles pour vous faire innocenter des coupables, des scélérats; devez-vous vous occuper des individus? Suivez votre marche et achevez la loi.' It was in these same months also that Barère, then trying to stay close to both Danton and the Mountain proper, persuaded the Convention to proclaim that France would refuse to deal with any foreign power which chose to entrust its diplomatic representation to an émigré.[36]

Osselin was another marginal leftist deputy who thrived at this time and whose case deserves special mention as a symbol of the dishonesty of many of those Conventionnels who were vocal members of the left but who were not Montagnards. The son of a *maître rotisseur*, Osselin was in 1789 a failure, about forty, and desperate to do well. In the autumn of 1792 the legislation on emigration became his eminent domain. For many months, his expertise remained unchallenged, a great irony since he would be executed in 1794 for having married and protected a former émigré, who had also hidden in Danton's house. In fairness to Osselin, however, it should be said that a number of rather seedy Conventionnels fell victim to the discreet charm of the aristocracy: Bentabole, Rovère, and Tallien also married noble women, with somewhat better luck; Julien de Toulouse, an equally unappealing man, took an aristocrat as his mistress. Soubrany, himself a noble but a very honest Montagnard also, was later shocked by the conduct of these fellow Conventionnels, 'plongés dans les voluptés, passant leur vie dans des orgies scandaleuses avec toutes les ci-devant marquises, comtesses'.[37] Nice Conventionnels, one might say, had nothing to do with aristocratic sirens, but their weaker colleagues were sorely tempted. The faded charm of noble women was difficult to resist, sufficient in fact to corrupt members of the Armée Révolutionnaire itself, one of whose officers at Villefranche named Dobigny was sent back to Paris in disgrace for having so succumbed.[38]

iii. The opportunistic radicalization of the Mountain's policy on nobles and émigrés in the spring of 1793

In the autumn of 1791, the Gironde began a hypocritical campaign against nobles and émigrés, a course that it continued to pursue for a few weeks after the fall of the monarchy. Then came the turn of the Dantonistes, who moved to the fore when the Gironde subsided. In the spring of 1793 began the last phase of opportunistic persecution when leadership on this issue passed into the hands of the Mountain proper, that is, of men who were far more resolute in their acceptance of popular sovereignty than were the Girondins.

The Dantonistes became less conspicuous, but the persecution of émigrés none the less commanded a wider base. In the autumn of 1792, as the Dantonistes stepped forward, the Girondins had stepped back. But in the spring of 1793, Dantonistes and Robespierrists moved in accord. For nearly one more year, Danton's friends would continue to push the Revolution leftward, and their émigré policy reflected this. On 9 April 1793, the Convention had carried the motion of Danton's friend, Delacroix, to deny the right of any formerly privileged person to join the 'army of forty thousand', which would be raised to guard Paris, and in August, Chabot, like Delacroix a venal man, was one of the first deputies to propose the blanket exclusion of nobles as a group, together with the deportation of all priests.

In the spring of 1793, however, the animosity of Dantonistes against the émigrés was no longer new. What mattered then was a shift to a stronger stand by the Mountain and its leaders. At first Robespierre opposed the passing of legislation against émigrés. In February 1791, Seagreen, as Carlyle called him, spoke against such a law; he also pointedly ignored the émigré problem in February 1792, when everyone seemed to care about it deeply. His position, moreover, was not unique, and was, in fact, comparable to that of Marat.

In the autumn of 1791, Marat unequivocally denounced the Girondins' persecution of émigrés. The Girondin decrees, he explained, were neither moral nor constitutional: people should be free to come and go as they pleased. More importantly, Marat also pointed out that such laws were irrelevant since they could have no effect. As a temporary solution, Marat incongruously proposed the publication of a list of absentees: 'C'est par l'infamie qu'il faut punir les scélérats que la loi ne peut atteindre.'[39] Middling steps were useless. Aware that this point of view was by Girondin standards positively counter-revolutionary, Marat forestalled his critics and went on to explain that he was right and they were wrong: 'Le lecteur irréfléchi aura sans doute été scandalisé de mon jugement sur le décret contre les fugitifs contre-révolutionnaires; et cela doit être, il faut des lumières que le commun des hommes n'a pas pour en appercevoir les vices, à travers des apparences de sévérité, bien propres à en imposer à la multitude qui ne pense pas.'[40] Marat certainly had no particular fondness for 'jadis nobles' as such, and it was his suggestion that those of them who were guilty should have their thumbs cut off.[41] But his point was that many who deserved to die were non-nobles and that only some nobles were guilty. In practice, it is true, Marat was quick to accept the need for bloodshed, but in theory, at least, his stand was more appealing and more sensible than that of the Gironde.

To persecute émigrés was beside the point. The problem of the Revolution was elsewhere. This had been Marat's view in 1791–2, and Robespierre defended the same line. In February 1791, he had denied the appropriateness of legislation that would make emigration illegal, and during the debate on declaring war in 1792, Robespierre consistently maintained that it made no sense to worry about the 'poignée d'aristocrates émigrés auxquels la France faisait à peine attention il y a quelques temps'. The threat was here, at home. Marat's solution had been strongly stated: 'tout mon espoir pour sauver la patrie est dans la guerre civile si toutefois le peuple a le dessus',[42] and characteristically, Robespierre said the same thing, but with more nuance: 'remettez l'ordre chez vous avant de porter la liberté ailleurs'.[43] The Incorruptible's contribution to the debate on emigration in 1791–2 was therefore extremely modest: in August 1791, Robespierre protested against the use of titles in addressing royal princes;[44] on 20 October 1792, he did not go much further when in a rare comment on this issue he complained that Pache in a message to the Convention had used the locution 'duc', which, he thought, 'semble attacher plus d'importance à la mort d'un ci-devant prince qu'à celle d'un émigré ordinaire'.[45]

In the spring of 1793, however, Robespierre reversed his tactic.

The key to his change of mind on émigrés lay in the sudden exacerbation of the conflict with the Girondins.

Like Cromwell, who would gladly have ruled with Parliament if its members had been more amenable, Robespierre was a parliamentary liberal who at first had no thought of purging the Convention. Eventually the Paris crowds were called in, but initially Robespierre assumed that his fellow deputies would of their own accord choose the Mountain rather than Brissot, Vergniaud, or the Gironde. In line with this tactic, Robespierre, though more tolerant of popular disturbances than nearly any of his colleagues, was less than favourable towards food riots in Paris. Political insurrection on behalf of the bourgeoisie was one thing; rioting for bread was something else. As late as 25 February 1793, when Parisian washerwomen invaded groceries in order to 'tax' or fix the price of soap at some price they could afford, Robespierre was not pleased: 'quand le peuple se lève', he sententiously remarked, 'ne doit-il pas avoir un but digne de lui? De chétives marchandises doivent-elles l'occuper?'[46] Robespierre was not sympathetic to the riots, and in fact gave guarded approval to the old Girondin tactic of associating citras and ultras. Just as Vergniaud had linked Coblenz and the Faubourg Saint-Antoine in September 1792, so did Dubois-Crancé, a Montagnard, suggest on 25 February 1793, that the émigrés had been behind the recent food riots:

Les besoins ne sont pas réels. Les émigrés sont cachés parmi vous, déguisés en sans-culottes et prêchant la liberté. Ce sont ces mêmes hommes qui poussent le peuple de Paris à des excès sous le prétexte de la disette des subsistances: allez à la halle, elle regorge de farine. Les anarchistes ont senti qu'il suffirait de faire prendre à une moitié de Paris une double provision pour faire manquer de pain l'autre moitié. Quoi! ce peuple qui s'est disputé en 1790, pendant six mois, le pain nécessaire à son existence, se livrerait au désespoir pour quelques moments d'engouement? Ces événements sont loin de nous, ils ne peuvent se reproduire.[47]

Robespierre concurred:

J'ai été témoin moi-même des mouvements. A côté des citoyens honnêtes nous avons vu des étrangers et des hommes opulents revêtus de l'habit respectable des sans-culottes. Nous en avons entendu dire: on nous promettait l'abondance après la mort du roi, et nous sommes plus malheureux depuis que ce pauvre roi n'existe plus. Nous en avons entendu déclamer non pas contre la portion intrigante et contre-révolutionnaire de la Convention, qui siège où siégeaient les aristocrates de l'Assemblée constituante, mais contre la Montagne, mais contre la députation de Paris et contre les Jacobins, qu'ils représentaient comme accapareurs![48]

Robespierre's distrust of popular extremism at this time is easily understandable. Until late February and perhaps even early March of 1793, neither Gironde nor Mountain had expected Paris to arbitrate their rivalry: the Gironde looked to General Dumouriez, and the Montagnards still expected to discredit their opponents within the walls of the Convention.

After March 1793, however, Dumouriez's defeat and betrayal followed by the Girondins' parliamentary manoeuvres against Marat forced on all parties a sudden realignment. On the right, the Gironde became more openly hostile to the sans-culottes and began to canvass for conservative support at large. On the left, the Mountain now looked to the crowd in order to use it against the right.[49] Just as Pétion had announced in February 1792 the indissoluble union of the Gironde and the people, so did Robespierre loudly proclaim in early May 1793 that 'la Montagne a besoin du peuple, le peuple est appuyé sur la Montagne'.[50]

In line with this new alignment of political forces, Robespierre, whether consciously or unconsciously is hard to say, trimmed his sails to the prevailing wind and altered his views on things that mattered to the poor, like food and nobles.

The supposed connection between citra and ultra which Robespierre had taken up a few weeks before was not forgotten—it was to be revived when Robespierre in the next phase of Revolutionary politics decided to attack the *enragés* in the summer of 1793—but the argument was shelved momentarily. The drive against émigrés was stepped up: in 1792, Robespierre disdained Condé's émigré army, then a coherent military force fighting alongside the Austro-Prussian army. Now, in the spring of 1793, when émigrés counted for nothing in the affairs of state, Robespierre proposed to reinforce the legislation against them, and he urged that severe penalties be imposed on those departmental administrators who were lenient in prosecuting fugitives.

The repercussions of Dumouriez's defeats were ominous for returning émigrés or for their relatives. The crisis had a two-fold effect. On the one hand, serious measures of national defence were rapidly adopted, of which the most conspicuous was the creation on 10 March 1793 of the Revolutionary Tribunal: 'soyons terribles pour empêcher le peuple de l'être'. And regular as clockwork, there appeared also a rekindling of the now ritual and demagogic denunciations of émigrés by aspirant revolutionaries, in this instance the Mountain, who were reaching for the top of the greasy pole. On 1 March, at the Jacobins, Robespierre already denounced the 'tracasseries de la part des nobles, des prêtres et des agens de l'aristocratie'.[51] Then, on 5 March 1793, came a more interesting exchange.

By now, the Girondins in Paris were thoroughly involved in their new policy of no enemies to the right. In a reversed stance, typical of the Gironde's involuted tactics, Lasource stood up to denounce the tyrannical implications of anti-émigré legislation. A young woman ('une enfant', really), who had left France, had just returned, been apprehended, and was by law under the penalty of death applicable to all returning émigrés. Lasource's conscience could not bear this: 'la loi ne peut subsister,' he argued, 'elle est injuste; la sévérité est inutile, barbare et dangereuse pour la liberté'. As a warning to the wise, he insisted on the general implications of the situation. Order in general, and not just the problem of émigrés, was at stake: 'Il en est de la théorie des principes comme du système du monde, il y a un équateur moral. De quel que côté qu'on y arrive, on agrandit le cercle des principes, et on avance jusqu'à ce qu'on touche la ligne; de quelque côté qu'on la franchisse, on rétrécit le cercle et l'on rétrograde.'[52]

The Dantoniste Thuriot concurred, his speech taking as its focus a consideration of pure principle. But Robespierre then rose and rejected Lasource's motion. Principle, as Lasource understood it, was irrelevant: 'La véritable humanité est celle qui sait sacrifier quelques intérêts particuliers à l'intérêt général.' The laws on emigration had less to do with principle than with expediency:

> On la regarde souvent comme un principe qui tient à la jurisprudence civile et criminelle, à l'exacte distribution des délits et des peines. Ce n'est au contraire, qu'une mesure vigoureuse qu'exigent les circonstances présentes, une mesure politique et révolutionnaire; sans doute il n'est pas douteux qu'un grand nombre d'émigrés ne soient très à plaindre, mais il faut nous armer d'une juste sévérité, et opposer la sagesse des législateurs, aux sentiments de commisération qui pourraient nous parler en faveur de tel et tel individu.[53]

Implicitly denying his earlier view that émigrés were of no consequence, Robespierre now held them up as the Revolution's first enemies, and on 13 March 1793, he explained what the purpose of the new Revolutionary Tribunal ought to be: 'Il faudrait que ce tribunal commençat ses opérations non par les Jacobins, non par les députés de la Montagne, mais par les émigrés, mais par les généraux qui ont trahi la patrie.'[54]

The same sequence of popular denunciation of nobles and Robespierrist indignation continued for some months. In the summer of 1793, Robespierre would turn the sans-culottes' hatred of nobles against the enragés; then, in the winter of 1793/4, his own grievances against nobles would take on a new, quite different, and more ideological configuration. But in the spring of 1793, his reasoning, half sincere and half opportunistic, was quite plain: the 'plebs' hated the nobles, and the Mountain needed popular support. The pattern could only be of popular complaint and bourgeois concession. On 25 March 1793, the Réunion section asked for the disarmament of all nobles; on 3 April, Claire Lacombe asked for the imprisonment of all Parisian nobles and their families. And on 27 March, at the Jacobins, Robespierre's resentment rose to fever pitch:

> Quoi! les prêtres, les nobles et leurs complices auraient plongé un fer sacrilège dans le sein de Pelletier [a Jacobin noble], et nous n'aurions pas le droit de nous défendre, nous n'aurions pas le droit de les bannir de nos sections; de mettre entre eux et nous les colonnes d'Hercule? Les traîtres adjournent-ils leurs complots, ont-ils invoqué les formes pour assassiner Michel Pelletier?[55]

His atypically vulgar and contemporary remarks on 'nobles et calotins' are likewise evidence of his desire to please in words and style, if in no other way.

It is true, of course, that the Incorruptible never completely lost sight of the principles in question here, and in May 1793, he once again reminded his fellow *clubistes* that the operative principle of Revolutionary justice was guilt and innocence, not birth or social condition: 'J'ai demandé que tous les citoyens suspects fussent mis en état d'arrestation. J'ai demandé que la qualité des citoyens suspects ne fût pas déterminée par la qualité de ci-devant nobles, de procureurs, de financiers, de marchands.' But at critical moments, Robespierre was more than ready to push these caveats aside to save the Revolution by posing for the 'plebs'. There was no other way. Although he had in earlier times merely despised the émigrés, he was able to conclude in May 1793 that their guilt was truly obvious: 'Celui-là est un insensé; celui-là ne sait pas combiner les premiers élémens de la politique qui ne voit pas la relation qui existe entre les révoltès et les Coblentiers; l'armée de la Vendée est un détachment de l'armée de Cobourg.'[56] And in June 1793, he abandoned General de Beauharnais to his fate. Robespierre acknowledged that Josephine's first husband, as he coyly put it, 'had not played a counter-revolutionary role' during the Constituent assembly: 'mais il est noble,' he lamented, and continued, 'il est d'une famille qui était très accréditée à la cour, et cela suffit pour m'empêcher de lui accorder une entière confiance'.[57] Custine fared no better. In December 1792, at the Jacobins, Seagreen had spoken warmly of him: 'J'ai connu Custine à l'Assemblée constituante, j'estime sa franchise, ce général a bien servi la patrie.' But by August 1793, Custine, he told the Convention, had become an 'assassin du peuple français'.[58]

The Mountain had decided to save the Revolution by working with the people. The people hated nobles, or so it was assumed. The nobles would have to suffer. The Mountain's opportunism was less transparent than the Gironde's. In late 1791 and early 1792, the Girondins manufactured the émigré threat out of whole cloth. This fabrication could no longer be undone, and in the spring of 1793, the Montagnards were in this respect faced with a *fait-accompli*. Their problem was to shut off the salt mill which Brissot, the sorcerer's apprentice, had started up. Yet there is a common denominator here in that the bourgeois revolutionaries' line on émigrés and nobles was, throughout this period, a tactic. The Girondins had hoped that it would please, and the Montagnards knew that it could not be ignored. This is an important difference. But in neither case can it be said that the bourgeois persecution of nobles was from 1791 through the summer of 1793 an integral part of the Revolutionary programme, as it would become in the autumn of 1793.

Between the breakdown of constitutional monarchism in the summer of 1791 and the development of the Terror in the autumn of 1793, most bourgeois anti-noble acts were strategic gestures designed to harness 'the people' to the bourgeois Revolutionary cause. To be sure, after the summer and autumn of 1793, the Mountain was to embark on a completely new anti-noble course, but in the earlier period, the difference between Montagnard and Girondin policy was not of kind but of intensity. What separated the two groups then were their varying views on the desirability of opportunistic persecution. Should the people be placated at the expense of nobles? The Girondins, who initiated anti-noble moves, were ultimately faint-hearted about this problem, the Montagnards more determined. If it was useful to hound nobles, if the people required it, it would be done. The issue in early 1793 was pragmatic rather than theoretical.

The Mountain's shift on nobles and émigrés was not conceptually novel, but Robespierre's turn round at this moment was of great importance. Henceforth, the most determined phalanx of the Revolutionary bourgeoisie would try to put into practice the anti-noble programme which the Gironde had invented but had not dared to carry out. Bourgeois revolutionaries would now take active steps to give lasting substance to the concept of popular sovereignty in this as in other matters. Moreover, unlike Barnave or Brissot or Danton, Robespierre would not be swamped on the left by any other bourgeois faction. With him, bourgeois 'Revolutionism' existed, so to speak, in a pure state because Robespierre enjoyed that tactical freedom which his own presence had denied to Brissot. To be sure, Robespierre's programme made no bourgeois sense, and it too would fail. But its contradictions would be exposed in a deeper and more telling way. It would collapse from within rather than from without.

iv. Rural and urban popular anti-nobilism as the background of bourgeois Revolutionary opportunism

In the autumn of 1791, when the Revolution began to falter, the dominant wing of the Revolutionary party decided to stabilize national politics by associating the bourgeoisie more closely with the people. When the Girondins, who had first adopted this radical tactic in 1791, shied away from its consequences in late 1792, the Mountain in the spring of 1793 took the lead in bourgeois Revolutionary politics. The people would be heard, and a necessary implication of this strategy was the curtailment by the bourgeoisie of the rights of nobles, for there is no doubt that plebeian anti-noble feelings continued very strong in 1792–3.

The most striking development of popular anti-nobilism in 1792–3, as shall be seen, was its politicization and spread to cities. But rural anti-nobilism certainly did not vanish after the summer of 1789 and the Assembly's theoretical abolition of feudalism. On the contrary, peasant feelings were in some ways sharpened, and geographically the sphere of rural disturbance was widened.[59] In early 1790, the Swiss press reported that more than forty chateaux had been burned since the beginning of the year.[60] In the south-west, rioting was endemic; in the Quercy, nobles formed a defence league, which did them little good.[61]

Those noble landlords who tried to collect the feudal dues to which they were still entitled by law often ran into trouble; in April 1790, for example, Jacques Roux was accused of having abetted such a riot, during which two chateaux were burnt down by peasants who had decided to stop paying any dues, regardless of what the bourgeois deputies had decided in Versailles and Paris.[62]

Each crisis, such as the flight of the King and the emigration of hundreds of army officers in the autumn of 1791, engendered another round of abuse.[63] After Varennes, chateaux in the Berry were searched for feudal parchments and nobles were ordered to report *en masse* at Bourges.[64] Similar incidents occurred near Lyon; near Villefranche, where the tocsin rang and peasants and national guardsmen invaded chateaux to burn feudal records; and, at Poleymieux, where peasants decapitated a noble landlord who had tried to resist.[65] In March and April of 1792, a *Jacquerie* broke out in the southern Ardèche and many archival records were destroyed.[66]

Rural anti-nobilism remained a force to be reckoned with. It was, however, redirected and made more manageable than it had been. Agitation tapered off after October 1792 (one author has even described the burning of feudal records in 1793 as 'symbolic')[67] because peasant grievances by 1792 were expressed in a different and more politicized way than they had been before. On both grounds, it became easier for bourgeois authorities in 1793–4 to cope with the peasantry's anti-nobilism than had been true in 1789.

The decline of overt peasant violence had a variety of causes. Of these, the plainest was that peasants after 1792 respected those rights of nobles which the law still upheld because they were more afraid of the law than before. In the cities, the Revolution had let passions fly, but in the countryside, the maintenance of law and order was gradually improved. In 1789–91, when the rule of law was associated with the existence of a suspect or despised monarchic executive, the left had often condoned disorder: 'Ce sang était-il si pur?' Barnave had asked. But with the fall of the monarchy, upholding the law at all levels became the responsibility first of the Gironde and then of the Mountain. In early September 1792, the *commissaires* sent out by Danton's Provisional Executive Council had done what they could to stop rural anti-noble rioting;[68] and when the Convention convened a few weeks later, law enforcement was given greater importance yet.

By late 1792, the issue of rural attacks against nobles was understood to be a part and parcel of the much larger problem of order in France generally. The Girondins were badly shaken by the massacres of September 1792, when, or so they thought, they had nearly lost their lives. The Mountain's refusal to condemn these outrages gave a much sharper relief to the problem of law enforcement, not only in the cities but in the countryside as well. The issue of illegal acts against nobles and émigrés came to a head in October 1792, with an incident which did not involve peasants directly, but whose implications eventually affected them also.

Discipline had been lax in the army, and some volunteers of the *Premier bataillon républicain de Paris*, drawn from the sans-culottes of the capital, had taken it upon themselves to execute four émigré deserters who had fallen into their hands. The high command objected. Marat took up the cause of the sans-culottes. Having secured the approval of the Jacobin Club, where the Mountain was methodically blocking investigations of popular excesses, Marat tracked Generalissimo Dumouriez to ground at a reception given by the actor Talma.[69]

He demanded to be shown the records of the soldiers' trials on the assumption that an impartial look would show the sans-culottes to have been unfairly persecuted by the generals. Having failed in this attempt, Marat then attacked Dumouriez in the Convention on 18 October, and eventually the Parisians were indeed released. But officially, at least, the Convention refused to condone the soldiers' act. Marat was shouted down. On 16 October, the Montagnard Ruhl had already set the tone of the debate: 'il faut que le glaive de la loi frappe la tête de ces traîtres [the émigrés] mais ce n'est que la loi qui doit les punir',[70] and one month later, the Convention again reminded the interested public that 'les voies de fait contre les émigrés sont défendues'.[71]

The message was clearly stated, and it was restated in mid-December 1792. French troops had once again shot some deserters, this time Prussians, and they had been reproved for this by their commander. In the Convention, Reubell rose to endorse his decision. Reubel did not do as well as he wished. The Convention did not dare to order the soldiers to be punished; but their commanding general was not censured as the sans-culottes had asked.[72]

It was now evident that the Convention would oppose further summary justice, even if a discreet veil was to be drawn over what had happened in the past. Garat, the opportunistic Minister of Justice, ever sensitive to the needs of the times, understood the new mood of the Assembly, and on 21 December spoke out ringingly in favour of rural order. It was his duty to remind the Convention, he explained, that although feudalism had been odious, unauthorized acts of violence committed in the countryside by peasants, the 'anciennes victimes de la féodalité', against their former masters were also intolerable:

> le droit de propriété doit être respecté, dans quelque main qu'il se trouve, et l'égalité des droits veut une égale protection pour tous. Dès l'instant qu'une portion quelconque des membres de la République pourrait être expropriée sans les formes de la loi, on ne pourrait plus dire que le droit de propriété existe, qu'il est sacré; et qui pourrait prévoir le terme où s'arrèteraient des prétentions qui ne seraient pas soumises au règlement de la justice?[73]

The law, then, and the rights of all owners of property, would not be flouted; rural popular anti-nobilism was for that reason alone redirected. To this must be added that the new legal structures at times enabled peasants to achieve peaceably in 1793 those same aims which in 1789 could only have been secured illegally. Why should men of violence thwart the police and deny the law when they could become the law by joining the newly created committees of surveillance? Why attack or even murder nobles who could now conveniently be brought to trial? The courts would serve where rioting had once been needed.

In the country north of Paris, for example, there was widespread agitation in the summer of 1789 against game laws and hunting rights and peasants had clashed with the *maréchaussée*, about rabbits especially. In 1793, new methods were of the essence, but the old grievances were still there. When the marquis de Grouchy, who lived in this same area, was arrested in 1793, the issue that had caused a riot in 1789 now resurfaced in legal form. The Public Prosecutor of the Commune of Candecourt was now the spokesman of the erstwhile rioters, and he began his prosecution accordingly: 'Primot en mil sept cent quatre-vingt-neuf tu étois le premier de la noblesse du bureau intermédiaire de l'assemblée du département de Senlis et nomée commissaire par le roi pour la destruction des lapins. . . .'[74] Grouchy, it seemed, had never destroyed the rabbits.

Peasants, then, were more afraid of the law; in some instances they had become the law. It may also be that the climate of these Revolutionary times enabled them to perceive their situation in a more sophisticated way, and it seems that we can point to a politicization of peasant grievances between the summers of 1789 and 1793.

By the end of 1791, many rural acts of violence carried a new and obviously political message, like the ravaging of Chantilly, which belonged to the émigré leader, Condé, or the murder of the Count of Dampierre after Varennes in June 1791. The same rethinking of what rural riots were about also emerged in the widespread disorders that broke out in the Ardèche in April 1792, which called forth a massive bourgeois show of force. This urban response was suggestive, to say the least, as was also the political discernment of the peasant rioters, for they did not loot indiscriminately: 'Tous les châteaux de nos environs', wrote some municipal officers, 'sont détruits ou démolis: et tous les citoyens qui ne portent pas la cocarde nationale sont insultés par cette armée. Tous ceux qui ont la réputation d'être patriotes sont épargnés et leurs propriétés aussi.'[75]

An even more extreme pattern of politicization was visible in the neighbouring department of the Gard. Peasants there had been quiet in 1789, and as late as 1792 political lines of cleavage in this region remained as they had always been, that is, aligned on the traditional split between Protestant and Catholic, a pattern that would be repeated in the late 1790s and in the nineteenth century. But in 1793–4, peasant politics took a different turn. Now, the animosity of peasants in the Gard region was directed to all reactionary landlords, regardless of religious consideration, on the new and striking political grounds that all of them were selfish and politically unreliable, no different really from avowed counter-revolutionaries and émigrés.[76]

As a rule, therefore, the peasants' hatred of landlords was thoroughly transformed. Chateaux might still be physically attacked, as happened in the Ariège in July–October 1792, but such occurrences were increasingly rare. Peasants were now able to put pressure on nobles by acting through local, and legal, Revolutionary institutions. Violence tapered off, not surprisingly after all, since many pre-Revolutionary peasant grievances had by now been met. Feudal dues had been abolished, and most French peasants, many of whom owned some property, did not wish to push beyond the abolition of dues towards a redistribution of land, even of common village land. As far as peasants were concerned, noble landlords might be left alone, provided that they did not give political offence. There was no need for riots, and, as has been said, rural law and order were in any case far better served in 1793 than had ever been true before or since 1789.

By choice and necessity, rural anti-aristocratism was very different from what it had been. Though certainly a force to be reckoned with, it was decidedly more manageable in 1793 than it had been since the early summer of 1789. The peasants' animosity towards nobles could not be ignored by either the Gironde or the Mountain, but the politicians in Paris were now better able to guide it than before. In the cities, however, the situation was difficult. There, the machine ran wild.

In 1789, the bulk of popular anti-noble disturbances took place in the countryside: 'Il faut pourtant convenir', wrote a young noblewoman to her brother in October 1790, 'que, s'il s'est commis des horreurs dans les villes, il ne s'en est pas moins commis à la campagne. Ce n'est pas dans les villes que les châteaux ont été brûlés, pillés, les curés massacrés'.[77] By 1792, however, the balance had shifted the other way and cities now became the focus of popular anti-nobilism.

Urban hatred of nobles developed steadily. Popular complaints about émigrés were ever more numerous than before and found expression through the provincial Jacobin clubs. After the fall of the monarchy, direct action became the order of the day, and the *sectionnaires* in Besançon, for example, pressured the municipality into ordering the arrest of the relatives of émigrés—which was done in part until Roland ordered their release.[78] In the same way, in the Doubs, at Salins, the municipality required all nobles to leave town and the local *conseil général* even ordered their arrest, for which they too were reprimanded by Roland.[79] Émigrés in 1792 were, to say the least, widely disliked in the cities, and there may have been something to Merlin de Thionville's later claim that he had in August 1792 proposed the arrest of their relatives in order to assure their protection.[80]

Quite regularly, from 1792 on and throughout the Terror, counter-revolutionary activity of any sort triggered popular demands in the cities for the incarceration of ci-devants.[81] Such demands were made in Nantes and Marseilles, in Lyon during March 1793, and at Lille in August. Similar complaints were also forthcoming from the cities where not much had happened but where opinion was thoroughly politicized, like Épinal, Dijon, or Clermont-Ferrand, where in April 1793, petitions were drawn up to demand the elimination of all nobles from public office and the army. But it was in Paris that hatred of nobles and émigrés rose to fever pitch.

By the spring of 1791, feeling in the capital against nobles was building up. In April 1791, the carriages of aristocrats on their way to balls that brought together notoriously reactionary nobles were stopped in the Chaussée d'Antin.[82] It was widely suggested that the army should be purged of counter-revolutionary noble officers, and the very successful Fête des Suisses de Chateauvieux on 15 April 1792 had as its theme the persecution of 'plébéiens patriotes' by ci-devant officers. Practical expression of these resentments emerged most brutally during the September massacres. Priests were the favourite target of the Septembriseurs, but their single most famous act was the murder of the Princesse de Lamballe. Her stripped body, it was reported, perhaps unreliably, was displayed for hours, then cut in pieces; her pubic hair, it was said, cut off and used as a moustache by one of her tormentors. To be sure, from the first moments of the Revolution, that fluid entity, the Paris crowd, had taken on some nobles. But men like Flesselles, Bertier, and Foulon, who were murdered in July 1789, were unusually conspicuous nobles who had become publicly notorious as agents of the state. It was only in 1792, when the sans-culottes became more conscious of their own collective existence, that nobles in Paris came under sustained pressure.

Popular urban anti-noble sentiment was a new phenomenon, distinct from rural anti-nobilism in both its trajectory and its origins. The difference was particularly obvious in Paris. For most peasants, nobles before 1789 had been a real presence; but in the capital, nobles on the eve of the Revolution were strikingly inconspicuous. Paradoxically, the capital of France under the Old Regime had been, to speak aphoristically, a city without nobles, just as it would become in the 1840s a city without notables.[83] Nobles were few and far between in Paris: estimates of their number in relation to the population as a whole in the 1780s vary from 1 per cent to one-third of 1 per cent.[84] In the 1780s, commentators on Parisian social hierarchy assumed as given that administrators and bankers were more important there than nobles who had no public function. Symbolically, Parisian aristocrats were tenants, not landlords, as Jaurès observed: 'Sauf quelques centaines de grandes familles, la noblesse elle-même était locataire de la bourgeoisie.'[85] Many Parisian nobles understood that their honorary distinctions had become supererogatory: at the assembly of the Parisian *tiers état hors les murs*, during the electoral assemblies of 1789, one noble, for example, explained that he had a right to sit with the third because he and his noble family had been in trade for many years.

The situation of nobles in Paris before 1789 was the opposite of what existed in the countryside, and the difference in the course of rural and urban popular anti-nobilism after 1789 was also striking. As peasants became more aware of politics, their hatred of nobles was cooled, or at least politically channelled. The reverse was true for the sans-culottes. As their self-awareness developed, their vision of nobles sharpened, and their hatred of aristocrats grew apace.

In the past, Parisian nobles had sometimes been disliked and, more commonly, ignored. Now they were hated. After August 1792, former ci-devants acquired a place of honour in the sans-culottes' view of the counter-revolutionary pantheon. In 1789–91, nobles were denounced as a sub-group of the counter-revolutionary party in general, but in 1792–3, the '*caste nobiliaire*' acquired a specificity of its own. There is no mistaking the deep if ephemeral hatred of the Parisian crowd for nobles in the summer of 1793, a hatred that was much more passionate and intense than the reasoned and frozen detestation of the noble-born that was felt by Saint-Just or Robespierre.

The causes of the sudden explosion of sans-culotte anti-nobilism are, however, by no means as self-evident as the phenomenon itself. The secondary literature on the sans-culottes is nearly mute on the subject. R. B. Rose's model essay on *The Enragés*, for example, illustrates the sans-culottes' detestation of the nobles with only four instances, none of them more than four lines long. The answer is opaque; explanations must be conjectural unless additional evidence is unearthed. At present, it is necessary to consider the problem in terms of historical categories.

In some respects, sans-culottes were definitely *sui generis*. Their sense of fraternity, their craving for direct action, their verbal excesses, their tolerance of drunkenness were so many traits that separated them from the *honnêtes gens*. But at the same time, the sans-culotte was, as Richard Cobb has emphasized, a political accident; and that accident was, after all, of bourgeois origin. Political goals like nationalism, anti-monarchism, anti-nobilism, and perhaps even anti-clericalism were in a way excrescences caused by events and by bourgeois cultural influence on the sans-culotte 'movement'.

It is therefore a central paradox of the period that the unique phenomenon of sans-culottisme should have come to political consciousness on the basis of political ideas that were of mixed origins. The sans-culotte complaint about *subsistance* was of course radically anti-bourgeois, and would, indeed, with Babeuf, provide the basis of the first concerted modern attack on property. But most of the sans-culottes' loftier concerns, like anti-nobilism, were largely derivative.

The cause of the sans-culotte loathing of nobles during the spring and summer of 1793 did not lie, therefore, in the material relationship of Parisian nobles and non-nobles before 1789. It differed from the peasantry's dislike of nobles which fluctuated closely with the weight and perception of feudal dues. Popular Parisian passion about aristocrats was an acquired characteristic which did not depend closely on an appreciation of what nobles had been in Paris before 1789 or were then doing as officers in the field. Sans-culotte anti-nobilism can best be understood as yet another example of the bourgeoisie's political and cultural hegemony. The emotion filtered down from above. For that reason, perhaps, it was also expressed in highly formulaic terms, quite comparable with the ritual denunciations of 'Pitt et Cobourg'. It was precisely because of its abstract quality that the popular hatred of nobles in Paris was as politically efficacious as it was: in 1793, when politics opposed one myth to another, it was the sans-culotte's ignorance of what nobles really were which enabled him better to mythologize their existence as the incarnation of all things evil.

The question of popular anti-nobilism, its genesis and development, has been as a rule neglected by historians of the sans-culotte movement, but it may none the less be a revealing one. If we accept the notion that 'the people' in Paris had little reason to detest nobles as intensely as they did (since Parisian nobles were few, powerless, and probably sympathetic to the goals of the bourgeois revolutionaries), the derivative nature of sans-culotte 'ideology' in the summer of 1793 becomes more understandable. And this same hypothesis, it may be added, is massively reinforced by the otherwise inexplicable reversal of sans-culotte opinion on nobles in the autumn of 1793. At that time, as shall be seen, at the very moment when Robespierre's persecution made the sans-culottes aware of their distinctness and their isolation as a

Revolutionary group, the most prominent of the extreme sans-culottes, Roux and perhaps Taboureau also, drastically re-adjusted their view of the noble-born. Nobles before had been the enemies of the people because they were the enemies of the bourgeoisie. But when the sans-culottes began to see themselves as the rivals of the bourgeois Montagnards, their views of nobles also changed.

Sans-culotte feelings about nobles mirrored the evolution of the popular movement as a whole. In its first phase, when sans-culottism developed in accord with bourgeois goals, the sans-culottes acquired a detestation of nobles which they had not had before. Then, after the summer of 1793, in a second phase, when sans-culottism gained in strength, its attention increasingly focused on those of its more sophisticated claims that were *sui generis*, like the control of food prices or pensions for the poor. At that point, acquired characteristics, like anti-nobilism, began to lose their appeal. This was a significant change, all the more striking in its originality for the fact, to be discussed later, that the decline of popular anti-nobilism in the autumn of 1793 coincided with a sharp rise of bourgeois feeling about the noble-born. The coherence of these various categories is suggestive. The evolution of popular Parisian anti-nobilism, at its height in the summer of 1793, followed by a brusque decline in the autumn of that year, reflects the emancipation of the sans-culotte thinking from its bourgeois models. That pattern in turn leads us to suppose that the causes of sans-culotte anti-nobilism are deeply embedded in the nature of the popular movement as a whole.

Historians will no doubt disagree about the causes of sans-culotte anti-nobilism. What is beyond doubt, however, is its strident tone during the summer of 1793. What had been somewhat erratic before suddenly became methodical. On 25 March 1793, the Réunion section demanded that all nobles and their domestics be disarmed. On 8 April, the section of the Mail asked for the dismissal of all nobles from the army. Inspired by Marat's growing concern, the Cordeliers took this up on 2 May: noble generals and especially Beauharnais ought to be dismissed; and the next day, Jacques Roux, an *enragé* sans-culotte, urged the *Conseil général* of the Paris Commune to come out for the arrest of all 'ex-nobles' as did another *enragé*, Varlet, at the Cordeliers on 22 May. On 2 June, the *Conseil général* of the Paris Commune decided to put its house in order on this score and it ordered the dismissal of all former priests and nobles from those public appointments that it controlled.[86] On 4 June, the Réunion Section asked that all nobles be barred from public office; and on 14 June, one of Garat's spies at the Section des Halles reported that an orator had spoken there to a similar end; if this were not done, he was reported to have said, 'la ville de Paris se regarderait de nouveau en insurrection et . . . il serait permis à tout citoyen de tuer et égorger tous les ennemis du bien public.[87]

On 15 June, Varlet again addressed the *Conseil général* of the Paris Commune on this same issue: if the army had failed in the Vendée, it was the nobles' fault. When reminded that the Convention was unlikely to do anything about this at the moment, he insisted that the ministry of war should draw up a list of noble officers currently serving and he was assured that this was being done.[88] That same day at the Jacobin Club, when Robespierre explained that it was premature to disarm all nobles still in the army, Hassenfratz complained: 'Qui avez vous à combattre? Qui avons nous pour nous commander? Des nobles et des prêtres. Des nobles.'[89] At that session of the Jacobins, Vincent insisted on presenting the petition of the Cordeliers demanding the dismissal of nobles, and Bourdon de l'Oise had to cut him off. Then, on 23 June, Roux once again asked the Paris Commune to ratify the plan he had presented to the Cordeliers in May: all noble officers were to be expelled from the army, and the parents of nobles and émigrés should all be arrested. This was also the drift of a petition submitted by the Panthéon section on 30 June,[90] by the Luxembourg section on 16 August,[91] and by a delegation from the *assemblées primaires* on 20 August.[92] Léonard Bourdon and Hébert joined this same chorus in late July and early August 1793. Indeed, from March to mid-September 1793, when such outbursts suddenly became very infrequent, complaints of this kind were put forward by genuine (and false) sans-culottes of all hues—like Hébert, Varlet, or Claire Lacombe ('Faites voir que vous voulez sauver la patrie par la destitution de tous les nobles');[93] and by a number of sans-culotte organs—like the new *Comité central révolutionnaire de Paris*.[94]

In fact, from the sans-culotte Cordeliers, the mood of panic and revenge about nobles affected even the Jacobins. In June, Vincent and Hassenfratz had been easily pushed aside when they had harangued this more bourgeois club about expelling noble officers, but on 28 August 1793, the Paris Jacobins were also swayed and decided to march *en masse* on the Convention to demand a purge of army staffs and the expulsion of all noble officers. For Hébert, even that was not enough: all nobles should be deported. Royer, who frequently spoke for delegations of sans-culottes from the *assemblés primaires*, was asked by the more respectable Jacobins to present their case as well: all nobles should be removed from office and the most unpatriotic ones deported.

The sans-culotte invasion of the Convention on 5 September 1793 marked the zenith of sans-culotte anti-nobilism. The importance of that *journée* is widely recognized, and many historians have dwelt at length on the social and economic claims which the sans-culottes made that day. But it should also be remembered that the first demand of the spokesman of the 'plebs' was not about food at all. It was, '*avant tout*', about the exclusion of nobles from public office. No exceptions could be made. For the sans-culottes, all nobles had now become the 'irréconciliables ennemis de l'égalité et de l'humanité entière'.[95]

In short, hatred of nobles had become in the spring and summer of 1793 *the* touchstone of popular Revolutionary zeal. Hébert had sensed this and had put it nicely some weeks before when, at the Jacobin Club, he had juxtaposed his claim to be Marat's successor with his hatred of the ci-devants:

S'il faut un successeur à Marat, s'il faut une seconde victime, elle est toute prête et bien résignée: c'est moi! Pourvu que j'emporte au tombeau la certitude d'avoir sauvé ma patrie, je suis trop heureux! Mais plus de nobles! . . . Plus de nobles! Les nobles nous assassinent! (Tout le monde se lève, et par un mouvement unanime promet d'appuyer cette juste demande.)[96]

A Parisian bonnet-maker named Auguste le Noble resurfaced as Artichaud le Libre, and Grelibre was floated as an alternative to Grenoble.[97] The town of Baron became Montagne-des-Piques; as Martigny-le-Comte was changed to Martigny-le-Peuple, and Bar-le-duc to Bar-sur-Ornain, after an initial mistake which had made it Bar-sur-Meurthe (choices, incidentally, that were ratified by a committee of Conventionnels, whose most prominent member was Antoine Mailly, a former secretary of Voltaire, who had begun life as Antoine Alexandre Marie Gabriel Joseph François de Mailly, marquis de Chateaurenaud[98]). To be a noble was horrid; and to associate with one a proof of *incivisme*. Incensed by the incursions of the sans-culotte *Armée révolutionnaire*, the citizens of Cambrai decided that their ravagers must be nobles in disguise. The commander of the Revolutionary unit was himself accused of being one: 'Moi-même, j'en suis un,' he complained; 'enfin, il n'est point de choses qui ne s'inventent chaque jour.'[99]

In a sense, everyone was cheated here, including the Revolutionary bourgeois politicians. Bourgeois passions in 1789–91 had pushed against the nobility as a corporate group rather than against nobles as individuals. That was a distinction which still mattered a great deal to Robespierre and many others in the summer of 1793, but which was now difficult to uphold. Girondins and Montagnards alike condoned rural anti-nobilism in 1791–3, but with a limited and demagogic purpose in mind. When anti-noble sentiment of a direct and personal sort developed in the cities, the ideologically minded bourgeoisie was faced with a problem it had not expected. Like the sailors of Odysseus, bourgeois politicians had unleashed a wind which they could neither guide nor control. Their anti-aristocratism was sophisticated and ultimately measured. The anti-nobilism of the Parisian poor, though derived in large part from bourgeois models, was violent and excessive. Tactical bourgeois manoeuvres against nobility and rural feudalism suddenly came home to roost as popular calls in the cities against nobles taken as private persons. In the summer of 1793, bourgeois politicians found themselves pushed to extremes in the name of ideas which they had spawned but whose practical effect they had not foreseen.

Even more cruel was the deception played on nobles themselves, of course, and on the sans-culottes as well. To be sure, popular hatred of the nobility was a positive force in so far as it contributed to the redirection of the popular movement. In a roundabout way, cries for noble blood did make it more possible for the sans-culottes to secure power and a lower price for bread. But in and of themselves, the varying prospects of the noble-born were strikingly irrelevant to the condition of the urban poor, as Marat had pointed out in 1790 when the abolition of nobility had been a subject of debate. True, Marat himself had rather lost track of this point in the summer of 1793, when he was closer to Robespierre than he had ever been. But his former message still made sense: ultimately, anti-nobilism was a blind alley for the sans-culottes, a fact that Roux, the most prominent of the *enragés*, would soon come to understand.

v. The resulting legislation on nobles

Given the popular passions of the day and the opportunistic tactics of Montagnard politics, it was only to be expected that a rich variety of laws would be enacted after February 1793. These laws fell under two headings: those that concerned nobles directly, and those that dealt with émigrés at a time when all émigrés were still thought to be noble.

Cases involving émigrés were placed in the jurisdiction of the Revolutionary Tribunal set up in March 1793; and in its first session, the court returned a verdict of death against one Guyot-Dumollans, a noble, who was convicted of having emigrated illegally and returned illegally. Émigrés who had chosen to come home were it seems guilty of a crime that was commensurate only to the misdemeanor they had committed when they had left in the first place.[100]

Émigrés were declared to be dead as civil persons. Their legal acts were declared null and void, and they were shorn of their familial rights as husbands and as fathers. The debts that were owed to them were cancelled, and those who would pay such debts regardless might be punished. Individuals accused of being émigrés were assumed to be guilty until proved innocent; it was not up to the courts to prove that a denunciation of some émigré was true or untrue. Accused émigrés were required to prove that they had never left, and the authorities took steps to improve the listings of émigrés by taking absence from domicile as proof of flight rather than as indication of absentee-ownership.

Accomplices of émigrés were severely punished; informers who betrayed them to the police received a reward of a hundred livres: 'Il faut', explained Chabot, 'qu'un enfant puisse envoyer un émigré à la guillotine.'[101] On 27 March 1793, with the passing of a new law defining the crime of emigration more clearly, émigrés essentially forfeited their right to inherit; one-tenth of confiscated émigré property was earmarked for those citizens who had denounced them to the authorities. Until July 1793, the Convention had continued to recognize the claims of the relatives of émigrés to hold some part of family estates, but this was ended on 13 September 1793. Dangerous anti-bourgeois precedent was also set in order to involve the population in the hunt for émigrés: the sale of ordinary *biens nationaux* was often rigged so that only the rich might buy them, but it was, by contrast, repeatedly suggested that the property of émigrés which had been ordered to be sold in July 1792 would go to the poor. In August 1792, a Conventionnel proposed that such confiscated holdings should be used to increase the number of '*petits propriétaires*', and in late September 1792, Cambon, in charge of the Revolution's finances, proclaimed that émigrés' lands would first of all be used to 'indemniser les malheureux habitants des campagnes qui sont en proie aux fureurs de ces brigands'.[102]

Émigrés were deprived of some of the most elementary rights otherwise recognized by all civilized nations. Though fighting in regular units under the orders of a government in exile, more or less recognized by some foreign powers (rather like the Free French in 1940), émigrés, if captured, were put to death, a rule which also applied to former émigré combatants captured abroad as civilians, in Belgium, for example.

Admittedly, the Convention did also decree that British prisoners of war should be put to death, but this was only carried out in the sense that prisoners were not taken when they could have been. Émigrés who fell into Republican hands, however, were killed in cold blood, and in a report from the Spanish front, Cavaignac could mention in passing that 'Cette infâme légion d'émigrés a laissé 80 de ces scélérats sur le carreau, 17 ont été fait prisonniers; ils arrivent dans ce moment, et le soleil ne se couchera qu'après avoir vu ces monstres expier leurs forfaits sur l'échafaud.[103]

More suggestive, however, than the legislation on émigrés—technically aimed at 'tout Français' guilty of having abandoned the country in its hour of greatest need—were the acts directed against nobles pure and simple. Some of the anti-noble legislation was symbolic: buildings from which chivalric crests had not been removed were ordered to be destroyed, as were the *chateaux-forts* of *ci-devants seigneurs*. Similarly symbolic was the destruction of feudal titles, decreed on 17 July 1793, by now a largely meaningless act, as was soon recognized by the Convention itself, which called a halt in October 1793 and January 1794 to these *autos-da-fé*. Nothing need be said about the law of 11 October 1793, which made it mandatory for Frenchmen to turn towards the wall any firebacks decorated with the fleur-de-lis.

But other anti-noble acts were more serious. On 17 December 1792, nobles were forbidden to join primary assemblies. On 19 March 1793, nobles were singled out for especial punishment should they become involved in rebellion. On 21 March, the Convention approved Debry's motion that all nobles be barred from membership in the newly created *comités de surveillance*. On 17 April, nobles were declared ineligible to receive passports. On 5 July, a judicial clarification established that all nobles involved in counter-revolutionary conspiracy, in whatever capacity, would be treated as leaders rather than as mere participants. Suspects would be tried within twenty-four hours by the departmental criminal tribunals. There would be no juries and no appeal. The death penalty also implied the confiscation of all property. Then, in early August 1793, the Conventionnel Gaston suggested that all ci-devants be declared ineligible for public office, and in September 1793, they were given a place of honour among suspects: any noble could now be arrested for not having been an active supporter of the Revolution. On 12 September 1793, nobles were required to reside in their place of domicile under the eye of the relevant municipalities. Being morally unfit, nobles were also declared on 7 brumaire an II unworthy of becoming *instituteurs nationaux*. On 28 brumaire an II (16 November 1793), at the prompting of Granet, Clauzel, and Bourdon, the Convention considered both the recall of all those Conventionnels on mission who were ex-priests or nobles and the possibility of excluding nobles from the Committee of Public Safety. Local authorities, as has been said, took spontaneous action against nobles; in the Ardèche, for example, it was declared illegal for more than three nobles to meet together for any reason whatsoever.

Much of the legislation passed against nobles centred on their fitness to serve the Republic as soldiers. The purging of the officer corps had long since been a standard item of popular demand. Robespierre and Roederer had spoken up for it in early June 1791, as had Albitte, himself a noble, in October 1791, and Basire in late August 1792; but until September 1793, a measure of this kind was supported by the parliamentary left as a measure of opposition that had no chance of success.

In the spring of 1793, however, after the defection of Dumouriez, these demands for blanket exclusion were made more earnestly by Albitte, again at the Jacobins, and more cautiously by Marat, who asked on 2 April 1793 that nobles not be placed in command of armies in the field unless they had shown themselves to be indubitably loyal, but this motion was shouted down on the suggestive and commonly invoked grounds that to exclude the noble-born would only pave the way for domination of public office by the rich.[104] The effects of this anti-noble campaign, however, soon became irresistible.

In the past, and until the first months of 1793, the officer corps had in fact been left to purge itself; commissioners had been empowered to dismiss noble officers at will, but an oath to the

Republic had usually been held to be a sufficient guarantee of Revolutionary loyalty. Beurnonville in February 1793, and Bouchotte in May and June were, it is true, more thorough in their purges, but even they continued to consider cases individually.[105]

In a letter to the future Marshal Davout, for example, Bouchotte stated clearly that, in his view, the exclusion of nobles was, at this point, an expedient rather than a question of principle. Bouchotte's tone was very friendly. He paid tribute to this noble's intrepidity. Davout's efforts to stop the fleeing traitor Dumouriez were particularly pleasing. Davout's future was promising, but present circumstances dictated a studious pause:

tout nous faisait espérer que vous pouviez rendre de bons services à la Patrie dans ce moment. Mais vous avez pensé que l'opinion générale et le vœu des sociétés populaires, fortement prononcées pour l'exclusion des ci-devant nobles des premières fonctions militaires, ne vous permettaient pas quant à présent d'aspirer dans l'armée au degré de confiance nécessaire pour y être aussi utile que vous le désirez. Je me rends avec beaucoup de regrets à la résolution que vous avez prise de vous retirer chez vous, en applaudissant à votre projet de vous y livrer à l'étude militaire et à la pratique des vertus civiques, jusqu'à ce que le souvenir de votre origine ne soit plus un obstacle à la confiance publique qui vous est due personnellement à tant de titres.[106]

But true to its pattern of opportunistic concession on this issue, the Committee of Public Safety (the CPS) drifted to a tougher line as the sans-culottes themselves became more vociferous. On 2 September 1793, the Committee decided to have lists of all noble officers drawn up[107]; and after the invasion of the Convention on 5 September, any officer who had served in the King's constitutional guard or bodyguard was dismissed on the spot. On 29 December 1793, commissioners were empowered to remove any officers for any reason, and all nobles were indeed purged from some of the army corps. Then an interesting exchange took place on 23 February 1794: Taillefer, a Montagnard, and Merlin de Thionville, at that time on the extreme left, moved for the exclusion of all nobles from the army. Suitably impressed—or terrorized—the Convention approved. Two minutes later, it reversed itself after a speech by Danton. Now the symbol of moderation, this great demagogue, who months before had criticized the execution of Custine, took it upon himself to remind his colleagues that it made no sense to exclude nobles from the army just as it made no sense to exclude them from public office: 'comme il est vrai de dire qu'il n'y a plus de nobles en France, qu'il n'existe plus dans cette république que de bons citoyens qu'il faut estimer et protéger et des traîtres qu'il faut punir, je crois qu'il est nécessaire, avant de rien décréter qu'un rapport préalable vous soit fait. En conséquence, je demande le renvoi de la proposition'.[108] But Danton's views did not prevail for long. By February 1794, he had nearly run his race, and he had not run it very well. He was near death. Like the constitutional monarchists in 1791, and the Gironde in late 1792, Danton in late 1793–4 wanted to break the back of popular sovereignty and stop the Revolution. Saint-Just and Robespierre did not disagree completely; the sans-culottes, they thought, should be muzzled, but the Revolution, they also thought, would go forward regardless.

So it came to pass that a few days after Danton's death on 27 germinal an II (16 April 1794), on a motion by Saint-Just, the Convention finally carried through what was ostensibly the culmination of the sans-culotte anti-noble programme, though one for which there was now little popular demand: all nobles as a class were, by implication at least, declared unfit to hold office; only those nobles who had been especially 'requisitioned' might still serve. Barred from attending the meetings of the Revolutionary sections or of the *sociétés populaires*, many nobles now found it difficult to obtain *certificats de civisme* and were exposed to a variety of predicaments, including imprisonment. Finally, all nobles were banished from Paris and from maritime or fortified cities. Assigned to forced residence in small towns and villages, they were expected to report daily at the local *maison commune*.

In fact, many nobles had already abandoned the capital. In the first two years of the Revolution, as has been said, cities had been the safer refuge, but after the September massacres, nobles had understood that an obscure rural residence was by far the preferable alternative. A police report of September 1793 pointed out that the Faubourg Saint-Germain had been purged of all 'noble citizens'.[109] But enough of them had stayed behind to make for long queues at the Paris city limits, their possessions piled high on top of rickety cabriolets, as described by Helen Maria Williams, 'which seemed from their tottering condition somewhat emblematical of decayed nobility; and many who found these vehicles too costly, journeyed in the carts which transported their furniture, seated upon the chairs they were conveying to their new abode.'[110]

By law, nobles were forbidden to reside in the western departments, and on 30 messidor an II (18 July 1794), the Committee of Public Safety ruled that all 'dangerous' nobles could be arrested anywhere.

vi. Nobles' reactions to the Revolutionary turmoil

An interpretation which defines the Girondins' and Montagnards' persecution of nobles as opportunistic, tactical, and demagogic rests, as has been seen, on an appreciation of the motives of the Revolutionary bourgeoisie. The principal argument must be that the bourgeoisie in 1791 reversed its stand on the acceptance of nobles as individuals because this switch was required by the logic of its populist principles. The accusation of opportunism is sustained by the timing of popular complaint and bourgeois action. The same accusation can be demonstrated in another way, however, by showing that nobles were not the dangerous opponents of Revolution which it is often assumed they were. Nobles did not do very much. When they did act in a counter-revolutionary way, it was often in self-defence: 'Ce chien est très méchant, quand on l'attaque, il se défend.' And nobles, though largely defenceless, were attacked. The hypothesis of opportunistic persecution is implied by the innocuous and collaborationist nature of noble acts.

On balance, it can certainly be said that nobles were no more and no less counter-revolutionary than non-nobles of similar wealth, education, and influence. When asked by her judges if she attached importance to her titles of nobility, Marie Dubusc replied that she did not: 'non, en vérité, je me soucie autant de la noblesse que de ma pantoufle'.[111] And though perhaps more aware than she of their former status, most nobles when faced with demagogic persecution simply withdrew, as did most sympathizers of political groups overtaken by events. Peace and quiet may well have been the nobles' fondest hope: 'Oh! mon Dieu,' wrote one aristocrat to his steward in March 1793, 'quand nous rendrez-vous la paix, la douce paix! Quand elle nous est la plus nécessaire, elle semble encore nous fuir et tous les honnêtes gens la désirent.'[112] Sieyes's 'j'ai vécu' holds for nobles as much as it did for him.

Many nobles did in fact manage to go on as before. From caution or scruple, many revolutionaries protected obscure nobles who had not given much offence. Barère claimed, after the fact, to have requisitioned 6,000 nobles, thereby placing them out of the reach of the law of 27 germinal.[113] Some of his protégés found refuge in theatres as actors, as did one noble, Leroux, who was 'requisitioned by the Republic' 'pour être employé à la composition d'ouvrages patriotiques et pour les fêtes nationales'.[114] Other nobles managed to find a niche in the bureaucracy of the CPS, a fact which Robespierre found particularly scandalous. Of the ninety-seven Parisian nobles who were sent to Belleville, twelve were let off, three of them as bureaucrats, and nine others for a variety of reasons, which included being a musician at the Théâtre des Italiens and a lemonade vendor at the Section du Temple.[115]

Other aristocrats sought refuge in the army,[116] shuffling about from unit to unit when their identity was uncovered, like the sans-culottes on the run in 1795. Some paid protection money to stay out of trouble;[117] others became active revolutionaries, terrorists, or police spies.[118] At Versailles, Mme d'Angivilliers, whose husband, the former *surintendant des bâtiments du roi* had emigrated, gave a bust of Marat to the local *société populaire*, and took to bed for the rest of her life, hoping in this way to evoke the pity of possible tormentors. Though less pusillanimous, most nobles were content to lay low, keeping down with the Joneses, as it were; knocking down the towers of their chateaux, even before they had been asked to do so.[119] The baron de Frénilly, in a comment on the life of nobles during the Directory which applies *a fortiori* to the more dangerous days of the Terror, wrote of an affectation of poverty: 'Pas de chevaux ni de voitures, pour ne pas insulter le souverain à pied, pas d'argenterie, pour l'avoir donné à la monnaie. On se faisait même, en public, un certain luxe de pauvreté assez plaisant, et par exemple, on mangeait dans des *culs noirs*, comme si la faïence eut été trop coûteuse.'[120] Generally speaking, most nobles, as far as we can make out, tried very hard to stay out of harm's way. When arrested, they tried to show that they were good nobles, or hardly noble at all: 'Je ne sais si je suis noble,' one Marseillais noble told his judges, 'j'ai fait gloire d'être commerçant . . . je ne me suis pas aperçu si j'étais noble; j'ai toujours fait des actes qui me rendaient incapable de le soutenir.'[121]

When the municipality of one small town which had received orders in March 1793 to disarm nobles went about its business and decided to disarm its eight resident aristocrats, 'encore qu'il n'ait pas d'autres motifs', its task proved more difficult than had been anticipated: the first two nobles who were arrested claimed not to be noble; the third was not at home that day; the fourth, found strolling on the village bridge, claimed to be a *roturier*; the fifth asserted that he was not sure that he was noble, but gave up his sword as a gesture of good will; the sixth claimed that none of his forebears had ever been a *gentilhomme*; the seventh produced documents issued by the Paris Commune as a proof of his *civisme*; and the eighth, though he had no such papers, flatly denied that he was of noble birth.[122]

Jean-Baptiste Radet, in his musical comedy *Le Noble Roturier* of ventôse an II, made use of the nobles' sudden dislike of nobility as a comic theme, and one of his characters, a genealogist named Furet, is made to decline a dinner invitation on the grounds of a busy schedule. He sings:

> Grand merci de tes politesses
> Je n'ai pas un moment à moi
> Avant la fin du jour, je doi
> Désanoblir quatre comtesses.[123]

Nobles were particularly quiescent in the suburbs of Paris to which they had been sent. Some municipalities, it is true, like the one at Passy, went out of their way to ask that nobles should be watched most carefully, but many local officials appear to have felt pity for this human debris that had floated to their shores. At Villejuif, local officers reported, for example, that although nobles were inactive, an eye would be kept on them none the less: 'Ils ne communiquent pas ensemble, sont peu fortuné, tout exacte à se conformer à la loi du 27 et 28 germinal, ne font aucun rassemblement, n'entravent en aucune manière les subsistances et vivent très sobrement; néanmoins nous les surveillerons avec la plus grande activité, et nous déjourons leur perfidie s'ils cherchent à nous en imposer.'[124]

Like most members of a civil minority suddenly singled out for punishment, most nobles passively awaited whatever fate would come their way. Abstention had been the nobles' tactic since the autumn of 1791, when they stayed away from elections, and this remained their most sensible option even when abstention became a crime. Many nobles ran away, and by the summer of 1794, about 20,000 of them had left the country, an act which *per se* had no direct political implication, although the reverse has often been assumed.*

If nobles had been frightened in 1789–91, they now had cause

* See Appendix 5.

to be terrified. The September massacres of 1792 were condoned and eventually acclaimed by the Mountain. Nobles could obviously infer from this that their lives could again be in danger. Massacres might reoccur at any moment, and of some nobles who were arrested in September 1793, one police agent reported that '[ils] craignent beaucoup le renouvellement de 7 bre 1792, du moins à ce qu'ils disent'.[125] Since all nobles were by late 1793 members of a 'classe proscrite', their fears can be readily imagined.

Although anxiety beset nobles over the whole of France, it became dramatically obvious only when brought suddenly into focus, as happened in Nice, when the unexpected appearance of French troops on 28 September 1792 led to the flight of 800 people in a single day.[126] Many nobles assumed that their departure was precisely what the authorities wanted, or so claimed an émigré from the Ain, where Albitte had ordered nobles to present themselves for arrest: 'n'était ce pas [là] inciter les gens à fuir, car quel est l'homme libre qui de son sang froid se décide à forger lui-même ses propres fers?'[127]

The gratuitous nature of the proscription of nobles is also borne out in the recent work of Olwen Hufton, Paul Bois, and Charles Tilly, which shows quite clearly that the involvement of aristocrats in counter-revolutionary movements was of marginal importance at most.

Some nobles, certainly, did lead counter-revolutionary insurrections, but so did many bourgeois in Bordeaux, Marseilles, Caen, and Lyon. In 1793–4, countless notables of all sorts would have liked to rebel, but only a few had the local support that enabled them to do so, and the presence of nobles in rural insurrections only shows that peasants were a better base for rebellion than shopkeepers. If the 'pères conscrits' of Brest and Nancy or Arras and Decize had been drafted as leaders by popular counter-revolutionary movements, our view of their 'class' loyalties would be very different from what it is.

Even in rural areas nobles were often inconspicuous, especially in the earlier phases of revolt when peasants had not yet conscripted them for military leaders, as happened in the Vendée.[129] In the 'petite Vendée' of the Doubs, only two nobles were involved;[130] and a lawyer, Charlier, was the head of an abortive rebellion in the Lozère, a department whose most conspicuous Montagnard was the Général ci-devant marquis de Chateauneuf-Randon. Some nobles, it is true, were involved in the *chouannerie* (though not enough of them in the eyes of the

British, who thought the movement lacking in noble leadership), but nobles there 'were neither the instigators nor the real leaders'.[131]

In Paris, it was convenient to assume that provincial insurrections had been fomented by nobles, but many Republican generals on the spot knew that this was not true,[132] as did also some nobles. The comte de Moustiers in April 1794 asked what would happen if noble seigneurs tried to reinstate the status quo in the Vendée, and answered his own question: there would be popular indignation and a strongly expressed desire to be rid of them.[133] It was from a similar perspective also that the former head of the Poitou *maréchaussée*, now a Vendéen rebel, de Solérac, suggested in mid-1794 that after the defeat of the Republicans, a special police force should be established to keep the victorious and supposedly pro-noble peasants from turning on their sometime noble allies.[134]

It was, and still is, possible to make a case of sorts for the counter-revolutionary intransigence of the noble class as a whole by focusing attention on the extravagant statements of selected émigrés in 1792–5. But again, there is no tangible reason to assume that most nobles ever were sympathetic with that extremist message.*

Nobles were on the whole quite passive; their persecution made little practical sense, and Michelet seized on this fact to support his view of the Terror as the handiwork of Robespierre, whom he disliked and held to be a tyrannical neo-clerical, an anational dogmatist. 'Il y avait dans la liste' (of nobles sent to the guillotine in the first week of July 1794),

> une masse imposante, tout le parlement de Toulouse, cinq ou six grands noms de la monarchie, une douzaine de nobles ou de prêtres; le reste était des gens obscurs. Mais ni les uns ni les autres n'étaient des hommes d'action. Qu'ils eussent désiré se sauver, cela se peut, mais conspirer, nullement. L'anachronisme était choquant. En 92, à la bonne heure, ou même en 93; mais en 94, l'abattement, la prostration étaient absolus, les courages à néant. . . . Les royalistes étaient brisés, et récemment encore, de la bataille de Fleurus. A Lazare, huit cents prisonniers, le croira-t-on? avaient en tout . . . *un* geôlier! et in n'y eut de désordre que des plaintes sur la nourriture.[135]

Michelet's problem was to assemble three pieces of a puzzle: the Revolution as a humane movement, the futility of the persecution of nobles, and his dislike of Robespierre. In that context, he had

* See Appendix 4.

no choice but to conclude that the gratuitous execution of ci-devants was due to the Incorruptible's personal cruelty. But this is not altogether convincing. Michelet was right to think that nobles were not being punished in 1794 for what they were doing at the time, but his diagnosis was too personal.

vii. The extent of anti-noble persecution

The extent of the persecution of nobles in 1793–4 is only of tangential relevance to the argument of this book. But some mention of it should be made, if only to demonstrate the seriousness of the Montagnards' intent.

There is no reason to suppose that most Conventionnels were unusually cruel about nobles, and it may well be that some of the revolutionaries decided to penalize the noble-born *en masse* because they thought that most aristocrats had left already, just as Louis XIV liked to think that the Revocation of the Edict of Nantes would not cause much damage since there were no Protestants left in France to exile. Numbers again are of relevance here: as it was sometimes supposed that France counted as few as 80,000 nobles, and since estimates of émigré defections were usually overblown, it did indeed make some sense to suppose that there were hardly any nobles still in France. Sautereau was perhaps in good faith when he asserted on 1 November 1792 that in his department of the Nièvre 'almost all' of the ci-devant *noblesse* had left.[136] Basire agreed and said that 'dans la classe des ci-devant nobles, presque toute la jeunesse est émigrée; il n'est resté que les enfants, les vieillards et les femmes pour gérer leurs biens et faire passer de l'argent aux autres'.[137] In the same way, the Girondins may have been more inclined to throw nobles to the wolves in August 1792 for thinking, as did Guadet for example, that all noble officers of high rank were bound to leave France anyway.[138] And of course in some places like the Artois, most nobles did in fact leave the country.[139] None the less, the least that can be said is that after having passed legislation against individuals whom they thought might not exist, many Conventionnels then proved very eager to enforce it.

In 1794, many of the *représentants en mission* spent a great deal of time tracking down ci-devants, very often ordering their arrest *en masse* at a time when imprisonment easily led to death: Élie Lacoste and Jean-Bon Saint-André did so in the Dordogne; Saint-Just and Lebas in the Nord, the Pas de Calais, the Aisne, and the Somme; Albitte in the Ain; Amar in the Isère; Dartigoeyte in the Landes; Lejeune, Lequinio, and Isoré in the Oise; Monestier in the Lot et Garonne; and Maignet in the Vaucluse. Many departmental and local authorities followed their example, some reluctantly, some with eager anticipation.[140] Nobles were at times convicted for reasons which even by contemporary standards were insubstantial (such as writing uncirculated royalist poetry or keeping family parchments), or for crimes which for others did not mean death (having émigré relatives or bad luck like Custine). Some were condemned for pre-Revolutionary offences.[141] Finally, nobles were convicted simply because they were nobles,[142] sometimes in whole batches, as happened on 29 germinal an II, when six noblewomen, one with her husband, and ten men, two of them with their sons, were lumped together in a single *fournée*: it was and is quite obvious that they were really killed as nobles and that the three non-nobles who accompanied them to the scaffold were there for variety's sake.

Many nobles fell victim to personal likes and dislikes.[143] Others were arraigned because they had been officials of the *Ancien Régime*. It is curious in this respect that former *officiers*, whether privileged *parlementaires* or *fermiers généraux*, were treated more harshly than former *commissaires*, like the state-appointed *intendants*.[144] It is of relevance also that nobles who were interrogated by Robespierre's police agents in the spring of 1794 were ritually asked if they had had relatives in the army or in the Robe.[145]

How widespread the persecution of nobles was cannot be gauged with precision, though it is clear that thousands of nobles did suffer in some way. Of the approximately 300,000 nobles who lived in France in 1789 (of whom a large number were very old, very young, or actively pro-Revolutionary, and therefore more or less excluded from punishment), 2,000 at least were executed in 1792–4, and another 1,000 or so were shot in 1795–9. About 20,000 more were arrested. Another 20,000 nobles left the country, of whom as many as 2,000 died in direct consequence of their exile from hunger, exhaustion, or suicide.[146]

There can hardly be a noble family that was left unaffected, and the gratuitous persecution of nobles during the Revolution goes a long way to explain the unreasonable adherence of so many nineteenth-century French aristocrats to throne and altar, in sharp contrast with what had prevailed in 1789–91.

If the punishment of nobles was often harsh, alternative proposals were even more severe. Outright deportation *en masse* seemed for some to be the only sensible way out. In 1789, Sieyes had suggested that French nobles of Frankish stock should leave France for Franconia, and the voluntary emigration of *some* nobles obviously reinforced the idea that there was no place in France for *any* nobles. Foreign to the body social, nobles ought not to be punished as bad citizens, but expelled instead as undesirable aliens.

Deportation to a distant isle—a romantic and recurring theme—was often the form attached to this projected punishment. In 1787, a respondent to Roederer's inquest on Jews suggested that these pariahs should be sent away 'dans les déserts de la Guyanne'; after the decrees of ventôse, some indigents were reluctant to sign up for receipt of lands confiscated from émigrés for fear that they too would end up as deportees to 'les îsles'; and, inevitably, similar suggestions surfaced about nobles, at Josselin in Britanny, for example, where a vocal and regenerated Jacobin society could hardly bear the presence on its territory of imprisoned priests and nobles: 'Déliverez-nous de ces monstres. Faites- [les] promptement juger. Envoyez cette exécrable cargaison de gens suspects à Madagascar. La terre des hommes libres ne doit pas être souillée par la présence des esclaves.[147]

viii. The dilemma of pro-Revolutionary nobles

Most nobles simply withdrew from the public eye in 1792–4. On the right, a minority opposed the Revolution with passion; but so did a minority of nobles on the left support the Revolution with equal zeal. Like all French social groups, it seems, the nobility fell into three parts, with an *attentiste* majority flanked on either side by ultra and citra minorities. If 20,000 nobles left the country, of whom perhaps a third went on to join a counter-revolutionary military unit, so did other thousands of the noble-born support the Revolution, even in its most terroristic phase. The approximately 8,000 officers of the royal army provide an enlightening cross-section.[148]

In October 1791, after Varennes but before the proscription of nobles as such, 1,932 of them had deserted. But at the other end of the spectrum, in September 1793, after repeated purges, 900 noble officers were still in the field.[149] Severely depleted during the summer of 1794 by official sanction, the pool of noble officers in Republican uniform rose again in 1795 to over 1,100, 100 of them generals.

The Royal Corps of Engineers (the *Ingénieurs du Roi*), who have been studied in great detail,[150] provide a particularly striking example of noble 'non-desertion'. One-half of these officers were nobles (48 per cent precisely), many of them from families ennobled before 1600. Of the 300 members of the corps in April 1791, only 50 had left by March 1792, and 153 were still serving in the first months of 1793, after the execution of the King. To be sure, the pattern of emigration was socially speaking somewhat skewed, since 60 per cent of the emigrating engineers were noble. But it is still clear that the number of noble-born engineers that chose to serve the Republic was at least as great as that of nobles who abandoned the Revolution in 1789–92. Moreover, since the number of former *Ingénieurs du Roi* in uniform rose again in late 1794, it can also be supposed that many of those who returned to civilian life in 1793–4 were forced to do so. It can of course be argued that the example of the Royal Engineers was unrepresentative since engineers, noble or not, were needed by the Republic or were likely to have a modern view of life. But that is the point: by 1789, there existed a large number of nobles, won over to the Enlightenment and ready to accept equality before the law, ready even to serve a regicide Convention.

Most ironic of all was the presence of forty nobles in the Convention itself, most of them advanced in their political opinions, and many of them men of great weight: Condorcet, Kersaint, Barras, Hérault de Séchelles, Soubrany, and Le Peletier de Saint-Fargeau were important figures. In view of the presence of so many noble deputies, the inconsequence of the Convention's anti-noble palavers was self-evident, and they were publicly mocked as such in messidor an II by the sans-culotte François Legray, who derided the role of Barère and Saint-Just, 'eux-mêmes nobles', and their law of 27 germinal.[151]

The Conventionnels were hardly blind to this anomaly, and some of them quite logically suggested that ci-devant deputies be disbarred. In November 1793, for example, Bourdon de l'Oise, then under a cloud and eager perhaps to refurbish his progressive credentials, recommended that all nobles be excluded from the Committee of Public Safety,[152] but Merlin de Douai countered this on the grounds that 'de motion en motion, on parviendrait à faire renvoyer de la Convention elle-même les nobles et les prêtres'.

So did Couthon successfully defend noble deputies in an early justification of Hérault de Séchelles.

Some months later, however, in germinal an II (April 1794), the issue came up anew. Bourdon, now became a sworn enemy of the ennobled, and especially of the *fermiers-généraux*, rose again, this time to ask his colleagues if the new law that banished nobles from Paris would also apply to former nobles currently members of the CPS, a thinly veiled reference to Barère and Saint-Just, who were not nobles but were often thought to be so. Couthon once more stood up for his colleagues. He ignored the barb about the *Comité* and concluded that 'l'observation de Bourdon n'a pas échappé au comité; mais il s'est rappelé que Lacombe Saint-Michel [a rather obscure Conventionnel] né noble, étoit en Corse à la tête d'un petit nombre de républicains. . . .'[153] With this lame excuse, Couthon asked for and naturally received the order of the day.

Many other pro-Revolutionary nobles fared less well than did the noble Conventionnels. The travails of opportunistic or incoherent nobles, victims of their own zeal, was sometimes comic, as was true of the marquis de Sade. In 1791, Sade was an ardent monarchist and in favour of a British solution, with a two-house parliament. 'Je suis anti-jacobite,' he wrote, 'je les hais à mort; j'adore le roi, mais je déteste les anciens abus.'[154]

Less than a year later, however, Sade approved of the September massacres: 'Rien n'égale l'horreur des massacres qui se sont commis mais ils étaient justes.'[155] Now a 'citoyen patriote', Sade wrote against the monarchy, supported Marat, harangued the Convention, assumed some judicial functions, and was elected president of the Section des Piques. But at the same time, he was horrified to hear that his chateau in Provence at Coste had been sacked, though he had done all he could to prevent it. He corresponded actively with the Jacobin Club at Coste, and pointed out to them that the destruction of noble property was not part of the Revolutionary programme at all:

> Pacifions en attendant, messieurs, et *respectons* les *propriétés*. C'est de la Constitution même que je transcris ces paroles; vous les vénérerez comme moi, j'en suis sûr, et vous vous souviendrez, ainsi que je l'écrivais hier à MM. vos municipaux, que Brutus et ses partisans n'avaient ni maçons ni incendiaires à leur suite quand ils rendirent à Rome cette liberté précieuse que lui ravissaient des tyrans.[156]

The plight of other, more sincere, nobles was more pathetic.

When pushed aside by the times, the marquis d'Antonelle, a member of the jury of the Revolutionary Tribunal, could hardly understand why it was that he should go. To be a priest, he explained, *was* truly culpable. One chose to be a priest. But what did it really mean to say of someone that he was a noble? The nobility in France had had no inherent function. It had been something 'indéfinissable'. Nobility he explained, was a vain word, 'une chimère dont on est désabusé. Cette chimère qu'on appella noblesse', he explained,

fut un caractère purement accessoire et tout-à-fait idéal, dont l'homme raisonnable et juste pouvoit se trouver investi, sans en être atteint, par l'erreur commune qu'il ne partageoit pas. Tant qu'a duré cette folie, le malheureux ainsi saisi, ou plutôt enveloppé, fut noble forcément, et peut-être à son insu. Si-tôt qu'elle cesse, il ne l'est plus. Cela le met à l'aise, et le voilà soulagé. Cette fiction bizarre n'avoit pu recevoir dans quelques imaginations, un dehors de consistance et quelque apparence de réalité, que par l'institution et l'opinion. Ainsi, du moment où l'institution est effacée et l'opinion guérie, il ne reste rien. C'est le souvenir confus d'un songe; et tel ci-devant pourroit sincèrement attester que celui-là n'entra jamais pour rien dans ses rêves de félicité publique et de bonheur personnel.

Antonelle did not know what nobility meant, and he thought it absurd to be attacked for belonging to a group that had no substance. 'Le sentiment de l'égalité', he went on, 'fut et sera toujours dans son cœur; qu'il n'a jamais rien pensé, dit ou senti, qui ne fut en accord avec ce sentiment, et en opposition directe avec l'orgueilleuse déraison du blason des parchemins, des crénaux et des privilèges.' Antonelle was particularly shocked by the Jacobin Club's exclusion of nobles in pluviôse an II: 'n'est-ce pas surtout aux Jacobins qu'il appartient de croire aux bonnes natures, aux cœurs inaltérablement amis de l'égalité? . . . Où donc est, je ne dis pas le motif, mais le prétexte soutenable de la proscription qui les afflige?'[157]

Felix Le Peletier was more gracious. A brother of the murdered Le Peletier, who had become a votive figure of the Revolution, this future Babouvist fund-raiser had a real claim to be considered as *the* personal exception to the Revolutionary laws on nobles. But he readily complied: 'Il avait espéré jusqu'ici que la Société ne reviendrait pas sur l'arrêté dans lequel elle avait déclaré qu'elle adoptait Félix Le Peletier comme un frère. Puisqu'il en a été décidé autrement, il rend sa carte d'admission, mais il assure que son cœur restera Jacobin jusqu'à sa mort.'[158]

Soubrany, who was excluded from the Jacobin society of Riom, was equally accommodating. He would gladly sacrifice his life to the Republic, he asserted, if his death could wipe out the memory of the nobility, a caste into which he had been born 'by chance', an approach to the circumstances of his birth which could hardly be denied. The whole business made him desperately unhappy: 'Me voilà donc . . . par un arrêté général confondu avec l'écume de la nation, que la fermentation de la Révolution repousse de son sein. Cette idée, sans cesse présente à mon imagination, fait le tourment de ma vie.' Soubrany's defence was both naïve and ingenious: ideologically, Revolutionary nobles were innocent; and tactically, he pointed out, what was the use of excluding such nobles from the Jacobin societies? Nobles as a group, he quite agreed, were obnoxious. Indeed, it was because they were obnoxious that so few of them had sided with the Republic and joined the Club. This in turn led to the next step: why bother to disqualify the few nobles who had opted for the Revolution? In Soubrany's view, it was paradoxically because liberal nobles had been a numerically insignificant quantity that an exemption should be made in their favour. Had there been more liberal nobles in the Jacobin Club, the presence of so many beneficiaries of the *Ancien Régime* would indeed have been embarrassing. But, as Soubrany pointed out, 'le nombre auquel je me glorifie d'appartenir n'eût pas été considérable'.[159] Liberal nobles could safely be ignored. Non-noble patriots would hardly be offended by the presence of an odd noble here and there.

The reasoning was tortuous, but Soubrany's position was difficult. In 1793, the most involuted ratiocinations of Republican nobles were, however, yet to come. The depths were reached in 1795, when the comtesse d'Harville set out her views on the release of her husband from prison in a letter to Romme: it had been absurd to imprison her husband in the first place, but neither could she approve of the spirit of reaction that had led to his release after 9 thermidor:

> Au cit. Gilbert Romme la cit. Harville salut. Dans ses affreux débats que l'intérêt de la République n'eût jamais dû commencer tu dois oublier tout intérêt particulier. Cependant! tu n'as pas pu confondre Harville avec cette foule d'anti-révolutionnaires qu'une faiblesse cruelle avait renfermer, qu'un plat esprit de vengeance, un autre genre de faiblesse non moins nuisible aux intérêts de la République a fait remettre en liberté.[160]

These were sophisticated thoughts.

The statements of pro-Revolutionary nobles suddenly made aware of their intrinsic immorality have a very modern ring, reminiscent of the confessions so commonly produced in more recent trials. Monet, the commanding officer of the First Régiment des Chasseurs à Cheval, began his letter of resignation with an invocation to 'liberté, egalité, fraternité ou la mort' and went on to explain that he would never have withdrawn: 'Si je n'étais persuadé que cet état n'a pour but que de mettre enfin à exécution la mesure révolutionnairement juste et sage d'exclure ces deux castes [les nobles et les prêtres] de tous les emplois, je te prierais, citoyen ministre, d'accepter ma démission, fondée sur la malheur de ma naissance et une santé détestable.' The comte de Béthune also apologized for the 'malheur de sa naissance. . . . J'ose le dire, j'en avais fait pour l'expier.' He approved of the exclusion of nobles from posts of command, and concluded: 'Vive la République une et indivisible, Vive la Montagne.'[161]

In 1793–4, Revolutionary-minded nobles were everywhere disliked, not only by the Republicans but also by the Austrians, who did not hesitate to prosecute them in those parts of France which they occupied at the time.[162] Liberal nobles did not fit; they deserved to be punished.

It was then assumed (as it has often been since) that nobles *ought* to have been against the Revolution. That the facts of the case might not apply was beside the point. In retrospect, however, the existence of many pro-Revolutionary nobles and the passivity of most nobles supports the hypothesis of opportunistic persecution. If all nobles had been against the Revolution, the curtailment of their rights would be easy to explain. But this was not the case, and that fact implies again that the background of their exclusion is more complex than has been allowed.

Chapter Four

The advantages and disadvantages of anti-nobilism in 1793–1794: The Terror

i. The advantages of opportunistic proscription

In some ways, the question of the rights of nobles in 1793–4 is embedded in the problem of the Terror as a whole. The pressures of war, class war, and counter-Revolution, as well as the hatred of the poor or the mediocre for the rich and talented, were all ingredients of the attack on nobles, just as they were of the Terror generally. Most historians agree to this and choose to go no further towards an analysis of the treatment of nobles: if the proscription of nobles flowed from the course of the Revolution as a whole, it necessarily follows that only the larger problem of the Terror deserves attention. The revolutionaries' indifference to the rights of nobles was to be expected. In the words of an ennobled Swiss army offcer, it was natural that *most* nobles should be jailed, not himself, of course, but others, 'dont on préjugeoit que l'intérêt majeur étoit le retour à l'ancien ordre'.[1] Hérault de Séchelles expressed the same idea: in November 1793, newly arrived at Belfort, he immediately ordered the surveillance first, of 'Les juifs qui n'ont aucun métier et qui ne feignent d'être soumis aux lois que pour exercer avec plus de sécurité un infâme agiotage'; and, second, 'Les ex-nobles . . . presque toujours inaccessibles à la philosophie et à l'humanité et nécessairement ennemis d'une révolution qui les dépouillent.'[2]

The fact, however, that Hérault was himself a great noble who had first achieved notoriety with his sketch, *Une visite à Buffon*, must give us pause. By November 1793, and *a fortiori* by the spring of 1794, the number of Frenchmen who were aghast at the course of political events was quite large, but it is not usually inferred that Girondins, constitutional monarchists, Feuillants, monarchiens, peasants antagonized by requisitions, or even Vendéen rebels desired a return 'à l'ancien ordre des choses'. The same is true of nobles. The real reason why we have supposed that nobles craved such a reaction is that a view of this kind fits rather well into preconceived, and rather shallow, *idées reçues* of what 1789 was about. But propositions such as 'The Revolution necessarily persecuted the nobles because it had overthrown an *Ancien Régime* which the nobility had dominated' are similar to those socio-economic verities stating that 'class-consciousness was the necessary consequence of the Industrial Revolution' or that 'consensus politics are characteristic of a modern political process'. Such assertions are not wholly false, but they do not say very much. They try to explain everything, but in so doing, they also fail to explain a great deal.

The straightforward conjunction of Revolutionary progress and of the persecution of nobles does hold rather well for the intermediate period that runs from the autumn of 1791 to the autumn of 1793. In these months, the opportunistic proscription of nobles and of émigrés (at that point mostly nobles) had as its immediate cause the bourgeois revolutionaries' essentially correct assumption that the proscription of the noble-born would help them to carry the Revolution forward: since nobles were disliked by peasants and later by the urban poor, to attack nobles was to gain a wider base of support for Revolutionary change. In that narrow sense, it can be argued that the progress of Revolutionary politics had as a self-evident concomitant some attack on the lives or property of nobles.

For the later phase of the Revolution, the problem is less tractable. It may then have been in the back of everyone's mind at those times that nobles were 'against the Revolution' and ought therefore to be punished somehow. But this was a vague feeling that might be expressed in many different ways. To say, merely, that the increasing persecution of nobles was a self-evident necessity in 1793–4 also makes it harder to see why the Revolutionary bourgeoisie should have gone to such lengths in 1789–91 to destroy nobility but to accept nobles. In any instance, such an explanation hardly accounts for the fact that the persecution of nobles was at its height in the spring of 1794, when the essence of Revolutionary politics lay in the tension between bourgeois politicians and sans-culottes, who were now interested in other things.

Without doubt, the persecution of nobles in 1792–3 was in many ways opportune: it helped the bourgeoisie to carry the Revolution forward, and in that phase, anti-nobilism did move hand in hand with the Revolution as a whole. But in 1793–4, these earlier conditions no longer held. Some other explanation must be found.

The practical disadvantages of the persecution of nobles should not of course be exaggerated. In some important ways, anti-noble laws continued to accumulate in the spring of 1794 because they were then, as they had been before, a convenient means of government. Many Montagnards may have continued to lobby for them because they genuinely believed that to imprison nobles would really make a practical difference. Moreover, the public tension that was sustained by the proscription of nobles or noble émigrés could be used for other ends, as Saint-Just tried to do, for example, when he explained in all seriousness that the fall of Danton and Hébert 'sont des coups de foudre pour les émigrés'.[3]

Laws on emigration were judicially useful for convicting enemies at random, since hundreds of thousands of persons were either related to émigrés or—like Danton, Hébert, Hérault, Osselin, Carnot, and Cloots—had some dealings with them. The confiscation of émigré property also made the Revolution more tangible for the 'plebs', and it was clearly with this idea in mind that the Convention decreed on 1 floréal an II (20 April 1794) that the confiscated property of émigrés should be sold in small lots, with payments spread over twenty years. Finally, the existence of the nobles issue was useful for heuristic and political reasons. In 1793, the Montagnards methodically blamed *urban* disorders on Girondins and their friends: if people rioted for food in Paris, Bordeaux, or Marseilles, it was because malicious men had put them up to it. Nobles were in the same way blamed for *rural* disorders: if peasants in the Puy-de-Dôme objected to requisitions, it could only be the fault, explained Couthon, 'des malveillans, prêtres ou ci-devant nobles [qui avaient saisi] cette occasion pour exaspérer les esprits. . . .'[4] Applicable everywhere, this type of reasoning was especially appropriate to the Vendée where so many Republicans had died, in Barère's words, because of the machinations 'de l'aristocratie sacerdotale et nobiliaire'.[5]

At a somewhat more complicated level, the persecution of nobles was also convenient as an ideological means of government. The argument here does not involve any structural explanation of the relationship of ideology to social class; it bears no similarity to the description of the role of ideology in Revolutionary politics presented by either Marx or Hegel.* The reasoning is far more rudimentary, stating simply that a particular perception of nobles enabled both the popular and bourgeois revolutionaries to act more forcefully as political figures. Ideology is at play, but only in

* See Appendix 1 and Chapter Five.

the context of tactical politics and not in any structural sense. There is no question here as there was for Marx of a social deadlock transcended by ideological escape. What matters in this instance is that the revolutionaries' abstract and negative view of nobles enabled them better to understand themselves, their place in politics, and the very nature of the Revolutionary struggle.

Self-identification was the most important of these uses of ideology. In the 'gothick' world of 1794, the varieties of political guilt were innumerable. But the stigmatization of the noble-born enabled everyone else to feel better about himself: nobles were bad, and by being bad, they allowed others to feel good.

At one end of the ladder was the archetypal revolutionary as Saint-Just portrayed him:

Il est inflexible, mais il est sensé, il est frugal: il est simple sans afficher le luxe de la fausse modestie; il est l'irréconciliable ennemi de tout mensonge, de toute indulgence, de toute affectation, . . . un homme révolutionnaire est plein d'honneur; il est policé sans fadeur, mais par franchise et parce qu'il est en paix avec son propre cœur, . . . il est intraitable aux méchants, mais il est sensible, il est si jaloux de la gloire de sa patrie et de la liberté qu'il ne fait rien inconsidérément; il sait que, pour que la Révolution s'affermisse, il faut être aussi bon qu'on était méchant autrefois. . . . Marat était doux dans son ménage, il n'épouvantait que les traîtres. J.-J. Rousseau était révolutionnaire et n'était pas insolent sans doute. J'en conclus qu'un homme révolutionnaire est un héros de bon sens et de probité.[6]

The self-image of the sans-culotte was much the same. Less well off and less restrained, the sans-culotte was more conscious of his direct political involvement and more proud of his terrorist past, but he shared with the bourgeois *patriote* a desire to be open, selfless, natural, industrious, vigilant, useful, and, in a word, *bon*.

All *aristocrates* were by direct contrast *mauvais*, but none were more *méchant* than nobles. Image became fanciful mirage as nobles became everything that the revolutionary did not want to be: *hautain*, *lâche*, *atrabilaire*, *l'homme le plus dur et le plus violent qui puisse exister dans la nature*, *pourri de luxure*, *ambitieux*, *orgueilleux*, *fier*, *impérieux*, *dangereux*, *froid*, *poli*, *égoiste*, *oisif*, *artificiel*, *méprisant le travail*, *stérile*, and a victim of *la paresse féodale*. Nobles were selfish and particularist; their very existence was a denial of community, and it is curious to see that the citizens of communes whose ci-devant names smacked of aristocracy, like Jouy-le-Comte and Fontenay-le-Comte, frequently chose metaphors of unity when they renamed their towns (in this intance, Jouy-le-Peuple and

Fontenay-le-Peuple).[7] Nobles were deceptive and scheming. The true revolutionary, like the child hero, Bara, never disguised his feelings, even to save his life, but nobles lied as a matter of course, and Robespierre described 'un usage exécrable' common to them all: 'On s'entendait sur le parti qu'on devait prendre dans une famille, et que le cadet, qui était ici sous le costume d'un sans-culotte, n'était autre chose que le soldat et l'espion de l'ainé, qui était à Coblenz.'[8] Where the sans-culotte dressed like a sans-culotte, nobles in order to run away disguised themselves even as women.

One might even say that the dichotomy between noble and sans-culotte was unconsciously paralleled by a similar contrast between the virile revolutionary and feminine aristocrat. Nobles might not, like priests, wear robes, but they were, like women, superficial, imperious, vain, foppish, and lacking in *gravitas*. André de Joguet, a noble converted to Republican principle, was on the right track when he decided to follow up his first drama, *l'Aristocratie des familles* with another five acts in verse entitled *L'Aristocratie femelle*, a fact, incidentally, which did not keep him from being arrested on the grounds that his sister's mother-in-law had neglected to remove her armorial shields from an unused carriage.[9]

Female nobles who combined the disabilities of their sex and caste were particularly hated: 'les femmes d'émigrés' were the most contemptible of all and held 'le premier rang parmi les ennemis de la patrie'.[10] Noblewomen were widely blamed for protecting the family and property of their émigré husbands, whom they occasionally divorced for show.[11] No one complained, therefore, when Maure in April 1794 asked that women be specifically included in the proscription of nobles: 'les femmes [nobles] sont très dangereuses et nous ont fait beaucoup de mal'.[12] Though women as a group constituted 9 per cent of the victims of the Terror, with averages ranging from 7 per cent for peasants and the upper middle class to 9 per cent for the working class, 20 per cent of executed nobles were female.[13]

Emotionally, it may be added, the revolutionary instinctively leaned to the persecution of nobles as he did to the disenfranchisement of women, and on the same principle: just as all men, it sometimes is said, find solace in the existence of an inferior second sex, so did all revolutionaries derive comfort from these 'others', a different but readily identifiable group whose existence gave consistency to their vision of their own ideal self. To be a revolutionary was to be strong. Nobles, corrupt and foppish, were in some deep sense at once guilty and feminine. The distinction was powerful, and was, as it happens, an assumption that underlay also Mary Wollstonecraft's own explanations of female frailty in her *Rights of Women* in 1792. There too, an analogy was drawn between privilege and bourgeois femininity: women, she thought, were so many 'Turkish bashaws, despots, kings and tyrants', and for a simple reason. Was it not true, she asked, that bourgeois women, like noblemen of privilege, led idle, pampered lives, the precondition of petulant self-indulgence? For her, the conclusion was obvious: both men and women should return to a more natural condition. Her analogy of women and nobles was one that sans-culottes might have understood, although they would have interpreted it rather differently.

Some women, it is true, did find grace, though both the sans-culottes and their historians have been hard on Mary Wollstonecraft and her feminist allies. But nobles could not be redeemed. Noble status and human decency were mutually exclusive. Nobles and sans-culottes were perfect opposites. This antithesis, quite commonly assumed, could become quite consciously absurd, as it was in the words of André Dumont, who explained to his fellow Conventionnels on 4 ventôse an II that if the Republic were like the monarchy 'appuyée sur les crimes, elle pourrait vendre la roture comme on vendait la noblesse; nos ci-devants achèteraient cher le nom honorable de sans-culottes'.[14]

The ideological function of the proscription of nobles was amplified by the identification of nobles as *inherently* and obviously guilty, an assumption which immediately lessened the burden of guilt which non-nobles had to bear. The background here was the general suspicion of all against all. 'On a cherché à consommer la Révolution par la Terreur,' said Vergniaud; 'J'aurais voulu la consommer par l'amour.' But the Revolution was 'frozen' and everyone lived in fear, and not love, of his neighbours. The basic premiss of the Revolutionary *fête* was brutally disavowed. Trust had become impossible, and although everyone by nature should have yearned for Republican virtue, it was with devastating ease that 'Pitt et Cobourg' could corrupt one's own best friends. 'Oui,' exclaimed Camille Desmoulins, 'je me suis souvent trompé! . . . Sept des vingt-deux furent mes amis. Hélas! soixante amis vinrent à mon mariage; tous sont morts ou émigrés! . . . Il ne m'en reste que deux, Robespierre et Danton.'[15]

The condemnation of nobles, like most political trials, including that of the King, was a symbolic gesture which would set such things right. The aim of the Terror would be improved. Just as the detective's apprehension of the criminal in the country house justifies his inquest and restores the other inmates to a state of grace, so did the opprobrium that was heaped on nobles help to explain the Terror and release non-nobles from fear and suspicion. Great insistence was therefore placed by revolutionaries of all hues on the inherent and manifest viciousness of nobles: 'leur cœur', explained Brissot, 'est endurci dès leur naissance'.[16]

To be sure, there were limits to what could be decently argued about the liabilities of genetic or racial origin. Faltering respect for the idea of the equality of men at birth did not allow Brissot or anyone else to condemn nobles outright as a race. Even at the height of the Terror, redemption was the message of those theatrical productions that had the role of nobles as their theme. The young heroine, for example, of *Les Crimes de la noblesse ou le régime féodal*, a play written by the Citoyenne Villeneuve in floréal an II, denounced her father, who had wanted to bury her alive; married a commoner; renounced her birthright; and was saved.[17] The same motif appears in *La Nourrice républicaine ou les plaisirs de l'adoption*, a musical comedy written by C. Piis and performed at the Théâtre de Vaudeville in germinal an II: the émigré father of the orphaned noble baby is guilty, but the infant child, once adopted by good Republicans, becomes (in every sense of the word) a genuine sans-culotte.

Innocent at birth, nobles became *méchants* in the cradle. Fouché neatly summed this up: 'L'habitude de la domination ne meurt jamais dans le cœur de l'homme; c'est une chimère qui nous a été funeste d'avoir cru que l'*égalité* pût pénétrer dans l'âme de celui qui apprit, dès le berceau, à traiter ses semblables comme des bêtes de somme.'[18]

Aristocrats were not totally anathematized, but they were in practice placed beyond the pale, and by being there, made it possible for other non-noble *aristocrates*, including priests, to be redeemed. Robespierre explained that idea at some length. It was not true, he said, 'dans le parallèle des nobles et des prêtres, que tout l'avantage est du côté des premiers'. Nobles were worse than priests, and the proof was that 'le noble est un homme dont tous les avantages sont des avantages politiques. Il les tire de sa naissance, et l'habitude des distinctions lui a fait mépriser tout ce qui n'est pas de ce qu'il appelle son rang.'[19]

The assumption of noble guilt had many uses. It made possible the creation of a distancing hierarchy of guilt (nobles, priests, and others) which was a source of comfort. It helped to rationalize the Terror as a means of government: 'Si la mort choisissait ses victimes,' said Augereau some years later, 'le crime seul serait bani du monde.' The identification of nobles as 'the guilty ones' enabled the revolutionaries to unravel unexpected and baffling situations: 'Plût à Dieu', implored Couthon in his apologia for the law that banished nobles from Paris, 'que l'on pût reconnaître les méchants à des signes certains et palpables, pour ainsi dire, aux yeux de tous. . . .'[20]

The argument of the noble's inherent guilt was clear and powerful. Couthon, the Terrorist, understood that it should be made, just as Beauharnais, the noble victim, had understood in June 1793 that it should be denied. Couthon's argument was that the guilt of nobles to some degree exonerated all those non-nobles who did not bear the palpable stigma of untoward birth; but Beauharnais's retort had been precisely that such an assumption made no sense. To persecute nobles, he had maintained, was useless because not all nobles were '*méchants*', though non-nobles often were. 'Si cette proscription politique [of nobles]', Beauharnais had explained,

> doit amener le calme dans la France, si elle peut mettre de côté tous les mauvais citoyens . . . certes on ne saurait hésiter à adopter une mesure aussi salutaire . . .; mais, citoyens, l'intérêt du peuple est loin, ce me semble, de commander une proscription qui envelopperait sans distinction ses amis et ses ennemis, les bons et les méchants, les courageux partisans de la révolution et ses laches détracteurs.[21]

The persecution of nobles made the Terror more acceptable to the bourgeois revolutionaries, as it made the Revolution itself more attractive to their popular allies on the left, because the need or wisdom of accepting aristocrats as individual citizens had hardly been understood by the population as a whole even in 1789–91. The expulsion of nobles from public office may have been particularly useful from this point of view since it made more comprehensible for the masses another notion which would otherwise have remained an empty conquest: careers open to talents. This goal had been from the first an essential part of the bourgeois Revolution, but its applicability had—necessarily—remained narrowly circumscribed. By persecuting and excluding nobles whose existence was judged to be a denial of that principle, the revolutionaries were suddenly able to give to equality of opportunity a practical meaning which it had before utterly lacked. Paradoxically, an ideological statement (the persecution of nobles) gave concrete value to what would otherwise have remained a meaningless abstraction: careers open to talents. 'Les nobles et les prêtres ont une manière de défendre la république,' reported André Dumont, 'ils violent les lois, et leur punition sert à les maintenir.'[22]

ii. Some disadvantages of proscription: the problem of definitions; *annoblis* and dependants

There were still good reasons to persecute nobles in 1793–4. But there were also more and more good reasons not to do so. Pillorying nobles may have soothed some Revolutionary anxieties, but it also raised new and thorny problems. Of these, the first lay in defining what a noble was.

Everyone knew in a general way that the enemies of the Revolution were *aristocrates*, but such men were not necessarily nobles, and some aristocrats, as has been seen, were definitely *patriotes*. The issue was quite confused, as Tom Paine had explained to Burke in a letter of January 1790. 'The term Aristocrat', he wrote from France, 'is used here similar to the word Tory in America; it in general means an enemy of the Revolution, and is used without that peculiar meaning formerly affixed to Aristocracy.'[23] So did Helen Maria Williams report in the same year that pedestrians thought the streets of Paris, encumbered as they were by carriages, to be *aristocrate*, as was 'everything tiresome or unpleasant'.[24]

In abstract terms, *aristocratie* was easily definable. It was as Buonarroti later described it, 'un pouvoir souverain exercé par une partie de la nation sur le tout', a state of being, he added, which flowed inevitably from the consecration of material inequality by selfish egoism.[25] Hence the harsh words hurled by the left at *l'aristocratie représentative*, *l'aristocratie bourgeoise*, *l'aristocratie insulaire* of Great Britain taken as a whole, or even of *l'aristocratie cutanée* which Camboulas mentioned in his address to a biracial delegation sent by Sonthonax from Santo-Domingo to Paris.[26] Hence also and somewhat paradoxically, the polemics of bourgeois Revolutionaries against *l'aristocratie sans-culotte*,[27] *l'aristocratie jacobine*, or *l'aristocratie de la pauvreté*.[28] *Aristocratie* was a flexible and useful word, but hard to define precisely, especially as it dealt with *l'aristocratie nobiliaire*, that is to say, with aristocracy in the ordinary sense of the word.

Two problems arose here, the first centring on individuals who belonged to a *noblesse de fonction*. Natural-born nobles were recognizably guilty despite the odd exception. Like the Action Française, with its 'bon sergent David', the Committee of Public Safety accepted the idea that there could be good native nobles as there would later be good Jews; on these grounds, for example, the Committee found it easy to exempt a young man who did not deny his noble birth but added that he had fled to Russia before 1789 to avoid the priesthood and would never have returned to an unregenerated France.[29] 'Wer Jude ist, das sage ich.' But the question of *annoblis*, that is, of non-nobles who had been made noble, was more delicate.

As a rule of thumb, the Committee applied here, if in reverse, the criterion that had been used in January 1789, when only hereditary nobles were deemed fit to vote in the elections of the Second Estate: in 1794 as in 1789, individuals who had acquired nobility were not considered true nobles.

The Committee took a while to think this through. At first, it seemed to them obvious, as Couthon explained on 28 germinal, that individuals who had chosen to become nobles should be considered morally more despicable and therefore politically more guilty than natural-born nobles who could 'imputer en partie leur orgueil incurable et leur antipathie invincible pour la liberté du peuple au hasard de leur naissance et au vice de leur éducation'.[30] But upon mature reflection, it became clear to them that ennoblement before 1789 had also been a meritocratic reward; Couthon's moral ranking would therefore have to be inverted as he himself admitted the next day. Even then, however, some doubts remained. For Robespierre, exemptions should be granted only to those on whom nobility had been thrust in the exercise of some *public* official function. Not everyone agreed, and in a letter to the Committee of Public Safety the future Thermidorian Lecomte, who represented the trading city of Rouen, considered the question in another way. Priests and men of noble birth deserved prosecution.[31] That was clear: 'Je vous abandonne ceux-là à discrétion.' But the nobility of talent was something else. Individuals who had been rewarded before 1789 for their *private* commercial virtues ought not to be punished; the problem was important, said Lecomte, who concluded: 'Il n'est point de ville commerçante où on ne compte plus ou moins de ces nobles; en les confondant avec les autres, ce serait évidemment confondre le vice et la vertu.'[32] Lecomte was not alone in pointing out the inconsistency of the law on nobles and the Committee was soon flooded with hundreds of petitions from nobles of all sorts who maintained that the law should not apply to them: artists, officials, merchants, nobles who were reborn, 'régénérés par la Révolution'; nobles who had always worked, some of them as glass-blowers; noble wives whose noble husbands had been fighting for the Republic and were now prisoners of war; widows; divorcees; and royal *domestiques* who insisted that they had only been '*des serviteurs distingués*'. An *auditeur des comptes* reminded the CPS that he had served fifteen years in a *charge* which conferred nobility only after twenty years. An *échevin de Paris* proved that he could not be proscribed since *échevins* were noble only when solvent and he had long since been proved bankrupt.[33] A nurse asked for advice about her noble ward, who was 'épileptique . . . et de plus dans un état d'imbécilité'.[34]

Necessarily, the plight of such victims elicited the personal sympathy of their friends, who, after all, would have been delighted to achieve a similar rank and status only five years before (there but for the grace of God go I), and it was perhaps for reasons of this kind that the non-noble majority of the *Commission Temporaire des Arts* took up the cudgels for their ennobled colleagues. The new ruling, they explained, did not actually apply to any of the Commission's members, but misunderstandings could arise:

Quoique aucun ci-devant noble d'origine ne se trouve dans la réunion de savants et d'artistes [composant la Commission], il s'en trouve cependant qui se croient placés sur la limite du décret, et que cette opinion jette dans la plus grande incertitude, on peut même dire dans l'inquiétude, attendu qu'ils ne se verraient pas sans peine écartés d'un travail dont un choix honorable les a chargés. Ce sont en quelque sorte des officiers de fortune de l'ancien régime qui auraient à se plaindre des rigueurs du nouveau, ce qui n'est point entré dans votre intention, lorsque vous avez présenté une mesure de police générale.[35]

All of these developments were more than the CPS could cope with, and it soon decided to exempt all ennobled persons *en masse*, a decision which annoyed those ennobled men of fashion who wanted to be exiled for reasons of prestige, like the son of an *échevin* who refused an exemption, and told Barère that he really was a noble: 'Non, monsieur, je ne suis point homme de lettres . . . je dois sortir et je sortirai d'après la loi.'[36]

The second and more difficult aspect of defining nobility involved the non-noble relatives of native nobles. Were non-nobles, adopted by nobles, noble? Or French-born nobles of foreign origin? Or illegitimate children? Or the off-spring of non-noble mothers presently separated from their ex-noble ex-husbands? More common were the cases involving non-noble women who claimed to have been forced, as minors, to marry nobles before 1789.

These were complex issues which the revolutionaries, on the whole, resolved in a way that was even less generous than that adopted by the National Socialists with the Jews. The juxtaposition may offend, but it provides the best standard of comparison because other racist states (like Tsarist Russia or Horthy's Hungary) have as a rule discriminated against their minorities in a different way, not on the grounds of birth plain and simple, but by making reference either to property or to voluntary participation in some religious group.

Like the bourgeois revolutionaries with nobles, the National Socialists did not deprive Jews of citizenship at a single blow. The process was gradual and began with selective exclusions from public and private functions, such as government, law, and medicine. Blanket denaturalization only came in 1935, with the Nuremberg decrees. By that 'law', all citizens defined as Jews were denaturalized, as were all French nobles in 1797. The question then arose of deciding who was Jewish. Hitlerian standards were racial and arithmetical: Germans with two non-Jewish grandparents could retain certain civic rights. These were the *Mischlinge*, first degree. Aryan wives and husbands of Jews were not considered Jewish.[37]

A different type of rule was applied by the more sexist Committee of Public Safety. Children of noble mothers and bourgeois fathers were not noble. Children of noble fathers were always noble. Noblewomen married to non-nobles were exempted, but non-noble wives of nobles were stigmatized. The legal status of the male line was the crucial variable. For some, the principle to be applied was that 'les mères n'ont d'autre patrie que la patrie de leurs enfants'.[38] More romantically, Barère justified that same ruling by considering the varying natures of mixed bourgeois-noble marriages, which included, though he did not mention it, the case of his own parents: 'Cette question', he explained, n'a pas été traitée au comité, parce qu'il a paru qu'elle devait être jugée suivant les principes de législation usités chez les Romains et les Français. Il n'y a pas de doute que la femme doit suivre le sort de son mari. La femme qui, pour flatter son orgueil, a épousé un comte ou un marquis, est comprise dans la loi; mais la femme noble qui, par des principes de philosophie et en suivant les impulsions de son cœur, s'est alliée à ce qu'on appelait autrefois un roturier, doit, comme son mari, rester attachée à la cause du peuple. Humiliez l'orgueil de l'une, récompensez les vertus de l'autre. Une autre considération doit vous déterminer: c'est que, si vous ne faisiez pas cette exception, vous forceriez au divorce des mariages heureux et fertiles.[39]

The most baroque complications necessarily ensued: non-noble widows of nobles relapsed to their previous status if they were childless, but they remained noble if they had mothered noble-born children. Exceptions, however, could be made for such non-noble, widowed mothers if their noble sons had served the Republic with *éclat*. The law was difficult to explain, difficult to enforce. Local *comités de surveillance* petitioned for clarifications, and in the Nord, Lebon decided for safety's sake to arrest all non-noble wives of nobles 'à moins qu'elles n'aient évidemment et constamment improuvé l'aristocratie de leur maris. . . .'[40]

Many people appear not to have known what the law was, and this confusion lay behind Carrier's complaint after Thermidor that the decrees against priests and nobles were, of all those passed by the Revolutionary assemblies, 'ceux qui ont été le moins exécutés'.[41]

From which cities were nobles to be excluded? What was a 'place forte', and was Abbeville a 'commune maritime'?[42] Even the experts lost track of what had been enacted or repealed. In December 1793, for example, Monmayou urged the Convention to deny nobles the right to sit on local *comités revolutionnaires*, but was then reminded by Merlin de Douai that this had already been decreed in March.[43] Hébert, also confused about what had been decided, attacked Fréron at the Jacobin Club in November 1793, asking why the man's brother-in-law, a ci-devant marquis, was still in the army when the law forbade it, although in fact, no such law existed.[44] Ministers invoked imaginary legislation. In December 1793, Destournelles reported that noble-born officials in the ministry of public contributions would be purged by virtue of the decree of 29 July 1793, although there was no such decree.[45] Since nobles 'ought' to have been outlawed, it was easy to suppose that this had in fact been done, as Duhem did on 12 fructidor an

II, when he asked at the Jacobins why it was the sentence of deportation against nobles and priests had not yet been carried out, though he later inquired of the Convention why such deportation had not yet been decreed.[46]

It was no wonder then that at the same session, Borie should have said that 'il faut une bonne fois fixer nos idées sur les prêtres et les ex-nobles',[47] but this was easier said than done. The relevant principles and issues were hopelessly contradictory, and the bourgeois revolutionaries would never sort them out, in either theory or practice.

iii. Military and civil disruptions

Anti-noble legislation in 1793–4 was cumbersome and difficult to apply. It may also have become tactically disadvantageous for both the 'people' and the bourgeoisie. For the *honnêtes gens* the exclusion of nobles was morally questionable and practically inconvenient. When popular pressure for the dismissal of noble officers swelled in the spring of 1793, the Conventionnel Blaux wrote to say that the prospective elimination of noble generals was causing consternation in the field. Stigmatized noble officers would become an easy prey. More blood would be spilt because excluding nobles from the army was tantamount to handing them over 'à la fureur du peuple et . . . au désespoir'. And to what end? Politically, the proscription of nobles made no sense: 'S'il ne se trouvait que des aristocrates dans la ci-devant noblesse, on serait excusable de la suspecter toute entière; mais à proportion du nombre, il s'en trouve au moins autant dans le ci-devant tiers état, et je pense qu'adopter la motion ci-dessus, c'est porter un coup mortel aux armées.'[48]

In the spring of 1794, some *représentants en mission* reported that the elimination of nobles was popular with the soldiers; others were more reticent. Pflieger balked at carrying out orders of this sort without specific instructions, and Choudieu wrote to Paris from the *Armée du Nord* in the Ardennes that

> Tout le monde parle ici avec estime et avec regret du général Béru qui a quitté l'armée en vertu de l'arrêté de Duquesnoy qui congédiait les nobles. On nous assure que cet officier a toujours montré beaucoup de civisme et de grands talents. Si vous avez les mêmes renseignements sur lui, mettez-le en réquisition et envoyez-nous-le. Nous avons bien besoin d'hommes à talents.[49]

In theory, the expulsion of nobles might seem to be a fine idea; in practice, it was less attractive. Bouchotte would have liked to expel all aristocrats but found that he could not do so; and he was after Hébert's fall accused of having protected them: Hébert's ultra-citra conspiracy, it was said in March 1794, had involved the army, and the proof of it was that Hébert's friend, Bouchotte, had not sacked all the nobles, as he had said he would: 'Bouchotte n'a pas retiré les nobles aux termes des décrets.'[50]

Carnot, on the other hand, thought in May 1794 that Bouchotte's enmity for nobles had, in fact, been one of his few strong points: true, Bouchotte had had 'une prédilection particulière pour les ignorants, mais [il] faisait au moins tout son possible pour nous débarasser des nobles. . . .'[51] But in the same breath, Carnot then went on to list his own suggested exceptions.

Doctrinally desirable, the expulsion of nobles from the army was, in fact, potentially disruptive, and Carnot, like Bouchotte and everyone else concerned, see-sawed throughout 1793–4 on this question. Ferocious in theory, Carnot was rather mild in practice. In a note which he drafted, the Committee of Public Safety ruled on 1 February 1794 that nobles who had been anti-Revolutionary should be kept on, in the artillery at least, where 'les connaissances de théorie et de pratiques sont longues à acquérir'.[52] This ambiguous stand was still his in May 1794, when he wrote to Garrau that nobles should be pushed aside, but only when it was safe to do so:

> Il faut que vous nous indiquiez les hommes que vous avez reconnus réunir les qualités nécessaires; il n'est pas que votre armée n'en fournisse quelques uns; en attendant, servez-vous de ce que vous aurez de mieux; tâchez de mettre de côté tous les nobles, à moins qu'ils n'aient un mérite qu'on ne saurait remplacer et un patriotisme sur lequel on puisse compter. Lespinasse paraît être dans ce cas. Enfin, mon cher Garrau, il faut chasser les traîtres, si nous voulons battre les ennemis.[53]

Indeed, Carnot personally protected some noble officers by finding them a place in the bureaucracy of the CPS.[54] Other Conventionnels did much the same. Romme said of the accusations brought against his former friend and protector, General d'Harville, that it was 'un assemblage monstrueux de ridicule et d'intrigues',[55] and Isoré wrote to MacDonald, 'ta naissance ne m'est pas suspecte. . . . Sois tranquille . . . si on te tracasse, je serai ton défenseur.'[56]

Noble officers could also count on the professional loyalty of their non-noble colleagues, the exact counterpart of what had been true in the summer of 1789, when some noble officers decided to accept the promotion of non-nobles on the grounds that the gain of greater efficiency would be adequate compensation for the loss of social privilege. General Krieg, for example, complained directly to Bouchotte about purges:

> Tant que je verrai à la tête des troupes des hommes qui, tout le long de leur vie, ne se sont appliqués qu'à quelque art mécanique, au commerce ou à la chicane, alors je plaindrai le sort des administrateurs et des armées de la République.
>
> Votre mode d'avancement, citoyen Ministre, ne peut rester tel qu'il est, si la République doit exister. . . . Quelle confiance voulez-vous que le soldat ait dans des chefs de cette espèce?[57]

Military necessity ran against an abstract view of the problem, to the annoyance of some like Tallien who simultaneously denounced at the Jacobin Club, the reintegration of rightist noble army officers as well as the campaign by anti-noble ultra-leftists (many of them, he argued, nobles) bent on purging the Convention of nobles only to destroy it.[58]

Confusing militarily, the proscription of nobles also disrupted civil affairs, as happened at Arras, where even the Terrorist Lebon was outflanked on the left. On 29 nivôse an II (18 January 1794), Lebon had appointed as mayor of Robespierre's home town one Ferdinand Dubois de Fosseux, a ci-devant. Very appropriately, the local *comité de surveillance* ordered the arrest of this man on the strength of Saint-Just's and Lebas's proscription of all nobles in the department; and it was only after receipt of an order from the CPS signed by Barère and Collot that Dubois was released.[59]

In those parts of France where nobles had been involved in trade, the law was economically disruptive as well. In the city of Amiens alone, the municipal council considered fourteen requests involving noblemen of business, most if not all from noble-born nobles. The unanimous decision of the councillors was to let the nobles off, all of them being bona fide 'commerçant . . . marchand . . . fabricant ou chef d'atelier' and all of them able to give proof of their usefulness and 'civisme'.[60]

Impractical in many ways, the proscription of nobles was, at times, plainly silly. Isolated nobles living in Paris were not very threatening, but when exiled to the distant, luke-warmly Revolutionary suburbs they formed little colonies and became more conspicuous.[61] If nobles were not conspirators, there was no need to push them together in Sèvres, Marly, Suresnes, Neuilly,

Auteuil-Antony, Clichy-la-Garenne, Choisy-sur-Seine, Créteil, Vaugirard, Villejuif, Sceaux, St. Maur, St. Maude, Antony, Vincennes, La Villete, Bourg-Égalité, and Franciade-Saint-Denis, where they might indeed conspire. The authorities at Belleville did in fact ask the CPS if it would not be prudent to send nobles further afield.[62] Besides, the concentrations of nobles in these small villages strained local resources and the authorities at Courbevoie complained, for example, that nobles were hoarding badly needed salted pork. Elsewhere, nobles were blamed for devouring the vegetables, eggs, and butter which these communes should have sent to the capital.[63] Parisian sans-culottes complained that the suburbs had been corrupted by the lackeys of the ex-nobles who had gone there 'pour être à l'abri de toutes poursuites et pour corrompre l'esprit des habitants. Ils leur insinuent qu'ils ne peuvent plus envoyer leurs denrées à Paris.'[64] It might have been easier to have left nobles where they were.

iv. The question of individual responsibility; the guilt of wives, children, and relatives

Difficult to define and militarily disruptive, the proscription of nobles was also ideologically difficult to digest. The violation of principle that it entailed was manifest. Popular denunciations of nobles, however useful in some respects, were not, as it were, ideologically cost-free. The idea of the individual responsibility of each citizen was after all a central premiss of Revolutionary politics.

Noble children were a minor but annoying aspect of this issue. Once it had been decided that a man or woman was indeed a noble, did it follow that their now indubitably noble children should also be punished? Where would the line be drawn between responsible noble *adults* guilty of belonging to a 'classe proscrite' and 'non-responsible' noble *children* not old enough to be guilty yet?

No clear answer ever emerged, but on the whole Revolutionary tribunals can be said to have been extremely reluctant to convict thirteen- and fourteen-year-olds.[65] Young émigrés who had returned to France, and had then been deported only to return again, were not executed if they had not yet reached their fourteenth birthday. In the same way, two seventeen-year-old girls, guilty of having offered candy and flowers to the King of Prussia at Verdun, were given a twenty-year jail sentence and not the guillotine as were their older friends. For lesser penalties, however, conviction at an early age was more acceptable. In some respects, ten-year-olds could be counted émigrés, and their property might be confiscated. In October 1793, it was ordered that they be subject to arrest and imprisonment. Even cleaner solutions were suggested. Billaud, in November 1792, moved the banishment of all émigré children regardless of their age, as the deputy Pons would later suggest to the Five Hundred on 15 frimaire an VI that the resident children of émigrés abroad should be taken from their families and re-educated in a Republican environment. Presumably none of this went down too well, and in April 1794, the Committee quickly added that the wives and children of at least those nobles who had been fortunate enough to be 'requisitioned' should also be allowed to stay home, though they themselves might not be essential to the welfare of the Republic.[66]

The principle of individual responsibility was also seriously violated by the condemnation on general grounds of noble adults who as individuals had not done anything. Noble children could not be punished because they had not reached the age of responsibility. But what of older nobles who had indeed reached the age of reason but had not committed any crime? Guilt by association was a principle of the *Ancien Régime* which had been formally denounced as barbaric by the National Assembly in January 1790, when the Constituants had solemnly affirmed the right of an innocent relative to inherit the property of a condemned criminal, a concept which Marat himself had endorsed.

This notion of individual responsibility could not be lightly discarded, an annoying hindrance, because the individual character of judicial responsibility naturally came to mind whenever the nobles problem arose. As one deputy put it, in this very context, 'l'assemblée me pardonnera de lui faire observer que les fautes sont personnelles. J'invoque ici la Déclaration des droits de l'homme, et je demande en son nom qu'on ne persécute pas les individus qui peuvent n'être pas coupables.'[67] And the Dantoniste Delacroix's complaint was echoed throughout the Revolution, by Feuillants in 1790, by Barère in 1793,[68] by moderates after 1794, and from time to time by anyone who for some reason placed morality over expediency.

The concept of individual responsibility was the very cornerstone of the new jurisprudence, and for that matter of bourgeois life in general. Its dismantling did not take place all at once; and in the winter of 1792/3, the Convention was still reluctant to give up this principle, though it had already begun to do so immediately after the fall of the monarchy. Thus in November 1792, at Osselin's request, and amid much laughter, the Conventionnels had at least considered the granting of exemptions to the wives of the émigrés who had followed their husbands to neutral countries, perhaps against their will. 'Il peut être juste', explained Osselin, 'de faire une exception pour les personnes du sexe. . . . Mais, citoyens, nous en avons tous un. . . . Eh bien, je veux dire pour les femmes, que des troubles intérieurs, des événements sanglants et désastreux ont forcées de fuir momentanément leur pays.'[69] One anonymous writer even suggested that female émigrés should not be punished at all: women, he explained, had been denied political rights because of their frailty, mental and physical, and did it not also follow that women émigrés should be considered more indulgently? 'Les femmes dont les nerfs sont plus délicats, pour être plus accessibles à la terreur, seroient-elles plus coupables? Non, sans doute; on connoît trop bien à quel point le physique influe sur le moral.'[70]

The Convention was less and less moved by such reasoning, and by the spring of 1793 guilt by association was assumed as a matter of course. The property of the relatives of émigrés was ordered to be confiscated, and all such people were decreed *ipso facto* suspect. From time to time it was suggested (by Merlin in late August 1792 and by Maure in April 1793) that the wives and children of émigrés be personally detained as hostages. A decree voted on 4 April 1793 ordered that the wives and children of officers in Dumouriez's army be placed under surveillance. One Montagnard, Lejeune, even suggested at the Jacobin Club that all relatives of émigrés be arrested and that 'des bouches à feu soient tournées sur la maison qui les contiendra. (Applaudissements.)'[71]

In the heat of the times, it took no great debating skill to justify abuses of this sort: as Robespierre explained, 'la véritable humanité est celle qui sait sacrifier quelques intérêts particuliers à l'intérêt général'.[72] But such violations of the principle of individual responsibility may none the less have been troubling for many revolutionaries, including Robespierre, who said in March 1794 that 'nous ne souffions pas que le glaive de la loi effleure un seul honnête homme'.[73] Indeed, the Incorruptible must surely have recalled that before the Revolution he too had written against guilt by association with eloquence and feeling, perhaps to assuage the shame and disrepute which his own unrespectable and physiologically unbalanced father had inflicted on his respectable self and family.

Salus populi suprema lex made sense of course, but it was an ideologically embarrassing defence. When all was said and done, the fact was that in Revolutionary French law, as Saint-Just asserted in 1791, 'les fautes sont personnelles',[74] a statement which he repeated on 17 ventôse an II (7 March 1794) when the Convention voted a pension for the children of proscribed Girondins: 'Les fautes sont personnelles, le supplice mérité du père n'empêche pas la nation de recueillir les enfants.'

With countless similar statements on the books, it was difficult for the *citoyens magistrats* to ignore the pleas of nobles like General de Beauharnais, who placed his defence on this obvious ground, and asked where the foundation of 'eternal justice' was 'si ce n'est pas sur cette incontestable vérité; que les fautes étant personnelles, les peines doivent l'être également'.[75]

The scope of individual responsibility became a problematic aspect of the nobles question. This was especially so because of the evolution in the popular revolutionaries' view of what the French Revolution was about. For the bourgeoisie, the idea of personal responsibility could be momentarily put aside, especially as regards nobles, but it could never be denied for long. Bourgeois individualism was the cornerstone of the Revolutionary settlement. As the Revolution progressed, the bourgeoisie understood ever more clearly that its emphasis on community had been misplaced, and that the claims of individualism came first. But the popular revolutionaries, significantly enough, followed an inverse course.

In 1790, Marat defended the concept of individual responsibility because he too assumed, like the bourgeois revolutionaries though from a different perspective, that true popular sovereignty and community could be secured within the context of a state that would be first and foremost the vehicle of individual rights. In his *Plan de législation criminelle*, published in 1790, 'l'Ami du Peuple' had insisted, therefore, that 'Les peines doivent être personnelles.' And Roux, as shall be seen, also invoked the principle of individual responsibility in late 1793 in his defence, as it happens, of nobles.

But after 1795, Babeuf was far more discreet. He did not deny that judicial guilt was a personal concern. This would have been too hard to explain. But he ignored the problem as logic decreed he must: if the struggle of politics opposed, as he said it did, the poor as a group to the rich as a group, the individual desires of this or that person were not at issue.

In 1790, Marat's paean to the bourgeois principle of individualism had made sense from a popular point of view. What progressive revolutionary of any hue would not then have agreed with his belief that every accused person was to be presumed innocent? 'Quant au coupable,' wrote Marat at that time, 'si la preuve de son crime est incomplète, et qu'il ne paroisse rien de grave contre lui, il sera absous et remis en liberté.'[76] But for Babeuf's fellow conspirator and chronicler, Buonarotti (admittedly writing in 1828 and more amicably disposed to Robespierrist terrorism than Babeuf had ever been), the situation in 1796 was very different from what Marat had envisaged some years before. 'La justice', wrote Buonarroti, 'et la nécessité de l'institution révolutionnaire étant reconnues, il ne s'agit plus d'examiner jusqu'à quel point l'autorité qui la dirigeait porta la rigueur dont elle fut forcée de faire usage; il importe seulement de savoir si elle répondit au but pour lequel elle avait été instituée.' The justice of any legal act depended on its social context, and it might well happen, explained Buonarotti, that innocents would perish. But this could not be helped: 'L'antiquité fit-elle un crime à Lycurgue de la mort de quelques aristocrates lacédemoniens? reprocha-t-elle à Brutus la condamnation de ses enfants? A-t-on blâmé la rigueur plus que révolutionnaire, par laquelle Moïse lui-même écrasa sans pitié tout ce qui s'opposait au succès de son institution?'[77]

The theoretical drift of popular revolutionaries on the question of personal responsibility is clear. How much difference such an evolution made to the practice of sans-culotte politics is hard to say. Perhaps none; but the change in theory is none the less undeniable.

By the same token, however, the drift of the popular revolutionaries away from the notion of individual responsibility could only serve to reinforce the bourgeoisie's devotion to this same idea. As the Revolution went on, the bourgeois revolutionaries were forced to choose between individualism and community, and if the ultra-left took up as its cry the rights of the community, the bourgeoisie was willy-nilly driven to argue for individualism unbound. 'Bourgeois thought', as Lukacs reminds us, 'judges social phenomena consciously or unconsciously, naïvely or subtly, consistently from the standpoint of the individual':[78] the notion of individual responsibilities could under no circumstances be given up, and yet the persecution of nobles necessarily worked to that end.

It cannot be categorically asserted that either Conventionnels or sans-culottes were clearly aware of these arguments in 1793–4. These were times when such issues were being sorted out. But it may hardly be doubted that it must have been a source of considerable embarrassment for bourgeois leaders to deny (even by implication and even for the nobles) that 'les fautes sont personnelles'.

v. Popular attitudes to the proscription of nobles after the autumn of 1793

Anti-nobilism had its bourgeois limits. It was embarrassing, hard to apply, hard to explain legally, and militarily disruptive. Finally, it became less popular than it had been.

In 1793–4, many people understood that the fate of nobles was no longer relevant to the day-to-day business of the Revolution. With threats of foreign invasion, food shortage, civil war, and economic breakdown, nobles seemed beside the point. This was the gist of a bold speech of Basire's on 5 September 1793. Many nobles, he said, had left already; some were plainly loyal; as for the others,

> presque tout ce qui reste de nobles est frappé depuis longtemps d'un effroi qui les paralyse. Leur cerveau est frappé de vapeurs (murmures); la stupeur de ces orgueilleux égoistes égale leur méchanceté; ce ne sont pas là les seuls ennemis de l'État, ce ne sont ni les plus dangereux . . . vous avez eu des feuillants, vous avez eu des brissotins, vous avez encore des hypocrites, et je vous demande si tous ces gens-là étaient nobles? Non. Il n'y avait pas deux nobles avec eux.[79]

Nobles should be watched, but the real enemies of the state were elsewhere. When a puppet show was staged in germinal an II to illustrate Jean Bart's successful refutation of l'abbé Maury, the police spy who reported the incident was not amused: 'A quoi servent aujourd'hui des plaisanteries sur les huit cents fermes et sur les vices de l'ancien clergé. . . . Le peuple a des ennemis plus dangereux.'[80]

There is of course evidence which suggests that the Convention's anti-noble legislation continued to elicit some popular support. The very complete edition of the Convention's debates and papers make available a wealth of affidavits from *sociétés populaires*, *comités de surveillances*, and local administrative bodies congratulating the Convention for its extirpation of 'la caste nobiliaire', 'le charlatanisme nobiliaire', or the 'vils intrigans . . . accapareurs de places'. But it is hard to know what to make of such statements, the likes of which were also sent by many Parisian sections to congratulate the CPS on its extermination of Hébert and his associates. Some of the statements sent to the Convention were in any case very faint; the best, for example, that the Tribunal and *société populaire* of Saint Quentin had to say about the anti-noble law of germinal an II was that it had made exceptions on behalf of those 'ex-nobles . . . qui peuvent être utiles à leur patrie; preuve sensible que ce n'est point leur naissance que vous abhorrez, mais leurs vice'. Nobles, they went on, should be given time 'de se corriger de leurs longs égarements, d'adopter d'autres mœurs et de rentrer en frères dans le sein du peuple qu'ils ont si longtemps méprisé, mystifié et tyrannisé'.[81] This was not a warm endorsement.

Nobles were not everywhere detested by the 'plebs', and paradoxically Lebon, in February 1794, justified Saint-Just's persecution of them on the grounds that some peasant women were still deceived by these so-called *pères du peuple*. Many nobles were given tacit protection by local authorities who were lax in keeping records of emigration.[82] In a related if different vein Barère in his memoirs, written long after the fact, maintained that he objected to Saint-Just's plan to send all imprisoned nobles on road gangs because of the nobles' subsisting prestige: 'la noblesse peut bien être abolie par les lois politiques . . . [he told Saint-Just] mais . . . les nobles conservent toujours dans la masse du peuple un rang d'opinion, une distinction due à l'éducation . . . qui ne nous permet pas d'agir à Paris comme Marius agissait à Rome'.[83] And in many places, the proscription of ci-devants was carried out with obvious reluctance. In one commune of the Nivernais, the *agent national* noted that he had indeed purged a noble from a municipal council, but that he had done so reluctantly: 'le citoyen potrelot Grillon, un de ses membres, n'a pas été proposé . . . attendu sa qualité de ci-devant noble, mais je lui ai rendu la justice que mérite son civisme'.[84] More unusually, the expulsion by the central authorities of nobles from

Revolutionary office elicited a response which was straightforwardly defiant. At Viry, for example, on the French side of the border with Geneva, the municipal council declared itself 'paralysed' by the removal of its mayor, the citoyen Viry, formerly Joseph-Marie de Viry,

> lui dont la vie privée et politique honore l'homme et le citoyen; lui le plus chaud défenseur de la liberté; lui qui s'est constamment identifié aux succès de la cause des peuples; lui qui n'a jamais dévié de la carrière du patriotisme; lui qui ne s'occupait qu'à faire marcher le gouvernement révolutionnaire, qu'à faire respecter les lois, aimer la vertu; lui, enfin, qui était l'*Hercule constitutionnel* de ce canton et le *limonier* de cette commune, qui chaque jour se distinguait par des sacrifices, tant en faveur de la République que de l'humanité souffrante. . . .[85]

Viry had been born a noble, but he was now a Republican citizen on account of 'sa métamorphose en homme libre'.[86] So did the municipal council of the town of Fabrègues in the Languedoc deliver to their ex-seigneur a *certificat de civisme*: 'il a fait de grands sacrifices pour la Patrie et . . . l'égalité était dans son cœur avant que cet heureux règne ait été établi'.[87]

Popular anti-nobilism, of course, did not die out completely either in 1794 or after. Traces of anti-nobilism appear, for example, in Babouvist propaganda, and especially in the appeals to the army by Grisel: 'Les nobles nous avaient toujours trahis,' he wrote 'et nous n'avons vraiment vaincu qu'après les avoir chassés de nos armées; aujourd'hui les braves b . . . d'officiers de tricot, qui nous ont conduits à la victoire, qui ont ainsi que nous, la peau toute recousue, sont indignement supprimés et remplacés par des chouans des castes nobles et musquées.'[88] But Grisel, it must be remembered, was also the man who betrayed Babeuf to the police. When some patriots appeared in December 1795 at the Panthéon Club, where Babeuf was regrouping opposition to the Thermidorian regime, to denounce 'priests and nobles', the Panthéonists invoked the Constitution and refused to hear them.[89]

Sans-culotte feeling about nobles, initially inconsistent, gradually acquired coherence. In the first phase of the Revolution, the urban poor had not paid much attention to the aristocratic *aristocrates*. In a second phase, the noble gradually became the archetypal anti-sans-culotte. But after the fall of Robespierre, the popular image of the noble appears to have shifted once again, and the noble now became a sort of super-bourgeois type rather than a counter-revolutionary villain in his own right. Roux, as shall be seen, was explicit about this: for him the enemies of the poor were the rich, and the nobles question was irrelevant. Babeuf's co-conspirator, Buonarroti, was no less clear. What were the Directorials and their praetorians if not an imitation of the old court and nobility?

Voyez ce directoire: à son faste insolent, à ses magnifiques palais, à sa garde nombreuse, à sa hauteur, à la lâcheté des courtisans, ne reconnaît-on pas la cour des Capets? Et nos généraux, si élégamment costumés, ne ressemblent-ils pas, par leur luxe et leur morgue, à ces nobles orgueilleux dont ils ont pris la place? Ah! vous le voyez, braves soldats, la révolution, qui devait rétablir l'égalité, n'a fait jusqu'ici que remplacer une bande d'anciens coquins par une foule de coquins nouveaux.[90]

For Babeuf's chronicler, the new and the old aristocrats were, in practice, a single group of scoundrels. After 1795, popular revolutionaries might still dislike nobles, but only because the resurgence of individual nobles was proof of the more important betrayal of the Revolution by the bourgeoisie. Many grumblers went so far as to claim that the *nouveaux riches* were even worse than the nobles they had replaced: 'Les esprits s'échauffent et s'aigrissent', reported one police agent in September 1795, 'contre les cultivateurs et les gros marchands, que l'on accuse de faire plus de mal à la société que n'en ont jamais fait les ci-devant nobles. On regrette tous les sacrifices faits jusqu'à ce jour.'[91]

The new realignment of popular revolutionaries with respect to nobles had important implications. Robespierre in the spring of 1793 was able to mobilize popular anti-nobilism in support of his own bourgeois faction, that is, on behalf of the Mountain against the Girondins. But a similar manoeuvre was not possible after 1794. In 1795, the Babouvists, or at least their more vocal leaders, among them Antonelle and Le Peletier, both of them great nobles, claimed not to distinguish between nobles and non-nobles, or for that matter between left bourgeois revolutionaries and right bourgeois revolutionaries. The possessing class was now declared by the extreme left to be a single bloc; this meant that no bourgeois faction could hope to bribe the 'plebs' by offering nobles to them as propitiary victims. Opportunistic bourgeois anti-nobilism lost its *raison d'être* in the winter of 1793/4 and declined even more after 1795.

It is difficult to say how distinctly this new situation was understood by all parties. The sans-culotte leaders were clearer about nobles than were their bourgeois enemies, since the Directorials did, after all, continue to persecute nobles through 1799. Only then did the bourgeois revolutionaries finally realize that nobles were, so to speak, their 'objective' class allies. The precise limits of such political and social consciousness are not to be found. But what does appear in any case is that the Revolutionary bourgeoisie had probably reached the limits of opportunistic persecution some months before the fall of Robespierre.

In summary, it is by no means obvious that the advantages of anti-nobilism outweighed its disadvantages after the autumn of 1793. The continued persecution of nobles had become a liability by the time of Saint-Just's law of April 1794. Anti-nobilism was embarrassing, hard to apply, militarily disruptive, and not especially popular. But despite such considerations, anti-nobilism did go on, and this inevitably leads us to look for some other explanation which will be more than a tally of tactical assets and liabilities.

In 1791–3, the Revolutionary bourgeoisie's persecution of nobles was readily understandable. It was an opportune means of government, and one which the bourgeoisie could readily take up because bourgeois anti-noble feeling had been widespread before 1789. It was the ideological incompleteness of the bourgeoisie's acceptance of individualism in property, together with its need to assuage the poor and its own latent suspicion of nobles which made possible in 1791–3 the drift to the left with its attendant anti-nobilism. Cause and effect are reasonably plain for those years. But after the autumn of 1793, the persecution of nobles made less and less practical sense from a bourgeois point of view. And yet, it did not cease to swell. The explanation, as I will try to show, is to be found in an understanding of the place and nature of Jacobin ideology.

Chapter Five

Ideological anti-nobilism

i. The nature of the argument

The traditional Marxist explanation of bourgeois anti-nobilism in 1794—that its fundamental goal was the extirpation of feudalism—is straightforward and, at first glance, highly plausible: from this hypothesis it naturally follows that the persecution of nobles should have been at its most intense when bourgeois Revolutionary fervour reached its climax during the Terror, in the spring of 1794. But much of the historical evidence does not accommodate itself to the traditional hypothesis, and a more plausible explanation of the Mountain's proscription of nobles must be sought at a deeper level, which, as has been said, closely corresponds to the young Marx's analysis of Revolutionary ideology.*

The general framework of such an explanation is the drift of Revolutionary politics from the concrete to the abstract, for surely, the greatest paradox of 1793–4 was the conjunction of an intense material reorganization of institutions (for which *l'organisation de la victoire* is a short-hand notation) with a drift towards the increasingly abstract justification of political acts. One example of this inclination to abstraction will suffice: the change in tone of Saint-Just's various apologia of parliamentary purges. In his speech of July 1793 against the Gironde, the young tribune flounders badly as he strains to find specific guilt: 'tous les détenus ne sont point coupables; le plus grand nombre n'était qu'égaré'.[1] But in his accusation of Danton, eight months later, this cruel twenty-seven-year-old is now completely vague and wholly ruthless: 'mauvais citoyen . . . faux ami . . . méchant homme . . . tu as dis que l'honneur était ridicule; que la gloire et la postérité étaient une sottise. . . . J'en ai trop dit: tu répondras à la justice.'[2]

But there is also a specific context to the drift towards abstraction, a context that centres on the role of ideology, which more than ever becomes in 1793 the Ariadne's thread of Revolutionary politics. This ideological explanation of anti-

* See Appendix 1.

nobilism in late 1793–4 falls into two divisions. In the first, as has been shown in the previous chapter, doubt is expressed about any explanation which holds the reason to be either self-evident or easily arrived at in material, positivist terms (i.e. nobles conspired against the Republic and were therefore punished). But a demonstration of the inadequacy of such an interpretation is only a first step. To show that many nobles supported the Revolution, or that it was embarrassing and difficult to punish them, or that neither peasants nor sans-culottes appeared to care much about nobles in 1794 makes another explanation possible, but hardly necessary. An ideological explanation may begin with a statement on the inadequacy of positivist explanations, but it must then justify itself in its own right by the greater plausibility of the new categories that it generates.

The starting-point of a counter-hypothesis is a discussion of what is described in conventional Marxist terms (or jargon) as the 'displacement of contradictions'. Unable or unwilling to proceed in one direction, bourgeois politicians shift the terms of the political debate to a field where they can hold their own. Social tensions are, so to speak, redirected towards areas where anodyne compensation can be more easily secured.

The approach, to be sure, cannot satisfy historians intent on 'wie es eigentlich gewesen'. But it is striking that assumptions about the displacement of contradictions have been, for example, the foundation of most contemporary work on the history of Bismarckian and Wilheminian Germany. Historians have commonly assumed that the key to German history was the incongruous domination of a modern, industrial society by an aristocratic Junker class, embourgeoisé in some ways, but in others feudal-minded still. The structure of German politics was in consequence 'unnatural', and for that reason the Junkers and their allies (the monarchy and big business) were forever driven in a restless search for alternatives to those social and parliamentary reforms which a more normal political arrangement would have naturally produced. German politics were a search for surrogates. Very convenient in this respect were the various disabilities heaped in turn on Catholics, Poles, Socialists, and Jews. Most dangerous were the foreign *Ersätze* to domestic difficulty: imperialism, a high seas fleet, and war.

The paradigm has gained wide acceptance in the works of Eckhardt Kehr, Hans-Ulrich Wehler, Reinhard Rürup, Jürgen

Kocka, and many others.[3] The argument postulates that certain types of political behaviour are normative and others not. It assumes also that the explicit motives of contemporaries must be drastically reinterpreted. German anti-Semitism, for example, has in actuality very little to do with Jews. What matters is less the existence of a traditional category (Jews) than the modern use to which that category has been put (in the case of Germany, the deflection of popular and middle-class animosity away from high capitalism towards a group marginal to the workings of the system).

A similar reasoning will be applied here to the nobility, which was, in my opinion, a traditional category manipulated by the Mountain to mask its own failure. Having drifted leftward since 1791 in the pursuit of community and of popular suffrage, the Revolutionary bourgeoisie found suddenly in the summer of 1793 that its primary goal, the defence of individualism and of private property, was being subjected to intolerable strain. In order to neutralize popular complaints on this score without forfeiting its Revolutionary stance, the Jacobin bourgeoisie redefined the purpose of the Republic as a war of virtue against vice. The question of property was side-stepped. The attack on nobles, who were the classical incarnation of vice, gave added plausibility to the scheme. The balance of individualism and community, which had been effortlessly decreed in 1789 but had broken down in 1791, was re-created, albeit on a terrorist basis and at the expense, on the right, of ideologically marginal groups like nobles, and on the left, of the socially marginal popular revolutionaries who had wanted to give a greater material embodiment to the concept of community.

In another and more mundane way, the persecution of nobles also helped the Mountain to make better sense of the apparent failure of Revolutionary consensus. The Montagnards' view of politics, like that of the Enlightenment, was organic and biological. Corruption rather than class conflict was identified as the cause of political strife; and in this view, the presence of nobles helped to explain the decay of Revolutionary zeal in the nation as a whole. The political vision of Robespierre, which presupposed the existence of social harmony and of politics by universal acclaim, could not absorb the modern fact of the sans-culottes' distinct position as a class. But it could focus on the traditional guilt of nobles. The persecution of nobles was for him an ideal tactical and doctrinal exit.

These arguments do not assume that Robespierre and the

Mountain consciously endeavoured to deceive the public or themselves. It is true that modern European history does present numerous instances in which 'displacements of contradictions' have been purposefully designed. War, for example, was explicitly accepted by some German statesmen in 1913–14 as the solution to the decay of the Bismarckian compromise. But in 1793–4, motivations lacked this clarity. It could hardly have been otherwise, as follows again from a German analogy.

Bismarck after 1848 (like Schwarzenberg in Austria and for that matter most conservative statesmen of the late nineteenth century) had a lively and even obsessive sense of the 'drift of History'. In the 1870s and 1880s, the relevant categories were very clear: the rise of the middle classes and of parliamentarism, the development of nationalism, industrialization, and socialism; these were the ABCs of politics. To juggle some of these developments in order to arrest others required skill and determination more than great intuitive insight. But the position of Robespierre and Saint-Just was not so clear-cut. It can be said, of course, that the need to find a palliative to pressure from below was more keenly felt by the French bourgeoisie in 1793–4 than it was by Bismarck and his king in 1862. Abdication is not execution. But the Revolutionary bourgeoisie's map of society and politics in France was far less appropriate, and their solutions were less neat.

All of the classic expedients of nineteenth-century conservative politics were, to be sure, unearthed by hard-pressed French Republicans in 1789–99: nationalism, imperialism, war, the persecution of religious and social minorities, fraudulent promises of economic redistribution, and the virtues of a technocratic, efficient administration were all weapons in the armoury of Brissot, Robespierre, Saint-Just, and Sieyes. But these political *Ersätze* were produced one by one, and as if by accident. Restated, the technique of the displacement of contradictions could come fully into its own only when contemporaries reached an intuitive understanding of what their class position really was. Once the script had been written, it was easy to act out, but the actors of the French Revolution had to make up their lines as they went along. Many of them were shocked by what they had done. As Marc Richir puts it, '1789 enabled the bourgeoisie to commit acts that would have made it . . . blush had it thought about them with deliberation'.[4] Bismarck did not blush; but many of the Conventionnels were dismayed and unable to accept, as was so easily done later, the inevitable contradictions of bourgeois life.

Others were simply mystified by what had happened. 'Qui a fait nos actes?' asked the Dantoniste Montagnard Marc-Antoine Baudot in his old age, 'nous n'en savons rien.'

The men of the French Revolution were caught up in a social drama whose true nature was very hard to grasp, and their confusion was further compounded by the dizzying pace of events, by the 'acceleration of history' during the first five years of the Revolution. In 1791, Fabre d'Églantine offered to the public a play entitled *Le Convalescent de Qualité*: a noble, seriously diseased, is for reasons of health sequestered in 1789–91. He then comes back to social life and is aghast. Can it be true that his noble daughter will marry a bourgeois officer of the so-called *Garde Nationale*? But all ends well. The Rip Van Winkle effect naturally came to mind in the turmoil of the Revolutionary decade, but not everyone evinced the equanimity and historical sense of Fabre's noble hero. Events moved very quickly in 1789–99. Bismarck after 1848 had more than a decade to discover that nationalism, which he had once detested, could be used to blunt the German bourgeoisie's desire for self-rule. Robespierre, who did not enjoy such leisure, had very little time to find his new balance. Readjustments were sudden; and it may have been difficult, perhaps even painful, for him to decide in the spring of 1793 that some of the sans-culotte economic goals would have to be met, or, in the spring of 1794, that those of his friends like Danton who had become useless would have to be executed. His actions do not have the clear Machiavellian quality of Bismarck's machinations.

We can, perhaps, make sense out of the French Revolution, but we should not ask too much help from those who lived it day by day. Their collective motives may seem plain to us today, but few periods of history can have been so bewildering for those who lived them.

ii. Two views of Jacobin ideology

The classic explanation of the decline of the rights of nobles is incomplete. The problem must be considered in the light of the political function of Jacobin ideology. That topic has been parenthetically discussed at various points of this narrative but must now be brought to the centre of the stage.

That the Jacobins had an articulated ideology is not, of course, at issue. Nor is there much dispute on the nature of its salient points. There is wide agreement that the Jacobins developed a unitary social and political philosophy which held that society was 'transparent'.[5] They assumed that the Revolutionary movement could durably unite two distinct social groups, that is to say, the Revolutionary bourgeoisie and 'le peuple'.

Historical disagreement centres on the function of this view. Why did Jacobins proclaim the unity of the poor and of the propertied, Revolutionary élite? Two explanations can be given: that the Jacobins did this because they needed the help of the poor to destroy feudalism; and that the Jacobins desperately needed to bridge the contradiction that had by 1793 become obvious between the Revolutionary bourgeoisie's ideological egalitarianism and its social conservatism. 'Il ne faut ni riches ni pauvres,' wrote Saint-Just in his *Institutions Républicaines*, only to add, 'Ne pas admettre le partage des propriétés.'

In the light of the second view, Jacobin ideology takes on a very negative cast indeed. It must then appear as a tactical gambit, a cheat for the sans-culottes and the source of a cruel and unjustifiable persecution of all those men and women who belonged to expendable social categories, like priests, monks, nuns, prostitutes, linguistic minorities, bankers, nobles, and, generally, deviants and suspects of every kind.

Jacobin ideology has usually been presented in a more positive light, by Claude Mazauric, for example, in an elegant and thoughtful essay entitled 'Quelques voies nouvelles pour l'histoire politique de la Révolution française'.[6] For Mazauric, the Jacobins were the part of the French bourgeoise which was in 1789–94 most able to understand its historical function, the destruction of feudalism and, in 1793–4, the defence of the nation. In order to achieve these goals, he argues, the Jacobin bourgeoisie found itself, time and again, forced to be tactically innovative and ideologically creative. As new situations arose, so did it discover new ideological constructs: 'la force des choses', declaimed Saint-Just in February 1794, 'nous conduit peut-être à des résultats auxquels nous n'avons pas pensé'. Carnot was more plain: 'On n'est pas révolutionnaire, on le devient.' Driven by political necessity to act on a broad front involving peasants and sans-culottes, the Jacobin bourgeoisie elaborated in 1794 a unitary metaphysics that embraced the cult of the Supreme Being, the Revolutionary calendar, the exaltation of virtue, national *fêtes*, and a neo-classical vocabulary of civic unity.

This is a highly suggestive interpretation. It underlies also the traditional Marxist interpretation of the events of 1789–91.

Conservative historians have stressed the solidarity of bourgeois and nobles that appears to have prevailed in these years, and have pointed to the reformist nature of most *cahiers de doléances*. But such early and conservative statements are taken by the Marxists to be superficial. The only valid ideological statements of the Revolutionary bourgeoisie, they say, are those made *after* 1791–2, when that class finally found itself in a political situation that enabled it to understand its true social and historical role. Only in 1793 did the Jacobin bourgeoisie realize its true nature as the scourge of feudalism and tradition. Only then was it able to renounce the basically pointless compromise that it had made with nobles in 1789, when it was still unable to see beyond its ahistorical alliance with the crown and the feudal-minded nobility.

Put simply, Mazauric's explanation assumes that Jacobin ideology was the expression of the bourgeoisie's felt need to unify the nation in order to carry out the destruction of feudalism. As Lefebvre explained, 'though the Constituants had read the philosophes, culture neither thwarted nor weakened their sense of reality'.[7] The key to the relation of ideology to social fact is the bourgeoisie's perception that feudalism was to be destroyed no matter how great the cost.

Ideology is not of much consequence in this view. The individualist ideology which the Feuillants had invoked to destroy corporatism (as well as the privileges of the nobles and, for that matter, the idea of nobility itself) is for these Marxist historians a transparent cipher, a superstructure that can be dismissed as the expression of the bourgeoisie's secular efforts to make of private property the cornerstone of economic life. The communitarian Jacobin ideology of virtue that prevailed in 1793–4 is differently explained but in ways which make it appear equally unsubstantial.

One kind of explanation, therefore, presents Jacobin ideology as an instrumental, tactical weapon designed to elicit the co-operation of the masses in the struggle against feudalism. A second line of argument, related to the first, sees Jacobin ideology as the expression of some ultimately useful but none the less vague idealism, the consequence of the 'influence of the Enlightenment'. Won over by their readings to a humanitarian philosophy of natural rights in general and to Rousseauistic fantasies about the General Will in particular, the Jacobins proclaimed and re-asserted the Rights of Man because it was useful for them to do so, of course, but also because of their generosity: 'In order to fight from above,' explains Jaurès, 'the Revolutionary bourgeoisie had to rise to the level of humanity as a whole, even at the risk of going beyond its own concept of right towards a distant and new right. . . . [The French Revolution] was never more grandly and gloriously realistic than it was when it affirmed its high ideals: "Men are born and remain free and equal in their rights." '[8] Lefebvre likewise related the Revolutionaries' communitarian vision of sacrifice to idealism, which, incidentally, he thought had been neglected by contemporary scholars:

Historians for a long time exaggerated the importance of [the] moral and ideological preparation [in salons, academies, cafés, masonic lodges, etc.] even to the point of seeing in it the sole cause of the Revolution. Reality is mutilated if we overlook the play of practical interests in producing the revolutionary spirit. For the last half century students have applied themselves, and rightly so, to the task of showing how the revolutionary spirit originated in a social and economic movement. But we should commit no less an error in forgetting that there is no true revolutionary spirit without the idealism which alone inspires sacrifice.[9]

It is ironic that the idealistic derivation of Revolutionary communitarianism has also figured prominently in the writings of some conservative historians. Crane Brinton writes, for example, that

in the persons of the patriots of the Constituent Assembly is to be discerned a milder form of that extraordinary gap between interests and ideas which was to appear at its fullest with the Montagnards, and which has always seemed an impossible, and therefore non-existent, gap to men of little imagination or of strong faith—that is, to the majority of historians. The interests of the patriots of this first Assembly were the interests of moderate men; their ideas were largely the ideas of immoderate men, of men determined once and for all to bring to earth those fair abstractions of Justice and Happiness, so dear to the race, so distant, so unattainable, so essential, so inevitable. Their ideas, fitfully but unmistakably, triumphed over their interests, made their constitutional monarchy impossible, and prepared for the first republic.[10]

In short, for both the Marxist and the conservative historian, the key is the reduction of ideology to social fact. Marxist historians, who demand that such a link be made, conclude from the idealistic motivation of their subjects that the revolutionaries' words were a tactic and did not mean very much. The reification of ideology by liberal or conservative historians who then interpret it as generous or foolish also serves to deny the causal power of ideas which are ultimately presented as epiphenomena.

Yet another conservative explanation of Jacobin ideology likewise denies its genuine connection to social fact, albeit in quite a different way. Jacobin collectivism in this view is seen as the unsubstantial derivative of rampant individualism. The argument suggests that the transition from the one to the other was implicit in the nature of individualism itself. Tocqueville, for example, sees a pattern in France, though not in America, which moves from the assertion of the rights of self, through envy, to the acceptance of an egalitarian and authoritarian levelling of all social conditions.

In the first two decades of this century, Augustin Cochin developed a similar, though more abstruse, reasoning.[11] The Revolution, he thought, had been the handiwork of the Sociétés de pensée, not in the narrow sense that Free-masons and others had conspired to bring down the monarchy but in the wider sense that the members of these societies had been the agents of a new and corrosive world view. For Cochin, writing in the shadow of Durkheim, the Sociétés de pensée were the laboratory of abstract individualism, and for that reason, the very antithesis of the organic and corporatist *Ancien Régime*. Crucial to Cochin's argument is the notion that this individualism, being abstract, contained *in ovo* the collectivism of 1794. Men as we know them, he explained in the manner of De Maistre, are made of unequal flesh and blood. But men considered as individuals, *in vacuo*, are necessarily endowed with equal rights. Modern democratic politics were in this perspective an unsubstantial, irrelevant field of action, destructive of what was true and real. Translated into other terms, democratic politics, one might say, were a manner of 'pays légal', where democratic, egalitarian individualism prevailed, in stark contrast to the variegated and organically integrated 'pays réel'. Such a view made considerable sense when considered from the point of view of the French centre-right, marked by a nostalgia for Catholic and organic hierarchy. To lump together socialistic communitarianism and bourgeois individualism was intensely pleasing. It is to be noted that similar arguments were later made in the 1930s by the polemicists of the Jeune Droite, like Jean Pierre Maxence, who liked to see the failure of Bolshevism and of American capitalism as two sides of the same coin. Judeo-Bolshevism and Judeo-capitalism were no more than Tweedledum and Tweedledee. In time, the second would necessarily emerge from the ashes of the first.

Jacobin communitarianism need not be derived, however,

from some vague idealism or from the *confusion chaleureuse* that so often characterizes revolutionary epochs. Nor should it be thought to be the paradoxically logical and inevitable derivative of rampant individualism. Jacobinism can be understood as the expression of the communitarian longings of a group incompletely won over to capitalistic individualism and still unaware of the threat to property which its principles would elicit in a society that had suddenly become articulated on lines of class.

That the social origins of bourgeois communitarianism should have remained opaque for Marxist writers is in some respects to be expected; the opacity derives from their skewed view of the inroads of capitalism in France before 1789. To say that the French bourgeoisie was won over to capitalism and individualism in property before the Revolution (and to ignore, for example, the critical absence of a widespread enclosure movement) is to foreclose the possibility that the bourgeoisie should after 1789 have earnestly and sincerely believed itself to be part of 'le peuple' and endowed as such with Revolutionary legitimacy. That Marxist historians should have ignored this aspect of bourgeois thinking is, however, odd in other ways, given the extensive and innovative work which they have done in uncovering the pre-capitalist and communitarian strands of popular urban and rural thought. All that was left for them to do was to see that this popular traditionalist nostalgia was still in some extensive part shared by a culturally erratic bourgeoisie, intent on the defence of property, but deeply involved in rural life as well. Such contradictions are not surprising: bourgeois *arrivisme* no more precluded a distrust of social mobility than the detestation of feudalism made seigneurial titles less desirable. To set Jacobin ideology in a dichotomous context of idealism and realism is to conclude, necessarily, that this ideology could not have much generative force. To place it in the context of the Enlightenment's hesitations between 'l'individu et le social', between individualism and community, and to see these hesitations as the expression of the incomplete development of individualistic capitalism in eighteenth-century France, is to realize at once that the effect of ideology could be immense, as it was.

Restated in the terms of contemporary sociological thought, Mazauric's argument, however ably stated, is limited by the constraints inherent in a view that considers ideology in terms of 'interest theory' or 'latent strain'. A more comprehensive view of the function of ideology is needed here. In the words of Clifford

Geertz, 'Both interest theory and strain theory go directly from source analysis to consequence analysis without ever seriously examining ideologies as systems of interacting symbols, as patterns of interworking meanings.' It is important to see that ideology should not as a rule, and certainly not always, be considered as a utilitarian epiphenomenon. It is incidentally of interest in this respect that Sartre arrived at a similar view of ideology, albeit from a philosophical rather than a sociological perspective, and it is more than a coincidence, perhaps, that he should have developed this view in relation to the events of the French Revolution. In a series of reflections on Guérin's interpretation of Girondism as the expression of the needs of the commercial class, Sartre rhetorically asks if it is 'indispensable to consider [the Girondins'] enterprise an insubstantial appearance, disguising the conflict of economic interests, when by itself, it proclaims its meaning and its goal through contemporary speeches and writings?'[12] The particular content of a cultural system, Sartre concludes, cannot be immediately reduced 'to the universality of a class ideology'.

To argue for a broader view of Jacobin ideology is not to deny that there is considerable merit in the narrower, instrumental view of Jacobinism that has been developed by Marxist historians. In some respects Jacobin ideology and bourgeois social fact certainly overlapped. The point, however, is that ultimately, the fit was not a very good one. It is difficult to argue that the egalitarian excesses of the Jacobins were, so to speak, oversights, brought into being by their need to go a bit further than they really wanted to in order to secure the utter destruction of their arch-enemy, feudalism. It is more plausible to suggest instead that the destruction of feudalism was only a first part of what the Jacobins, for a complex set of reasons, gradually decided ought to be a moral restructuring of French society, now intended to become a genuinely virtuous community where the ancient dream of civic humanism would finally come to fruition.

From a bourgeois point of view, the instrumental pursuit of a virtuous community made sense only during the destructive phase of the Revolution, that is to say, during those first years of 1789–91, when the bourgeoisie was gripped by its desire to destroy the remains of traditional rule. As soon as the Revolutionary bourgeoisie seized control of politics in 1792, its ideology began to be, in instrumental terms, a dead weight, a source of contradiction, as an ever greater number of bourgeois revolutionaries came to understand.

The destruction of traditional ties of deference was bad enough; the terrorist defence after 1793 of the Rights of Man and of the claims of virtuous community were much worse, since all over France sans-culottes now suddenly bubbled to the surface, wild men of no substance who might otherwise have led more or less normal lives on the fringes of respectability. There were rumours of an impending *loi agraire*. Bourgeois universalism had consequences that were unforeseen.

It is the Terror which brings to a head the conflicting interpretations of Jacobin ideology. For Mazauric, these months witnessed the culmination of the entire Revolutionary effort to destroy feudalism. In the second view, which I have presented here, these same months witnessed the dwindling away of bourgeois support for the Jacobin's mixed vision of a society that did respect private property but which would also be virtuous and communitarian. As I see it, by late 1793, the mass of the French bourgeoisie had finally come to understand what its true situation as a class now was. A similar understanding had been reached in late 1791 by the Feuillants, who then did what they could to stop the Revolution: their enlightened sensibility and nostalgia for community led them much further than they had wished to go. So in late 1792 to early 1793 did the Girondins finally understand that a policy of no enemies to the left was dangerous. During that time, only a small part of the Revolutionary bourgeoisie (i.e. the Jacobins in France at large, and in Paris, the Mountain) persisted in demanding a bourgeois but morally egalitarian society, an objective now suddenly rejected as inadequate by the sans-culottes and as too threatening by a growing section of the bourgeoisie.

In describing Condorcet's decision to open the franchise to men of no property, Keith Baker writes that 'it seems likely that [Condorcet] did so less in response to a single event than in the constant search for theoretical consistency'.[13] So no doubt, did many Jacobins. But more and more owners of property chose instead to put practicality over logical consistency.

Mazauric says of the successive purges of the Jacobin societies in 1793–4 that by their practice of exclusion the Jacobins 'were trying to eliminate not only certain individuals but also the kernel of political division'.[14] Exclusion was, to speak irreverently, a method of unification. It may be equally sensible to take these purges at face value. The purification of the Jacobin clubs was probably less an effort to maintain a united front of bourgeois and sans-culottes than a reflection of the disintegration of support within the propertied class for the Jacobins' unrealistic programme. In short, although the Jacobins of 1794 have been seen by some as the most historically conscious part of the bourgeois class, so can they be judged to have been the most confused. Caught between bourgeois exigency (represented by the need to bring sans-culottism and Hébertisme under control) and egalitarian principles which they would not give up, the Jacobins found themselves forced to rush in where more sensible social conservatives or more sincere social reformers would have feared to tread.

The results of the Jacobin policy of exclusion combined with ideological radicalism were highly paradoxical. An excessive concern for virtue and community had brought into being a threat to property, but the Jacobins' response to this threat was contradictory: they denied the need to restructure property, but they assumed an even more egalitarian stand in theory, as proof of their continuing allegiance to the concept of community. In other words, the Jacobins' short-run solution to the breakdown of bourgeois politics led to its long-run aggravation. By taking up the vocabulary of equality, the cult of a Supreme Being, the defence of the united nation, or the persecution of nobles, the Jacobins did maintain some credibility as defenders of equality; but in doing this they also legitimized the notion that virtue and community ought indeed to be the bases of social life.

The equilibrium which ensued was precarious. The popular revolutionaries, for whom Jacobin promises were not enough, had to be repressed, as did those bourgeois for whom even the promise of equality was too much. Terror was the necessary weapon that was used by the Jacobins like Robespierre who were sincere in imposing this solution on a nation which was equally sincere in its detestation of it.

Jaurès, it may be said in passing, also thought like Mazauric that a link could be made between terrorism and the Montagne's aspiration for a better world: 'The more the Convention was forced to fight and kill, the more it had to show that it possessed a deepened thought of gentleness and peace.'[15] But I would reverse the relationship and suggest instead that it was the irrelevance of the Convention's message 'de douceur et de paix' which forced the Conventionnels to terrorize the nation. Georges Sorel, Jaurès's arch-enemy, was more correct when he wrote that

Pendant la Terreur, les hommes qui versèrent le plus de sang furent ceux qui avaient le plus vif désir de faire jouir leurs semblables de l'âge d'or qu'ils avaient rêvé, et qui avaient le plus de sympathie pour les misères humaines: optimistes, idéalistes et sensibles, ils se montraient d'autant plus inexorables qu'ils avaient une plus grande soif du bonheur universel.[16]

The negative view of Jacobin ideology central to my study is sharply distinct from both the Marxist interpretation and that of authors like Cobban, Furet, and Richet. For the Marxists, as has been shown, ideology was no more than the expression of underlying class differences. It had no real specificity. The same is true in a different way of those historians who subscribe to the *dérapage* theory. Jacobin ideology was for them from the first pure theatre, because it never had any relevance to the existence of the new, united, and composite élite which, they say, had come into being by 1789. The view of Jacobinism that is presented here holds, to the contrary, that ideology was not a cypher.

It holds also that the unusual autonomy of ideology in 1793–4 could hardly have come into being if French social structure had been more clearly delineated before the Revolution. Had the French bourgeoisie in 1788 been more aware of its situation as a propertied class (which might well have happened if capitalist involvement in trade had had a bigger impact on the nation as a whole, as had happened in Britain), the adoption of an extreme egalitarian ideology in 1793 could hardly have taken place. The ideological escape of Jacobin politics in 1793 towards virtue and community has as its pre-condition the survival in the 1780s of the vision of civic humanism. The incompleteness in that decade of the bourgeoisie's pre-Revolutionary class-consciousness, in the form of its latent hostility to nobles as well as of its articulated concern for virtue, provides the background of the particular solution that was taken in 1793 by the Jacobins to the appearance of autonomous sans-culotte political concerns.

For a variety of reasons, then, Jacobin politics can be seen as a desperate effort by bourgeois Revolutionary political figures like Saint-Just and Robespierre to impose on French society an egalitarian vision which had a narrow and shrinking relevance to bourgeois social reality. This was, it may be added, the first interpretation that was given, historically, to Jacobin ideology in the works of Hegel.

Hegel of course did not derive Jacobinism from some pre-capitalist communitarian bedrock. Idealism was for him the mainspring of Robespierre's concerns. But the ideological motivation of the Jacobins was not to be doubted, as appeared, he thought, from a comparison of French and American revolutionary politics. In America, which was ensconced in its Lockean tradition, 'revolutionary force [was] mobilized for the restriction of despotically unrestrained power'. The French vision, however, was very different; and, in Hegel's view, the French Revolution was a world-historical event precisely because it was in 1789 that an effort was first made to create 'a total constitution in accordance with Natural Law against a depraved society and a human nature which had been corrupted'. In the French situation, revolution meant the mobilization of moral forces, as yet undeveloped, whereas revolution in America had meant only the mobilization of existing interests.[17]

Whether Hegel's views of American politics are of substance is only of indirect importance.[18] What matters here is his estimate of the causes of the success and failure of the French Revolution. Especially relevant is his belief that the French bourgeois revolutionaries, like Robespierre, failed because their moralistic goals went beyond the material possibilities of the time; in Hegelian terms, Robespierre's undoing was implicit in his excessively abstract view of freedom.

Hegel did not go on to use the vocabulary of class; he referred only to the gap which existed between Robespierre's subjective consciousness and French social forms in general. But he laid out clearly the basic outline of the revolutionaries' dilemma: a Revolutionary consciousness which appealed to the abstract principles of natural law would appear impotent if it did not overcome the contradictions between what it wanted and those forces which resisted its demands. Yet to overcome these forces, as happened during the Terror, meant that Revolutionary consciousness would go beyond what was feasible and in so doing destroy its own hopes. Robespierre could not bring himself to choose between these alternatives, and it was, incidentally, by finding a median way between them that Napoleon, in Hegelian perspective, derived his historical significance.

The young Marx completed the Hegelian argument. Starting like Hegel from the idealistic foundation of revolutionary communitarianism, Marx did not move the debate further in that respect; but he advanced it by providing a class analysis of the mechanism of revolutionary politics *after* their inception. Hegel had explained the Terror and its failure by describing a communitarian philosophy that had outstretched its social foundations. Marx's elaboration made it possible to define more closely what was subjective and what was objective in Robespierre's thinking. A more coherent description of the revolutionary drama as a whole now became possible. In the Hegelian–Marxist scheme, it could now be seen that the great paradox of the French Revolution lay in the conjunction of particularism and universalism. A bourgeois particularist class came to power and justified its existence by referring to egalitarian themes drawn from natural philosophy. Ideology in this interpretation did not reflect social forces as Mazauric would argue. Instead, it was ideology which created politics and indirectly affected social forms in a durable way by creating the circumstances that made possible the transition from the latent concept of 'class in itself' to the conscious fact of 'class for itself'.

This explanation can be applied in an analysis of the function of Jacobin ideology in 1793–4. It can also be used to explain the passage from an opportunistic alliance with the sans-culottes in 1793 to the redefinition of the purpose of the Revolution in 1794 as the war of virtue versus vice: in the spring of 1793, the full implications of the gap between bourgeoisie and sans-culottes were still hidden from the Mountain, though they had long since become obvious to both Feuillants and Girondins. In the autumn of 1793, however, the Mountain itself came face to face with the problem of social division, but unlike the Feuillants or the Gironde, the Mountain did not decide that the Revolution had ended. It moved forward instead. Still intent on realizing a society that would be at once hierarchic (with rich and poor) and egalitarian (with participatory democracy), the Jacobins now had no choice but to elaborate a moral reconstruction of the world that left intact differences in wealth. Material distinctions might be modulated by the destruction of the very rich (bankers) or by the reduction of prominent 'hommes à talent' (no more academies) or in a variety of other minor ways (the confiscation of the property of émigrés). But the thrust of the Revolution would be towards moral and political equality. Everyone would be *tu*, no one would be *vous*, and the constitution of 1793—never to be enforced—clearly stated that all men were entitled to vote and to rebel against unjust authority. At the same time, there would be no *loi agraire*. Indeed, there would be no need for one since distinctions of property would become irrelevant.

The Mountain's ideological solution was elegant. Unlike the Feuillants or the Girondins, the Mountain did not withdraw with unseemly haste from a policy of opportunistic progressivism to one of opportunistic reaction. It continued to move forward, although, of course, the direction of its trajectory was drastically amended. The goals of the Revolution became abstract and, in truth, meaningless. In an earlier phase, when the Mountain had relied on the 'plebs' to topple the Gironde, Jacobin egalitarianism had true material substance, most notable in the regulation of trade and prices. But the limits of such concrete action were reached as soon as the Mountain took control of bourgeois politics. In the autumn of 1793, the Jacobins did make progress, though in a novel way, by moving from the genuinely to the falsely democratic.

This was the setting of the nobles question in late 1793–4.

iii. Anti-nobilism as a symbol of political regeneration in late 1793–1794

In the spring of 1794, Saint-Just concluded that the Revolution was 'frozen'. The Jacobins had fallen into a trap from which there were two exits. For some, the way out was easy: The Revolution should aim, as Danton said, for 'l'égalité des droits, [et] non à l'égalité impossible des biens' which meant in the winter of 1793/4 that the Revolution was over. For men of a more abstract or determined temperament, the pursuit of Terror was a better exit, and Terror became progressively more necessary as the universalist goals of the terrorists became increasingly unrealistic. No longer the reflection of any practical bourgeois need, especially after the military successes of the winter of 1793/4, the actions of Robespierre and Saint-Just became increasingly unrestrained. The Revolution was indeed frozen: its central contradiction sprang from the very nature of French society, now understood by most to be a hierarchy of classes. Unable to affect this social substance, which they would not accept, Robespierre and Saint-Just instinctively pushed social concerns aside, actively suppressed sans-culotte institutions, and pointed to a principle, corruption, as the cause of the Revolution's immobility.

The situation of nobles in 1794 can best be understood as a consequence of this theoretical impasse for the actual business of politics. Nobles were not proscribed because they were unusually dangerous or because the 'plebs' thirsted for their blood. The attack against nobles was a symbolic representation, a displace-

ment of contradictions from a social level to an ideological one.
The nobility was obviously no threat in 1794. Robespierre in October 1792 had said already that 'la noblesse et le clergé ont disparu'[19] and he had not changed his mind in floréal an II (May 1794) when he compared France to the rest of Europe; there, 'un laboureur, un artisan est un animal dressé pour les plaisirs d'un noble; en France, les nobles cherchent à se transformer en laboureurs et en artisans, et ne peuvent pas même obtenir cet honneur'.[20] Saint-Just concurred. In 1791, he too had remarked that 'la noblesse et le clergé, qui furent le rempart de la tyrannie, ont disparu avec elle; l'une n'est plus, l'autre n'est que ce qu'il doit être'. 'L'esprit de l'aristocratie française', he concluded, 'est le repos,'[21] and in the late spring of 1794, while reflecting on the puzzling luxury displayed by audiences at Paris theatres, he wondered who these people might be: 'autrefois, la noblesse, la cour, remplissaient les spectacles; celle ci est bannie, l'autre est peu nombreuse'.[22]

Robespierre and Saint-Just recognized, then, that in a material sense nobles were of no consequence. Since 1789, nobles had been more worthy of contempt than hatred. But in the spring of 1794, nobles suddenly became the first enemies of the state, and from this new perspective Saint-Just reinterpreted their role. In 1792, Saint-Just, taking a view that might have been espoused by d'Antraigues, a noble traditionalist, thought that it was the absolutist King who had in 1789–90 manipulated the hapless nobility, and the King who had eagerly accepted the fall of the second order: 'la royauté, isolée, accabla les ordres par le peuple', a clever plan had it not been for the fact that Louis 'n'avait pas calculé que la chute des ordres entrainerait celle de la tyrannie'.[23] But in 1794, when political concerns yielded in importance to social ones, Saint-Just inverted his earlier description: under the monarchy, he now wrote, 'la noblesse se moquait des rois, qui n'étaient comme ils le sont encore, que les premières dupes de leurs empires; l'aristocratie abhorée pour ses crimes, pesait sur la terre'.[24]

In the main, as shall be shown, the persecution of nobles was a stratagem that arose from the Jacobins' need to find a way out of their political impasse. Nobles were not proscribed for what they had done or because the destruction of feudalism required that feudal lords be once and forever brought to heel. It was to the logic of political necessity that the rights of nobles were sacrificed.

To this general statement, some exception can be taken however. Though nobles in 1794 were in a material sense powerless, it may well be that the *idea* of nobility retained enough importance to elicit the thunder of the Conventionnels. *Per se*, nobles were a *quantité négligeable*, but as the ornament and symbol of traditionalism, they did have some importance, more importance in fact than they had had since 1789. The reasoning here brings us back, in an indirect way, to the Marxist analysis of revolutionary ideology: when the Mountain attacked nobles in 1794, it was in part because the humiliation of the aristocracy could forcefully illumine the chasm that lay between the new order and the order that had been forever destroyed. 'Ce qui constitue une République,' said Saint-Just on 8 ventôse, 'c'est la destruction totale de ce qui lui est opposé.'[25]

In a round-about way, the symbolic humiliation of nobles in 1794 did have a practical political purpose. It was important in 1794 to underline once again the distinction between feudalism and revolution. Now that the Revolution had ceased to move forward and was once again defining itself in relation to the past, the spectre of the *Ancien Régime* was more haunting than it had been in 1791–3. Since Robespierre, Danton, the Mountain, and the Plaine were all trying to stabilize the Revolution, each in his or its own way, all previously closed issues were now reopened.

From the beginning of the Revolution—even of the 'pre-Revolution' in 1787–8—France had lurched forward from crisis to crisis and *journée* to *journée*. Through the first years of the Revolution, the problem of politics had been to sustain the *élan vital* of movement. At the height of this period, in 1792–3, the *Ancien Régime* appeared to be an antique system that had been destroyed forever; the idea that some parts of it might survive was unthinkable; the question then was to see how far away from older social forms the Revolution could still go. But in late 1793–4, the Revolution ceased to advance as a social movement; and the limits of its economic action were apparent: there would be, for example, no *loi agraire*. The problem of Revolutionary politics was drastically altered; the aim of politics was no longer change but stability. 'Formons la cité,' reflected Saint-Just, who added naïvely, 'Il est étonnant que cette idée n'ait pas encore été à l'ordre du jour.' Robespierre concurred and declared in floréal an II (7 May 1794): 'Le moment où le bruit de nos victoires retentit dans l'univers est celui où les législateurs de la République française doivent affermir les principes sur lesquels doivent reposer la stabilité et la félicité de la République.'

What would the new regime be like? Had its social and economic foundations been self-evident, the prospect of a return to the status quo would have been unthinkable. But, to the contrary, the Republic of Virtue was cursed by the existence of a yawning gap between its social basis (property) and its political goal (equality). Where it should stop was by no means obvious. This uncertainty affected the image that was held of nobles.

While the Revolution had moved forward, nobles became progressively more insignificant. But when the time came to stabilize the Revolution, nobles once again became a subject for concern: in early 1793, nobles were of no consequence to the bourgeoisie, except as a sop to be given to the 'plebs'. At that time, it had been the Girondins or the sans-culottes who were a threat. Even in the Vendée or at Toulon, nobles had only been important because they had received the help of Pitt and Cobourg or of misguided men, superstitious peasants, irreconcilable Catholics, perverse *fédérés*, and the like. But in the spring of 1794, when the Mountain decided to institutionalize the reign of virtue, nobles suddenly mattered once again: as social models, they retained an archetypal symbolic value. 'La république', asked Saint-Just, 'ne doit-elle donc exister que dans la tribune aux harangues et dans la charte de nos lois? La monarchie restera-t-elle dans l'état civil?' Nobles became a touchstone of comparison to gauge Revolutionary France, and Robespierre instinctively referred to the condition of the noble-born in other countries to illustrate how egalitarian France had now become:

> Le peuple français semble avoir devancé de deux mille ans le reste de l'espèce humaine; on serait tenté même de le regarder, au milieu d'elle, comme une espèce différente. L'Europe est à genoux devant les ombres des tyrans que nous punissons. . . .
>
> L'Europe ne conçoit pas qu'on puisse vivre sans rois, sans nobles; et nous, que l'on puisse vivre avec eux.
>
> L'Europe prodigue son sang pour river les chaînes de l'humanité, et nous pour les briser.[26]

The creation of a new order required as its prolegomenon the annihilation of the old. The pharaohs had erased the names of their rivals to push them to oblivion and Saint-Just would do the same for nobles. Michelet perspicaciously reconstructs what he supposes to have been the steps of Saint-Just's thinking:

Il faut exterminer l'ancien monde. . . . Mais par un procédé plus définitif que la mort. La mort le réhabilite et le fait revivre.

Il faut l'exterminer par la honte.

Droit, morale et révolution, trois choses identiques. Le contre-révolutionnaire et l'homme immoral, qui sont le même homme, doivent, également flétris, traîner le boulet, casser les pierres sur les routes, former un peuple d'ilotes. Ils faisaient travailler le peuple par corvées. Eh bien, à leur tour! . . . Les privilégiés, nobles et prêtres, seront, de droit, galériens.[27]

Consciously in Saint-Just, less consciously in others, the exclusion of the nobles became in the spring of 1794 the symbolic representation of social regeneration. In the autumn of 1792, he had argued that 'la cause de nos malheurs est dans notre situation politique'.[28] The King would have to die because the choice, as Saint-Just saw it, was a practical *political* one between the Republic and the tyrant. Séleucus had asked of his murderous queen and mother, in Corneille's *Rodogune*, 'Ne saurais-tu souffrir qu'on règne innocemment?' Saint-Just did not think so. In January 1793, his eyes were on the King and on his death as a ritual sacrifice. Louis would die so that the Republic might live: 'on ne peut règner innocemment'. But at the height of the Terror, Saint-Just, incensed by the refusal of his colleagues on the Committee of Public Safety to order the drafting of imprisoned nobles as labourers on road gangs, presented a new and abstractly *social* dichotomy between the Republic and a now rather ragged nobility:

Eh bien! s'écria Saint-Just, Marius était plus politique et plus homme d'État que vous ne le serez jamais! J'ai voulu essayer les forces, le tempérament et l'opinion du Comité de salut public. Vous n'êtes pas de taille à lutter contre la noblesse, puisque vous ne savez pas la détruire; c'est elle qui dévorera la révolution et les révolutionnaires. Je me retire du Comité.[29]

Robespierre's and Saint-Just's fear of nobles had its limits. Whether they really feared that they would not succeed in creating a new Jerusalem and that nobles might in consequence once again achieve some real prominence is doubtful. To connect their fear of failure with a fear of nobles is hazardous.

It would indeed be convenient to conclude that the destruction of nobles in the early summer of 1794 was for the Mountain a form of insurance against a sense of impending failure: oppressed by an understanding that the reign of virtue could only be a phase of

Revolutionary history (or so would run the argument), the Jacobins turned with particular savagery against the leaders of the regime they had destroyed for fear that some parts of it might survive. But in 1794 nobles were too weak to elicit a response of this sort. As a symbol for ideologues, they were feared, but as the flesh and blood leaders of counter-revolution, they did not signify.

In 1793, the persecution of nobles had been a marginal but tactically useful manoeuvre in the Jacobin political arsenal. In 1794, however, a new set of concerns gave to the nobles question a renewed and contrapuntal value: on the one hand, as has been said, the problems posed by the creation of a new regime had brought to mind the memory of the old regime. The idea of nobility had become more important because the revolutionaries had decided to stabilize the new order in opposition to the *Ancien Régime* of which nobles were a symbol. But what mattered most for nobles was that the bourgeois revolutionaries wanted to stabilize the Revolution in a particular way, as a Republic of Virtue, where the virtuous poor and the property-owning but virtuous Jacobin would unite to strike down the forces of darkness. Unable to resolve the social problem which their own policy had contributed to bring to the fore, bourgeois Jacobins in 1794 adamantly maintained that property was not at issue. It was virtuous fraternity and not social equality that was the Revolution's goal. In that context, the no longer latent conflict of rich and poor, of Jacobin and sans-culotte was side-stepped; and in that same context, nobles suddenly became the expression of anti-Jacobinism in particular and of 'anti-Revolutionism' in general.

The political purpose of the Mountain in 1794 was to create a new moral order. The principle of this social organization would be virtue; the enemy of such a regenerated France could only be corruption; the nobility was the embodiment of that vice. In this perspective, the persecution of nobles now began to make sense as the mainspring of bourgeois revolutionism. In the past, it had been a mere expedient designed to bind the 'plebs' to the Revolutionary bourgeoisie. In late 1793–4, however, the persecution of nobles became the highest expression of the people's will as the Jacobins had chosen to define it. Anti-noble propaganda now took on a new and greater dimension.

In the first years of the Revolution, the myth of noble depravity was not much bruited, because it was not at that time of particular significance to bourgeois Revolutionary goals. In early 1794, however, the supposed corruption of nobles became more critical. The philosophes had laid great stress on the corruption of nobles and the Enlightenment's *discours* on nobles now acquired a renewed significance.

Equations such as 'nature equals simplicity equals bourgeois mores' or 'noble equals *mondain* equals artifice' had been the clichés of eighteenth-century social literature. 'L'ambition dans l'oisiveté,' Montesquieu had written,

> la bassesse dans l'orgueil, le désir de s'enrichir sans travail, l'aversion pour la vérité, la flatterie, la trahison, la perfidie, l'abandon de tous ses engagements, le mépris des devoirs du citoyen, la crainte de la vertu du prince, l'espérance de ses faiblesses, et, plus que tout cela, le ridicule perpétuel jeté sur la vertu, forment, je crois, le caractère du plus grand nombre des courtisans, marqué dans tous les lieux et dans tous les temps.[30]

Bourdaloue agreed and wrote that 'A force de vivre à la cour, on se trouve rempli de ses erreurs. Quelque droiture de conscience qu'on y eût apportée, à force d'en respirer l'air et d'en écouter le langage, on s'accoutume à l'iniquité, on n'a plus tant horreur du vice, on le souffre, on l'excuse, c'est-à-dire qu'on se fait, sans le remarquer, *une conscience nouvelle*'.[31]

Nobles were, to be sure, elegant, polished, and at ease with *les usages*, qualities that were in some sense desirable but dangerous also since, as Marivaux conceded, 'l'âme se corrompt à mesure qu'elle se rafine'. Regardless of their intent, pastoral elegies, bucolic fantasies, and Rousseauistic praises of the good and the natural implied a critique of aristocratic life as it was understood—wrongly—to exist.

The same message emerged from the many novels in which noble elegance was juxtaposed to sexual licence. In Choderlos de Laclos's description of a sexually corrupt and self-seeking *beau monde*, a great noble, Valmont, the villain-hero of the *Liaisons Dangereuses*, pursues his victim, Mme de Tourvel, a noblewoman, to be sure, but of the *noblesse de robe*, a provincial, and a woman whose virtue is presented as highly untypical of her milieu. Many *libelles*, like those of Thévenau de Morande, dwelled at length on the sexual debauchery of both male and female nobles. As if this were not enough, great nobles were also commonly assumed to be either impotent or deviants of some sort.[32]

Nobles, in short, were thought to be idle and corrupt both

morally and sexually. As the fanatic anti-noble Conventionnel Dulaure put it in 1790, the nobility was a vicious institution which in all likelihood would produce 'des hommes vicieux',[33] and necessarily, when Robespierre began in the summer of 1793, to reassert his bourgeois rule over that of the sans-culottes by attacking the *enragés* the theme of noble corruption immediately came to his mind. Brushing the Hébertist Vincent aside, the Incorruptible tore at Roux (a former priest) and at Leclerc: 'le second est un jeune homme qui prouve que la corruption peut entrer dans un jeune cœur. Il a des apparences séduisantes, un talent séducteur, c'est Leclerc, un ci-devant, le fils d'un noble.'[34]

Nobles were corrupt; the Republic was virtuous. The implications of that world view were unavoidable.

In late 1793–4, nobles suddenly became the ideological and class enemies of a more virtuous French nation. Nobles would be pushed aside, perhaps banished or destroyed. This state of mind has wide implications for an understanding of both French social structure before 1789 and of Revolutionary politics.

Obviously, the eagerness with which the Revolutionary bourgeoisie threw the nobility to the wolves after 1791 must lead us to question the solidity of the élitist alliance before 1789. *Post hoc* is not *propter hoc*, but the intensity of feeling in 1794 must have had very deep roots indeed, and this must say something about the existence of a single noble-bourgeois élite on the eve of the Revolution.

The inability of the nobility to act as a corporate group and to fight back is also instructive. Contrary to what is often assumed, what is striking about the behaviour of nobles during the French Revolution, as has been said, is not their aggressiveness but their passivity. Here again, it is tempting to go back to pre-Revolutionary days in order to explain the feebleness of nobles in their time of trouble: nobles before 1789 had lost their corporate sense of identity, but they had not yet understood their dependence on the bourgeoisie. As a social group, they were neither class nor caste. In consequence, noble seigneurs were unable both to resist revolution in 1789 and to provide in 1791 as owners of property a pole of attraction which would have given the bourgeoisie cause to reflect on the strategic desirability of a policy of 'no enemies to the left'. Before 1799, nobles were neither in nor out of the new notable class. In 1794, they could neither resist the Republic's armies nor deny the ideologues' view of their distinctness. They were expendable, and as such they deserved to be humiliated, imprisoned, and in some instances, put to death.

iv. Thought and matter; corruption and decadence

The redefinition of the Revolution, and with it the heightened importance of nobles as the symbolic enemies of the new Republican state, have as their first cause the nature of the particular ideological compromise that was reached in the 1780s between individualism and community. In 1791, Barnave took up one of these two messages and tried to stabilize the Revolution around the joint defence of bourgeois and noble property, as well as of constitutional monarchy and parliamentary institutions. In 1793–4, Robespierre attempted instead to stabilize the Revolution as a Republic of Virtue, in which a sense of community might transcend the irremediable differences that would have separated rich and poor in any other institutional setting.

Both solutions were implicit in the world view of the Revolutionary bourgeoisie before 1789, as was also the uneasy conjunction of the two extremes that had prevailed in the euphoric months of 1789–90. The fate of nobles varied accordingly. Equal citizens in 1789–91, they became important conservative allies for Barnave in late 1791, and conspicuous enemies of virtue for Robespierre in late 1793.

The ideological balance of the 1780s is the origin of the vicissitudes of nobles' rights in 1789–94. Two other ideological, or perhaps cultural, concerns were also of relevance: namely, the relation that was held to exist in the early 1790s between thought and matter, and the role that was attributed to corruption as the motor of political change.

Robespierre's redefinition of the purpose of the Revolution provided an ideal way out for the Jacobins, much pressed to give more substance to the Revolutionary struggle by their popular allies on the left. That the Mountain wanted to accept such a solution is not surprising, and that the Jacobins were able to impose this solution is no less interesting.

Terror of course was their principal argument, but although the use of terror explains the Jacobins' ability to impose their views on the now chastened bourgeoisie, it does not explain their own good faith, for it seems likely that Robespierre and Saint-Just, among so many others, did not think of themselves as unusually honest men.

How then were the Montagnards able to explain to themselves the shift in the stated purpose of the Revolution from the elaboration of new social and institutional forms to the defence of a highly abstract view of the nature of the state, or stated more simply, the passing from the concrete to the theoretical?

In our own age, to pass from a practical political dilemma (i.e. material equality versus inequality) to an ideological solution (the defence of virtue against vice) would appear to be transparent. But such a transition was perhaps more acceptable culturally in the 1790s than it would have been in any of the preceding or following decades. Mind and matter were in these years very much of a piece. Cabanis in 1795 still argue that the physical and the moral were indistinguishable in both their manifestations and their substance—the elaboration of thoughts by the brain, for example, being rigorously comparable to the digestion of food by the stomach. Similarly, Schelling in the same years could proclaim that

> Now, after long wanderings [philosophy] has regained the memory of nature and of nature's former unity with knowledge. . . . Then there will no longer be any difference between the world of thought and the world of reality. There will be one world, and the peace of the golden age will make itself known for the first time in the harmonious union of all sciences. . . .[35]

Diderot's purpose in his study of diseases had been to show the identity of physical, chemical, biological, and spiritual phenomena. So was Marat's when he published in London in 1773 his *Philosophical Essay on Man, Being an Investigation of the Laws and Principles of the Reciprocal Influence of the Soul and Body*.

In a more specific way, the same interweaving of moral and material phenomena as both cause and effect also runs through a great deal of eighteenth-century political thought. Montesquieu, Voltaire, Rousseau, and Volney all characterized societies as embodying simultaneously some particular social or material configuration (such as the preponderance of nobles, a rough identity of material interests, or the size and climate of an empire) and a corresponding moral principle (honour, terror, virtue, and so on). A change in the one would affect the other:

> Je sais bien, [explained Montesquieu] que, si des causes morales n'interrompaient point les physiques, celles-ci sortiraient et agiraient dans toute leur étendue. Je sais encore que, si les causes physiques

avaient la force d'agir par elles-mêmes (comme lorsque les peuples sont habitants de montagnes inaccessibles), elles ne détruisissent bientôt la cause morale: car souvent la cause physique a besoin de la cause morale pour agir.[36]

When faced with the material particularism and hostility of their bourgeois audience, Robespierre and Saint-Just could therefore, and in good conscience, change their tack and argue that the French Revolution was after all about principle (morality) and not about social class (the *loi agraire*). In this scheme, a countervailing conservative principle—corruption—proved to be the enemy that was to be destroyed. The slide of the Mountain towards a terrorist ideology which accepted the social status quo but included the proscription of nobles was eased by the amorphous nature of Enlightenment culture.

A second ideological concern of relevance to the identification of nobles as the class enemies of the Revolution was the particular importance given in Enlightenment thought to corruption (of which nobles were the social embodiment) as the source of political decay. Virtue and corruption were established political categories, virtue as the moral foundation of the public good, and corruption as the cause of political degeneration

Methodologically, eighteenth-century political thought remained thoroughly Aristotelian in its conceptualization of political systems. Movement was seen to exist from type to type and invariably as a deviation from one principle to another. In its upward trajectory, social change was variously explained, but a negative trajectory was always ascribed to corruption. 'Un état', wrote Montesquieu, 'peut changer de deux manières: ou parce que la constitution se corrige ou parce qu'elle se corrompt. S'il a conservé ses principes et que la constitution change, c'est qu'elle se corrige: s'il a perdu ses principes, quand la constitution vient à changer, c'est qu'elle se corrompt.'[37] For some, like Rousseau, corruption was irreversible: once introduced, it could not be arrested. As John Brown put it in his book on English manners, which was translated in 1758 as *Les Mœurs angloises, ou Appréciation des mœurs et des principes qui caractérisent actuellement la nation britannique*, societies inevitably fell prey to moral degeneracy and then proceeded through various phases: 'rude, simple, civilized, polished, effeminate, corrupt and profligate'. Britain, he thought, had now run this course. That country was now irretrievably corrupt. But other writers were more optimistic about the inevitability of decay and Montesquieu, for example, assumed that corruption could be stamped out, though the cost might be high: 'quand une république est corrompue, on ne peut remédier à aucun des maux qui naissent qu'en ôtant la corruption et en rappelant les principes.[38]

The precise nature of corruption was likewise as disputed as its effects: Voltaire wrote of trade in England that it had 'enrichi les citoyens . . . contribué à les rendre libres et cette liberté à étendu le commerce à son tour', though Montesquieu said of the Dutch that 'le cœur des habitants des pays qui vivent du commerce est entièrement corrompu'.[39] What matters here, however, is that it was a denunciation of corruption, curable or incurable, that was the Enlightenment's immediate response to the appearance of political decline.

The relevance of these views to the course of Jacobin politics is clear. Because they lacked a class, or for that matter a social analysis of politics, such as Barnave had already conceived, the Jacobins would have been hard put to say why it was that the Revolution had become 'frozen' had they not been able to point to corruption as the source of their difficulties: 'le peuple est bon, juste, magnanime', said Robespierre. '[La] corruption et la tyrannie sont l'apanage exclusif de tous ceux qu'ils dédaignent.'[40] In Jacobin perspective, the extirpation of corruption (and therefore of nobles) was the necessary precondition for the re-creation of Revolutionary unanimity.

Ironically, this false interpretation of corruption as the motor of politics was, it may be added, reinforced by the minutiae of Revolutionary intrigues. In retrospect, it is the divergences of class interest between bourgeois and 'plebs' which explain for us the flow of politics in 1789–99. But what many contemporaries saw instead were plots and dishonesty.[41] What seems to us to have been the froth of politics appeared to them to be its essence. That the machinations of the liquidators of the *Compagnie des Indes* were of consequence now appears questionable. But that Robespierre thought such machinations important does make sense and is important because the accident of genuine corruption served to confirm the validity of a political theory which now appears to us to have been manifestly inadequate.

Over all, the fit was tight. A straight line ran from the breakdown of bourgeois universalism to ideological escape, to corruption as the enemy of the state, and to nobility as a symbol of corruption. Though individual nobles tucked away in their country houses might hold very still, the logic of Revolutionary politics necessarily placed them in the public eye.

v. The simultaneous reversals of sans-culottes and Jacobins on priests and nobles in the winter of 1793/1794

The growing predominance in the Jacobin politics of late 1793 and early 1794 of ideological and anti-noble motivation was evinced in many ways, but one aspect of the problem stands out: the simultaneous attenuation of the persecution of the clergy and the intensification of the campaign against nobles. The circumstances of 1794 were in this respect the opposite of those of 1792–3. In the earlier period, it was the clergy that had been most fiercely persecuted. In late 1793, the pattern was reversed. Though Catholic priests were now more hated by the urban poor than were the nobles, the nobles were more actively proscribed by the Revolutionary bourgeoisie.

Though often linked in Revolutionary parlance like Castor and Pollux, the 'caste nobiliaire' and the 'classe sacerdotale' (or as Barnave put it, 'l'aristocratie équestre et sacerdotale') were in fact handled very differently. Inevitably, the persecution of the Church was in the first years of Revolution intense and more quickly organized. Nobles, as enlightened individuals, had a distinct and useful role to play in the new order; but the ideological place of the Church within the bourgeois universalist vision in 1789 was as unclear as the institutional role of Romish priests within a sovereign nation. The resulting ambiguities enabled the Constituants to settle religious matters quite arbitrarily, and it is difficult to endorse Aulard's and Mathiez's view that the intent of the National Assembly had been to affect the Church as a civil institution only.[42]

Powerful in its own right, bourgeois anticlericalism as a political force was also amplified by popular hatred of the Church, especially in Paris, where it peaked twice, during the September massacres of 1792 and in October 1793, with the campaign of dechristianization, when priests were humiliated as had been 'no other enemy of the Revolution, no noble, no returned émigré, no rebel, no conspirator, no hoarder, no enemy of the people'.[43] Nothing seemed more important at that time than to wipe out superstition in all its forms—Catholic, Protestant, or Jewish.

Priests were more repulsive than nobles, and Antonelle, a juror on the Revolutionary Tribunal and himself a titled noble, accurately expressed this feeling: 'en me supposant ici membre d'un jury révolutionnaire, appelé, pour prononcer révolutionnairement contre les prêtres et les ci-devant nobles restés en France, je sens que dans ma conviction je déclarerais, quant au passé, les prêtres plus coupables; quant au présent, les prêtres encore plus dangereux et plus suspects.[44]

In the autumn and winter of 1793/4, however, when the popular and bourgeois Revolutions visibly diverged, the relative rights and wrongs of priests and nobles were reconsidered by all of the involved parties. Surprisingly, anti-nobilism once again became a predominantly bourgeois concern, and anticlericalism tapered off.

Instances of violence against clerics of all sorts continued to occur during the Terror, to be sure, some of them at the direct prompting of individual Conventionnels. The abbé Grégoire thought that in the summer of 1794 mass was being celebrated in only 50 of France's 40,000 parishes.[45]

None the less, historians who follow Soboul and Plongeron would agree that in the spring of 1794 both the Mountain and the Committee of Public Safety were trying to slow down popular, anticlerical excesses. Robespierre, in late November 1793, gave the signal; on 6 December 1793, the Convention as a whole reaffirmed the freedom of religion, and on 26 frimaire an II (16 December 1793) during a debate on the exclusion of nobles from the Jacobin Club, Robespierre explained the need to reverse the policy of anticlericalism:

> On pouvait sans inconvénient chasser tous les nobles des sociétés populaires. On pourrait les chasser de partout. Il n'en serait peut être pas de même des prêtres. Les campagnes ont été induites en erreur par les ennemis du peuple, toujours prêts à profiter de la moindre de nos erreurs. Rappelez vous les malheurs qui ont été la suite des mesures violentes qu'on avait prises à leur égard dans certains pays, et craignez de les voir se renouveller.[46]

Official governmental sanction for the new religious policy was also forthcoming, and in January 1794, the CPS urged the provincial *sociétés populaires* to be cautious in dealing with the last 'convulsions du fanatisme expirant. . . . Pénétrez vous bien de cette vérité: qu'on ne commande point aux consciences.'[47]

The Mountain's decision to stop or at least control anticlerical agitation is revealing of its very awkward situation in the early winter of 1793/4. It was then drawn towards two conflicting poles. The temptation of ideological escape was strong: why not anti-clericalism as a solution to the social deadlock? A renewed persecution of the Catholic clergy was definitely within the logic of a Jacobin policy that would culminate a few months later in the creation of new religious forms. Such a persecution would in fact take place in 1797–9 after the coup of fructidor, when the socially conservative Directorials purged the right, attacked the Church as it had never been attacked in modern times, and in so doing emerged, or so they thought, as defenders of the purest Republicanism.

A policy of this sort, however, was rejected by Robespierre in late 1793. The persecution of the Church, however tempting it may have been ideologically, could not be allowed in 1793–4 because it was tactically undesirable. Dechristianization had become the banner of the so-called 'sans-culotte movement', and because of this the persecution of the clergy by the bourgeois Jacobins would have had as its first effect a freer rein for the sans-culottes whose autonomy Robespierre was above all determined to destroy. The toleration of anticlericalism would have made more visible the gap between the bourgeois and the popular Revolution, a gap which the Jacobins' ideological 'flight forward' was intended to mask. Acceptable in principle, dechristianization was unacceptable in practice because of the simple fact that the 'plebs' wanted it. Because Robespierre's first aim was to bring the sans-culottes under control, he was bound to oppose whatever distinct platform the popular revolutionaries might adopt.

To make matters even more complex, Robespierre did not have much room to manoeuvre: in order to thwart the sans-culottes, he had to restrain the persecution of the clergy, but he also wished to uphold the need for the Terror, which was for him an irreplaceable means of government. Danton would have had it the other way. For him a gentler handling of the priests would have signalled the beginning of the end of the Terror. Danton's was the more consistent approach, but Robespierre was fighting a two-front war.

The precise meaning and extent of dechristianization at the local level has been questioned. It is also true that the more extreme forms of Parisian anticlericalism were abetted not only by the neo-sans-culotte Hébertists but by the more conservative bourgeois Indulgents also. None the less, and in spite of these ambiguities, it is reasonably clear that Robespierre personally equated dechristianization with *sans-culottisme* and thought it necessary to stifle or at least channel this latest popular complaint. Robespierre's solution was ingenious: he played down dechristianization as an ideological issue and presented the suppression of popular anticlericalism as a strictly political move. In this way, both of the Mountain's fundamental goals would be reached. Politically, the sans-culotte movement could be bridled. But this pause would not preclude ideological persecution in other realms; for in condemning dechristianization, Robespierre was very careful to point out that he did not object to it in principle. Paradoxically, Robespierre's denunciation of an ideological campaign (i.e. popular anticlericalism) was presented to the Mountain as a political step which did not imply any denunciation of ideological goals.

Robespierre developed this *distinguo* in some detail. As a smoke-screen, he sententiously explained that his desire to stop dechristianization had nothing to do with sans-culottes at all; it was caused, he said, by his concern for foreign policy and in response to local complaints. But it was easy to read between the lines of his speech:

> Qu'avez vous à faire dans ces circonstances? *Parler en philosophes? Non, mais en législateurs politiques*, en hommes sages et éclairés. Vous devez protéger les patriotes contre leurs ennemis, leur indiquer les pièges qu'on leur tend et vous garder d'inquiéter ceux qui auraient été trompés par des insinuations perfides; protéger enfin ceux qui veulent un culte qui ne trouble pas la société. Vous devez encore empêcher ces extravagances, ces folies qui coincident avec les plans de conspiration, il faut corriger les écarts du patriotisme, mais faites-le avec le ménagement qui est dû à des amis de la liberté, qui ont été un instant égarés. . . . [Italics mine.][48]

Restated *en clair*, Robespierre's message was that anticlericalism ought not to be considered in an ideological context. The question was a political one. Extremists would be forgiven on condition of future good behaviour. The Mountain would not rule against the sans-culottes; a discreet veil would be drawn over those acts of dechristianization which had already taken place. But neither did the Mountain intend to share power with the sans-culottes. After November 1793, independent sans-culotte political action was a thing of the past.

The joined persecutions of priests and nobles which had progressed apace in 1792–3 now diverged. In the past, both priest and nobles had been simultaneously pilloried for largely opportunistic reasons by a Revolutionary bourgeoisie intent on capturing a popular rural and urban audience. But with an economic crisis and the disjunction of the bourgeois and popular Revolutions, in late 1793 nobles and priests found themselves in very different situations: because they were attacked by the popular revolutionaries, priests fell under a manner of officia bourgeois protection. Nobles, to the contrary, came under renewed pressure as the bourgeois revolutionaries were forced to give a new and more ideological definition of their purpose.

The nobles lost what the clergy gained, and in the province those agents of the CPS who did not understand this realignmen were brought to heel. On 2 May 1794, Mallarmé wrote to Paris to explain that he was doing all he could to persecute the clergy, who were 'des hommes plus faux, plus scélérats que les nobles' becaus they united 'la fourbe hypocrisie' to the characteristic pride o nobles.[49] Mallarmé concentrated his energies on priests and explained proudly that he had also done all that was humanl possible to destroy the 'pagodes extérieures du culte papiste' a well as the 'boutiques de fanatisme chrétien'. But on 15 May, he was recalled to Paris, much to his surprise and anxiety. On 28 May the Committee of Public Safety then laid out that even in the Vendée priests ought not to be prosecuted as priests, 'cette qualit inconnue dans l'ordre politique ne devant attirer à ceux qui la possède ni indulgence, ni sévérité, c'est comme rebelles ou factieu qu'ils doivent être punis',[50] a surprising statement coming as it di little more than a month after the decree dismissing all nobles from public employment, though nobility was certainly more than priesthood a 'qualité inconnue dans l'ordre politique'.

Michelet was puzzled by the Jacobins' exclusion of nobles and their tolerance of priests, since he rightly thought that priests wer a far more coherent social order than nobles: 'combien les noble généralement formaient moins un corps! combien ils étaient moin serrés, moins habiles à combiner, à calculer d'ensemble leu efforts et leurs intrigues! Les prêtres, ce corps redoutable, gardien fatal, immuable, de toute la tradition contre-révolutionnaire pour un serment (dont ils sont, par leurs règles, déliés d'avance) les voilà bons républicains, jugés et acceptés tels.'[51]

The idiosyncracies of Robespierre's character must, he though explain the persecution of nobles and not of priests, which woul otherwise make no sense. But the coupling of anti-nobilism and neo-clericalism does in fact make better sense when placed in the double context of the bourgeoisie's tactical political battle against the sans-culottes and of the ideological crisis in Revolutionary politics.

The position of the Mountain and of the sans-culottes with regard to nobles was now reversed. Nobles had become the ideological enemies par excellence of the Revolutionary bourgeoisie. Conversely, for the sans-culottes, pushed out of active politics by Robespierre and his allies, nobles lost the meaning they had had earlier, in the spring of 1793. Nobles then had been the first enemies of the people. But now, it was the Revolutionary bourgeoisie itself which stood in the way of sans-culottes; nobles suddenly became irrelevant, almost to be pitied by the poor as fellow victims of bourgeois greed. This was almost certainly the most astonishing *renversement des alliances* of the entire French Revolution, though curiously it has been neglected by historians of the period.

In the spring of 1793, it was the Mountain that temporized about excluding nobles from the army, something which the sans-culottes at the time were intensely eager to secure. Marat, who now sat in the Convention with Robespierre, did not ask for the removal of all noble generals, but Roux, the leader of the *enragés*, vociferously and repeatedly demanded at that time the expulsion of all nobles without exception from the officers corps, together with the head of Custine: 'Les traîtres ne se convertissent jamais. . . . Sous le règne des lois fondées sur la liberté et l'égalité, c'est une erreur, c'est une folie, c'est un crime d'élever aux fonctions publiques ceux qui portent en naissant la livrée de l'esclavage. . . . Les *nobles* ne sont pas des citoyens, mais des janissaires; ils ne sont pas de soldats, mais des assassins.'[52]

In December 1793, however, positions were reversed. On the right, Robespierre sharpened his attack on nobles, whose existence was now incompatible with the deceptive ideological radicalism of the Jacobin Revolution. On the left, Roux, in a truly amazing change of heart, now took up the nobles' cause.

Roux's reasoning was explicit. In the past, it had made sense for the people to attack the nobles: 'Pauvre peuple, lorsque tu gémissais sous le joug des rois, il était naturel d'attribuer à l'abus des pouvoirs, à la digestion des mauvaises lois, aux caprices du despote, à la perfidie de la cour, à la corruption du gouvernement les malheurs sans nombre qui t'accablaient.' But who were the enemies of the people now? 'Ce sont . . . les traîtres, les monopoleurs, les agioteurs, les accapateurs, les sangsues publiques. . . .' What was the point of imprisoning nobles? It did no good and some harm. Where was justice if innocents were imprisoned because they had been born nobles?

This passage is central to the explanation of the nobles problem presented here, and it deserves to be extensively quoted in its own right. Nobles ought not to be imprisoned, Roux explained, if they have not personally committed some offence:

Il y a oppression, contre le corps social, lorsqu'un seul de ses membres est opprimé, et vous signeriez l'arrestation de cent mille citoyens, dont la plupart sont demeurés armés dans leurs foyers, ont fait de grands sacrifices à la chose publique, et n'ont à se reprocher d'autre crime, que d'être nés d'une caste privilégiée qu'ils abhorrent, et d'avoir hérité des domaines de leurs aïeux? . . .

To do so was to revive the most vicious practice of pre-Revolutionary legislation:

C'est ressusciter le fanatisme que d'imputer à un homme les crimes de sa naissance. C'est le comble de la cruauté de faire incarcérer, comme suspects à la République, ceux qui ont eu le malheur de déplaire à un commissaire de section, à un espion de la police, à un garçon de bureau, à un secrétaire de la trésorerie, à un huissier de la Convention nationale, à un guichetier, au président d'une société populaire, et à la catin d'un homme en place.

Roux felt deeply about the question and in mid-September 1793 devoted most of an issue of his *Publiciste* (Number 265) to the unjust persecution of nobles. The Mountain was implored to be more just to ci-devant nobles:

Députés de la Montagne, qui avez posé les bases de notre bonheur dans une constitution qui a fixé les regards des savants, et l'approbation de l'homme vertueux; vous devez être sévères envers les fédéralistes, les contre-révolutionnaires; envers ceux qui s'opposent à la levée des troupes, au paiement des contributions, envers ceux qui calomnient l'évangile des lois républicains, ou qui fomentent l'explosion de la guerre civile.

Some people should be punished: federalists, hoarders, conspirators, but not nobles *per se*; and Roux reminded the Convention that the nobility no longer had legal substance as a corporate order:

s'il n'y a plus d'autre distinction entre les hommes, que celle qu'engendre l'innocence ou le crime, l'insouciance ou l'amour de la patrie, regardez-les tous du même œil, dès qu'ils adorent l'étoile de la constitution républicaine . . . le génie de la liberté a frappé d'anathème les privilèges et les corporations; vous ne devez plus reprocher à un individu les vices de la caste à laquelle souvent il appartenait, malgré lui; la nature n'a pas donné à tous les hommes, des organes révolutionnaires; mais elle les a tous créés pour l'humanité de pour goûter les charmes de la vertu.[53]

Taken at face value, Roux's turn-around on nobles is indeed, as Walter Markow remarked, astounding. But it is too easy to conclude as Markow does that Roux had been 'gripped' by an emotional sympathy for the innocent nobles he had met in prison[54] or as did Mathiez that 'since he [had been] imprisoned at Sainte-Pélagie', Jacques Roux appreciated legality and blamed excesses.[55] To my mind, a purely personal explanation of Roux's dramatic reversal is not sufficient. Roux, in fact, was not the only *enragé* who showed sympathy for imprisoned nobles during the autumn of 1793. Taboureau, an important figure at Orléans, whom Mathiez described as 'much superior to the Parisian *enragés*', the only one of them, he thought, whose name would survive for posterity, was following a similar tack.[56]

Taboureau, or as he called himself before 1789, Taboureau de Montigny, may have been a noble himself, since his wife was exiled from Paris when, according to the law, the noble status of married women depended on that of their husbands. Before the Revolution, Taboureau had been an outspoken enemy of grain merchants and of what he called 'la liberté fatale du commerce'. Far from allowing *laissez-faire* and *laissez-aller*, the State, he thought, should regulate the grain trade on behalf of the poor: 'Et vous, grand Roi,' he wrote, 'souvenez-vous que vous avez le glaive du pouvoir entre les mains pour nous soutenir contre ceux que l'inégal partage des richesses nationales a rendus nos maîtres.'[57]

His very well developed ideas were, as Mathiez, points out, a blend of traditionalist anti-commercialism and of a more novel appreciation of the class of producers. In 1792, he lambasted 'la fange commerciale' and the men who had acquired 'le titre d'honnête gens qu'à force scélératesse', which was not altogether new, but he also spoke of 'La misère des ouvriers [qui] les soumet toujours à l'arbitrage de ceux qui les emploient.'

His views on the representation of the poor at the Estates General were of a piece. Just as some merchants then claimed that commerce deserved a special representation, so did Taboureau foreshadow the disintegration of the Third Estate as a social entity by denouncing in 1789 the right of the merchants to represent the poor. The rich should be excluded, whether traders or landlords, all of them lumped in one category, which was made up, he thought, of 'tous ceux qui sont intéressés au désordre actuel'.

With the Revolution, Taboureau soon became prominent: he even became notorious in 1792 when he wrote a pamphlet on behalf of rioters who had succeeded in forcing grain sellers to lower the price of bread in a very wide area running from the Seine to the Loire; and in a letter to the Girondin Minister of the Interior, Roland, the politically moderate mayor of Orléans denounced Taboureau's essay as an 'écrit infernal'.

When the Montagne supplanted the Gironde, Taboureau's behaviour did not improve, and he soon quarrelled with the Montagnard Conventionnel who had been sent on mission to Orléans. In October 1793, Taboureau was arrested on two charges, a vague one of stirring the people up against the authorities, and a more specific one of pro-nobilism. His greatest fault, it seems, was that he acted on behalf of the marquis de la Tour du Pin, then imprisoned at Orléans:

Considérant qu'en se constituant le défenseur officieux d'un ci-devant noble détenu dans la maison d'arrêt comme suspect, le citoyen Taboureau s'est immiscé dans des fonctions absolument inutiles, puisque l'arrestation est prescrite par les lois contre cette classe dangereuse;

Considérant enfin que la malveillance, dont les subsistances sont le prétexte, se manifeste depuis quelques jours d'une manière inquiétante et qu'il est temps de faire connaître au peuple qu'il est trompé et de l'éclairer sur le compte de ceux qui, par des motions incendiaires, écartent les subsistances en alarmant le cultivateur. . . . [Le comité] est d'avis de faire mettre en arrestation le citoyen Taboureau comme suspect par ses relations secrètes avec les ci-devant nobles et par ses écrits sur les subsistances, pour être ensuite ordonné par le représentant du peuple ce qu'il jugera convenable pour la sûreté de la ville d'Orléans.[58]

Subsequent events are hard to follow. Taboureau is not on record as having denied the charge outright, but he was later cleared from the accusation of pro-nobilism by the Revolutionary Committee of Surveillance of the Loiret, which attested that Taboureau had not accepted payment from La Tour du Pin and that he had refused to become his 'défenseur officieux'. This in turn, however, leads us to suppose that Taboureau had indeed acted on behalf of the marquess as his unpaid, unofficial defender, an even more revealing commitment.

Various interpretations of Taboureau's arrest are possible. One of them, of course, is that the charge was wholly trumped up and should be seen as an aspect of the bourgeoisie's efforts to denigrate the popular revolutionaries by dreaming up charges of ultra-citra conspiracy. But Taboureau's case is too specific to be seen in this way. In all probability, the man was guilty of something, and it is altogether possible that Taboureau had followed in the autumn of 1793 an intellectual evolution similar to Roux's.

Taboureau's case is not completely clear, but then it must be remembered that evidence about the *enragés* is generally scanty. We know nothing, for example, about Taboureau's politics during the critical months when the Montagnards defeated the Girondins. Indeed, there was no *enragé* 'movement' (Varlet and Roux hardly knew one another), and only four men achieved prominence as *enragé* spokesmen. But given the paucity of information and the small number of people involved, it is quite remarkable that even two instances of *enragé* pro-nobilism, one explicit and the other one at least implied, should have come down to us.

The motives of the actors in these weeks of intense crisis are difficult to unravel. Some statements and actions appear to have been deliberate, like Robespierre's conclusion that dechristianization should be considered politically and not ideologically. Other gestures are more complex, such as Robespierre's decision to step up the persecution of nobles as an ideological solution to a social deadlock. Inference here is of greater use than direct evidence, since it was very difficult for even Robespierre fully to understand why it was that he was doing what he did. But Roux's shift on the ci-devants was highly explicit, and its significance lies precisely in the apparent anomaly which it represents.

In the autumn of 1793, Roux clearly understood that the continued proscription of nobles was, in popular perspective, conceptually useless and tactically pointless. Earlier in the year, in the spring and summer of 1793, the push against nobles had been the useful means of mobilizing sans-culotte energies. But by late 1793, the situation was reversed: to encourage anti-nobilism made no strategic sense from a popular point of view. It was no longer in the sans-culottes' interest to insist on this platform which the bourgeoisie had taken up in order to justify its pose as a friend of the people, a pose which Roux of course denied. His tactical stance on nobles mirrored in reverse that of Robespierre on the clergy. Roux's reversal on the nobles problem is revealing, not only as it relates to the rights of nobles during the Revolution but as an indication also of the nature and tempo of political thought during the Revolution.

When placed in the context of French history before or after the Revolution, a reliance on the vocabulary of social class for 1789–99 must seem wrong or offensive. Social structure before 1789 was fluid, and the undeveloped nature of class and class consciousness in nineteenth- and twentieth-century France is also well known. But the French Revolution was unique, not in any trivial sense, but because the frantic rhythm of change in 1789–99, especially in 1791–5, brought into sharp focus loyalties or fears which in other times were much less keenly felt. As Dr Johnson remarked, the prospect of hanging wonderfully concentrates the minds of men. The transition from a vision of social harmony to one of class warfare, which might take decades elsewhere, took place in Paris in the space of months. In 1790, all men were brothers; estates had ceased to exist; but by 1794, class had suddenly and undeniable emerged. As a moderate Republican publicist, Lenglet, put it in 1798, 'D'un côté, on entendait répéter: *l'inégalité des fortunes ne peut être garantie que par l'inégalité des droits politiques*; de l'autre, on criait: *l'égalité des droits ne peut être garantie que par l'égalité des biens. . . .*' For a brief moment, there seemed to be no middle course.

Robespierre's change of mind on economics and *subsistance*, in the spring of 1793, like Roux's reversal on nobles in the autumn of 1793, must be placed in this context of a growing and even overwhelming sense of the existence of class, a sense whose ephemeral nature ought not to mislead us about its vividness and importance. To be sure, Robespierre and Roux may have had private motives. But their change of views were also reflections of a world-historical event, that is, of the momentary appearance of a new social structure, an event which transcended their private wills. More often than not, history works through agents who are unable to understand the historical importance of their own actions: this is the sense of Hegel's Cunning of History, 'der List der Vernunft', and it is often true that political figures in difficult times achieve meaningful historical stature precisely by going against their private inclinations in order to reach goals that are imposed on them by the logic of events.

A word can be said about the relevance of Roux's change of heart to the nature and method of argument that has been used in these pages. The fact of Roux's reversal on nobles—and perhaps of Taboureau's also—has been available to historians for some decades, though little has been made of it, and the lacuna here brings to mind again the question of historical categories.

Every approach that has been brought to bear on the history of the Revolution has yielded critical insights. It is essential to understand, for example, that the economic origins of sans-culottes were widely divergent, as it matters also to realize that sans-culottes, taken one by one, were often unstable, marginal men, on the edge of social life.. But these categories, for all of their undeniable and crucial value, do still leave a few blanks.

One of these voids relates to the sans-culottes' obsession about nobles in the summer of 1793, and their striking turn-around in the autumn of that year, accompanied by the parallel, though inverse, change of mind of the Montagnards. The usefulness of any theoretical approach lies in the light it throws on previously puzzling facts. It can, I think, be argued that the heretofore ignored girations of both sans-culottes and Montagnards on the nobles issue produce under inspection a useful theory. The event acquires a greater meaning when set in its theoretical framework and the theory of a declining and contradictory bourgeois universalism acquires greater plausibility for its ability to explain this discrete event.

vi. Robespierre and Saint-Just on nobles

The views of Saint-Just and Robespierre on nobles were much of a piece, but they were not completely alike, and the nuances that separated them are revealing of Robespierre's greater awareness of the contradiction that had developed between Jacobin theory and practice.

Of the two men, it was Monsieur le Chevalier de Saint-Just, as Camille Desmoulins called him, who had the more trenchant view of nobles, and it was with some justice that Barère could write of the younger man that he execrated 'la noblesse autant qu'il aimait le peuple'.[60] The differences between the two tribunes, locked in Revolutionary friendship, was not properly understood at the time. In an omitted section of his farewell address of 8 thermidor, Robespierre complained of his 'bad press' on this issue: 'on répandait le bruit que Saint-Just était noble, et qu'il voulait sauver les nobles; on répandait en même temps que je voulais les proscrire'.[61]

Robespierre's annoyance was partly justified. Barère's memoirs make it plain that it was Saint-Just and not Robespierre who pushed for anti-noble laws. A small incident bears Barère out: though both men were ideologues in the grand manner, neither despised mundane police work of a trivial sort, and Saint-Just, in his *Bureau de Police Générale*, found time to deal with the case of an army officer who had refused to put away his gold-framed cross of Saint-Louis, a military decoration that Saint-Just *père* had himself received. Saint-Just *fils* was not amused, and very peremptorily required that the '*coquin*' be arrested and traduced 'à la Conciergerie de brigade en brigade'.[62] It is at least curious that Robespierre should have demurred, first by suspending and then by rescinding the order. In short, Robespierre was more hesitant on nobles than was Saint-Just, but in one way at least, more constant also. For Robespierre, nobles had rights as individuals even if they were dangerous as a group, and some compromise would have to be made between the theoretical need for tolerance and the practical need for exclusion.

To be sure, in 1791 already, even before Varennes, Robespierre had demanded that the army be purged of counter-revolutionary ci-devant officers:

> Tous les gens de cette caste funeste, qui joignent à la maladie incurable de l'orgueil et des préjugés quelque franchise et quelque fierté se sont rangés en bataille contre nous. Tout ce qu'il y avait parmi eux de plus bas et de plus pervers courtisans ont continué de nous caresser pour nous trahir, pour attiser, au milieu de nous, le feu de la guerre civile, pour séduire l'armée, pour opprimer la patriotisme. . . . Décrétez le licencement de l'état-major de l'armée. . . .[63]

Obnoxious nobles, then, deserved to be dismissed. But at the same time, good nobles deserved protection, and on 8 thermidor, Robespierre was still adamantly denying that it was his wish to proscribe all nobles. Some nobles were guilty, but others were innocent: 'Le Peletier était noble.'[64] So did the Incorruptible in July 1793 take pains to protect the General marquis de la Valette who proved, one year later, to be very loyal. Imprisoned by the Convention, la Valette was ordered to be released by the rebellious Robespierrist Paris Commune on 9 thermidor at 9.30 p.m. and lived to share his master's fate on the next day.

For Robespierre, nobles were to some extent protected by

Revolutionary principle, as they were also by practical necessity. Pushing nobles out of the Jacobin Club was a politically advantageous move that would disarm the ultra left. Pushing nobles out of the army was something else. In the late summer of 1793, Robespierre, then under much pressure from the sans-culottes, did recognize the desirability of such an exclusion. But his endorsement of this 'grande mesure révolutionnaire' was a calculated statement designed to appease the 'plebs', and he had no intention of doing much about it.[65] The problem was that although his double standard made sense in practice, it was difficult to explain: on 20 August 1793, Robespierre refuted Hébert, who wanted to deport all nobles, but he then went on to admit that all nobles should be barred from public office. If ci-devants were allowed to hold a position in the government, Robespierre explained, the administration of the state would soon be theirs. The proper path between the Scylla of deportation and the Charybdis of participation, he promised to define in some 'mesure générale', which, noted the *Journal de la Montagne*, 'il ne désigne pas pourtant, mais dont il établit la nécessité'.

Robespierre could not make up his mind, and in December 1793, he went so far as to fall back on the thought that nobles themselves should resolve the nobles problem. True, he said, there were patriotic nobles, but on balance nobles today were 'aussi perfides, aussi insolens qu'ils le furent toujours'. Ci-devant nobles were especially obnoxious for their leadership of ultra factions. Good nobles would understand, therefore, that the safety of the Republic demanded the exclusion of all nobles from the Jacobin society. In short, the law should not banish nobles but nobles should be treated as if they deserved to be banished. Patriotic aristocrats would realize that this had to be the case.[66]

On the face of it, Robespierre was more confused about nobles than was Saint-Just but more steady in his devotion to principle and less swayed by the political evolution of the times. A different argument can be made, however, to show that because the views of Saint-Just were less subjective, he was equally consistent, though to another, shifting standard.

Although the purpose of the Revolution veered dramatically in 1794, Robespierre continued to pay some heed to the principles of 1789. Saint-Just, by contrast, was more faithful to the spirit of Revolutionary change. For if the purpose of the Revolution had become to make men really equal, the individual responsibility of nobles was now irrelevant. Did it make sense to protect individual

nobles and to defend the idea that 'les fautes sont personnelles' i
the true purpose of the Revolution was to assert not the rights o
man but the rights of men, of collectivities, of classes, and of the
poor against the rich? In this perspective, the rights of nobles hac
to be sacrificed if the progress of the Revolution required it. The
greater intransigence of Saint-Just on the nobles issue in Apri
1794 parallels his determination in March 1794 to give substance
to the decrees of ventôse on the redistribution of property. There
also, Saint-Just had gone further than his colleagues when he
urged that the confiscated property of suspects be given away tc
the poor, a suggestion that was not taken up in the decree
presented by the Committee of Public Safety to the Convention

More than Robespierre, Saint-Just understood in the spring o
1794 that the Revolution had come to a standstill. The formalistic
bourgeois definition of universalism had proved insufficient. The
ways in which Saint-Just intended to transcend the deadlock tha
he now apprehended were contradictory. He wished to give
bourgeois universalism more material content through a
redistribution of some property, but he also intended to accentuate
the compensatory ideological universalism of the Republic o
Virtue by destroying even the memory of nobility. Although the
solutions differed radically, both had their origin in his basic
apprehension that the bourgeois Revolution had come to a deac
end.

From one perspective, Robespierre can be given credit for
having remained faithful to the principles of bourgeois
universalism as they were understood in 1789; from another, it i
Saint-Just who can be said to have had a deeper understanding o
the Revolution's need to transcend a social stance that was made
obsolete by the drift of events.

vii. Jacobin ideology in a social void

What nobles were or were not doing in the summer of 1794 wa
largely irrelevant to their fate. What mattered was the image tha
was held of them by men who would have liked to make society
more just but lacked the power and, ultimately, the desire to do so
For that reason, a connection exists between the thought o
Robespierre and Saint-Just on nobles and their wider under
standing of politics. It was hardly accidental that Saint-Jus
should have been at once more bellicose about nobles and more
determined to do something for the poor. It was also revealing tha

Saint-Just developed a more abstract justification of government than did Robespierre. The views of the two men on nobles were a reflection of their more general concern for the nature of government and of the social good.

The political programmes of both Robespierre and Saint-Just were by 1794 cut loose from any social basis, as was also their ideological vision of what France should become. For Robespierre, the justification of a minority and terrorist government lay in Rousseau's dissociation of the general and of the majority will. Saint-Just was even bolder: for Robespierre, some connection, however lax, would eventually relate institutional and social forms; but the younger man brashly separated governmental institutions from any social forms whatever and linked them instead to nature: 'puisqu'il n'est point de société si elle n'est point fondée sur la nature, la cité ne peut reconnaître d'autre lois que celles de la nature. Ces lois sont l'indépendance et la conservation. La loi n'est donc pas l'expression de la volonté mais celle de la nature.'[67] In some respects, Robespierre and Saint-Just were pragmatists who, for some months, succeeded in humbling their enemies at home and abroad. But both men were also utopians.

Most historians of the Montagnard dictatorship have dwelt on the realism of the Committee of Public Safety. They have likewise stressed the practicality of the Jacobins' social vision, and especially of Robespierre's goal, which one historian has described as a 'society of small producers, owning some land, a small shop, a boutique'.[68] In a literal sense, such an interpretation cannot be denied, although the emphasis on the relevance of the word 'small' to the plans of Robespierre and Saint-Just is anomalous. In any case, the France of yeoman farmers and small landowners which the Incorruptible and his friend would have liked to see had very little resemblance to France as it then was, a country where most men by far were landless and where most land by far did not belong to those who worked it. It is true, but only partly true, to say as did Lefebvre that Robespierre's social programme was 'in accord with the economic conditions of his time'.[69] The 'realism' of Robespierre's stand was more apparent than real.

Nor does Robespierre really differ from Saint-Just in this respect. On the face of it, Robespierre's vision was more restrained than the *outré* designs of his younger friend, which were intended to offend. But the difference was of degree rather than of kind. Robespierre, more politic, proposed an egalitarian solution which would not overly deny 'l'inégalité inévitable des biens'; Saint-Just, more wild, spun out dreams of moral equality and of children socialized in a Spartan environment of vegetarian militarism. But as neither view corresponded to any social bedrock, Robespierre's perspective was, in the end, just as unacceptable as Saint-Just's. The flaw in both approaches was the same. That Robespierre's vision was expressed in Jeffersonian terms, where for the other man 'nature' alone could provide a key, is in the main irrelevant. Robespierre's vision appears to be more balanced, but it flies forward towards egalitarian theory in an escape from the social realities of the time.

It could in fact be suggested, half-seriously, that a true continuum extends from the speculations of Saint-Just and Robespierre to those of, let us say, Sade, who stands to Saint-Just as Saint-Just does to Robespierre. For once it had been decided that politics ought not to be the expression of some social force but should deal instead with the imposition on bourgeois society below of some subjective egalitarian vision; any man's fancy could readily become a political programme of sorts. It was nature and equality which Sade invoked also to justify access not just to property, but to sexual fulfilment as well: 'les femmes naissent vulgivagues', he wrote, 'c'est-à-dire jouissant des avantages des autres animaux femelles et appartenant, comme elles et sans aucune exception, à tous les mâles; . . . aucun homme ne peut être exclu de la possession d'une femme, du moment qu'il est clair qu'elle appartient décidément à tous les hommes.'[70] Sade then went on to consider man's natural right to theft, calumny, rape, and murder ('j'ai promis partout le même logique et je tiendrai parole').

Such elaborations were, in 1794, quite sterile, though they appear to have acquired greater relevance in recent years. Robespierre's efforts to reconcile virtue and community with individualism and property were no more fruitful. Subjective desire was their mainspring, also, rather than an objective respect for social fact as it then was.

Two years later, in 1795–6, Babeuf clearly grasped this fact and then pitched his programme to the wishes of another, more popular audience. But in 1794, Saint-Just and Robespierre remained, in a way, ideological innocents. Though their constructs now offended the propertied bourgeoisie and no longer pleased the poor, they persisted in going on, convinced to the end of the lasting power of ideas. The hollowness of their programme was made all too obvious on 9 thermidor when their regime collapsed from within, on the Convention's floor, amid general indifference and relief.

viii. Jews and nobles: social and political cross-currents in France and Germany

This discussion of the place of nobles in the Revolutionary politics of 1793–4 was introduced by a comparison of the historical method used here and that used in current German historiographical work. The discussion can conclude with a juxtaposition of the persecution of nobles in 1794 and of Jews in Hitlerite Germany.

The analogy involves the intersection, common to both cases, of short-run and long-run perceptions of Jews and nobles. The travail of French nobles had its deepest roots in the disintegration of traditional French society, and so did modern German anti-Semitism have its secular origins in a very rapid and socially disrupting industrialization, a nostalgia for traditional values, as well as in the machinations of German political élites eager to circumscribe universal suffrage.

But anti-Semitism in 1933 was also reinforced by the intersection of these secular racial and economic views with the German bourgeoisie's diagnosis of its immediate problems. The fit was perfect between the short-run perception of Germany stabbed in the back, of crumbling bourgeois values with little men squeezed by financiers, and the longer view of Jews as duplicitous, corrupt, and avaricious. In the same way, the longer Enlightenment view of the particularism and corruption of nobles overlapped in 1794 with the Mountain's diagnosis of the Republic's many problems. As egalitarians who were unable to achieve equality and as virtuous, enlightened enemies of immorality the revolutionaries instinctively leaned to the exclusion of the group which had become in the eighteenth century the symbol of inequality and corruption.

Another analogy lies in the relevance of the two groups, nobles and Jews, to the societies which persecuted them. Both categories were ancient and familiar, but by that same token, ironically irrelevant to current social strain. The selection of Jews (or of nobles in an earlier setting) as a source of evil was a natural response to the appearance of social problems whose root was social change, a social change which in turn had emptied older social groupings (like Jews and nobles) of their social substance. The irony of history in this instance was that the strains of modernization were incomprehendingly blamed on older categories which modernization was making obsolete. The German *Mittelstand*, saturated with a traditionalist mythology of *Blut und Boden*, explained the convulsions of capitalism by making reference to a traditional category, Jews. In the same manner, the modernizing Revolutionary bourgeoisie, faced with the breakdown of its universalist programme and politics, found in an established, almost ancient category (the corrupt nobility) an immanent explanation for its current failure. 'Dans le système de la révolution française', explained Robespierre, 'ce qui est immoral est impolitique, ce qui est corrupteur est contre-révolutionnaire.' Nobles, as was well known, were the embodiment of corruption. To destroy corruption would break up the dam that had stopped up Revolutionary fervour.

The animosity of bourgeois for nobles and of 'Aryans' for Jews has a further point of contact in the disproportion between the punishment and the crime. The hatred of the victors for their victims can be understood as a displacement from one sphere to another of new types of frustrations created by a changing social structure. In other words, bourgeois detested nobles not only because nobles were a marginal and traditional category, as were Jews, but because their own situation in the new class structure, which they did not fully understand, created within them an unprecedented anxiety that was real but which they could not fully articulate. The persecutions of Jews in the 1930s and of nobles in the 1790s came at moments when the fears and hatreds that characterized social life at the time were apprehended but not understood. The sudden swelling of feeling against a society of orders in 1789 implied the existence of a new web of tensions different from those that had existed in a society of estates. Paradoxically, the trappings of a society of orders focus hatred precisely at the moment when they become definitively irrelevant. In France, a more organic and traditional society would not have generated the bitterness which nobles elicited in 1789–99, while a more mechanistic one would have produced new categories (like the celebrated *classes dangereuses*), which would have channelled bourgeois fears and anxieties.

Another analogy, though of a wholly different sort, can be drawn between the actual fate of Jews and nobles, not in Europe where the disproportion is ghastly and enormous, but in the French context, where it makes more sense. About one-half of the Jews who resided in France in 1940 died in concentration camps. But because the great majority of Jews handed over by Vichy to the Germans were foreign-born, only 10 per cent of French-born Jews were deported and only 4 per cent of native-born French Jews were put to death in 1942–5. The figure is much closer to the 3 per cent of nobles who died in 1789–99 than to the figure for Jews residing in Holland, let us say, of whom only 15 per cent survived the war. The proportion of French nobles and French Jews imprisoned in their respective times of persecution are similarly comparable.

Historically, however, the interesting analogy between anti-nobilism and anti-Semitism does not lie in some comparison of suffering, obviously much greater for the victims of German than of French brutality, but centres on the place of dissidents in a bourgeois but non-mechanistic state. In that respect, the comparison is a fruitful one, which is symbolized by the use of common stereotypes. Nobles in 1794, like Jews in Dreyfus's time, were thought to be cosmopolitan, politically unbalanced (extreme left or extreme right, citra and ultra, Rothschild and Trotsky), sly, cowardly, sectarian, selfish, godless, degenerate, hostile to manual labour, and sexually perverse, a set of similarities which was skillfully drawn out by Jean Renoir in his *Rules of the Game* of 1939, whose protagonist is that *rara avis*, a titled Jew.

Like German Jews in 1935, French nobles during the Revolution were, so to speak, *nationsunfähig*. Their corporate distinctiveness was indelible, and the comparison has specific application. The Directorials' detestation of corporate survivals, as is well known, ran deep, but it did have two exceptions: Jews and nobles. Nobles were considered as a group; their rights as individuals were waived, and so to some extent were those of the Jews. This point emerged in connection with the nationalization of the Jews' corporate debt, inherited from the *Ancien Régime*. As Saladin vainly argued to the Five Hundred, this corporate debt, like all other debts, was now the responsibility of the national French State. It could not be treated differently. To refuse nationalization, he explained, would be unconstitutional and tantamount to recognizing that Jews had 'la faculté ou le droit de s'agréger encore en corporations; et ce droit ou cette faculté ne peuvent plus appartenir en France à aucune portion de citoyens, qui ne sont plus que des individus, et qui n'ont plus chacun que les droits d'un seul'.[71] This same argument might of course have applied to nobles. But though all men were created equal, some, it appears, were decidedly more unequal than others. Saladin's plea was rejected. There are exceptions to every rule.

Chapter Six

1795–1799: The ideological failure of the Directory and the renewed persecution of nobles

i. Class, caste, and ideology during the Directory

The uninterrupted decay of nobles' rights from the summer of 1789 to the summer of 1794 was expressive of the evolution of French politics as a whole. The evolution and re-establishment of some of these rights during the next five years was equally representative but more confused. The relationship of bourgeois and nobles before 1789 was ambiguous. Though lines of caste had largely broken down, an awareness of surviving distinctions of status remained sharp. Nobles could be seen as models of bourgeois success in a society which would reward individual achievement; both bourgeois and nobles shared a common concern for the defence of property. But at the same time, the bourgeoisie of the late Enlightenment was ideologically inclined to consider 'le peuple' (rather than class) as the self-evident matrix of political action and social life. The bourgeoisie's purse was to the right, but its heart was to the left. From these confused premisses, various policies emerged.

For some months, it seemed possible to have the best of all possible worlds. In 1789–91, nobles and bourgeois were theoretically reconciled as a benevolent élite whose rule was freely accepted by a nation of equal citizens, where differences of wealth no longer mattered. The *Fête de la Fédération*, Lafayette's finest hour, and 14 July 1790 were the expression of this mood.

In 1791, the arrangement broke down. Now the revolutionaries decided that they would have to choose between Barnave's conservative policy ('La Révolution est finie') or Brissot's 'popular front' solution: the worsening of the nobles' place in French life was an inevitable result of the bourgeois revolutionaries' decision to follow the more daring, progressive course. Then, in a third phase, from late 1793 to the summer of 1794, when the consequences of this democratic policy emerged, the bourgeoisie made up for the failure of its universalism in practice by accentuating it in theory. But the effects on the rights of nobles were the same. For one reason or another, aristocrats in 1791–4 had proved steadily more expendable.

The evolution of the rights of nobles in the following period (1795–9) reflected similar lines of fundamental social and ideological divisions but in less linear fashion. These were years of uncertain transition, when the relation in France of class and caste to ideology and politics was unusually confused. Social tensions between rich and poor had reached an intensity in 1793–4 that was perhaps greater than it had been at any other time of French history. Social conservatism ought therefore to have become the alpha-and-omega of politics. But the rhetoric of universalism had by now become second nature for the Revolutionary bourgeoisie. It was hard for them to disavow in 1795–9 what had been so strongly stated in 1789–94. Personally honest men, like Sieyes, Cambon, or La Revellière, could hardly burn the idols they had so recently adored. 'Je me suis trompé, je ne l'aurais jamais cru,' said in 1795 the Conventionnel Sergent, a writer, an artist, and a man close to the sans-culottes. This was hard to admit.

In retrospect, we can see why this delicacy of feeling was inappropriate. The bourgeoisie's egalitarian pose in 1794 was, after all, a compensation for its social impotence and for its inability as a particularist class to carry through a universalist programme. Bourgeois egalitarianism reached its climax during the Terror not as an affirmation but as a denial of social justice. The bourgeoisie denied equality in practice, praised it in theory, and was able to do the one for having done the other. But this mechanism could hardly be apprehended at a personal level by individuals who had often been completely sincere in their beliefs and actions. With historical hindsight, it is easy to see that the exacerbation of ideological bourgeois universalism in 1794 was the preface to the particularist rule of a consolidated propertied class in 1795; this, however, was a sequence which individual politicians could not immediately perceive and found hard to accept when they came to see it.

Social fact had changed; the bourgeoisie was now more aware of being bourgeois. But the greater practical awareness of this fact was balanced by a nostalgia for its denial in 1793–4. The resulting situation was highly volatile and contradictory. Present circumstances were overwhelming, but so were ideological memories. The Directorials were unable to disengage themselves from their past. This was true in an immediate and practical sense for the regicides who would have suffered personally if the direct or indirect consequences of bourgeois universalism (like the Terror or the execution of the King) had been repudiated. But the same inability to deny the past affected the political class as a whole, committed as it had been to a vision of natural equality.

Hence there was some ambiguity in the meaning of 9 thermidor. Engineered in large measure by the ultra-left—by terrorists and men sympathetic to the sans-culottes like Collot d'Herbois and Billaud-Varennes—Robespierre's downfall none the less signalled the rightist drift of the Revolution. One group of Conventionnels understood this nearly at once. These '*réacteurs*', personally inconsistent but historically logical, realized that the Terror had been a dead end. They quickly recognized that the verbal egalitarianism of 1793 should now be supplanted by the naked rule of property, however cruel.

A second group, many of them leftist opponents of Robespierre, like the Montagnard Romme and for some months Babeuf also, hoped, though in vain of course, that the rule of virtue might persist without terror. A third and dominant group of Conventionnels and bourgeois revolutionaries generally, like Sieyes, tried to straddle the issue. They wanted to remain roughly faithful to the Republican, anticlerical ideology of 'l'An II' without for all that endangering the interests of the propertied bourgeoisie. Here, the reality of the new class structure was at once accepted and denied. The essence of Directorial rule lay in this mixture of ideologically progressive and bourgeois concerns. The real logic of Directorial politics was that the French State should now become the avowed agent of a particularist class. But the ideology of the regime remained universalist, and by that same token a threat to social order, since popular revolutionaries like Babeuf could continue to justify their opposition to the regime by invoking the egalitarian spirit of the Constitution.

The situation was in many ways a *reductio ad absurdum* of what had prevailed before the Revolution, when the bourgeoisie's vision of community and ideological egalitarianism obscured its true interests as a class. Now, after the fall of Robespierre, a similar confusion prevailed, a confusion made worse by the events of the preceding five years. The need to defend property had been made much sharper in 1793–4 than ever before, as the Thermidorians understood fully, but so had the mystique of community acquired greater specificity for having been the rallying cry of bourgeois politics from the Bastille to Thermidor.

The resulting inability of the Directorials to come to grips with their situation as a class was a crippling liability. Before 1789, bourgeois universalism for all its faults had enabled the bourgeoisie to involve enthusiastic 'plebs' in its attack on the *Ancien Régime*. From 1791 to 1794, this same doctrine had in one way or another enabled the bourgeoisie to galvanize itself and, in some measure, the poor, in the struggle of France against Europe. But after 1795, the irrelevance of virtue and community to bourgeois politics was ever clearer. Its costs were obvious, and by continuing to subscribe to the letter but not the substance of the doctrine, the politically active part of the Revolutionary bourgeoisie gradually cut itself away from its base in the nation at large. The gap widened unceasingly between the mass of the politically conscious particularist bourgeoisie at large and its neo-universalist leaders in Paris, who soon came to represent nothing but themselves. Republican institutions were emptied of social substance, and it is fair to say that the Directory was not so much betrayed as it was gradually abandoned, first by the poor, then by the mass of the bourgeoisie, and eventually, in 1799, by the politicians themselves.

More aware of the practical requirements of law and order than the former Conventionnels, and less compromised by an extravagant past, the *bourgeois moyen sensuel* was after 1795 quick to reflect on the inconsequence of Jacobin (and after 1795, neo-Jacobin) ideology. The Directorial leadership soon found itself in the position which had been Robespierre's in July 1794. The regime lost credibility, and despite its innovative administrative policies, many of which were continued by Bonaparte, it ceased to govern. France became a conglomerate of provinces, regions, or even towns, often thrown on their own resources and removed from a government whose principles and practice were hopelessly at odds.

Nobles were caught in this cross-fire. The need to involve them in a defence of property ought to have been obvious; and in fact there never could be a sustained persecution of nobles after 1794. But at the same time, to frustrated bourgeois universalists like Sieyes and La Revellière, the idea of nobility was after 1795 more hateful than ever. The conflicting theory and reality of the persecution of nobles reflected the bastard nature of Directorial rule.

ii. Anglo-royalist conspiracy versus Republican ideology as the cause of Directorial failure

The history of the Directory and with it the fate of nobles have as a rule been presented in an altogether different light from that in which they are seen here. Though most historians have shied away from this period, which has been rightly described by Marcel Reinhard as the 'parent pauvre' of Revolutionary historiography, those who have dealt with it have explained its failure in a variety of ways which do not as a rule involve ideology.

The fundamental problem of the period is plain enough: if the first consequence of the French Revolution was 'the crowning of a long social and economic evolution which made the bourgeoisie the master of the world',[1] and if the Thermidorians had as their first purpose the consolidation of 'the social pre-eminence [and] political authority of the bourgeoisie',[2] why then did the Directory not succeed? One of the simplest of the answers that have been suggested has an institutional focus. It holds that the Directory did not succeed because its attempt to rule was set within the context of a cumbersome, bicameral liberal political system of mixed Franco-British parentage. Another institutional tack is to suggest, as has been done by Professor Godechot, the most eminent authority in the field, that the ultimate cause of the Directory's failure was its inability to control the army. The regime was inefficient. Much might have been achieved, Professor Godechot holds in his admirable *thèse de doctorat*, if more reliance had been placed on the work of the *commissaires aux armées*.

A different approach was followed by Robert Schnerb, who emphasized economic dislocation. No regime could have survived, he said, so radical a depreciation of its currency, or the crisis that followed when metallic currency was reintroduced, a crisis whose effects vitiated the positive influence of the good harvests of 1797 and 1798.[3] Each of these explanations has much to commend it, but none of them is wholly convincing, if only because we do not know very much about the details of economic life during the Directory. The consequences of even massive economic facts, such as the return to metallic coinage, are obscure. It can also be supposed that the administrative inefficiency of the regime was not a critical factor since it was at the request of those who ran the state that the army became an active force in the politics of the nation.

The incomplete explicative power of the classic model appears also in Albert Soboul's narrative account of bourgeois-noble relations in this period; anti-aristocratic legislation was not abandoned by the Thermidorians, he explains: 'the meaning of the class struggle remained unaltered'.[4] This was true in 1795 as it was also in November 1797: the law against nobles was not enforced, but its purpose was none the less 'evident' and 'significant'.[5] 'Significant', certainly; but 'evident' is perhaps less clear, since when all is said and done, only two years later, as Professor Soboul himself points out, 'the possessing bourgeoisie and aristocratic émigrés came together after a decade of Revolution'. Given the short lapse of time between the anti-noble law of hostages of July 1799, and the Consulate's first laws on the return of noble émigrés in January and February 1800, Soboul's rather Burkean explanation of the shift is not as satisfying as it might be: 'In spite of everything which had set them at odds, these two groups [bourgeois and nobles] had come to understand, thanks to the secret voices of the native soil and of landed property, that they should identify as one the land of France and the French nation'.[6]

The facts do not coalesce as firmly as might be wished; and, as if aware of the flaw in the model, many Marxist historians of the period have then gone on to give a somewhat anomalous importance to the weight of conspiracy in their explanation of the politics of the Directory.

The fear of conspiracy, like the delight in mask and back-door intrigue, are themes that are well known to historians of eighteenth-century England and America also; but paradoxically, few historians of those countries have ascribed to plots and the fear of plots the importance which they have in the work of many French Marxist historians, who are somewhat at a loss perhaps to account for the inapplicability here of the 'Social Interpretation of the French Revolution'. Conspiracies, one might say, are a surrogate whose use enables historians of this epoch to persist in their explanation when political behaviour is not what it should be.

Mathiez's belief in a wide conspiracy centred on the trial of Chabot was too precisely drawn not to appear far-fetched;[7] but his approach was made much more credible when raised to a higher plane by Lefebvre, who correctly emphasized the belief in the existence of conspiracy rather than the conspiracy itself. Much reliance was placed by this great historian on such fears to explain the *Grande Peur*, or the mentality of sans-culottes, or even the

Terror which he once held to be 'a punitive reaction indissolubly tied to the defensive *élan* against the aristocratic plot'.[8]

But it is the Marxist explanation of the Revolution *after* 1794 which ascribes the greatest causal importance to conspiracy. Aulard, Mathiez, Lefebvre, Soboul, and (to a certain degree) Woronoff have in essence a common explanation of Directorial failure: the right and even the centre right were conspiratorially intransigent; the Directory, however socially conservative it wished to be, had no choice but to fight back; the obstacle to the consolidation of the regime was not its own ideological obdurateness; it was instead the uncompromising attitude of the rightists, borne out at every step by their participation in anti-Republican intrigue.

It is a fact that the theory of conspiracy does have *some* substance. Plots did exist. Conspirators like Brottier and d'Antraigues thought themselves to be important people, and many of their Republican enemies concurred. That many Frenchmen should have conspired and should have attached great importance to intrigues is hardly surprising. A belief in the efficacy of conspiracy comes naturally to those who deny the relation of politics to society and class.

Having accepted the idea that some plots existed and perhaps also that the culture encouraged belief in plots,[9] we must go on to ask why it was the Republican statesmen were so prone to accept the reality of a conspiratorial threat and so eager to react to threats in a counter-productive way. Robespierre used the latent fear of plots to consolidate his terrorist rule. But for fear of machinations which were not in fact dangerous, Reubell and La Revellière destroyed the constitutional basis of their regime. This was a great step, which was taken by men who *needed* to believe in plots and repression because their situation had become politically untenable.

The importance of conspiratorial intrigues is questionable, because it is by no means self-evident that the Directorial élite was bound to take them as the starting point of its political calculations. The likelihood that the conspirators might succeed was low, and in 1797, for example, Barras was fully cognizant of Anglo-royalist intrigue, such as it was.[10] Revealing of the Directorials' basic doubts about the whole business is Bailleul's report to the Chambers on the connection between the coup of fructidor and the plot which it had been designed to avert. He could say no more than that 'Votre Commission aurait mal saisi votre intention si elle se présentait pour apporter des preuves, pour fournir des justifications. . . . *On ne cherche pas à prouver la lumière.*'[11]

More plausible than the conspiratorial explanation of Directorial failure is the thesis that the Thermidorians and their successors had placed themselves in a political dead end. Another explanation suggests, first, that a compromise acceptable to most owners of property was possible and, second, that it was the Directorials themselves who made agreement impossible by insisting on maintaining the now empty symbols of Republican ideological intransigence. Having thus antagonized both the poor and the rich, the men of the Directory had no choice but to sabotage the electoral basis and with it the legitimacy of their regime. Fear of conspiracy justified steps which had become necessary for other reasons.

Mathiez, Lefebvre, and Soboul insist on the unrelenting intransigence of émigrés and nobles. The alternative explanation focuses on a variety of points which have often been neglected. More can be made of the fact, for example, that many rightists were eager to work through the Directorial system, rather than against it. This was true of Mallet du Pan[12] and of Wickham, the English *maître d'œuvres.* Much can be made also of the willingness of the Church to find a compromise with the Republican state, as witnessed by the brief *Pastoralis Sollicitudo* of July 1796, which advised French clerics to accept the authority of the Republican state.[13] Hundreds of priests came home in 1796, and many royalists were afraid that bishops would follow suit: 'il n'est pas concevable', wrote an agent of Louis XVIII to his master, 'qu'en promettant d'être fidèle à une Constitution qui consacre l'usurpation des droits de la royauté, l'on ne fasse rien de préjudiciable aux intérêts du légitime souverain'.[14]

To the same end, it can also be said that Carnot's critical role in this period has been consistently misinterpreted. Ordinarily presented as a dupe ('L'ennui pour lui, c'est que ce tiers parti n'existait pas'),[15] Carnot must be seen instead as his biographer Marcel Reinhard described him: flexible, perspicacious, and ultimately consistent. Reinhard's conclusion deserves to be recalled:

> It was possible to manoeuvre. The royalists were divided and included those who spoke for a *coup d'état* as well as partisans of a legal solution, absolutists, constitutionalists, many of them divided by personal

animosities. In addition, there were the moderates, who were willing to serve under a pacific Republic which would guarantee order if not prosperity. These were the men who tried to avoid a break between the [conservative] councils and the [Republican] Directory, and who turned towards Carnot. Only he could have acted as an intermediary.[16]

The first part of an alternative view of Directorial failure insists on the possibility of compromise. The second deals with the Directorials' ideological intransigence, which made compromise impossible. For it is reasonably clear that the Thermidorians were unusually provocative in their devotion to the trappings of communitarian Republicanism, that is, to the subsisting forms of Revolutionary sensibility, now devoid of substance.

This stance was politically destructive in every way. It antagonized many members of the possessing class who might otherwise have accepted a conservative and strictly constitutional Republic of the kind that was favoured at the time by Benjamin Constant and Mme de Staël. Secondly, it legitimized the universalist complaint of the surviving Baboubian popular left as well as that of the neo-Jacobin, bourgeois, but democratic left, which still took the principles of the Enlightenment seriously.

The varied symbols of Republicanism which the Thermidorians were determined to uphold fell to pieces because Directorial Republicanism was in its essence false and without social meaning: a war of liberation became a war of rapine; cosmopolitanism turned into a nauseating nationalism; *tutoiement* resurfaced as an injunction to suppress the use of *sieur* and *monsieur* in letters of credit;[17] the cult of the Supreme Being became theophilanthropy; and the destruction of corporatism, an excuse for plundering (in messidor an VI) the pathetic remains of charitable institutions. And true to form, the Directory also used the supposed threat of émigrés for foreign aggrandisement; but whereas Brissot had declared war on empires, Reubell disrupted a city-state, Basel. The reform of education was the most positive achievement of politicians who shared this world view,[18] the proposed banishment of the nobility perhaps the most trivial, and the evolution of the Revolutionary *fête*, its most telling symbol.

Never was so much attention given to *fêtes* as during the Directory. This passion deserves attention because its vicissitudes are symbolic of the decay of the bourgeois universalist world view during the last decade of the eighteenth century. Long before 1789, the traditional and religious *fête* had fallen into disrepute.

The *encyclopédistes* had had to rethink it completely. Their *fête*, socially integrationist and respectful of the established order of things, emphasized the praise of work and of communal repose. Ritualized and *dirigiste*, writes one historian, the Enlightenment *fête* fulfilled 'a socially integrative role and always aimed to buttress the existing social order'.[19] The Revolutionary *fête* took this up but added to it an element of 'organized spontaneity' best represented by the emphasis on music and collective song, at once enthusiastic and rehearsed.[20] This was far removed from La Revellière's conception of the Directorial *fête*, whose aim was a Jesuitical suffusion of the senses. The need for collective forms, thought La Revellière, was beyond the grasp of the masses: 'La multitude ne peut s'élever à ces idées d'ordre et de convenance.' The Directorial *fête* became at worst a deception and at best an empty ritual: the *législateur philosophe* took the place of the priest which the *lumières* had briefly exorcized. Spontaneity was excluded; the minutiae of celebration closely regulated. Symbol became debased allegory, and the *fêtes* of David became—literally—the circuses of François de Neufchateau.

In April 1794, Robespierre attended a tragedy of Legouvé in which history was rewritten: Lucan triumphed and Nero died. This was the measure of the Montagnards' terrorism: history would be rewritten as they willed it to be. The best pendant no doubt was the Directorials' make-believe Roman costumes adopted after 18 fructidor: a tragic image degenerated to comical mirage. Benjamin Constant put it nicely apropos of left, bourgeois radicals, but in words that would have been more suitable to the more moderate Sieyes: the Jacobins of the Terror have died away: the Jacobins of 1798 have all of their vices but none of their virtues.[21]

In 1793–4, the ideologically motivated persecution of nobles had a certain grandeur, as did the moral egalitarianism of Robespierre. Terror dignified these futile efforts. But the persecution of nobles in 1795–9 and their denationalization in 1797 were shabby acts, a mask for corrupting impotence.

iii. Anti-noble legislation in 1795–1797

The passing from opportunism to ideological panic that marked the evolution of the rights of nobles from 1791 to 1794 was repeated from 1795 to 1799, but in a more confused form. After tragedy comes farce. Both instances were conceptually comparable, since nobles were proscribed in 1797 as they had been in 1794 for reasons which were embedded in the nature of the Revolutionary movement; but the results were very different. After 1794, penalties were less serious and the phases of persecution less clearly distinguishable. Conservative pro-nobilism and opportunistic proscription often overlapped, especially in 1794–6, when the Thermidorians hesitated in their handling of the problem: they had rejected terrorism and, theoretically, would have liked to unite with anti-popular constitutionalists—some of them monarchists, others Republican, many of them noble. But their past and their ideas made such an alliance problematic.

As politics fluctuated, so did émigré legislation. From the summer of 1794 to the summer of 1795, penalties were lessened in theory as they already had been in fact by local criminal tribunals.[22] Individuals who managed to have their names removed from the émigré lists had their property returned to them. The relatives of émigrés were given better treatment. In November 1794, émigré legislation was codified. Certain categories of émigrés were allowed to return, and many did so in the spring of 1795 and again in late 1796 and early 1797.[23]

At the same time, however, émigrés, and especially noble émigrés, were hardly readmitted to the bosom of the nation. The question of their presence was truly an obsession for the Thermidorians. From September 1792 to September 1794, the Conventionnels drafted 63 texts on this matter, but in five successive years, they and their successors found time to draw up 87, 34, 10, 18, and 12 more laws about this issue, or 224 in all. The Swiss border was carefully watched for fugitives, and in the late spring of 1795, a special bureau 'contre les émigrés' was set up by the Committee of General Security.[24] Émigrés were political untouchables. Even royalists were unwilling to defend those of them who had served in counter-revolutionary military units. In January 1796, for example, Cadroy, a constitutional monarchist, abandoned them altogether: 'Une barrière insurmontable . . . sépare [les émigrés] de nous; ce n'est pas pour les émigrés que vous avez ouvert cette discussion, mais bien pour les citoyens français qui, n'ayant jamais perdu ce titre, ont pourtant été inscrits sur la liste des émigrés.'[25]

After ordinary counter-revolutionaries were more or less reintegrated into French society in 1795, it became doubly important for prospective heirs to show that their deceased benefactors had been ordinary conspirators and not émigrés whose right to will their property was still suspended. Widows produced documents to show that their husbands had not been lukewarm conservatives who had left France in a panic as émigrés, but genuine counter-revolutionaries who had been shot *manu militari*, or as Charrier's widow insisted, guillotined for having led an insurrection *inside* France: 'Charrier n'a jamais quitté le sol de la République.'[26]

Whenever the gap widened between the Thermidorians and the right, émigrés were invariably squeezed. In the summer of 1795, after the 'royalist' coup of vendémiaire, penalties against émigrés were refurbished; and their readmission to France was specifically forbidden by a constitutional act. Émigrés alone were not pardoned when the Convention dissolved itself in October 1795. Other see-saws took place in late 1796 when the drastic law of 3 brumaire an IV (25 October 1795) was modified, and again when its more repressive provisions were repealed in April and May 1797. The pattern lacks the clarity of its earlier counterpart in 1789–94, with its almost linear decay of nobles' rights. This same confusion exists for legislation on nobles as such, which also went through numerous phases in which the reintegration of élites was from time to time countered by opportunistic persecution.

With Robespierre's death only five days behind them, the Conventionnels, at Monmayou's prompting, reaffirmed the exclusion of all nobles from public office and even worsened their situation by withdrawing from the Committee of Public Safety the right which it had had since March of 'requisitioning' useful nobles. But the next day, on 16 thermidor, Merlin de Thionville, then inaugurating his career as an unusually pliable Thermidorian, asked for the repeal of the law passed on the previous day. He did not even bother to justify his plea, which he held to be self-evidently just: 'je n'en dirai pas les motifs, tous mes collègues les pressentent; je me servirai d'un motif général: c'est l'égalité que je veux ramener. . . .'[27] The motion, which let off nobles and priests, was quickly passed and confusedly commented on by a former priest, Villers, who praised the leniency of his colleagues and tried to establish parallels among nobles, priests, and men of law. All of these people had done the Revolution great harm, but did it make sense to proscribe them as groups?[28] On the same day, Casabianca, a Montagnard Conventionnel, asked the CPS to take steps on behalf of pro-Revolutionary

Corsican nobles (like himself).[29] On 23 thermidor, non-noble women in the process of divorcing their noble husbands were allowed to return to Paris, and the same relaxation was allowed in provincial cities. When asked by the Committee of Public Safety to check into the presence of nobles in the cavalry near Cherbourg, Guimberteau replied that he had lost his instructions,[30] and Berlier in the Nord decided to repeal some arrests made by order of Saint-Just and Lebas, measures which now appeared to him 'hors des termes des lois générales de la République . . . je ne conçois dans toute espèce de governement, même révolutionnaire, point de bonne législation sans uniformité: si je me trompe, je désire en être promptement informé'.[31] Acting according to these same rights, local authorities released nobles everywhere, as was done in Orthez, for example, by the municipal Comité de surveillance: 'since the times have changed, the committee foresees no danger or inconvenience in granting this noble his liberty'.[32] In early October 1794, the Comité de surveillance at Rennes released ten nobles who had been imprisoned for some months. Although it had continued to arrest nobles in August and September, it now decided to release those noble prisoners who had no émigré relatives and whose 'mentalité était assez punie par une longue détention de neuf à dix mois'.[33]

Not everyone concurred. In fructidor an II, the Jacobins counter-attacked. In Dijon, the local Société Populaire drew up an address urging the preservation of the state's terroristic apparatus and the continuation of the 'war on nobles'.[34] Forwarded to Paris, the programme was widely advertised in the capital by the Jacobin Club, and Levasseur hailed the continued persecution of nobles as 'le grand ordre du jour de la Société'.[35] His motives were very different from those of Saint-Just. In germinal, the young man's excommunication of the ci-devants was an honourable ideological statement, but Levasseur's proposal was frankly opportunistic. The problem as he saw it was obvious: since *l'aristocratie* was 'plus insolente que jamais', it was necessary to restore the 'courage abbattu' of good citizens everywhere and the proscription of nobles would do nicely. This opportunism harked back to the policy of the Montagne in the spring and summer of 1793.

For some weeks, the rump of the Mountain more or less held its own on nobles. In October 1794, the Convention listened patiently while Borie and Duhem explained that aristocrats should be excluded from public office. It was also Duhem's belief that a distinction should be made between the more culpable relatives of noble émigrés, and the less culpable relatives of non-noble émigrés. Only non-noble émigrés, he thought, should be given back those of their estates that had not yet been sold. Bentabole objected.[36] This former friend of Marat's, now married to a ci-devant, defended nobles on the curious grounds that non-noble émigrés were the ones who ought to be the more severely punished because it was, after all, normal that nobles should have fled the fury of a Revolution that had been made against them. Neither man swayed his audience. The debate was a draw, and Cambacérès ended it by tabling Duhem's motion on the grounds that some middle position should be found which would wound 'ni l'intérêt de la patrie, ni celui de l'humanité'.

Some weeks later, however, the current began to run the other way. In October 1794, Bourdon had still been on Duhem's side: 'on s'élève contre cette dénomination de nobles,' he had said. But the fact was that nobles were guilty *qua* nobles: 'quand on punit un homme d'un délit qui tient à des préjugés de naissance autant qu'à la méchanceté de son cœur, il faut bien dire qu'il est ci-devant noble, si vraiment il est né noble'.[37] Two months later, in December 1794, the scales had fallen from his eyes. Two important items were placed on the Convention's agenda for 18 frimaire an III (8 December 1794): the first concerned the readmission of the famous seventy-three deputies who had signed a petition on behalf of the Gironde in June 1793; the other was the repeal of the law of 27 germinal against nobles. On behalf of the Committees of Legislation, Public Safety, and General Security, the same Bourdon moved the suspension of this act which he now held to be of barbarous brutality. In all seriousness, Bourdon then went on to show that a law which exiled nobles was really directed against the 'classe des nécessiteux', 'l'armée des gens à 40 sous' who depended on the rich for patronage and trade.

In the same vein, some days later, a general named Pille, who was a friend of Carnot's and had been before 1789 the secretary of a royal intendant, suddenly thought to remind the Committee of Public Safety that many officers had been dismissed unjustly 'par la seule raison qu'ils étaient ex-nobles',[38] and on 20 frimaire an III the Convention ordered the gradual reappointment of such men. Nobles were also allowed to creep back into the bureaucracy, especially at the Treasury (Dufresne, Faipoult de Maisoncelle, Amelot de Chaillous, a former intendant) and at the Foreign Office (Gérard de Rayneval).

These were important steps, but it should also be remembered that even at the height of Thermidorian reaction nobles were still actively, if indirectly, persecuted. Crucial in this respect was the distinction commonly made between non-noble 'fugitifs' (sometimes called 'réfugiés') and noble émigrés; or more bluntly between real and false émigrés, indistinguishable in all respects but one, birth.

Originally, and through 1792, the term émigré had been understood to mean noble.* In 1793–4, however, when all manner of people fled, nobles were no more than one in five of the émigré population. Since then, however, the Directory had worked with reasonable success to clarify the lists, so that anti-émigré legislation in 1795–9 was again primarily directed against nobles. Many revolutionaries understood this, and some did not bother to hide it, as the moderate deputy Philippe Delleville pointed out in the Assembly of the Five Hundred, where he stated that in his department, 'un individu fut inscrit [as an émigré] parce qu'il était gentilhomme; on croyait qu'émigré et gentilhomme étaient synonymes'.[39] Émigré nobles who returned to France, especially after they had sought refuge in England, might well be shot, as happened in the winter of 1795 and after September 1797. By contrast, avowed counter-revolutionary but non-noble émigrés like the former Conventionnel Chasset could be elected to the Five Hundred. In the same way, everyone knew that Louvet had fled to Switzerland; but everyone pretended to believe that he had merely found refuge 'dans les cavernes du Jura'. For these non-nobles, the law could be violated; and so was it in a way for nobles, but in another direction, best illustrated by the celebrated case of a group of ci-devants shipwrecked at Calais in 1795: four of them chose to drown in order to avoid capture, unwisely so, since the others were ordered to be released by a local court, which accepted international law and declared itself incompetent to judge these men who had fallen within its jurisdiction by an act of God. This judgement, however, the Directory suspended for two years. In July 1797, the Five Hundred then reaffirmed it; but after the coup of 18 fructidor, this decision was ignored as well. Moreover, when in 1799 both Chambers once again acquitted the culprits, the Directory once again refused to let them go, and they were only set free after brumaire by Bonaparte. Laws against émigrés, like all Revolutionary laws, were hardly ever enforced across the board: still, most of the émigré nobles captured at

* See Appendix 2.

Quiberon were shot (non-nobles were as a rule let off), and after Fructidor, as shall be seen, military commissions handed down about 160 death sentences, most of them against nobles.[40]

iv. The law of 9 frimaire an VI (29 November 1797)

For three years after the fall of Robespierre, anti-noble and anti-émigré feeling moved back and forth. In the autumn of 1797, however, the legislation against nobles took a wild step, which likened it, in theory at least, to the first ideologically motivated proscription of nobles that had climaxed in April 1794.

In the background of the law was the coup of 18 fructidor (4 September 1797). In 1796, under the lead of Carnot, Catholics, constitutional monarchists, and conservative Republicans were granted *de facto* tolerance. In consequence, a majority of conservative Republicans and neo-royalists was returned in the elections of March 1797, and the former Conventionnels who dominated the five-man Directory (Barras, Reubell, La Revellière, and Carnot) were forced to choose between conciliation and repression. Carnot inclined to a compromise. But Reubell and La Revellière, joined finally by Barras, decided that an agreement was impossible. They chose instead to stage a *coup d'état*. On 18 fructidor, Augereau, one of Bonaparte's generals, directed the military occupation of Paris. The assemblies were shut down. The powers of the Directory were reinforced. The regime took a sharp turn to the left.

At the same time, the new Directors were as determined as they had ever been to maintain the social status quo. Great efforts were made to balance the budget. Indirect taxes were reintroduced. Sans-culottes did not starve as they had in 1795, but this was purely fortuitous and was only due to the abundant harvests of 1796, 1797, and 1798. Economically, the state limited itself to the encouragement of manufacturing and trade, notably with the first national exposition, in Paris, in the autumn of 1798.

The regime's relationship with the left was tortuous. Having purged the right, it was logically held to favour at least the neo-Jacobin, bourgeois left. But the essentially conservative nature of the regime could not allow the resurgence of any leftist movement, however bourgeois, which might co-operate with the popular left. In May 1798, the neo-Jacobins were therefore purged in turn.

The first purpose of the plotters of Fructidor, however, was to thwart the right. A new persecution of priests and nobles was decreed. Such acts did not cost very much, and they gave to the regime a pleasingly progressive look. The laws of 1792 and 1793 against the non-juring clergy were reinvoked. In late 1793, it will be remembered, Robespierre had deplored dechristianization because to accept it would have encouraged the sans-culottes. But because the sans-culotte 'movement' was defunct in 1797, priests were now expendable; and so were the other enemies of this supposedly leftist regime. Émigrés who had returned were given fourteen days to leave; their relatives were excluded from public office. More dramatic yet was the legislation passed against nobles.

On 19 fructidor, the Five Hundred carried Bailleul's motion to set up a commission to consider the exclusion *de jure* of all nobles from public office, a step which even Saint-Just had not dared to take. Dominated by the shadow of Sieyes, the commission duly reported that it was struck by the incompatibility of Republicanism and inherited nobility. A state of war existed between the two. Nobles at home were plotting with émigrés abroad. All over France, claimed Bailleul, 'les imbéciles et les lâches' were still under their sway, and with an eye perhaps to winning such people over to the Directory, the commission urged a clean break. Nobles as a class should all be deported. Necessity decreed it, and one deputy announced that in his department alone, nobles had massacred more than a thousand Republicans.[41] Creuzé-Latouche, a running dog of Girondism, defended the law of proscription as a measure of national security: 'il faut prendre ce parti ou périr'. Oudot concurred, and taking up Saint-Just's old distinction (immoler pour ne pas être immolé), but in a more mundane manner, maintained that either the nation or the nobles would succumb: 'Il faut . . . que la caste dont il est question anéantisse le peuple, ou que le peuple parvienne enfin à anéantir ses efforts toujours renaissants et toujours contre-révolutionnaires.'[42]

This was an argument that would have surprised the defeated veterans of Condé's émigré army, who were then winding their way from Krems to Olmutz to the Bug, in Poland, some distance removed from the borders of the Grande Nation, which on the face of it did not have much to fear from them.

Many of Oudot's colleagues remained sceptical. In the Chambers, deputies rose to point out, once again, that 'les fautes sont personnelles'; former nobles were citizens with rights. To forbid them access to public office was to '[renverser] ces principes inviolables de la sociabilité'.[43] One deputy thought the project unconstitutional, and another reminded his colleagues that many nobles had genuinely accepted after 1790 the decree of the National Assembly abolishing nobility. To push these citizens out of the body politic was to dissolve the social contract: 'cette rupture n'est ni au pouvoir du corps législatif, ni même au pouvoir du corps de la nation delibérante immédiatement'.[44] Besides, as one deputy put it rather brusquely, there had been no nobility in France for the past six years: 'quand on y poursuit les nobles, on court après des fantômes'.[45] A Belgian deputy, Beyts, was less sure about France, but he knew that, in his bailiwick at least, nobles were quite harmless: 'Je crois aussi qu'il y a des pays infiniment étendus, la Belgique par exemple, où les nobles ne conspirent pas. . . .'[46] Other critics were sympathetic to nobles on the supposition that the new regime needed them. Nobles, explained one deputy, had as a rule remained 'étrangers à toutes les factions, constamment soumis à vos lois'. Many of them had given proof of their fidelity by accepting the constitution, and many of them had given 'de signalés services à la cause de la liberté. Bannissons donc', he concluded, 'de cette tribune des craintes pusillanimes sur les conjurations et les conjurateurs.'[47]

The law was passed none the less on 19 November 1797, ironically enough, only two weeks after the Director had once again reaffirmed the illegality of strikes. Public opinion at large was not enthusiastic by any means, and Thibaudeau described the reception of 'cette loi violente et atroce' as one of great stupour.[48] For some weeks, it was the subject of much political speculation: 'cet objet', noted a police report, 'continuant à former le fonds de tous les entretiens politiques'.[49] The law failed to reassure anybody on either the left or, more importantly, the centre.[50] Regrettably, from the Directors' point of view, the idea of deporting nobles only appealed to the partisans of the constitution of 1793 and to officers on half pay. It did not please the patrons of even those cafés 'd'un patriotisme connu'.[51] The Director, Barras, a ci-devant viscount, was, like his 'court', appalled. Benjamin Constant, who on 18 fructidor had approved the coup which he soon came to regret, was in a quandary. Born a baron, his solution was to claim that his family, forced into exile with the Revocation of the Edict of Nantes in 1685, had by virtue of that royal law forfeited its claims to nobility. The French Revolution had restored him to his rights of citizenship, as it had done for all the descendants of such French Protestants, but could the Revolution restore him to noble status? The new law could not apply to him. Few people were as ingenious.

Boulay and Sieyes responded to these criticisms by diluting their first proposal. Nobles would not after all be deported; they would merely be deprived of their civic rights, as Boulay had originally intended. Other amendments further restricted the measure: nobles who had sat in national representative bodies were exempted, as were the Directors themselves, ministers, soldiers, and anyone who had been faithful to the Republican cause, a vague condition which was to be made more specific at some later date.

Despite such amendments, the law remained in theory more strict than the one of 1794, which had specifically empowered the Committee of Public Safety to employ or 'requisition' any and all nobles, including those who had never done anything on behalf of the Republic. This had been a loophole as wide as the law, and one that was convenient for men of influence who had friends to protect. In thermidor an II, this exception had been momentarily suppressed, but it was once again revived and extended in September 1795, to cover the deserving parents of selected émigrés.[52] In 1797, however, Sieyes and Boulay went out of their way to eliminate the practice of requisition. Indeed, they used the existence of past exemptions to justify a more complete exclusion. Previous practice, they argued, had been arbitrary and therefore un-Republican. By accepting these *ad hoc* arrangements, which placed them *de facto* in a particular category, nobles had shown themselves to be incurably selfish. Once again, their inability to live under universal laws had been revealed; their souls fitted them to be either slaves or tyrants. They should be deported; and the indignant but somewhat naïve Barante could later write that it was in this devious manner that a whole class of individuals was proscribed in the name of equality: 'Ce sophisme n'était qu'une cynique ironie.'[53]

The law was to be applied as soon as exceptions to it had been defined, and in December 1797, the Directory urged the Chambers to do so immediately. It was important, they said, to determine precisely which nobles had really disavowed 'la caste où le hasard les avait jettés, pour s'allier d'intention et d'effet, à la grande famille de la liberté'. If this were not done, the Directory rightly pointed out, 'l'exécution de la . . . loi se [trouverait] entièrement paralysée'.[54]

Their prediction proved correct and the law was never given

much practical effect, nor could it be, as Mme de Staël pointed out, now that Terror had been ruled out.[55] None the less, the law remained on the books; an attempt to repeal it in germinal an VI (April 1798) was shouted down. Some noble-born local officials were removed.[56] Other anti-noble laws were enacted in subsequent months also: rather comically, on 19 nivôse an VI the Directory reminded the nation that various members of the same family could not add a name to their surname: all Duponts would be Duponts; none could become Dupont de Nemours.[57] Less comic was the law of hostages: as it had become customary in the Sarthe to arrest nobles as hostages, the Directory and the Chambers in July 1799 decided to legalize the practice. Henceforth, in any 'disturbed' department, four nobles or relatives of émigrés might be arrested for every murdered patriot. Hostages would be collectively responsible for damages caused by royalist attack. In June 1799, it was also suggested that the complaints of noble émigrés who wished to return to France would only be considered after those of all other émigrés: that is to say, never.

The desire of the Directorials to persecute nobles was unmistakable. But the logic of their political situation dictated that they should both want to persecute aristocrats and be unable to do so. Anti-noble laws might be enacted and selectively applied but a general proscription was fundamentally impossible. Regardless of their intent, Sieyes and Boulay in 1797 could not afford to launch a widespread attack on nobles who were, after all, a subcategory of the propertied class. Such a move would have been unacceptable to the dominant landlord class. As Morellet pointed out, to assault nobles once again would make it more difficult to resolve the military conflict that opposed France to the other countries of Europe where nobles were politically powerful.[58] More critically, a renewed persecution of nobles would be, at home, a dangerous precedent. Dufort de Cheverny, a liberal noble and admittedly a man with an interest, said of Boulay's proposal that it had thrown all of France into despair: 'le cri général en fait justice. Mais les gens qui réfléchissent juge que la propriété n'est plus tenable, que l'on viendra d'une manière ou d'une autre à la loi agraire. . . .'[59] Mme de Staël, *the* reflective woman of her age, was in complete agreement: she decried the 'absurd policy' of the Directory on nobles in an essay of 1799, and asked in the same breath: 'Comment donner à la propriété la stabilité nécessaire pour la prospérité de l'état lorsque telle propriété n'est point protégée?'[60]

The debate on nobles in 1797–9 paralleled, with one basic change, the debate of 1791–2 on emigration. At that time, legislation against émigrés had been set in a political or even moral context: the safety of the state versus the rights of individuals, and it was in vain that defenders of principle and nobles had made their point. 'Qu'est qu'une nouvelle constitution', one of them had written, 'dans laquelle on peut condamner sans preuve et sans jugement, non pas quelques citoyens, mais des classes entières et nombreuses de citoyens?' That political argument had fallen on deaf ears; but after Robespierre and the sans-culottes, when the political debate had come to centre on the material question of property, the cause of nobles suddenly appeared more just. The respect for property, Mme de Staël explained, was after all the greatest creation of the social order, and the cause of property could not be dissociated from that of the noble-born: 'Il ne faut pas se jouer trop longtemps avec ce merveilleux résultat et, pendant que les vainqueurs s'occupent à dépouiller les vaincus, une troisième classe pourrait annéantir l'édifice social en réclamant contre toute espèce d'inégalité de fortune.'[61]

The heart of the bourgeoisie was no longer in this business, and perception of the decay of bourgeois aggressiveness and self-confidence emerges from a comparison of the justification of persecution of nobles in 1794 with that in 1797. For Saint-Just, the existence of ex-nobles was an intolerable denial of virtue, community, and moral equality. Nobles would have to be destroyed so that Republican society might live. But the arguments of Sieyes and Boulay were of a much humbler sort. Although their hatred, or envy, of nobles was great, it could no longer be expressed in the Catonian terms of Robespierre and Saint-Just. The justification of Saint-Just, like his goals, was sincere. Those of Sieyes were much less honest. His campaign against nobles was something of a fraud, and so was his principal intellectual justification of it, the racial distinctiveness of nobles, which held that the nobles were the descendants of the ancient Francs, just as members of the Third Estate were the heirs of the ancient Gauls.

The argument was plainly absurd. It had, to be sure, been defended by Boulainvilliers, Montesquieu, Alès de Corbet, and Jaucourt in the *Encyclopédie*. But it had also been denied by Dubos, Mignot de Bussy, and Linguet, who had sarcastically heaped ridicule on the nobles' manifestly spurious claims. The theory was at best a *vue de l'esprit*, and little more than an entertaining debater's point designed to amuse a public whose true motivations had little to do with race. 'Je ne vous dirai pas', wrote Lafayette, 'si je suis Gaulois ou Franc. J'espère être Gaulois parce que très peu de Francs s'établirent dans les montagnes d'Auvergne. J'aime mieux Vercingétorix défendant ses montagnes que le brigand Clovis et ses abominables successeurs.'[62]

The argument was not really serious, and it had not been invoked when the imprisonment of nobles had been a truly deadly business. Then, as has been said, emphasis was placed instead on the character faults of nobles, corrupted by secular habits of amoral authoritarianism. Saint-Just, in fact, mocked the racialist explanation altogether when he commented on the origins of monarchs who claimed to rule by divine right. All states, he explained, were in flux, and the ancestors of great monarchs may well have sat under rather modest trees: 'je voudrais savoir quels étaient, du temps de Pompée, les pères dont descendent les rois nos contemporains',[63] and his point also was that the trees in question were those 'de la Germanie *et* des Gaules' rather than of Germany *or* the Gauls. In other passages written in 1792 and 1793, he likewise lumped in a single group 'les anciens Francs, les anciens Germains, très voisins de nous'.[64]

References to the racial distinctiveness of nobles were of course made from time to time throughout these years. In a letter to the departmental directory of the Vosges, for example, an amateur historian explained in May 1794 that the conquest of Gaul by the Franks had been the first manifestation of a conspiracy that brought together the clergy and nobles of foreign birth: 'ce n'est que la fourberie, l'avarice et l'ambition des prêtres qui nous ont livrés sans défense à une nation dont tous les individus sans exception étaient dignes du dernier supplice'. The citizens of Lorraine, he went on, had always detested the Franks or French, in the original sense of the word, and it would require no great effort to convince them that 'ce nom soit a jamais proscrit et que nous reprenions le nom de Gaulois'.[65] *Mutatis mutandis*, that in fact is what happened at Francey (in the department of the Loir-et-Cher), which became, for a time, Gaulois.[66]

Similar ideas were floated on the national political stage by the journalist Guffroy, in his paper *Le Rougyff* or *Le Frank*. But Guffroy seems to have had the racial argument upside down, as appears from the title of his paper and from his claim that the war against

Europe would only end when the French attacked their neighbours with *francisques*.[67] For him, it seems, it was the revolutionaries who were the descendants of the Germanic Franks. Guffroy, in any case, was not a respectable individual, and was much given to excessive statements: 'Abattons les nobles, et tant pis pour les bons, s'il y en a; que la guillotine soit en permanence dans toute la république; la France a assez de cinq millions d'habitants.'[68] The men of 1793–4, Robespierre, Saint-Just, and the Mountain, were above using the type of argument on which Guffroy relied, and so were in 1795/6 serious popular revolutionaries like Babeuf: when Drouet proposed on 8 May 1795, that the Equals demand that the name of France be changed to Gaul, Babeuf abruptly cut him short.[69]

It was indeed a cardinal point of Jacobin ideology that nobles were a distinct group within the nation: 'L'émigration', said Barère, 'parle allemand.'[70] And it was often said that French nobles considered themselves to be the peers of nobles in other countries rather than of non-nobles in France.[71] In the same way, much was made of the connection between émigrés and foreign courts, as well as between émigrés and sans-culottes, all of them participants in the citra-ultra conspiracy denounced by Barère during the food riots of February 1793, and after this by Robespierre, who dwelt on it at length.[72] But to claim that nobles had voluntarily chosen to place themselves outside of the national community was one thing; to say that they were *racially* committed to do this was another. The theme of racial distinction was hardly in keeping with the principles of 1789, and it is therefore revealing that it was only in November 1797 that this idea finally came into its own, as if to underline the inanity of the measure that it aimed to justify.

Much was made of the racial theme in these days. In his presentation of Sieyes's law of deportation to the Five Hundred, for example, Boulay de la Meurthe dwelt at length on the peaceful character of the Gauls at the time of the barbarian invasions. Reprisals for their destruction were now in order. The Teutons, he explained, had reduced 'us' to the most humiliating servitude: 'Ils nous traitaient comme des bêtes de somme; ils avaient éteint le flambeau des arts et des sciences; il avaient établi leur règne sur celui de l'ignorance et de la barbarie. Voilà comme nous avons été traités par eux pendant des siècles; c'est cela qui était de la proscription et du brigandage.'[73]

And with equal seriousness, conservative publicists took pains to refute these allegations. In his *Sur le projet de bannir ou déporter la ci-devant noblesse déjà spoliée et décimée*, one Toustain-Richebourg, for example, showed that it was a 'grossière erreur de représenter les barbares insurgés contre l'Empire romain comme les fondateurs de la noblesse'. Moreover, nobles taken as individuals were not descendants of Franks since 'quantité de nobles d'aujourd'hui, même entre les illustres, descendent de ces braves et laborieux serfs ou affranchis'. Unstoppable, Toustain went on to prove that nobilities everywhere were based in part at least on merit, and compatible presumably with *la carrière ouverte aux talents*: feudalism, he explained, ought not to be confused with nobility, and had been, originally, an alternative not to freedom but to slavery.[74]

The reutilization of the racialist argument in 1797 is suggestive. To secure the expulsion of the nobles from society, Sieyes and his friends had to convince the surviving and anxious Revolutionary bourgeoisie that no help was to be found on the right and that nobles would not be of any use to the bourgeoisie in its efforts to contain the Jacobin and popular left. Since this was not in fact true, imaginary arguments had to be used to convince the bourgeoisie that, all appearances to the contrary, nobles were of a different species and would never unite with their bourgeois neighbours. Nobles, explained Sieyes, had nothing in common with non-nobles: 'Quand on n'est pas de mon espèce, on n'est pas mon semblable; un noble n'est pas de mon espèce, donc c'est un loup; je tire dessus.'[75]

Speculation on the nature of noble turpitude reached a high level of fantasy. A deputy named Rousseau, whom the noble-hater Dulaure described as a man 'd'une probité sévère', arranged to have inserted in *Le Moniteur* of 20 germinal an VI a long letter in which he showed that Robespierre had been a tool of the émigrés in Coblenz: 'J'étais persuadé depuis longtemps qu'une main invisible avait souvent dirigé Robespierre et ses abominable suppôts. . . .' To be sure, explained Rousseau, such a thought might at first seem 'absurd', but was it not striking that liberal nobles had been among the most conspicuous victims of the Terror? 'Vous verrez toute la ci-devant haute noblesse et tous les membres du parlement, restés en France, punis de même [by émigré nobles] de leur non-émigration.'[76] The more prominent deputy Oudot was even more categorical. Nobles were not just responsible for Babeuf or Brottier or Robespierre and the Committee of Public Safety. They were responsible for everything that had gone wrong since 1789. Necessarily, his was a long list:

Qui a suscité des ennemis à la France, et la coalition de Pilnitz? . . . Ce sont les émigrés, . . . c'est la noblesse. . . .
Qui a porté les armes contre la patrie? C'est la noblesse.
Qui a conspiré à la journée des poignards et du 10 août 1792? . . . La noblesse. . . .
Qui a trahi dans les armées de terre et de mer? . . .
Qui a entretenu la division dans l'intérieur?
Qui a livré Toulon, . . . excité les troubles de Lyon, de Marseille? Qui a fait la Vendée, organisé la chouanerie, compagnies du Soleil et de Jésus? . . . C'est la noblesse. Soyez sûrs que si le clergé ou le fanatisme y a pris tant de part, c'est encore la noblesse qu'il faut en accuser.
Qu'auroit pu faire le clergé sans les évêques réfractaires, sans les possesseurs des grands bénéfices, qui tous étoient de la caste des nobles? le Clergé du second ordre n'étoit-il pas en opposition avec eux en 1789? C'est donc à la noblesse que l'on doit tous les maux de la Révolution.[77]

Oudot's reasoning was patently inane, as was that of Sieyes. Nobles in 1797 were not antisocial wolves lusting for bourgeois blood. The argument of racial distinction had been historically silly, since only a handful of nobles could trace their line to the middle ages, much less to the times of Clovis and Pharamond; and the argument was also practically absurd, in contemporary terms. To exclude nobles was, manifestly, to weaken the bourgeoisie, as had been pointed out by a rightist paper some time before with regard to the relatives of émigrés: 'La Convention vient d'éloigner des fonctions publiques et de réduire à la classe de simples propriétaires tous ceux qui ont des parents chez l'étranger. Si cette loi subsiste . . . les sans-culottes auront donc seuls dans les mains le gouvernail de la France.'[78] With this law on nobles, Sieyes had placed ideological self-indulgence above practical necessity. This was a luxury which the bourgeoisie could no longer afford in 1797.

v. Directorial ideology in historical perspective

In traditional perspective, the law against nobles of November 1797 is easily explained: 'An aristocracy that refused to yield', explains Albert Soboul, 'remained the essential enemy [of the Revolution]. The law of 9 frimaire an VI . . . conceived by Sieyes, proved this since it reduced nobles to the status of foreigners.'[79] But it may well be that nobles were not in fact the 'essential' enemy of the Directory. The sans-culottes, Austria, Louis XVIII, Babeuf, and Bonaparte could all lay better claim to that title. The key to the passing of the law, and to its non-enforcement, it must be repeated, is not to be found in aristocratic conspiracies but in the ideological origins of the French Revolution.

Every society is in some sense a set of symbolic systems, more real in many ways than the situations which they symbolize. But seldom can this have been so true as it was of France in 1789–99. Ideology showed the way forward when the Revolutionary movement came to some critical dead end, as happened when constitutional monarchism failed in 1791 or in the autumn of 1792 and spring of 1793, when old friends somehow proved to be irretrievable liberticides. And in the autumn of 1793, when bourgeois revolutionaries continued to deny the increasingly evident nature of bourgeois particularism, ideology lay at the heart of Revolutionary politics. The Revolution had finally become pure theatre and was, in the words of François Furet, 'l'imaginaire d'une société devenu le tissu même de son histoire'.[80] If romantic terrorism is the product of infantile proletarian consciousness, so was ideological terrorism the fruit of senescent bourgeois universalism. This was apprehended by Babeuf. His defence at Vendôme was in part an exegesis of eighteenth-century thought with its emphasis on community; but Babeuf at his trial also denied the claims of the heirs of the philosophes, of the men who had betrayed their ideals. In his rage, he did not stop short of denouncing the power of thought itself: 'La supériorité de talents et d'intelligence n'est qu'une chimère . . . ce n'est qu'une chose d'opinion que la valeur de l'intelligence . . . il est peut-être encore à examiner si la valeur de la force toute naturelle et physique ne la vaut point.'[81]

The fate of nobles in 1789–99 reminds us of the scope that ideology can have in the politics of a society whose class lines are in a state of flux. Had the limits of class been more closely drawn in 1789, had the irrelevance of the tradition of civic humanism been more clear, the leftward drift of the Revolutionary bourgeoisie could hardly have occurred. The importance of the social substratum is not to be denied, but neither is the autonomy of ideology. As Marc Richir has observed in his excellent introduction to Fichte's *Considérations sur la Révolution française*, it was not so much the bourgeoisie which made the French Revolution as it was the Revolution which made the bourgeoisie.[82]

Considered in the abstract, the ideological stance of the Directorials was highly respectable: the Ideologues of the late 1790s were carrying over into positivism the legacy of the

Enlightenment. But in the context of the times and of the divisive political purpose of the Directorials' egalitarian pretence, the ideology of the regime appeared at once irrelevant and repelling. 'L'universalité du peuple français', thought the officials of a village in Cantal, 'est également attachée à la République et à la religion de ses pères,'[83] and writ large, this complaint held for the whole of France: extreme anticlericalism did not please; theophilanthropy fell flat; the use of the Revolutionary calendar was resented; war was unpopular. By linking Republicanism to ideological radicalism, the Directorials merely discredited the Republic. To the unsophisticated, the regime made little sense. Richard Cobb has rightly written that the Thermidorian reaction and Directory are of great interest to historians interested in individuals because men and women were then left to their own devices: 'the recognition signals had been lost, without being replaced by others, so that people had to grope along a narrow ledge, uncertain of the direction in which they were going or of what they might meet round the corner'.[84] One might also say that there were signs, but ones which pointed left although the road went right. The words of the terrorists of 1794 expressed a genuine will to rule; the words of the Directorials were mere self-indulgence. These were indeed men who deserved to be called '[des] grands diseurs de rien'.[85] Ideology in its normal role is the cement of social life, but in 1795–9, it was at once the *raison d'être* and the solvent of Directorial rule.

In 1789–94, the revolutionaries waged ideological warfare with great skill by draping their programme in a rhetoric which their enemies could not deny with ease. In 1789, the rights of man were declared to be embedded in 'nature'; French social and political institutions, it was said, would express the ordered harmony of man and the universe.

When these principles lost their edge, the left in 1792–4 fell back on the cause of nationalism and on accepted views of virtue, vice, and corruption. In succession, Feuillants, Girondins, and Montagnards struck chords which the French nation could understand. But in 1795, the one ideological platform that could make sense was the defence of order. Republicanism as a simple alternative to monarchy was tolerable: the uncompromising royalism of Louis XVIII's proclamation at Verona did not win him many friends. But Republicanism as an egalitarian ideology and a potential threat to order was worse than useless. It did not seduce the poor, and it made the rich anxious.

Directorial principles fell between two stools. As Stein observed in 1850, the Constitution of the year III 'expressed only the general principles of the Revolution but not any of its social elements'.[86] He might have gone further to say that in fact it stood for nothing at all.

In a satire on French politics which he wrote shortly before his death in 1797, Edmund Burke drew up a number of hypothetical constitutions that the French might use. One of them revolved around the idea that it was the representatives who should choose the voters, and Burke's fantasy would in a way have been realized had Bonaparte followed the advice of Sieyes, as Boulay reported it: the right to elect a parliament was taken away from a 'foule d'assemblées sectionnaires' and handed over instead to a 'Collège des conservateurs', . . . véritablement représentatif de toute la France, et le plus capable d'en exprimer les vœux qui ne pouvaient jamais être que conformes à l'intérêt général.' Sieyes would choose the 'conservateurs' who would choose the deputies who would choose Sieyes.[87] The arrangement was, in its way, straightforward; but the relevance of such principles to the life of the nation was less clear.

Former philosophes, now become conservative apologists of the Directorial status quo, but unwilling to give up their principles, understood that the explosive implication of their communitarian principles was at the heart of the problems of the regime. Morellet, for example, conceded that the Enlightenment had roused 'une grande agitation dans les esprits', and he tried to emphasize the 'constructive', conservative aspects of that doctrine: 'on y trouve aussi de la bonne foi, un grand désir d'étendre les lumières, une grande horreur de toute oppression, une grande passion pour tous les genres de liberté compatibles avec l'ordre public. . . .' It was wrong to make a connection between those constructive principles and the socially destructive acts of the Revolution: 'il ne s'y rencontre aucun des principes destructeurs des societés qui ont été depuis répandus et même pratiqués par des ennemis de tout ordre social. . . . [C'est] un torrent d'aveugles disciples, de fous et de furieux qui inondèrent l'empire, l'évangile de leurs maîtres à la main.'[88] This was a point which Mme de Staël also made: '[Les crimes de la Révolution]', she wrote, 'ne sont en aucune manière une conséquence des principes dont ils se sont si injustement appuyés.' Her motivation here was explicit: 'Qui pourrait, en effet, consacrer ce qu'il a de forces à soutenir le système républicain, si l'on pouvait lui attribuer la moindre analogie avec les atrocités inouies qui ont précédé? But Babeuf's reliance on the teachings of Rousseau, Mably, and Morelly was proof that the communitarian principles of the Enlightenment *were* a threat to order. Morellet's defence opened up as many problems as it resolved.

In an unpublished essay which she wrote in the summer of 1799, Mme de Staël described the situation of the Directory with remarkable accuracy. *Des Circonstances actuelles qui peuvent terminer la Révolution et des principes qui doivent fonder la République en France* was a thoughtful piece, 300 pages long, and to a large extent focused on the question of nobles.

The great and irreversible principle of the Revolution, she explained, was 'non-heredity'. Unlike her father, Necker, Mme de Staël did not think that nobility as a legal order could be restored in France: 'La royauté, la noblesse, la pairie, le clergé, la superstition catholique, tout cela peut aller dans les pays où le temps les a consacrés, mais aucune de ces institutions *poétiques* ne peut se transporter dans les nations où elle n'existent pas'.[89] By sapping the traditional belief in the crucial concept of inherited nobility, the philosophes, she admitted, were indeed responsible for the Revolution. That in itself, however, was not to be deplored. The trouble was that the salutary and modern principle of non-heredity had been carried to excess by the Babouvists who had, falsely, presented themselves as the heirs of the Enlightenment: 'Le très petit nombre de démocrates babouvistes . . . veulent que la destruction de la propriété soit fondée sur les mêmes raisonnements qui ont renversé l'esclavage, la féodalité et l'hérédité.'[90]

The Babouvist claims to respectable lineage were, she thought, manifestly unreasonable. Material egalitarianism was not a legitimate derivative of Enlightened thought. Nor for that matter was the excessive philosophical egalitarianism that had found expression in the law on nobles. The key was to consolidate the position of the various élites which had provided the philosophes with their audience before 1789. To banish nobles was simple folly. To recall the name of the man who had proposed it, she wrote, would be ungenerous.[91] The measure was senselessly cruel, and in a passage which Benjamin Constant urged her to delete, Mme de Staël observed that if the law were enforced, one thing leading to another, the French would soon be murdering children: 'bientôt, on sentirait la nécessité de tuer tous les enfants, tous les amis d'une race ainsi proscrite'. Such a law could not be enforced save by terror, and terror was an abomination. The law against nobles was typical of what the regime had come to. The Republic, she thought, had to be redirected. Its emphasis on community was excessive. The state should no longer make demands of the citizens: '[La République doit prendre] pour guide une morale préservatrice plutôt qu'un système de dévouement qui devient féroce lorsqu'il n'est pas volontaire.'[92] The only way out was to bring together nobles and Republican owners of property. 'Il faut . . . que les Républicains deviennent riches, et les riches, républicains.'[93]

Mme de Staël's statements were remarkably prescient. A consolidation of élites was indeed the event that would finally signal that 'la Révolution est finie'. Where she erred, however, was in thinking that such a reconciliation could take place within the context of a Republic and, rather fancifully, a Republic which had made Protestantism its official religion. Her diagnosis was accurate, though her cure was absurd. Mme de Staël over-estimated the popular resonance of Republicanism and anti-Catholicism, but she did clearly see the futility of the Directorial persecution of the noble-born.[94]

vi. Reprise: social class and ideology during the French Revolution

Ideology has been presented in these pages as an aspect that is central to an understanding of Revolutionary politics. This insistence on the importance of ideology is intended not to deny, but to complement the so-called 'Social Interpretation of the French Revolution'.

The argument duplicates, albeit inversely, the classical Marxist view of this question. Marxist historians do not debate the fact that each group which successively came to the fore in 1787–94 expressed its class interests ideologically. Conservative nobles in 1787, like liberal nobles and notables in 1789–91, or Girondins and Jacobins after that, all tried to justify their social claims by making reference to some particular principle: the natural order of an organic state; liberal pluralism; or popular sovereignty, expressed indirectly for the Gironde or directly for the Mountain. The Marxist thesis, however, holds that such ideological claims were derivative and transparent.

The argument of these pages holds instead that the Revolutionary bourgeoisie as a group in 1789 subscribed to an ideology which ran against its basic interest: though committed to the defence of individualism and private property, the Revolutionary bourgeoisie looked forward to the creation of a virtuous communitarian state. But there is a critical point of contact between this view and the Marxist interpretation, because the phasing of disenchantment with virtue and community was, within the Revolutionary party, related to social fact.

Though the bourgeoisie, and with it the liberal aristocracy, fully accepted liberty, equality, and fraternity in 1789, different social groups within that reformist party were at different times disillusioned with this ideological stance. Indeed, by propelling the political system forward and by creating situations which had been inconceivable in 1789, the ideological thrust of Revolutionary politics brought to light social cleavages which would otherwise have remained opaque for decades, cleavages which were barely perceptible in 1789 and were definitively established only in 1848, when a capitalistic form of industrialization gave durability to what had been before ephemeral social forms.

Disenchantment with the possible costs of ideological and Revolutionary communitarianism set in very quickly, and was, from the first, if not class-specific, at least explicable in social terms. The first group to deny communitarianism were the Monarchiens. In June 1789, Mounier, their spokesman, proposed, and the Assembly accepted, that the deputies vow not to dissolve until a constitution was firmly established. In July 1789, it was Mounier again who insisted on the drafting of a declaration of the rights of men: 'Pour qu'une Constitution soit bonne, il faut qu'elle soit fondée sur les droits de l'homme et qu'elle les protège.' But in October 1789, Mounier decided that the Revolution had gone too far, and withdrew together with some of the most conspicuous leaders of the liberal court nobility like Clermont-Tonnerre, Lally-Tollendal, and Virieu.

More revealing yet was the defection in late 1791–2 of another social group which had been even more whole-heartedly committed to reform, the mixed group of Feuillant liberal nobles and *grand bourgeois* notables who stood behind Lafayette, Barnave, and Duport. These Orleanists before the fact were men of social substance who, as a rule, had achieved prominence within the *Ancien Régime*. Well-to-do and established, they differed markedly from their successors, the Girondins, who before 1789 had often been middle-class publicists without an audience and small-time lawyers without clients.

Then, in 1792–3, the running war of Girondins and Montagnards had social undertones as well, and there are many reasons which account for the fact that it was the Girondins who first gave up on the Revolutionary policy of 'no enemies to the left'. The Girondins were a distinct social group. Though far less prominent than their Feuillant predecessors, whose agents they had been at first, the Girondins soon became the proxies of the more modern, sophisticated, and ideologically radical part of the bourgeois reformist élite. In his provocative book on the Girondins, Professor Sydenham has, to be sure, skilfully marshalled all of the arguments that can be used to show that the 'Girondins', as he refers to them, that is, within quotation marks, were not a group, did not know each other well, did not vote as a party, did not represent the *grande bourgeoisie*, and were in critical ways similar to other Conventionnels. Some objections, however, can be raised to Professor Sydenham's statement, especially if the Montagne is compared with the inner core of the Gironde, rather than with a diluted, heterogeneous group of deputies who were subsequently accused of Girondism by the victorious Montagnards. In 1793–4, the Montagnards did in fact significantly differ from their Girondin foes. Montagnards were as a rule provincials, won over to the principles of the Enlightenment. Montagnards were more respectable socially than Girondins and came from more respectable families. The ties of Montagnards were to the smaller towns and to the more established bourgeois professions, like the army or the service of the state; the Girondins, on the other hand, were more often sons of tradesmen and small merchants, like Vergniaud, whose father was a failed entrepreneur, or Brissot, the heir of a pastry cook.

Lines of geographical differentiation were not neat, but the Girondins were also likely to have passed over from their small home towns to the growing cities of the coast or to Paris. Although the Girondins were not rich, they were closer to the rich than were the Montagnards and therefore more afraid than the Mountain of the poor and the sans-culottes, the likes of which did not exist in the small towns where the Montagnards grew up. The Girondins were *arriviste* and well-connected modernizers, 'des hommes à talent' who lacked bourgeois *gravitas*. As intellectuals and publicists, they drifted to the fore of a radicalized Revolution in 1791, but they fell back in late 1792 when more serious problems arose.

Objections to a class interpretation of the Revolution cannot be ignored, and caution must be used in referring to the Monarchien 'nobles', Fayettiste 'notables', Girondin 'bourgeois arrivistes', and the Montagnard 'provincial bourgeoisie'. It has been sensibly suggested, for example, that class did not exist in 1789–99 because it did not exist either before or after that decade, and it cannot be denied that the Revolutionary social fetus was, as it were, still-born. But that is not to say that it never existed. It is not surprising that class could not remain after 1789 the matrix of politics in France: French society in the 1780s had hardly reached a level of economic development capable of sustaining in ordinary times a modern political structure based on the phenomenon of class division. Indeed, when Revolutionary fevers abated, it became difficult to remember that these divisions had ever existed: the *enragés*, for example, whom Robespierre in the summer of 1793 had branded as one of three principal enemies of the Revolutionary state, along with Austria and Pitt, vanished from the historiography of the Revolution for nearly half a century, and were only given their rightful importance in the history of the period by Mathiez, in the 1920s. The larger message here may well be that 'classes are not things'. They are not to be thought of as elements of a static structure, but as fluid categories that stand in relation, and, at times, in political relation to each other.

The class politics of 1789–99, however ephemeral, are historically crucial as a forerunner of modern European political life.[95] Only with the Industrial Revolution was the transitory quality of class consciousness based on political cleavage replaced by a more durable awareness of class conflict, based in part on political memories, to be sure, but based also on newer concerns such as the division of labour, more visible differences of wealth, access to education, the curtailment of civil rights, or legal discrimination by the rich against the poor. None the less, the fact remains that it was in 1789–94 that these differences of class first appeared. That the appearance of new social forms could not be sustained does not mean, in the words of Alfred Cobban, that the sans-culottes were a red herring drawn across the path of history. It is to say instead that the conjunction of events which dominated politics during the Terror was simultaneously fortuitous (because it was due to unique historical accidents) and prophetic (because it gave a brilliant relief to a stratification of classes which would otherwise have remained, despite its exemplary nature, latent and obscure).

Objections to a class interpretation of the French Revolution can to some degree be met if certain factors are kept in mind. The first is the unusual weight in this decade of ideological considerations. In 1789–99, small differences of class were given great prominence because they were magnified by ideological concerns. Both before and during the Revolution, material circumstances, like the structure of property or the relationship of the bourgeoisie to the burden of the seigneurial system, were constantly amplified by ideological concepts, which themselves could be apprehended in divergent ways: Robespierre and Brissot were both bourgeois men of law but the relatively slight differences in their status were greatly magnified by being set in the dramatic contrast of their divergent views of what the structure of French society ought to be.

A second important factor when gauging the role of class is that concerns of class, symbolized and magnified by ideological concerns, did not focus on material issues as much as they did on the basic question of how far the Revolution might go. The results were often paradoxical. Deputies who were socially at odds might at different times make identical economic pronouncements because their main preoccupation was the larger issue of the movement of the Revolution. Statements on specific material problems cannot be taken as a litmus test of politics or class, because the principle concern of the participants was the single and all-important issue of the progression of Revolutionary movement. On that question, on the extent to which the Revolution should proceed in accord with the 'plebs', the revolutionaries did divide along class lines, but the varying and contradictory verdicts which they might make in passing on this or that problem are not significant. It does not really matter, therefore, that Montagnards and Girondins may have made similar statements about price controls at different times. As Mathiez pointed out, the only Conventionnel who truly favoured government regulation of prices was not a Montagnard, but a Girondin sympathizer, Viger. And it is also of little consequence that Saint-Just in November 1792 gave an impassioned apologia for *laissez-faire* which earned the plaudits of the Girondin leader Brissot: 'Saint-Just traite la question à fond, et sous tous les rapports politiques et moraux; il déploie de l'esprit, de la chaleur et de la philosophie, et honore son talent en défendant la liberté.'[96]

Such statements do not prove that Saint-Just and Viger were of the same class, or that the Girondins were more or less radical than the Montagnards. Nor does it matter very much that Brissot and

Vergniaud were varyingly Republicans or royalists. As Carnot put it, 'lorsque vous avez votez la loi du maximum, par exemple, la question n'était pas de savoir si vous, négociants ou philosophes, trouviez cette loi mauvaise, mais si le peuple la voulait oui ou non'.[97]

The crucial issue was the point at which the players decided that 'la Révolution est finie', which in turn meant that no further attention would be paid to popular insistance that ideological equality be given political and practical embodiment; and on that overriding issue, social lines of division were clear-cut, or rather became so as the Revolution progressed. Initially, the propertied revolutionaries, whether noble, notable, or bourgeois, had been communitarian universalists, committed to the creation of a fraternal state. But with the passing of years, or even months and weeks, some social groups were far more quick than others to abandon their earlier ideological vision. It is difficult to separate Montagnards and Girondins if we concentrate on their day-to-day pronouncements, but it is less difficult to see that by the autumn of 1792 the Girondins, a particular social group, had tired of community, just as Barnave and the Feuillants had wearied of it in the summer of 1791—and Robespierre and the Mountain felt in the autumn and winter of 1793 that the popular movement had got out of hand.

The interweaving of ideology and class in the early years, that is, in 1789–94, also follows from a comparison of Revolutionary politics before and after Robespierre. In 1789–94, different reactions to the political implications of ideological statements brought social differences into the open. In 1795–9, the situation was reversed. In these later years, all shades of the bourgeoisie were united in the defence of property. And in this period ideological differences were no longer creative socially. Anti-clericalism and antimonarchism did still matter, because they made it impossible for one part of the bourgeoisie to come to terms with some other bourgeois factions, but these same ideological concerns had no bearing on the relationship of the bourgeoisie to the poor. Though equality was everywhere proclaimed, it was also flouted in every instance. Vapid logomachy necessarily ensued. The expression of ideological concerns in 1789–94 draws our attention, because words then had social consequence. But in 1795, the same words counted for very little, and the men who spoke them cannot arouse our sympathy. Indeed, the Directory can be seen as the emptiest phase in the political and cultural evolution of the French social élite in the last decade of the eighteenth century.

In 1789, despite the existence, on the extreme right and left, of dissenting minorities whose role has been exaggerated by most historians of the period, despite the Parlementaires and Marat, let us say, the broad majority of the French bourgeoisie and aristocracy were increasingly coming together as a new social élite which expressed itself uncertainly through an ideology that placed community above the defence of individualism and property. (Indeed, it can also be suggested that even the Parlementaires and Marat accepted large parts of that ambiguous message as well.) In 1800, that same élite, politically chastened, was reconstituted on a new ideological basis: though the foundations of nascent capitalism had been set back by the events of the times, the élite was now far more thoroughly committed to individualism and property than it had ever been; 'La propriété, ou la société', wrote Mme de Staël in 1799, 'c'est une seule et même chose.'[98] Admittedly, irreconcilable minorities still existed in 1800 on the far right and left, minorities whose opinions had crystallized around the humiliating experiences of emigration and repression. But most of the propertied French bourgeoisie-nobility was now of one opinion again, as it had been in 1789, though of course the opinion of 1799 was the opposite of what had been believed ten years before: community was forgotten, individualism was extolled. Piece by piece, the constituent parts of the élites had moved from the pre- to the post-Revolutionary model: Barnave and the Feuillants, many of them liberal nobles, had done this in 1791; Robespierre and the moderate Republicans, many of them drawn from the provincial bourgeoisie, had begun to do so in 1793. The years of the Directory were the period in which the whole of the Revolutionary bourgeoisie, already won over to social conservatism, finally adapted its principles to its practice, albeit in a circuitious way, since the passion of anti-nobilism and anti-corporatism rose to fever pitch only months before the final break.

In 1791–4, the political life of France became ever more serious and tragic, because it was in these years that the modern problem of class confrontation arose, and that one segment after another of the French social élite reluctantly came to understand that community and the defence of property did not overlap. In 1794–9, by contrast, intra-bourgeois politics became ever more trivial because they were emptied of their social content. The suppression of Babouvism was a world-historical event, even though Babeuf's audience was probably minuscule. But Sieyes's war on nobles, or for that matter against the left and right bourgeois Republicans, was trivial, regardless of its apparent importance at the time, because it was about words only. To consider the minutiae of the social distinctions that separated Girondins and Jacobins is meaningful; to consider the larger gap that separated the friends and foes of the coup of fructidor is less rewarding. The quarrel of Brissot and Robespierre, both of them mediocrities, has a grandeur that is not equalled by the rivalry of Sieyes and Carnot, both of them men of talent and distinction.

vii. The abbé Sieyes as Revolutionary archetype

The law against nobles of November 1797, in its motivation and inapplicability, is revealing of the nature of Directorial rule, and of the interplay during those years of ideology, politics, and social structure. Equally indicative, it may be added, is the personality of its maker, the abbé Sieyes, 'the key figure of an entire political generation'. No more representative figure of the Revolution as a whole could be found than this man, whom Lefebvre aptly described as the 'soul of the French juridical revolution'.[99]

Sieyes has two faces, and more than any other political figure straddles the fundamental contradictions of Revolutionary bourgeois universalism. There is a chauvinist, budget-balancing, centralizing, socially conservative Sieyes, recognized in 1815 as the spokesman 'de la bourgeoisie et des propriétaires' by none other than Guizot, a certified connoisseur in the field.[100] This is the same Sieyes who, before he thought of deporting nobles or depriving them of their citizenship, also dreamt of deporting the unemployed to the colonies.

But there is a second Sieyes, a true child of the Enlightenment who holds the past to be irrelevant. For him, the law, which he likens to an immense globe, in the manner perhaps of Boullée's sketches, treats all citizens equally. In relation to the State, all citizens, without exception, stand at the same distance and occupy equal places.[101] The general will does not encompass all particular wills completely—each individual has inalienable rights—but the general will must be the will of all. 'Tous les pouvoirs publics, sans distinctions', he wrote, 'sont une émanation de la volonté générale; tous viennent du peuple, c'est-à-dire de la nation. Ces deux termes doivent être synonymes.'[102] The general will transcended the juxtaposition of individual desires, and it was with regret that Sieyes accepted the need in 1790 to suspend the equal voting rights of the poorest citizens, very much as he deplored also the selfish way in which Constitutants had assigned to landlords—and themselves—the gains that flowed from the abolition of feudal dues.

Very interested in *fêtes*, a partisan of women's rights, an advocate of free education, and suspicious of the unlimited applications of *laissez-faire*, Sieyes was also struck by the necessity of co-operation in modern society. No one else in the Terror had a reputation so far removed from fact: 'J'ai vécu' is what we remember of this man whom Robespierre aptly labelled 'la taupe de la Révolution'. But what contemporaries imagined instead was a ferocious power behind the Revolutionary throne: 'je jugeais mal', wrote Louis XVIII in 1794, 'l'âme de tigre de l'abbé Sieyes'.[103]

The two sides of this man appear to be far apart, but there is a link between them, which is his unrelenting hatred of the ci-devants. On this issue, the growing intensity of his feelings parallels the decline of his Revolutionary zeal and the rise of his complacency. In 1789, Sieyes the Warrior leaned to the left socially and struck a countervailing, middling stance on nobles: as a caste they must metaphorically return to Franconia, but as individuals they had a role to play. In 1797, when his hesitations on the disenfranchisement of the poor were long since gone, Sieyes's hatred of nobles was drastically radicalized. The one made up for the other.

Barante, in his account of the anti-noble law, described Sieyes strolling on the Champs Élysées and puzzling on the fact that the rich had carriages though the poor must walk; although deplorable, such inequality was none the less, he felt, a fact of life: 'C'est à cause de cela que notre loi sur l'expulsion de la noblesse sera rejetée.'[104] If nobles were banished, the inequalities of life would lessen; if the citizens of France were less selfish and more civic minded, nobles would long since have been excluded from the body politic. For Sieyes as it had been for Saint-Just, the expulsion of nobles was at once a positive social act and a symbolic gesture. Anti-aristocratism—real in 1794, trivialized in 1797—was the last refuge of bourgeois universalism come face to face with social inequality.[105]

Chapter Seven

Epilogue

i. The changing place of nobles in French life

The question of the rights of nobles has historical importance in its own right, but its principal interest lies in its implications for an understanding of French society and politics at the end of the eighteenth and the beginning of the nineteenth century. The rhythm of economic and social change in eighteenth-century France, as was pointed out in the first pages of this book, was neither insignificant nor overwhelming. Although France was not so modern a society as Britain was, French social structure in the last decade of the *Ancien Régime* was changing rapidly. France was increasingly a society of class where differences of status based on birth were losing their edge. Conditions in France were more mixed than they were in Britain: north of the Channel, the land-owning gentry had become a class of rural capitalists; in France, by contrast, many bourgeois had become land-owning seigneurs. But within the context of a semi-capitalist society, lines of caste in France were blurring. Economic corporatism was practically defunct. Many modern-minded aristocrats were involved in banking, manufacturing, and trade. Owners of property, regardless of status, were more aware than they had been earlier of the problem of urban poverty and were more afraid of the poor. France in the 1780s was not yet a capitalistic society, but neither was it still a society of Orders.

Ideologically, however, the consciousness of whatever social realignment had taken place was not fully realized. The institutions of the *Ancien Régime* which discriminated against the *roturier* gave to traditional barriers against social mobility an appearance of strength which they did not have. Many nobles, who otherwise accepted the reality of economic and social change, retained a traditionalist sensibility which gave offence. In some ways, then, the bourgeoisie and the aristocracy were becoming a single propertied élite; but this fusion was far from complete when the Revolution broke out.

The ambiguity of the bourgeoisie's relations to nobles was compounded by the ideological climate in France in the last years of the *Ancien Régime*. In Britain and America, the classical balance between the rights of the citizen and his civic obligation had yielded to the assertion of the rights of the individual and of private property. The French were less decisive. A small minority did follow the Anglo-American example, while, on the other side, another minority chose instead to reassert civic obligations, now set in a socialist or even collectivist context. But most literate Frenchmen preferred to think that the old balance might be preserved. The result was an unstable compromise which re-asserted the rights of individualism and of property without rejecting the longing for a state that would be at once virtuous and communitarian. In that context, the bourgeoisie found it difficult to abandon its vision of a united people. When political circumstances forced it to choose between property and community, the bourgeoisie chose an entente with the 'plebs' in the name of community in preference to an entente with nobles in the name of property.

Bourgeois-noble relations in 1789 were thus doubly precarious, in both fact and theory. Two political resolutions could emerge. The first was a tentative alliance of all owners of property, regardless of caste. The second was an alliance of the Revolutionary bourgeoisie with the 'plebs'; and imbedded in that policy was the gradual deterioration of nobles' rights, although ultimately, of course, the limits of bourgeois Revolutionary action were clearly drawn. Though the nobility as an order could never be revived, nobles as individual owners of property could not be enduringly oppressed.

Initially, therefore, the French bourgeoisie in 1789 did make room for nobles, taken as citizens. Though nobility could be no more tolerated than any other corps, nobles as individuals were made full partners of the new régime. But when this entente broke down in the autumn of 1791, the Revolutionary bourgeoisie, true to its communitarian principles, altered its course and gradually sacrificed the rights of nobles in an opportunistic effort to please the crowd. This was an alliance which did not make much sense socially but which appeared to be politically astute. It was also ideologically acceptable because the cultural expression of the pre-Revolutionary bourgeoisie's latent existence as a class was, paradoxically, the assertion of the intrinsic harmony of society as a whole, and a belief in the similarity of interests between rich and poor.

In late 1793, this view began to decompose as well. The

bourgeoisie was repelled by the social claims which the poor were entitled to make as citizens of a bourgeois but universalist state. The tension between social reality and the bourgeoisie's egalitarian principles soon became intolerable. For some, the message was that the Revolution had gone too far. For others, like Robespierre, the solution consisted in drastically accentuating the purpose of the Revolution as the triumph of virtue over the vice and corruption that were embodied, as it happened, by the nobles and in finding an ideological egalitarian solution, like the persecution of nobles, to a difficult social problem. Terror was used to enforce this solution on that part of the bourgeoisie that no longer supported egalitarian principles, and on the 'plebs', for whom equality in principle only was not enough.

The results were self-defeating, especially after 1794, when the use of terror was ruled out. After the appearance of the sans-culottes on the far left, the bourgeoisie, however Revolutionary it might be, understood that communitarian principles were potentially dangerous. But before 1799, it could not for all that bring itself to give up antimonarchism, anticlericalism or the pretence of social equality which remained in theory the very foundation of the regime.

The options of the Revolutionary bourgeoisie in 1795–9 were severely limited. In consequence, its quest for ideological surrogates became more acute than it had ever been, especially after the coup of fructidor in September 1797. The Directory's policy on nobles came out of this impasse. Nobles were persecuted, as proof of the bourgeoisie's commitment to egalitarianism, but in a half-hearted way. Committed to defend property in any form, the Directorials could not envisage the confiscation of even the suspects' property, as Saint-Just had done with the decrees of ventôse. The contradictions of Directorial policy were blatant, and, here as elsewhere, point to Bonaparte's suspensions in 1799 of the political debate.[1] It may well have been with some secret relief that the regicides themselves accepted in 1800 the return of nobles from abroad when they had been émigrés, or from their absurd isolation, if they had stayed at home. After the constipating reign of virtue, in 1794, comes the 'lâche soulagement' of Napoleonic rule.

The place of nobles in France after 1799 and the rule of Bonaparte can be considered in this same perspective. In both material and ideological terms, nobles were more secure after 1799 than they had been before; but at the same time, their role in French life was closely circumscribed. In a material sense, nobles in 1814 were much as they had been in 1789. Because most of them had not left France, where many of them supported the Revolution, the nobles' loss of property was much less than it would have been if the French Revolution had really been a war of progressive bourgeois versus feudal nobles. In some ways, it is true, the material gaps between bourgeois and nobles did widen, since many of their common interests were destroyed, like ownership of the royal debt, loans to peasants, seigneurialism, venal offices, or overseas and colonial trade. But on balance the structure of property in France in 1799 remained *grosso modo* as it had been in 1789. The bourgeoisie did not gain very much, because the French Revolution retarded economic growth, even if it made subsequent growth more feasible; and most nobles managed to stay afloat during their time of trouble.

Materially, then, conditions were as they had been and in 1799 no more dictated or precluded an alliance on the basis of property than they had in 1789. But what did change and what made an alliance of the two groups far more workable was the drastic ideological realignment of all parties. Most studies of the nobility after the Revolution have taken as their starting point Marc Bloch's concern with the extent of noble landed property after 1789. 'There are few problems', wrote this eminent historian, 'whose solutions are more important to our exact understanding of nineteenth-century France.'[2] This is true, without a doubt, but it is less perhaps than the whole truth: the extent of noble property *per se* could be unusually revealing only if it had been altered drastically, which it was not. An appreciation of the place in society of nobles must indeed begin with a true reading of their landed wealth, but this is only a first step. An equally important second step is to see that in 1799 the bourgeoisie's perception of social structure, of nobles, and of the scope of community in French life was palpably different from what it had been ten years before. After 1799, the bourgeoisie understood that it could not afford to persecute nobles, and in any case, it no longer wanted to.

In some important ways the French Revolution did show, it is true, that the bourgeoisie did not need the help of nobles. It could, if need be, rule without them. As Mme de Staël observed, emigration had sapped the prestige of the nobility. After 1789, a bourgeois generation 'a vécu, prospéré, triomphé sans les privilegiés[;] elle croit encore pouvoir exister par elle-même'.[3]

The 'plebeian' generals of Napoleon's army (many of them, as it happens, nobles) were proof that non-nobles could rule not only France, but Europe.

At the same time, the memory of 1793–4, far more than that of Austerlitz or Jena, remained the pivot of French political thinking. To be sure, the French bourgeoisie knew that it could manage on its own, but it also seemed to many (quite wrongly again) that the race between the *honnêtes gens* and the *canaille* in 1793–4 had been very close. French nobles were perhaps more necessary than had been thought, and in any case less to be envied. Socially and politically, the bourgeoisie after 1794 could not afford to humiliate or even to ignore nobles, and culturally it did not need to do so. The costs could only be greater than the gains, and in consequence the bourgeois image of nobles steadily improved. The eighteenth century had seen a steady deterioration of the nobles' reputation, which reached its nadir with their denaturalization in November 1797. But after 1800 the pattern was reversed. In the 1780s the average bourgeois had thought of himself as a non-noble, quite close, really, to 'le peuple', in spirit if not in fact. After 1799, the bourgeois became a non-worker, whose aim, now openly avowed, was 'vivre noblement'.

From the other side, so did most nobles also understand what had happened. Some of them, to be sure, steadfastly adhered to a 'politique du pire', and remained loyal to Church and King. Just as some nobles, and some bourgeois, too, had refused before 1789 to become part of a single, new élite, so did some noble royalists and many bourgeois Republicans continue to squabble even after 1870 when socialists had long since been knocking at the gate. Nor is this particularly surprising, since the social bases of aristocratic exclusivism and Catholic traditionalism were to survive well into the twentieth century, when they found their last expression in the Vichy government of 1940–2. It can in fact be supposed that the archaic tradition of exclusivism was exacerbated by Revolutionary persecution, so that its votaries were after 1815 even more determined than they had been before 1789.

In the main, however, most nobles complied. Equality of taxation was after 1800 universally understood to be inevitable, as was the rationalization of administrative institutions, the tolerance of religious sects, and the juridical irrelevance of birth. All the institutional issues which had kept bourgeois and nobles apart before 1789 were resolved. The lines of class between rich and poor were more closely drawn, and the importance of wealth over birth was more widely accepted.

Nobles rallied overwhelmingly to Napoleon I. Most of them abandoned Charles X in July 1830, and most of them accepted Louis-Philippe, the Second Republic, and Napoleon III in turn. Like the Orleanist bourgeoisie, nobles after 1815 understood the need for élitist solidarity. Their place in bourgeois life was important, and the July Monarchy was in many respects their regime as much as it was that of the bankers. It may well be that *embourgeoisé* nobles, like Louis-Philippe himself, held their place on sufferance, but what matters here is that they held it.

A 'dialectical compromise' is discernible: the bourgeoisie, after 1799, shared power with nobles in a way that could hardly have been imagined some months before. But in the same way, nobles now had to frame their manner to the times, not only by accepting the laws of the market as the principle of social life but by accepting in government a position of dependence which even liberal nobles would have found hard to swallow ten years before, and which the British aristocracy, by contrast, managed to avoid for another century at least. The will of the actors yielded to historical constraint. No single better instance can be found of this than the fate of l'abbé Sieyes, ennobled in 1808, a count of the Empire and a *grand officier* of the Legion of Honour. 'Avez-vous vu Sieyes', said Doulcet de Pontécoulant at a Napoleonic ceremony which the former abbé attended in court dress, 'Avez-vous vu Sieyes? *Qu'est-ce que le Tiers-état?*'[4]

More consciously bourgeois than before, and far less communitarian, the French bourgeoisie shifted its grounds on nobles accordingly. Essentially, the shock of the Revolution reversed the importance of the two *discours*: of exclusion (which led the bourgeoisie in the name of virtue or community to choose the 'plebs' over the nobles) and of inclusion (which united bourgeois and nobles in the common defence of the propertied interest). The bourgeoisie became more cautious, and most nobles became more humble. For most owners of property, quarrels of birth and precedence were, after the French Revolution, a luxury which no one could afford.

The manifestly irrelevant curtailment of the rights of nobles during the Revolutionary decade in a society that was increasingly obsessed by the problems of property and class was the precondition for the partial acceptance, at least after 1799, of the theory of converging élites. The material preconditions for the existence of an élite existed before 1789, but only with the French Revolution did an awareness of this social reality become a self-evident assumption for most propertied Frenchmen.

Morellet's mournful ululations, in his memoirs of 1825, illustrate the enormous gap which, after the Revolution, separated Frenchmen from their past. A disciple of the philosophes, a publicist in Turgot's time, Morellet *after* the Revolution could hardly understand why the nobility, which he had known so well, could have been so obtuse *before* the Revolution. The nobles and the clergy, he wrote, fought for their privileges, which they held to be just. What they should have done instead was to underscore their rights as owners of property: 'ils ne faisaient pas valoir leur véritable titre, leur véritable droit, celui de la propriété, et la nécessité de la défendre pour le bien de tous'. Had the nobles been less proud, he went on, they surely would have understood how wise it was for them to make common cause with the propertied but common herd. Nobles, merchants, lawyers, and manufacturers would then have sat in Parliament together as owners of property. 'Et ils ne voyaient pas qu'en les y admettant,' he concluded: 'Ils eussent acquis autant de défenseurs de leurs droits réels et légitimes.'[5]

Morellet was right in a way. Noble pride and bourgeois prejudice did have something to do with the breakdown of the Revolution. But what he forgot was that, before the sans-culottes, the costs of self-indulgence had seemed bearable enough for all parties concerned. In retrospect, however, it can also be said that everyone was right here, not just Morellet, but the subjects of his scorn as well. With political hindsight, the memoirist could see with blinding clarity what was before the Revolution hidden in the sometimes conflicting flow of social history. But neither the nobles nor the bourgeois of 1789 can be blamed for the existence of that opaqueness. The point is of general significance, perhaps, since it illustrates the fact that economic and social events do not speak for themselves, and that no historical investigation that limits itself to such facts and their presentation can yield much more than a disembodied truth. The most sophisticated and quantified investigations of our cultural and material past can be quite as unrewarding as those arid discussions of diplomacy which once delighted the practitioners of the historian's craft. Identical social, economic, or cultural events can have radically different meanings in contexts that are not politically the same. Truly understood, social history must involve politics, just as political history, properly understood, must involve the study of society in all its forms.

ii. Bourgeois universalism in historical perspective

The evolution of the rights of nobles tells us a great deal about the French Revolution. It also tells us something about the limits of community in an individualistic social context. All modern societies are blends of *Gemeinschaft* and *Gesellschaft*; 'There is irreplaceable truth in both tendencies.'[6] The most totalitarian systems of government accept the inalienability of some individual rights, and the economic and social scope of government in Peel's and Gladstone's Britain was, as we now know, quite extensive. The question is, of course, where, precisely, ought the state and community to stop and individualism begin?

Caught as they often were between their particularist leanings and their craving for virtuous community, the French *classes moyennes* rummaged for ersatz solutions which would not endanger their social supremacy but might placate *le peuple*. The anti-nobilism of the French bourgeois Revolutionaries was *per se* something of a curiosity, but as a harbinger of frustrated universalism, its implications were very great indeed. A parallel readily springs to mind with the false democracy of nationalism which time and again has been the final bourgeois answer to social conflict—as anti-aristocratism was in 1797—a solution as disastrous for the bourgeoisie as it has been empty for the working class. Anti-Semitism falls under the same rubric, less a socialism of fools than the socialism of a bourgeoisie intent on diverting the attention of the electorate away from its complaints about the particularism of the possessing class towards a marginal, expendable, and defenceless group.

By and large, the experience of French society in the nineteenth and twentieth centuries has been that the more the bourgeoisie has strained to create a communitarian polity, the more ideologically vacuous its aims have been and the more politically helpless its chosen victims have become. The persecution of nobles in 1794 and 1797 is in that sense at the fountainhead of a long tradition, in other settings, of great brutality, and in France, of empty words: 'tu causes, tu causes', says Zazie's parrot to her uncle, 'c'est tout ce que tu sais faire'.

Implicit in the nature of French citizenship were the prospects of future alliances between workers and bourgeoisie, alliances which could never succeed. Conceptually, the situation of the Gironde in 1792, of the Mountain in 1793, or of Ledru-Rollin in 1848 was also that of Gambetta (*première manière*) in 1869 and of Léon Blum in 1936.

Before the Revolution, bourgeois universalism was an appealing doctrine. The advantages which it held out were considerable, including as they did careers open to talents and the prospect of a more just and harmonious world. The possible gains were high, and there would be no costs. Quite obviously, however, bourgeois universalism lost much of its appeal with the Terror and the farce of Directorial politics, which brought class tensions to fever pitch, not yet the tensions of proletariat and bourgeoisie, of course, but none the less, of *le peuple* against *l'aristocratie*, of the Babouvists against the *honnêtes gens*, and of the haves against the have-nots. Since then, bourgeois universalism has been more properly seen as an oxymoron, by the right, for whom it is dangerous, and by the left, which has derided its emptiness. Babeuf understood this in 1796 with complete clarity. When tried for rebellion, he asked where the legitimacy born of adherence to the principles of the Enlightenment now was? Had not the Directors betrayed the egalitarian principles of the philosophes and thereby forfeited their right to rule?

Change here was swift, and in a single decade of Revolution the epistemologically varied fund of bourgeois universalism was drastically reduced. Though the negative defence from oppression did of course remain, its positive social content was largely abandoned. Adam Smith was dethroned by Malthus.

Bourgeois idealism did not by any means disappear. Guizot's 'instruisez-vous et enrichissez-vous par l'épargne et par le travail' was still a moral injunction and quite close in spirit to Condorcet's opinion of the 1790s: 'Tout citoyen, artisan, cultivateur marié peut être citoyen actif; il suffit qu'il soit laborieux et économe.'[7] But the imperiousness of Guizot's injunction is the measure of his unease. After the French Revolution, bourgeois universalism no longer flowed smoothly. The heroic Graeco-Roman mould of David yielded to the sterile and domesticated classicism of Ingres.

In retrospect, what had gone wrong was clear for all to see. With inimitable and untranslatable Teutonic grace, Goethe's patron Prince Carl August succinctly summarized the problem when he wrote in March 1793 that the aim of the 'Free French' had appeared to be liberty but that it had really been '[den]

Besitzern die Hosen ausszuziehen, um die Unbehossten damit zu bekleiden'.[3] The French bourgeoisie as a whole might have underwritten Dumouriez's similar understanding of its failure: 'la liberté et l'égalité . . . adoptés dans un sens trop matériel, et poussés à l'excès par le peuple, ont amené la subversion de tous les états et l'anarchie'.[9] But what was obvious in 1799 was opaque in 1789. It is only at the dusk of History that the owl of Minerva takes flight.

iii. Some general thoughts: historical method and the guilt of nobles

Removed from the historical implications of the problem, but o interest none the less, is the relative indifference which many historians have shown to the sufferings of individual nobles, surely no more or less guilty than most. Living in exile at Fribourg Mme de Montagu heard first of the execution of her great aun and uncle, and later, in a single day, of the killing of her grand mother, mother, and sister: 'Mme de Montagu pensa mourir d douleur, puis la religion la sauva du désespoir, et elle ne voulut plu vivre que pour la charité'.[10] But the plight of such people does not on the whole, elicit our sympathy. Richard Cobb, a writer o great finesse and sensibility, has described these effete nobles i rather ironic terms:

> In the year II . . . elderly aristocratic ladies of the *faubourg*, abandoned b their children, who had emigrated, and living in the maids' attics of thei former palaces, requisitioned for the expanding needs of a revolutionar bureaucracy, committed suicide by throwing themselves out of hig windows, after leaving notes for the *commissaire de police*, asking him t provide for a pet lap-dog or for a canary, left behind from the genera wreck of life. . . . In 1795–6, suicide takes a further toll, but this time poor women, driven desperate by hunger and seeking an end for them selves and for their children in a conveniently-placed Seine.[11]

Some suicides are tragic; others are almost comic, and the tone o this passage is all the more remarkable for Richard Cobb' humanistic view of the French Revolution. From his very rea sympathy for the flotsam and jetsam of life whose private calendar are out of step with history's 'vast impersonal forces' might hav emerged a more lenient view of innocents who happened to b noble.

Albert Soboul is even less attentive to the plight of the noble-born. His account of the 160 émigrés shot mostly for no reason after fructidor takes up three lines, two of them a description of one such victim as an insurgent. But a whole page is awarded to the 36 people shot after prairial, with 6 Conventionnels listed one by one. 'Ce sont les *martyrs de prairial*.'[12] Who died in 1795? 'Primarily', says Cobb, 'the women and the small children of the urban *petit peuple*, of the *faubouriens*, and of village artisans, weavers, and shipwrights. Many urban artisans and elderly *indigents* also died: the rich did not die.'[13] This is not altogether so: 748 prisoners captured at Quiberon, half of them nobles, also died that year.[14] Revolutions are dreadful things where rich and poor alike are maimed, the latter more than the former as always. But my point is not to cheapen the sufferings of the poor; it is instead to emphasize that compassion cannot be rationed by class.

Albert Soboul writes of the 'contained emotion' that Georges Lefebvre felt when he cited that speech of Robespierre's which he preferred above all others, in which the Incorruptible explained that

> Ce qui est plus dur pour un patriote, c'est que, depuis deux ans, cent mille hommes ont été égorgés par trahison et par faiblesse: c'est la faiblesse pour les traîtres qui nous perd. On s'attendrit pour les hommes les plus criminels, pour ceux qui livrent la patrie au fer de l'ennemi: moi, je ne sais m'attendrir que pour la vertu malheureuse; je ne sais m'attendrir que pour l'innocence opprimée; je ne sais m'attendrir que sur le sort d'un peuple malheureux qu'on égorge avec tant de scélératesse.

These lines, writes Professor Soboul, depict for us not only the Incorruptible, but his historian.[15] It is sad to think that this was so.

The persecution of nobles during the French Revolution should certainly not be made more ferocious than it was. In the end, as has been said, only 2 or 3 per cent of French nobles were killed with official sanction. There is no cause here for wailing or the gnashing of teeth. Quiberon was not Auschwitz. But the death of nobles was sufficiently embedded in the fabric of Revolutionary thought and politics to warrant our attention. Although the numbers involved were small, they were not insignificant, and numbers in any case are not everything. By the standards to which we have become, alas, accustomed, the 40,000 victims of the Terror as a whole are themselves a minuscule group. The principles involved are none the less of enduring interest as regards both the Terror and the nobles. A moral problem does exist and must be considered here, even if apologists for Revolutionary violence and crime have as rule ignored it. The numbers are very small, they say. Or the problem is held to be a *faux problème*. A variety of arguments have been brought to bear on the issue.

The most common justification of punishment has also been the most simple: nobles were justly punished because they were individually guilty of counter-revolutionary acts and of being personally hostile to the Revolution as shown by steps taken during or before the Revolution. This was the reasoning of Lefebvre in his well-received essay on the murder in June 1791 of Dampierre, a count who had taken it upon himself to make a show of loyalty to Louis XVI during the monarch's return from Varennes. With great skill, Lefebvre describes Dampierre as an unusually unpopular man who had made a fetish of collecting feudal dues. Quite obviously, then, the victim's reputation, as well as the atmosphere of fear and suspicion which followed Louis's flight, explained the peasantry's murderous intent. The Count was an enemy of the Revolution. His past and present were there to prove it. His assassination was purposeful, and although Lefebvre did not by any means explicitly condone it, he describes the murder without much passion and shows it to have been readily understandable: 'the men who surrounded him on 22 June . . . considered that his attitude had been provocative. [His murder] can doubtless be seen as another episode of the Great Fear that followed the flight of the King. But as is always true, through the political event, one can see the social unrest which was the mainspring of the Popular Revolution.'[16]

The same reasoning can be applied in a more general way. Nobles who disapproved of the Revolution or who had been hateful seigneurs before 1789 were bound to suffer, and nothing should be made of it. Such nobles may have felt innocent, but were in fact culpable. The nation, in a sense, had no choice. The people had been provoked and were now fighting back. Their enemies should have had sense enough to yield. The reasoning is not new and was in fact commonly used at the time by moderates to explain excesses from which they had benefitted but of which they were not proud. As Nodier put it in his *Souvenirs de la Révolution française*, 'Ce qui stimule les grandes cruautés, ce sont les grandes résistances'.[17]

Another line of justification has been to emphasize the historical need for persecution. To be sure, Dampierre deserved his fate, but even if he had been personally innocent, his death would still have served a useful purpose. It neutralized his class and paralysed the enemies of a Revolution which was historically a necessity. Some of its victims were innocent perhaps, but their anguish must be set in the larger context of 'world-social-justice'. Lefebvre, for example, admits that some émigrés left France simply because they were afraid. But, he then adds, persecution still made sense because most émigrés hoped to return to France by force of allied arms. 'On these grounds, the rigour of the revolutionaries can be explained.' To be sure, most émigrés could or would not personally become combatants and to punish non-combatants might seem wrong. But it could not be helped: 'to persecute such people was an inevitable inconvenience. Otherwise, anti-émigré legislation would have become inefficacious, something which the revolutionaries could not accept.'[18]

Some collectivists (social democrats) and some revolutionaries (Proudhonists) have, it is true, consistently disavowed the use of violence. It is also true that nearly all revolutionary groups have disavowed political assassination on strict instrumental grounds: to believe that political murder might do some good is to be politically naïve. It is great forces, not great men, that move the world. Moreover, even the most adamant collectivists today would not accept as justifiable the level of violence involved in Stalin's forced collectivization programme of the 1920s.

But most revolutionaries, like most Marxists, including Marx himself, have accepted the idea that revolution can often be the only way to social change and that all revolutions imply some violence, however deplorable. Danton put that case pungently when he cut short the comte de Ségur's complaints about the September massacres: 'Monsieur, vous oubliez à qui vous parlez; vous oubliez que nous sommes de la canaille; que nous sortons du ruisseau; qu'avec vos principes, nous y serions bientôt replongés, et que nous ne pouvons gouverner qu'en faisant peur!'[19] Saint-Just was to put the same idea more nobly: 'immoler pour ne pas être immolé', as has been said; and Barras, more practically: 'il faut guillotiner, ou s'attendre à l'être'. Revolutions cannot be avoided, and they do mean blood: 'on ne fait pas de procès aux Révolutions'; this cannot, and, more importantly, should not be done. The violence of revolutions must always be placed in a historical context. To reject violence is to reject revolution, and to reject revolution is to accept another sort of violence, for if some men were guillotined in 1794, other men had been broken on the wheel in 1788. Violence is part of politics. It cannot be avoided. A world-historical felicific calculus justifies executions which count for nothing in comparison with the blood that is spilt in wars, exploitation, and in the day-to-day business of bourgeois life.

A similar reasoning also holds that the liberal critique of revolutionary violence makes no sense, since bourgeois liberalism and respect for the rule-of-law are themselves the fruits of revolutionary violence. To speak of the model of nineteenth-century England, for example, is unjustifiable because it is to forget the bloodshed of the English Civil War. To criticize violence from a liberal point of view is to ignore the circumstances which made liberalism possible.

Finally, the Revolutionary violence of 1794 can also be justified by making reference to yet another consideration of a more narrow historical sort. Here the reasoning suggests that to feel horror today at the bloodshed of the French Revolution is historically anachronistic. What contemporary liberal bourgeois politician would dare to say in our own day of the victim of a popular riot, as Barnave did, 'Ce sang était-il si pur?' French society in the eighteenth century, though less brutal than it had been, was still violent. 'C'est au manque absolu de morale particulière et publique dans la nation française', wrote Mme de Staël, 'qu'il faut surtout attribuer les horreurs de la Révolution.'[20] No social movement of any consequence could have taken place in France at the end of the eighteenth century without bloodshed. 'It is increasingly difficult', wrote Mathiez, 'to say that such a Revolutionary figure was naturally more cruel or mean than another. Girondins and Dantonistes alike could at that time think of only two types of measures: proscription or death.'[21] In this view, the violence of 1794 has less to do with the Revolution itself than with the evolution of French customs and mores over the centuries, an argument which contradicts the view that Robespierre and others were kindly men who wished to stop the Terror as soon as this could be safely done.

All such statements obviously make an assumption about the inevitability of violence. The assumption is shared by some historians, like Richard Cobb, who base their argument not on historical necessity but on an appreciation of the darker side of man's nature, especially as it shows itself in chaotic times. Revolutionary crimes are not in their essence revolutionary. They are accidents that flow not from zeal but from the restlessness of the times. Wild men vent their passions in a lawless world, in this instance as terrorists of the left in 1793 and then as terrorists of the right in 1795:

> pleasure-seekers could find their way through any régime, even the pleasure-hating one of the Incorruptible. The anarchical Terror of the autumn and winter of 1793 had as much to offer as the White Terror of 1795–1802 (or the Counter-Terror as it has sometimes, and most aptly, been described) to the simple, resourceful man out for a good time, concerned with the satisfaction of the baser needs and with any occasion for self-dramatisation. Indeed, both Terrors were likely to appeal to the same sort of people, at least at ground-level activism; and, sometimes, the same sort of people, even the same people, served both in succession. There was nothing very remarkable about that.[22]

For some, victimization was somehow inevitable; for others, it is almost banal, the consequence of politically meaningless, random events. In both cases, however, the casualties lose their substance and are no longer seen as the very real victims of a dishevelled political process.

Each man is his own historian here, and my own view is categorically different, for as I see it the gratuitous violence of the Revolution was intolerable and cannot be justified or excused in any way, however admirable, or necessary, or 'world-historical' the Revolution may have been. That violence was brought to bear in cold blood against individuals who had committed no legal wrong, even by the loose definition of the term 'wrong' that prevailed in 1793–4, was particularly inexcusable. Individual responsibility must remain the touchstone of political punishment. 'Les fautes' are indeed 'personnelles'. In all likelihood, most victims of Revolutionary violence, including most of its victims who were noble, had committed no crime, and the memory of their persecutors should bear that burden.

Finally, though virtue is its own reward, it may also be argued that historians would have been better placed to consider the question of the place of nobles in French politics during the Revolution if they had had a less dogmatic view of the supposed guilt of the noble-born. An eagerness to see the problem in abstract terms and to condemn nobles as reactionaries and conspirators may well have led writers to ignore the implications of the historically important fact that most nobles did not act against the Revolution and that many welcomed it. Abstract views about the nature of the bourgeois Revolution have enabled historians to distance themselves from the suffering which many innocent noble-born persons were made to endure. The mechanism of abstraction and removal is not in fact much different from what often occurred during the period: 'Nous traversâmes les rues voisinantes de notre habitation,' wrote a Parisian priest after his arrest in August 1792,

> celle des postes, celle des fossés Saint-Jacques où nous étions connus. Le peuple en nous voyant passer gardoit un morne silence. J'apperçus même des artisans qui s'enfonçoient dans leurs boutiques pour n'être pas témoins de ce spectacle et pour cacher leur douleur. Mais, loin de notre demeure, nous fûmes beaucoup hués, beaucoup injuriés. Nous trouvâmes à la Section plusieurs autres prêtres qui avoient été arrêtés en divers endroits. . . . On nous envoya tous à l'hôtel de ville. La Section, comme je l'ai sçu après, n'avoit pas voulu se charger de la honte de notre emprisonnement.[23]

To those who are of a teleological frame of mind, metaphysical justifications of political persecution may appear convincing. But the danger of such explanations is that they can at times be misused to justify useless, cruel, and malicious acts. All men live in suffering, but justice requires that we distinguish between punishment and persecution.

Appendix 1

Marx and Hegel on the Terror and on the goals of the Revolutionary bourgeoisie

Most Marxist explanations of Revolutionary politics, and of the Terror also, start from the historical work of the older Marx. The Terror is essentially described as 'a plebeian way of completing the French Revolution'. Marx developed this idea by 1848, and Engels in later years evolved a similarly positivist view of the question at greater length. In 1870, for example, Engels argued that the Terror was the work of men who were themselves terrorized and whom he characterized as 'petit bourgeois philistines who were soiling their trousers'. (For a discussion of Marx's and Engels's views, see J. Bruhat, 'La Révolution française et la formation de la pensée de Marx', *Annales historiques de la Révolution française*, Apr.–June 1966, XXXVIII, No. 184, pages 125–70. Marx's views are also discussed in F. Furet, 'Le Catéchisme révolutionnaire', *Annales*, Mar.–Apr. 1971, No. 2. See also S. Avineri, *The Social and Political Thought of Karl Marx*; R. Unger, *Knowledge and Politics*; and E. Schmitt and M. Meyn, *Ursprünge und Charakter der Französischen Revolution bei Marx und Engels* (Bochum, 1976), pp. 63–71.)

The explanation of Revolutionary politics to which the younger Marx subscribed was more sophisticated and hinged on the subjective nature of bourgeois egalitarianism. Marx's argument was in turn derived from Hegel.

In Hegel's view, the failure of the French Revolution ought not to be ascribed to its inherent principle. It lies instead in the revolutionaries' determination to apply this principle immediately and abstractly. Within the corporatist *Ancien Régime*, Hegel explained, artisans and bourgeois had developed a morality born of their limited spheres of social action. Only nobles and soldiers could comprehend the whole, since only they had as their material task the defence of society as a whole. In the course of time, Hegel argues, these limiting divisions lost their practical purpose and served only to alienate individual wills from the universal will. Concept (the corporatist organization of society) had been the object (the prescription of individual social tasks); but as object (a disaffection with prescribed social roles) became a concept (the yearning for a more equal society) and as the Spirit became Science ('der Geist ist Wissenschaft') each individual conscience rose from its prescribed sphere, understood itself as the Concept of the Will, and strove for the Universal. Unbeknownst perhaps to its makers, this elaboration of the progress of the Universal was the task of the French Revolution. In 1789, the social substance (the monarchy, the law courts) subsisted only because of its vestigial material usefulness, but such institutions were no longer beings in themselves (i.e. the monarchy's claim to rule by divine right was now irrelevant). The task in 1789 was to create a new social substance penetrated by consciousness of self. In 1794, however, this new substance became once again irrelevant since the Will, in a revolutionary situation, does not tolerate any form of material alienation: when the men of the Revolution, vessels of the universal Will, strove to realize their goals in the excessively egalitarian state of 1794, the concrete achievements of 1789 disappeared, as it were, and only the abstract universal remained. Terror necessarily resulted from such an attempt to construct a political system abstracted from historical reality:

For this reason, when these abstract conclusions came into power they afforded for the first time in human history the prodigious spectacle of the overthrow of the constitution of a great actual state and its complete reconstruction *ab initio* on the basis of pure thought alone, after the destruction of all existing and given material. The will of its refounders was to give it what they alleged was a purely rational basis, but it was only abstractions that were being used; the Idea was lacking; and the experiment ended in the maximum of frightfulness and terror.

(See S. Avineri, *Hegel's Theory of the Modern State* (Cambridge, 1974), p. 184.)

Hegel's approach was taken up in modified form by the young Marx in 1844. The author of the *Holy Family* neither approves nor condemns the Terror, but declares it to have been a dead end. Political terror is for him neither moral nor immoral, but useless. Subjectivism is the most heinous of offences in the Hegelian code, and reliance on terror is for the young Marx a subjectivist fallacy. His explanation here, as shall be seen, dovetails neatly with his view of the Revolution as a whole.

In the Marxist perspective, the French Revolution was a world-historical event because it brought about that separation of the State from civil society, which exposes the mechanism of class.

The social movement of 1789 was a class revolution because it was carried forward politically by the bourgeoisie and, more importantly, because it made obvious the existence in society of different complementary and warring classes: by definition, bourgeois could only exist when others were not bourgeois; 'careers open to talents' meant that some talents would not suffice.

But in a crucial way, this bourgeois revolution was also a universalist movement because it carried forward 'ideas which lead beyond the *ideas* of the entire old world system' and contained within its bourgeois self the communist idea: 'This idea consistently developed is the idea of the new world system.' (Quoted by S. Avineri, *The Social and Political Thought of Karl Marx* (Cambridge, 1971), p. 186.)

For Marx, the great paradox of the French Revolution lies in this conjunction of universalist message and particularist class. The limits of the bourgeoisie's ability to realize its ideological programme are obvious. Janus-faced, this class was genuinely universalist in its determination to destroy the corporatist *Ständestaat*, with its prescriptive restriction of the rights of individuals and its denial of equality before the law. But nearly at once, the bourgeoisie (defined by acceptance of the laws of the market rather than by vestigial distinctions status) revealed itself to be particularist; and for Marx, the Le Chapelier Law of 1791 against workers' guilds was in this respect an unusually significant turning point. The rank and file bourgeoisie now began to set itself against the 'plebs', who by reason of this opposition would become the proletariat, that is to say, the one truly universalist class. Unable to grasp this new situation, the Jacobin bourgeois Revolutionaries strove none the less in 1794 to impose social equality on the particularist bourgeois class that had assigned a limited 'night watchman' role to the State. But the centre could not hold: terror and collapse necessarily ensued.

Arguing more explicitly from similar premisses, Lorenz von Stein reached similar conclusions in 1850:

> The basic tenet of the Constitution of 1793 was absolute personal equality. Public law, the right to vote, public representation and legislation were established according to this principle. The state did not want to recognize, still less create, any differences. This state form, according to the law which determines the relationship between state and society, is based on the assumption that society too is not differentiated. But did social equality really exist side by side with political equality?

(Lorenz von Stein, *The History of the Social Movement in France 1789–1850* [1850], Kaethe Megelberg, ed. (Totowa, NJ, 1964) p. 145.)

In the perspective of the young Marx, the Jacobin programme was subjectively fallacious, and a determination to enforce it could only be done through terror. Equality and universalism did not coincide with bourgeois particularism and could not exist spontaneously in a modern bourgeois state as they had in the ancient polis where, to speak in Rousseauistic terms, a universal collective *volonté générale* transcended but did not deny the sum of individual wills or *volonté de tous*: 'Terror', writes Marx, 'wishes to sacrifice [civil society] to an ancient form of political life.' (Quoted in Avineri, *Social and Political Thought*, p. 191.)

Von Stein in 1850 developed the argument in greater, if less subtle, detail:

> Pure democracy is unable to rule . . .; a result of thought, it is valid onl in the realm of thought . . . terrorism was in fact a necessary consequenc of the situation in which state power was exclusively in the hands c democratic extremists. Terrorism, for most people an excess of ma blood-thirst, was quite a natural result of the revolution, comparable t a crisis during serious illness. Its explanation rests on the foregoin analysis.

(*History of the Social Movement*, p. 146.)

The argument would be suggestive even if it did no more than to illustrate the complex interplay of infrastructure and superstructure in the thought of Marx.

Appendix 2

The social origins of emigration in 1789–1799

The question of emigration, its causes and extent, is a vast topic which has been thoroughly examined by E. Daudet, D. Greer, and J. Vidalenc, among others. My purpose is not to comment on this problem as a whole. It is instead to touch on its direct connection with the question that is of concern here, namely, the changing definitions of the rights of nobles. The first aspect of relevance involves the social origins of the émigrés. To what extent can we equate noble and émigré? And is it fair to say that, at some moments during the Revolution, to speak of émigrés was really to speak of nobles? The question has an obvious bearing on the interpretation of anti-émigré legislation. Should such laws be understood to have been a disguised form of anti-nobilism? Or did émigrés exist, so to speak, in their own right, as reactionary Frenchmen rather than as nobles pure and simple?

My suggestion is that at the beginning and end of the Revolutionary decade, anti-émigré laws were aimed against nobles exclusively; such laws can therefore be used as a barometer of anti-noble feeling. This interpretation is somewhat at variance with commonly accepted views.

Thinking on this question has been dominated by D. Greer's *Incidence of Emigration* (Cambridge, Mass., 1951), whose aim was to show that the social origins of émigrés were varied, and that only a small minority of them were nobles. These conclusions were at once true and misleading, though not on account of the objections recently brought to bear on the essay. (See G. Shapiro and J. Markoff, 'The Incidence of the Terror: Some Lessons for Quantitative History', in the *Journal of Social History*, vol. IX, no. 2, Winter 1975.) Greer realizes, of course, that the social composition of emigration varied greatly from time to time (p. 34). But his perspective is skewed by his uninterest in the problem after 1794. He writes, for example, that 'emigration ran its main course from the fall of the Bastille to the fall of Robespierre; then it diminished to nothing because the struggle that had fed it had ended' (p. 37). This is not altogether so, and in consequence Greer presents a biased interpretation of emigration as a whole.

For him, the flight of nobles in the earlier period is presented as a mere prologue to full-blown cross-class emigration in 1793–4 rather than as a distinct phase of a long process. Emigration during the Terror was indeed cross-class, as Greer rightly emphasizes, but flight during the Terror was also a phenomenon quite distinct from emigration before or after 1792–4. It is therefore somewhat misleading to proceed from the socially variegated nature of emigration in 1794 to the social purpose of legislation in 1792 or in 1797, when the aristocratic nature of emigration was distinct and well understood by everyone. Emigration in its social composition, went through three distinct phases, the first and the last of which can be said to have been periods of predominantly aristocratic emigration.

In 1789–92, most émigrés were nobles and were thought to be nobles. In late 1791, Brissot, for example, considered it self-evident that émigrés were aristocrats and foolish ones at that, 'Une foule d'hommes enthousiastes de leurs vieux parchemins. Le néant est là: il attend ou la Noblesse ou la Constitution, choisissez (vifs applaudissements).' (*Archives parlementaires*, vol. 34 (Paris, 1890), 20 Oct. 1791, p. 311.) Barère made the same assumption: all émigrés were nobles; they were 'mauvais citoyens, qui furieux d'avoir perdu les hochets de la vanité, ne vous pardonneront jamais, ni le décret du 19 juin 1790, ni les lois sages que vous donnez à la France'. (*Archives parlementaires*, vol. 28 (Paris, 1888), 9 July 1791, p. 82.) All émigrés, or so the revolutionaries assumed, were nobles, and on the right Calonne in this respect mirrored the ideas of the left when he urged the Princes in late 1792 to be worthy of 'cette noblesse . . . qui a mis sa confiance en vous'. (Lacour-Gayet, *Calonne*, p. 432.) The proclamation of the prince de Condé of 1790 ran in the same vein: 'La noblesse est une, c'est la cause de tous les Princes, de tous les gentilshommes que je défends, ils se réuniront sous l'étandard glorieux que je déploierai à leur tête.' (Prince de Condé, *Mémoires*, p. 45 [texte du Manifeste de SSS le prince de Condé.])

In short, from 1789 to 1792 it was widely assumed in both Paris and Coblenz that all émigrés were nobles and that all nobles were potential émigrés. The social equation 'émigrés equals nobles' no longer held in 1792–4, and was then understood to be irrelevant, but the realization that many non-nobles had also emigrated was slow in coming.

Admittedly, allowances were made from the first for wayward, non-noble soldiers: on 9 February 1792, privates and noncommissioned officers, who were assumed not to be nobles, were allowed to return from abroad even if they had deserted. They might even be paid to come home. Initial legislation regarding non-noble emigration was, however, quite harsh as a rule. In November 1792, Boudin, a convinced enemy of noble émigrés, proposed that their non-noble servants who had left France since 1789 be given special treatment because they were, after all, no more free than children whom the law had exempted from its 'juste vengeance'. But he was overruled. Non-noble émigrés were freaks who deserved no more sympathy than did dissident nobles. In essence, laws on emigration in 1791–2 were understood to be aimed at one group only, nobles.

In 1793–4, however, it no longer made sense to suppose that all émigrés were nobles. It may have been feasible even then to think that most nobles had left or wanted to do so, but it was no less clear that thousands of ordinary Frenchmen had also fled.

A rethinking of the question was in order, and this was all the more imperative because of the very haphazard way in which the label 'émigré' had been attached by the more pure to the impure. Even in the febrile atmosphere of the Terror, it was difficult to use as working documents lists of émigrés which included Louis XVI, imprisoned criminals, Conventionnels, paralytics, diplomats, and military men who had left France in the armies of the Republic or as prisoners of the Allies. Many so-called émigrés had been listed from pure malice, and many others from genuine mistake because they were non-resident landlords. It was, incidentally, for reasons of this sort that on 23 germinal an II, some sales of émigré property were suspended, 145 names being removed from the list in one department alone. (Sangnier, *Les Émigrés du Pas de Calais* (Langermont, 1938), p. 144.)

In its technical aspects, the émigré question had got out of hand. But even if émigré listings had been correctly made, difficulties would still have been insurmountable because by 1793 and 1794 all sorts and manner of people were officially declared émigrés. Since the culpability of people called 'émigrés' was legally set already, it was tempting for victors to pronounce any of their vanquished foes to have been émigrés. So labelled, for example, were those individuals who had been summoned by the Revolutionary Tribunal but had failed to show up, Vendéens, captured rebels from Toulon, Girondins, *sectionnaires*, and state accountants unable to square their accounts. In addition, during the turmoil of 1792–4, tens of thousands of non-political individuals technically qualified as émigrés by fleeing war-torn areas, especially in the border areas, sometimes for a few hours only in moments of military crisis. Alsatian refugees were prominent in this respect. Account also had to be taken of the thousands of Frenchmen who either resided abroad on business or who went abroad year in and year out as seasonal workers, to Spain especially. In short, by 1795, the term émigré was completely devalued, much as happened at various times to other categories, like *aristocrate*, *girondin*, *modéré*, and *suspect*.

In 1789–91, 'émigré' meant noble. By 1794, the term had lost that meaning. During the Directory, however, the overlap became once again more meaningful. The identity of noble and émigré in the late 1790s never acquired the strength that it had at first, but it almost did, and the authorities endeavoured to see that it should. Listings of émigrés were methodically purified of their non-noble accretions. There were, it must be said, occasional lapses. In brumaire an VII, for example, unarrested but, as was said at the time, 'fructidorized' right-wing deputies were decreed to be émigrés. But on the whole, Thermidorians were selective, and no general trend can be derived from the sudden shift in standing of Admiral Truguet, for example, who fell from governmental favour and was in a single day stripped of his ambassadorship to Spain and labelled an émigré, since he was now abroad without diplomatic rank. Generally, both the national Directory and local authorities worked fairly steadily, regardless of drifts to the left or the right, to make sure that only nobles were listed as émigrés.

This was done in two ways, first, by simply keeping nobles on the lists, and second, by granting exceptions to specific non-noble social or professional groups, such as former Conventionnels (1 frimaire an III), veterans, sailors, artisans, husbandmen from the Haut-Rhin, and farmers from all of France. Swollen émigré listings from southern France were brought under special scrutiny, because it was held that many citizens there 'n'osant se mettre en état d'arrestation par la crainte de perdre la vie, ont été mis sur la liste des émigrés' (*Le Moniteur*, 17 frimaire an III). Such refugees, from Lyons or Bordeaux, for example, were now said to have been victims of 'artificial emigrations'. Most incongruous, perhaps, was the reprieve given in fructidor an IV to notaries, as compensation perhaps for their unusual travails during the Reign of Terror.

Nobles were shut out, non-nobles were let back; and by 1797, non-nobles may well have become once again a minority of émigrés as they had been before 1793. In this line, Greer estimates in his *Incidence of Emigration* (p. 99) that in the Var, most non-privileged émigrés had already come home by September 1795. Morellet was completely on target when he denounced the hypocrisy of the Directorial verbiage on émigrés and attacked the laws against this supposed political faction as a screen for unavowed anti-aristocratism.

The particular class bias of emigration during the Directory would be even more evident than it now is if the Directory's intent had been efficiently carried out. Many of the non-nobles still listed as émigrés after 1797 were in fact victims of clerical errors, as appears from the curious case of Jean François Bureau, *homme de loi*, a resident of Sens in the Yonne since 1787.

Bureau's 'inscription fatale aux livres des émigrés' was decreed on 11 March 1793 by local authorities in the neighbouring department of the Aube, where he owned property. But Bureau, as it happens, was an active revolutionary. A member of the *société populaire* at Sens from start to finish, he had also directed for five months the local *Bureau des Subsistances*, and on 10 August 1793, had been sent to Paris as a representative of Sens to congratulate the Conventionnels on the occasion of the anniversary of the fall of the monarchy. Untouchable, or so it seemed, Bureau neglected in 1793–4 to take steps to have his name removed from the émigré list.

Stirred somewhat by the law of 3 brumaire an IV (October 1795), Bureau did make some desultory efforts to clear this up in May and August 1796, and he secured letters and affidavits from the municipality of Sens that certified his non-emigration. But he did not see the matter through, and his name was still on the 'liste fatale' when the laws of 1795 were revived in September 1797. This was the source of his undoing.

With the coming of the 'Directorial Terror' in 1797, the authorities of the Aube now advised him of his condition as an émigré, an offence punishable by deportation. Appalled, Bureau on 30 September 1797 (8 vendémiaire an VI) submitted to the minister of police incontrovertible proof of his non-emigration in the form of letters from some Conventionnels of the Yonne, affidavits of his presence at various Republican functions, and a petition signed by over 100 Republicans of Sens. As a first step, he was ordered placed in *résidence surveillée*, which was done two days later (on 7 October 1797) by the *Commissaire du directoire exécutif près l'administration de Sens*. A month later the minister of police wrote to the commissioners on emigration in the Aube, asking them for advice. Their reply was decisively ambiguous: Bureau had most certainly not emigrated, but he was guilty. To be sure, the commissioners were in their own words 'frappés des preuves incontestables qu'il présente de sa résidence en France pendant toute la durée de la révolution'. But his name was on the list and it was therefore with an 'extrême amertume' that they found themselves in November 1797 condemning this man whom they recognized had served the Revolution 'dans le lieu de son domicile'. Though obviously innocent, he was also obviously guilty according to the letter of the law.

On 2 December 1797, Bureau appealed to the minister of police in Paris: he did not blame the commissioners, 'esclaves de la Loi dont ils sont les organes'. But he did insist that he was innocent, and he would not give up. On 2 July 1798, he tried again, this time in a letter to the national executive itself: 'Cette pétition est peut-être la vingtième que j'ai l'honneur de vous présenter pour obtenir ma radiation de la liste des émigrés.' Moved by the plea, the Directory referred the case to the Third Division of Ministry of Police, which now considered the whole imbroglio from start to finish. Their decision was admirably bureaucratic: they referred the matter back to the executive itself. Bureau's name was undeniably on the list, but the Directory might also want to 'pezer dans sa sagesse les moyens de considération qui s'élèvent en sa faveur'. To Bureau's immense relief, the Directory did do just that, and on 5 September 1798 (19 fructidor an VI), by a direct order of the National Directory, his name was removed from the list. The decision was forwarded to the Commissioners of the Aube with copies to the Ministry of Finance. But of course the record of his having 'emigrated' was not removed. In a tally of émigrés after fructidor, Bureau counts as a non-noble émigré since his name figures on printed lists drawn up in 1797. Were such cases to be identified (an impossibly laborious task), our impression of a post-fructidorian overlap of noble and émigré would be even stronger than it is.

(The vicissitudes of Bureau's career as an émigré can be traced in AN F^{7} 4885 no. 1121, F^{7} 7374 no. 8969, F^{7*} 116, fol. 178, and in État général des émigrés et de leurs propriétés dans le département de l'Aube (s.l.n.d.), Bibliothèque Nationale Lb 3034.)

In conclusion, it appears that the question of the social origin of émigrés can be seen to have gone through three distinct phases: most émigrés in 1789–92 were nobles; in 1792–4, the social background of emigration was much more mixed; in 1795–9, because non-noble émigrés were allowed to return, the equation 'émigré equals nobles' took on a renewed meaning. The implications of the varying social meaning of the word 'émigré' have an important bearing on the question of the rights of nobles. The overlap between the conditions of noble and émigré in 1789–92 and again in 1795–9 (and more particularly in 1797–9) and a reminder that the legislation on emigration has an obvious relevance to the nobles question. The laxness of the Constituant Assembly, like the harshness of the Directory, is an indication of the different ways in which the problem of the rights of nobles was envisaged in these two periods.

Appendix 3

The extent of aristocratic emigration

The legislation on emigration is an indication of the bourgeoisie's perception of the place of nobles in society. The extent and causes of emigration by contrast reflect on the nobility's reaction to the ups and downs of Revolutionary politics. Did the prospect of civil equality so disgust most nobles that they decided to leave *en masse*? The answer here is clearly no.

The precise number of émigrés (both noble and non-noble) is unknown; and it is forever to be regretted that 40,000 letters and petitions of émigrés were burnt in 1808. (See *État sommaire des versements faits aux Archives Nationales par les ministères et les administrations qui en dépendent* (Paris, 1924), p. 292.) To those who suggest that official estimates of the number of noble émigrés are more accurate than those for non-nobles because the ci-devants were more conspicuous and easily numbered, others reply that there were many noblewomen and children whose departures were never recorded. Many local authorities were reluctant to list nobles whom they knew were abroad, while others were quick to decide that absentee noble landlords must surely be émigrés. No set of figures can claim to be wholly exact.

Greer's over-all estimate (more or less followed by Vidalenc) of 129,099 (on p. 126 of his *Incidence of the Emigration During the French Revolution* (Cambridge, Mass., 1951)) is perhaps too low. Castries's estimate of 250,000 to 300,000 is certainly too high (*La Vie quotidienne des émigrés* (Paris, 1966), p. 16). In ventôse, an V, the Directory asserted that it had 250,000 names on the list, but this figure, too, is unreliable: some departments were not represented in this tally; many people were listed twice; and some of those listed had never emigrated at all. Equally untrustworthy are the estimates made in 1805 by the chief of the émigré bureau at the ministry of police, who thought that 200,000 people had been affected by émigré legislation, and that 145,000 were on police lists, of whom 80,000 had actually emigrated (Grégoire, *Mémoires* (Paris, 1837), pp. 172–3). It would seem that perhaps 150,000 to 200,000 people emigrated, of whom approximately 25,000 were nobles.

The problem arises of deciding what proportion of the nobility as a whole such a figure represents. Unfortunately, estimates of the size of the nobility as a whole vary from 200,000 to 350,000. (See R. Dauvergne, 'Le Problème du nombre des nobles en France au XVIIIe siècle et au XIXe siècle' in *Hommage à Marcel Reinhard, sur la population française au XVIIIe et XIXe siècles* (Paris, 1973), pp. 181–2.) None the less, it is manifest that the great majority of nobles never left. Their desire to stay in France, and, in most instances, to make their peace with the Revolution, is significant. In revolutionary times, most people can vote only with their feet. This is not to say that most nobles supported the Revolution, but it is to argue for the unrepresentativeness of the émigré propagandist who thought non-emigration to be dishonourable and collaborationist.

Appendix 4

The causes of emigration

Most nobles stayed home. But some did leave, and it is instructive to reflect on the causes of their departure. Did nobles leave because they were dyed-in-the-wool reactionaries or because they feared for life and limb?

Historians who deny that most nobles were ready to accept civic equality have, logically enough, also interpreted emigration as a wilful manifestation of counter-revolutionary sentiment. How else can we explain, for example, the departure of hundreds of noble officers in the autumn of 1791, when conditions had momentarily stabilized, and when the King needed the help of nobles who were no longer being threatened physically and had no personal reason to leave?

A number of possible motives should be considered. Some nobles left for frivolous reasons: to escape from boredom or to avoid creditors. Many intended to return within three months, a lapse of time that is often cited in émigré accounts. (See, for example, vicomte de Broc, *Dix ans de la vie d'une femme pendant l'émigration* (Paris, 1894), p. 51, and d'Haussonville, *Souvenirs et mélanges* (Paris 1878), p. 23.) Others left merely to conform or for honour's sake. (See Alexandrine des Echerolles, *Une femme noble sous la Terreur* (Paris, 1879), pp. 12–13, and Pierre de Vaissière, *Lettres d'aristocrates* (Paris, 1907), p. 325.) In this context, mention should be made of the intimidation of moderate nobles by their ultra friends, a process that was almost institutionalized, as Ferrières, who did not leave, describes: 'On forçait les nobles d'abandonner leurs femmes, leurs enfants, leurs propriétés et de fuir en bannis dans une terre étrangère.' (Ferrières, *Mémoires*, vol. II, p. 414.) Many nobles also left because they were afraid, especially when they had been conspicuously connected to the more unpopular parts of the political apparatus of the *Ancien Régime*, as were the Parlementaires, who emigrated in unusually large numbers. Generally speaking, there is a great deal to Gain's idea that the aristocracy even in 1789–91, not to speak of 1791–2, was swayed by undefinable fears of terrorism, economic hardship, and administrative sanctions that are very reminiscent of the

Great Fear of 1789. (A. Gain, *Liste des émigrés* (Metz, 1925), vol. I, p. 76.) It is to something of this sort that Mirabeau referred in July 1789:

Rien ne frappe d'avantage un Observateur que le penchant universel à croire, à exagérer les nouvelles sinistres dans les temps de calamité. Il semble que la logique ne consiste plus à calculer les degrés de probabilité, mais à prêter de la vraisemblance aux rumeurs les plus vagues, sitôt qu'elles annoncent des attentats et agitent l'imagination par de sombres terreurs. Nous ressemblons alors aux enfants de qui les contes les plus effrayants sont toujours les mieux écoutés. [*Courrier de Provence*, no. 21, p. 1.]

Matters did not improve after 1789. Many nobles, for example, were made particularly anxious by the prospect of war. In August 1790, Ferrières wrote to his wife that some conservatives did think that a war would make possible a return to the status quo. They were wrong: 'Ils se trompent. Une guerre, dans les circonstances actuelles, acheverait de ruiner le pays, et serait le signal de plus grands excès contre la Noblesse et le Clergé; car les démagogues regarderaient les nobles et les prêtres comme les instigateurs de cette guerre.' (Ferrières, *Correspondance*, p. 263.) This was a theme dear to his heart and in June 1791, he bitterly reproached the King for abandoning nobles and clergy to the 'fureur du peuple' by banking on a foreign war; if war broke out, he wrote in September 1791, it would certainly endanger nobles in the provinces. Some nobles doubtless thought that war was the way out for them, but more perspicacious observers did not agree, and Barnave predicted with striking accuracy that a war would be disastrous for aristocrats:

Comme la force contre laquelle ils [i.e. the radical leaders] auront à combattre ou plutôt qu'ils devront attaquer, sera composée de la noblesse et du roi et aura pour elle le gouvernement établi, ils auront pour se faire des partisans contre elle un moyen presque infaillible, ils appelleront le peuple des campagnes à la suppression totale des droits féodaux et l'inviteront à refuser l'impôt et se trouveront toujours soutenus dans les villes par le sentiment qui seul y a fait la révolution, l'amour de la liberté. Ils commenceront une guerre dont les effets certains seront les ravages les plus horribles dont l'histoire ait jamais offert le tableau, et dont le dernier résultat probable sera la spoliation générale des nobles et le détrônement du roi.

(G. Michon, *Essai sur l'histoire du parti feuillant: Adrien Duport, Correspondance inédite de Barnave.* (Paris, 1924), 4 March 1792, p. 33.)

Many nobles thought that the declaration of war itself, regardless of its consequences, would be the signal for a wholesale massacre: and one of them reminded his daughter abroad that

> Une augmentation de terreur a saisi les habitants de Paris; tous les gens riches ou aisés quittent cette malheureuse ville, et l'on ne voit plus dans les rues que des fiacres. Une inquiétude, je crois déplacée, est la cause de cette émigration; on annonce avec affectation une guerre prochaine; on croit ou l'on veut faire croire que les puissances étrangères veulent se mêler de nos affaires et l'on assure qu'à la première nouvelle d'une invasion en France, les maisons et leurs habitants nobles seront livrés au meurtre et au pillage; voilà les spéculations amusantes qui occupent la société; aussi est-elle bien triste et la conversation bien monotone. Adieu, chère enfant; mes lettres sont comme les conversations, mais quand les faits dominent la pensée, ils laissent peu d'activité à l'imagination.

Quoted in Henri de Miramon de Fitz-James, *Lettres du comte de Thiard à sa fille la duchesse de Fitz-James (1790–1793)* (Aix-en-Provence, 1943), p. 22.

Even those nobles who were abroad occasionally admitted that unalloyed royalism alone had not caused their departure. In December 1791, the report in Coblenz of a commission of Norman nobles, who had an obvious interest in appearing to be militant, stated as a matter of course that 'Spoliation, violation de propriété, meurtres, incendies, voilà ce qui vous a fait quitter votre patrie.' (Abbé Hébert, *La Noblesse de Normandie en émigration* (Évreux, 1902), p. 38.) In 1796, Mallet du Pan, Louis XVIII's spokesman, and no one's fool, summed up the motives of his audience in no uncertain terms: 'Quiconque considérera impartialement les seules et véritables causes de l'émigration les trouvera dans l'anarchie. Si la liberté individuelle n'eût pas été formellement menacée, si l'on n'avait pas mis en pratique le dogme insensé prêché par les factieux que les crimes de la multitude sont les jugements du Ciel, la France eût conservé les trois quarts de ses fugitifs.' (Quoted in Castries, *La Vie quotidienne des émigrés* (Paris, 1966), p. 13.) It is useful in this respect to look at the chronological conjunction between flight and disorder, as happened in November 1790, when 1,100 people left in one week after the sacking of the Hôtel de Castries in Paris.

Fear was probably the single most important cause of emigration, a fact which the involved parties were obviously eager to conceal. Once abroad, nobles found it in their interest for both psychological and material reasons to claim that they had left for the sake of throne and altar. Gentlemen could not own to having been afraid. Many nobles were also penniless and depended on the subsidies doled out by the Princes, and it is perhaps significant that Louis XVIII did not rescind the rules of *dérogeance*, which barred nobles from finding employment, until 1795.

In short, émigrés often lied about their motives. The comte de Thiard, who had refused to leave and was guillotined on 8 thermidor, wrote as much to his émigré daughter, who was cool in her reply. 'Mon interminable affaire', he explained, 'seul bien qui me reste, ma misère actuelle et d'autre combinaisons me retiennent ici, où je suis fort fàché d'être dans un moment où peut-être on nous fera un tort de délicatesse d'être restés; les autres l'ont quitté par peur dans des temps bien orageux; ils diront que c'est par honneur et par courage; ils mentiront.' (See Fitz-James, *Lettres du comte de Thiard à sa fille la duchesse de Fitz-James*, pp. 48–9.) The same discrepancy between real and avowed motive emerges from a comparison of the rodomontades which émigrés published after 1814 with the unpublished petitions which they had filed in the late 1790s when they were desperate to go home.

Many nobles were forced to leave, in some instances, by revolutionaries intent on legal theft. Such was the view of Morellet, a typical apologist of the class of *propriétaires*, a man for whom material lust explained most human acts. It was greed, he thought, that explained the revolutionaries' 'système de dépopulation' and greed also that had driven innocent nobles abroad:

L'incendie des châteaux, le pillage des propriétés mobiliaires, la dévastation des bois, les enlèvemens de denrées de toute espèce, sous le nom de réquisitions, les taxes exorbitantes, les incarcérations arbitraires, etc.; la chasse donnée aux nobles, aux prêtres, aux riches, avoient pour but de les porter à fuir en pays étranger, et à laisser ainsi leurs biens sous la main de la nation. On rendoit l'émigration nécessaire, parce qu'on vouloit arriver à la confiscation.

Supplément à la cause des pères (Paris, an III), pp. 76–7. Morellet's tirade has to be taken for what it was, but instances of forced emigration certainly did occur. M. de Dangeville, imprisoned at Dijon for seventeen months, discovered on his release that his goods had been sequestered on grounds of emigration (Forneron, *Histoire général des émigrés*, vol. 1, p. 206). Forneron also cites the case of a landlord who was ceremoniously given a passport he had not requested and sent with two gendarmes to Geneva. Charles Gravier de Vergennes protested to the Convention against such a manoeuvre and, after having produced a certificate from the authorities of the Brutus section, was taken off the list of émigrés. (Wallon, *Histoire du Tribunal révolutionnaire* (Paris, 1881), vol. V, p. 113.) In 1795, the conservative deputy Calès described the way in which, he claimed, such practices had been carried out:

> Ils faisaient mettre sur la liste des émigrés, beaucoup de citoyens qu'ils savaient bien ne pas l'être. . . . Lorsque le prévenu se présentait à sa section, on intimidait les témoins par de menaces, on les récusait souvent sans aucun motif: le chef du bureau des émigrés de l'administration du département tachait d'influencer l'administration pour faire prendre des arrêtés défavorables aux réclamants; lorsqu'il ne pouvait y parvenir, alors il changeait lui-même l'arrêté du département et le présentait à la signature; quand il ne pouvait réussir ainsi, il essayait de violenter l'administration en la menaçant de la dénoncer; . . . trois ou quatre jours d'intervalle de la date d'un certificat à l'autre, temps employé à un voyage ou exigé par l'affiche, ou les retards nécessaires et inévitables amenés par les circonstances ont souvent et presque toujours suffi pour faire déclarer un homme émigré. Ajoutez à cela que l'arrêté du département condamnait l'homme, puisqu'on a déclaré au tribunal qu'il n'avait que l'application de la loi et qu'il a été menacé par un représentant parce qu'il avait donné à un prévenu vingt-quatre heures de sursis pour prouver sa non-émigration. Cet exposé, que j'affirme vrai d'après les pièces et dénonciations que j'ai entre les mains, vous engagera de suite, j'en suis sûr, *à mettre fin à ces atrocités, qui n'auraient pas dû être connues en France, qu'on ne soupçonnerait pas chez un peuple de cannibales.*

Cited in Marcel Marion, 'L'Application des lois de l'émigration', *Revue historique* (septembre-décembre 1911), pp. 34–5.

Of relevance to the question of the émigrés' motivation in leaving France was the industry which they demonstrated in trying to secure official permission to do so, in order to cover their bets or to be able to return in quieter times. Talleyrand, for example, was very careful on this score. In the first months of 1792, he was against emigration altogether, and he would later, as foreign minister in 1797, be very harsh on émigrés. To one of his friends who asked his advice, he replied: 'je ne vous conseille pas de rester à Paris, puisque vous êtes effrayée, ni même de vous retirer dans l'une de vos terres; mais allez passer quelque temps dans une petite ville de province où vous ne serez point connue', an opinion which Mme de Brionne rejected with contempt: 'fi . . . paysanne tant qu'on voudra, bourgeoise, jamais'. (Cited in

Beugnot, *Mémoires* (Paris, 1868), vol. I, pp. 157–8.) And when the time did come for him to leave, Talleyrand took especial pains to obtain Danton's signature; in order to secure it, he hovered for days in Paris at a time when it was very dangerous for him to do so.

Nor was Talleyrand alone in his desire to be *en règle*. In the earlier period, many officers did not leave until the Assembly's decree of 23 February 1791, which made them eligible for early retirement as *maréchaux de camp*. Two years later, Roland in the same vein reported to the Convention that 3,000 persons had requested official permission to take the waters in Germany (*Archives parlementaires*, vol. 56 (Paris, 1899), 9 January 1793, p. 687). Again, my aim is not to deny that many émigrés were counter-revolutionary. It is instead to suggest that the stated motivations of many émigrés cannot be taken at face value, and, *a fortiori*, should not be taken to represent the views of the silent majority of nobles who stayed in France.

The point is an obvious one: it makes no sense to infer the opinions of the 90 per cent of French nobles who stayed at home from the fact that 10 per cent of them left, especially as they often did so under duress, or because they were none too brave. The fact of emigration has little bearing on the supposed opinion of nobles in France. Once again, the conclusion is the same. There is no reason to infer from the evidence at hand that the French nobility bitterly opposed the French Revolution. Before and after 1789, the motives of nobles were probably comparable to those of non-nobles of similar wealth and importance. In all likelihood, most nobles were shocked in 1792 by the collapse of the monarchy, and by the Terror in 1794; but, in all probability, so was the mass of the provincial, land-owning bourgeoisie.

Many émigré nobles lied about their motives, and too many historians have taken them at their word. They have also looked at this matter with considerable *arrières pensées*, and the historiographical reflex here has been identical with the one which has so often obfuscated the true nature of the Vendéen rebellion, where both right and left historians had a vested interest in placing throne and altar at the centre of the rebellion, the right to dignify it, the left to explain the otherwise inexplicable refusal of peasants to accept the Republic. So it is with emigration. Emigrés who left for doctrinal reasons are, for the right, more elegant, and for the left, more worthy of detestation. But human motives are seldom quite so neat.

A small slip in Lefebvre's review of Greer's book on emigration

(*Annales historiques de la Révolution française*, no. 127, July–Aug. 1952) is revealing of the way that historians have considered the issue. Lefebvre interprets Greer's figures to show that Taine was wrong in writing that most émigrés left from necessity rather than choice. But Lefebvre puzzles over the small number of nuns who emigrated, and speculates that former nuns were described on official lists according to their old, or new, social status. Another explanation is possible: priests left because they had to; their choice was to take oaths which were repugnant to their conscience or to emigrate. They chose emigration. Nuns were not required to take all of the oaths that were required of the secular clergy. In consequence, they did not feel that they had to leave; and so, they stayed behind. Lefebvre's hypothesis reveals his desire to believe that most émigrés left because they wanted to.

Appendix 5

The politics of emigration

A cascade of unwarranted assumptions has veiled the problem of emigration. One such mistake has been to take the extreme statements of émigré spokesmen in Coblenz as representing the views of those nobles in France who could not speak, just as Radio London during the Second World War is said to have spoken for the millions of anti-German Frenchmen who could say nothing. A better analogy might be Radio-Patrie of the French fascist refugees in Germany in 1944–5, which spoke for hardly anyone at all.

Most nobles did not leave; those who left did so for a variety of reasons, and even those who expressed themselves politically once abroad were not the consistently unalloyed counter-revolutionaries which they have been assumed to be. It is in fact quite striking to see that in 1789–94, nobles were prominent in all political groups without exception. On the pro-Revolutionary side, some aristocrats opted for the extremes of the popular left (Saint-Huruge and Cloots), for the Mountain (Le Peletier, Soubrany), the left generally (Hérault de Séchelles, Égalite), the Gironde (Condorcet, Valady), and the Feuillants and Fayettistes, whom they dominated. No greater consensus existed on the conservative side. In the National Assembly, the *côté droit* was divided over the advisability of oath-taking or emigration, which Artois had recommended in the first days of May 1791. Ferrières reported that the *Aristocrate* party in the National Assembly was torn: if noble officers were advised to refuse to give their oath, the ranks of emigration would swell, but there would be a price to pay, namely, that the army would fall in the hands of the *Démocrates*. (Ferrières, *Correspondance*, p. 352.) In the same way, the nobles who had assembled at Jalès refused to have dealings with the Tuileries, just as the nobles of the King's Constitutional Guard distrusted Coblenz; and there were rumours in Parisian and in émigré circles in late 1791 that Condé had agents in Paris whose work it was to keep the King from leaving. The same divisions existed abroad. Émigré nobles in London, Hamburg, and Philadelphia were far more moderate in their opinions than those of their brethren who had gravitated to Coblenz, Rome, and Vienna. Mathiez was quite right to write in a review of Gain's books on emigration that 'one cannot insist too much on the fact that the different categories of émigrés detested one another, and that they were handled differently by the successive governments of Revolutionary France' (*Annales historiques de la Révolution française*, vol. 6, 1929, pp. 507–8).

Within the camp of official emigration, at Coblenz, the spectrum was obviously far more narrow but quite real none the less. Unrepentant 'counter-revolutionism' was well represented by the Princes of the Blood, and exclusive aristocratism could become under their aegis quite absurd, as happened when the Corbehem brothers were declared unfit to serve in one of the more élitist units of Condé's army because they descended from a mere doctor ennobled in the sixteenth century by Charles Quint. On the other hand, Calonne, the Princes' spokesman, never wholly betrayed his earlier advocacy of Enlightened despotism. In his appeal to the French aristocracy of 8 August 1792, he urged them to be moderate:

> Vous ne serez que trop vengés. A votre approche, les factieux, législateurs, philosophes, beaux esprits, et toutes les pestes de la démocratie se hâteront de purger la France de leur aspect. . . . Que vos mains ne soient pas souillées de leur sang et que des supplices toujours trop doux n'abrègent pas leur vie! Des remords sans vertu les attendent. . . . Quoique la monarchie déchirée réclame vos efforts, dites-vous bien que c'est plutôt au secours du monarque que vous courez.

The French nobility, he concluded, was in the nation and not above it: 'Souvenez vous, noblesse française', he concluded, 'que vous n'êtes ni souveraine comme en Allemagne, ni féodale comme en Pologne, ni législatrice comme en Angleterre, ni caste sacrée comme dans l'Inde, mais que, née de l'honneur, vous devez vivre et mourir sur les marches du trône.' (Quoted in Lacour-Gayet, *Calonne*, p. 425.) So would Calonne in his *Tableau de l'Europe en novembre 1795* protest against the confiscation of émigré property, but discreetly glide over the question of confiscated clerical lands.

Opinions at any one time were widely separated. The political programme of emigration was in constant flux, as was its membership, and it was only gradually that extreme statements became predominant. Émigré strategies were forever changing: in 1790, great hopes were pinned on the Languedoc plan, which culminated in the demonstration at Jalès in August; in 1791, under Calonne's guidance, the focus of counter-revolutionary hopes shifted to the émigré army assembled in the Rhineland. Another critical point was reached in June 1792, when the uncompromising plan of the Princes finally took precedence over the King's own scheme. Out of that manoeuvre came the Brunswick manifesto, which was infinitely harsher in tone than what Louis XVI had intended. The King's plan, drawn up with the help of the foreign minister, Montmorin, Bertrand de Molleville, and Mallet du Pan, had been very cautious. Only the very wicked would be punished; it was important to 'séparer les jacobins et les factieux de toutes les classes du reste de la nation ... et de rassurer tous ceux qui, sans vouloir la constitution actuelle, craignent le retour des grands abus'. (Lacour-Gayet, *Calonne*, p. 421.) But when Mallet arrived in Frankfurt on 21 May 1792, he was short-circuited by the more extreme émigrés. He failed to persuade Brunswick, who signed Geoffroy de Limon's absurd manifesto. The ferociousness of that pronouncement set the tone of émigré propaganda for the next three years. From this extreme point emigration would continue to see-saw, a conservative nadir being reached with the proclamation of Verona, and a liberal apogee with Louis XVIII's *de facto* acceptance of the senatorial constitution in 1814.

What emerges is that the opinions of émigrés, and *a fortiori* of the nobility as a whole, were hardly of a piece. To read back from Louis's views at Verona in 1797 to what most French nobles may have thought about civic equality in 1789 is to be very daring indeed. And the same, it might be added, was true of the political goals of the allied powers. They too varied considerably, though it should be said that both Austria and Prussia showed in their negotiations with Danton and Dumouriez in 1792 and 1793 (or for that matter with Napoleon's successors in 1814 and 1815) that they preferred constitutional monarchy to restoration plain and simple.

Appendix 6

The crown's view of emigration in 1789–1792

One last irony, which has often been described, but which none the less deserves mention here, is that the supposed entente of crown and émigrés did not exist, contrary to what was assumed by everyone from the Feuillants to Marat. Mindful of aristocratic dissidence in 1787–9, eager to maintain their independence, and afraid of feeding claims which would later be costly to reward, the King and Queen were genuinely distressed by both emigration and the claims of the French Princes. The monarchs' repeated insistence that they were acting freely had in its background their desire to avoid a possible regency of the King's brothers; and royal agents worked methodically to destroy the credibility of the claims of Artois and Provence in Sweden and Russia, where the Princes' cause had been particularly well-received.

The court in Paris and the Princes in Coblenz had different plans. In 1791, Breteuil, whom the King and Queen trusted completely, was opposed to a military intervention in which Calonne had great faith. Breteuil's intention at the time was to work quietly at home and to encourage divisions in the Revolutionary camp in order to bring about the disintegration of the Revolution from within. Only then would the allies come into play. At the crucial moment, a joint statement by the Powers of Europe, possibly accompanied by a military intervention, would allow order to arise from disorder. (Lestapis, 'Royalistes et Monarchiens', *La Revue des Deux Mondes*, 15 Sept. 1960, part 1, p. 279.) In a letter of 21 March 1792, to Gustavus III, the Queen's lover, Fersen, spelt out the royal plan. The royal pair would not try to find allies in the Assembly. They would instead do what they could to encourage confusion. Theirs was a *politique du pire*:

Le roi et la reine, ayant senti tout l'avantage qu'il y avait à fomenter dans l'Assemblée l'esprit de parti pour mieux la perdre et entraver la Constitution, ont pris celui de rester liés avec les constitutionnels et de régler leurs actions et le choix des ministres d'après leurs avis, bien persuadés cependant de leurs mauvaises intentions et de l'impossibilité e gouverner avec cette constitution mais trouvant dans cette conduite avantage d'augmenter la confusion et les désordres de tout genre dans : royaume.

uch a policy would 'prepare minds to discontent' and facilitate foreign intervention; it also implied public adherence to the rogramme of the constitutional monarchists. (Lestapis, *Revue es Deux Mondes*, 1 Oct. 1960, part 2, p. 512.) Since this plan was ot to the émigrés' liking, Breteuil, who was in charge of it, ecame the butt of their sadly disparaging sobriquets: *Chef-uprême des monarchiens*, *Deux-Chambres*, and *mezzo-termine*.

Here as in so many other respects Gouverneur Morris in 1791–2 ucidly understood what was happening and observed that neither he French King nor his fellow monarchs had cause to be nterested in émigré politics. Nobles, he remarked, were in a weak osition, but the King's hand might yet be played successfully ince it was:

otorious that the great Mass of the french Nation is less solicitous to reserve the present Order of Things than to prevent the Return of the ncient Oppressions, and of Course would more readily submit to a ure Despotism than to that kind of Monarchy whose only Limits were ound in those noble, legal and clerical Corps by which the People were lternately oppressed and insulted. . . . a great Question occurs. What ings will exert themselves to raise abroad what they labor incessantly o destroy at Home, and more especially as the french Revolution having een begun by the Nobles, the Example will be so much the more striking they become the Victims of it.

Gouverneur Morris, *A Diary of the French Revolution*, vol. II, p. 440–1, June 1792.) In Morris's view, the King and his nobles ad naturally divergent interests.

There is no reason to suppose that the more rabid émigrés were nything but sincere when they accused the King after Varennes f having genuinely accepted the Constitution and derided him as *pauvre homme*, *le béat*, and *le soliveau*.

As it happens, they were wrong about Louis's devotion to onstitutionalism, but they were right about the King's low pinion of Coblenz, since it was only *in extremis*, in early 1792, that he court fell in behind the émigrés. When the Feuillants lost ontrol of the Legislative Assembly and Barnave left for Grenoble, he King and Queen finally rallied to the more desperate policy f allied military intervention with émigré participation. But

even then, on 30 March 1792, three weeks before the outbreak c
the war, their emissary, Goguelat, told Kaunitz that, 'un
contre-révolution opérée par les Princes serait . . . plus fatale a
roi que la situation actuelle. . . . Tout ce que les Princes avancen
de l'autorisation qu'ils ont de la part du roi d'agir en son nom es
faux.' (Lestapis, p. 508. See also Mme de Tourzel, *Mémoire*
(Paris, 1969), p. 461, n. 1.)

Viewed in this light, the anti-émigré measures passed by th
Legislative Assembly take on an ironic colour. The distrust by th
Monarch of his self-exiled nobles must surely have been one of th
very few points on which the crown and even the 'Republicar
party were in genuine accord. The ensuing *mésentente* underscore
once again the importance of perception over reality. Wha
nobles did mattered less than what nobles in the abstract *ought* t
be doing. The King, the émigrés, and those nobles who stayed i
France had very divergent views of what was to be done, but thi
was overlooked by their opponents, as it has often been since b
contemporaries and historians all too eager to see in th
protagonists of the Revolutionary drama the decided friends c
foes of feudalism.

NOTES TO CHAPTER ONE

[1] Kant, *An Answer to the Question: What is the Enlightenment?*

[2] Gabriel Bonnot de Mably, *De la législation ou principes des lois* (Amsterdam, 1776), vol. 2, pp. 94–5.

[3] Diderot, *Œuvres politiques*, ed. Paul Vernière (Paris, 1963), p. 404.

[4] *La Signora d'Épinay e l'Abate Galiani. Lettere inedite (1769–1772)* (Bari, 1929). 29 Sept. 1769, p. 27. The definition of the problem of politics as the reconciliation of individual and community was hardly new, and J. G. A. Pocock, in his provocative *Machiavellian Moment* (Princeton, 1975), has described English and American analogues of this same assumption, whose origins he finds in the thought of Machiavelli and which he describes as a modern adaptation of Renaissance civic humanism. In this view, a virtuous man, who is the citizen of a virtuous state, can harmonize his private goals with his public responsibilities: The individual, writes Pocock, 'knew himself to be rational and virtuous, and possessed what we can now call *amour de soi-même*, inasmuch as he knew himself to be a citizen and knew how to play his role and take decisions within the *politeia* or *modo di vivere* of a republic.'

The prospects, and the problems also, of this world view were second nature to the philosophes, who read Machiavelli with great care. Montesquieu was steeped in the thought of the Florentine, and Rousseau claimed to have taken Geneva as his practical model and Machiavelli as his theoretical guide (see Maxime Leroy, *Histoire des idées sociales en France de Montesquieu à Robespierre* (Paris, 1946); p. 192).

[5] Pocock, *The Machiavellian Moment*, p. 548.

[6] Ernst Cassirer, *The Philosophy of the Enlightenment* (Boston, 1951), p. 240.

[7] Quoted in Leroy, *Histoire des idées sociales*; p. 251.

[8] Isabel F. Knight, *The Geometric Spirit* (New Haven, 1968), p. 274.

[9] Mercier de la Rivière, in *L'Ordre naturel et essentiel des sociétés politiques* (Paris, 1767), ed. Daire, p. 633.

[10] See Jean Starobinski, *Jean-Jacques Rousseau, la transparence et l'obstacle* (Paris, 1971), pp. 44–8.

[11] Judith N. Shklar, *Men and Citizens* (Cambridge, 1969), p. 66.

[12] Ibid., p. 64.

[13] Ibid., p. 18.

[14] The dilemma of man in society was one which Rousseau as a person felt as acutely as anyone possibly could. Professor Pocock envisages correctly that if Jean-Jacques had indeed gone to see Hume in Scotland, he would have appeared among his hosts as 'an accuser of the brethren, paranoiacally proclaiming that the tensions between personality and society did have apocalyptic possibilities, that the apocalypse had arrived in his own person, and that if properly understood it would be seen to have been present since before the beginnings of human society itself'. (*The Machiavellian Moment*, p. 504.)

[15] Ibid., p. 466.

[16] Quoted in Leroy, *Histoire des indées sociales*, p. 71.

[17] Rousseau, *Discours sur l'origine et les fondements de l'inégalité parmi des hommes*, ed. Garnier (Paris, 1954), p. 77.

[18] Lester G. Crocker, *Diderot's Chaotic Order* (Princeton, 1974), p. 133.

[19] Quoted in J. L. Talmon, *The Origins of Totalitarian Democracy* (New York, 1961), p. 52.

[20] Quoted in Isser Woloch, '*Jacobin Legacy*', *The Democratic Movement under the Directory* (Princeton, 1970), p. 153.

[21] E. G. Lenglet, *De la propriété et de ses rapports avec les droits et avec la dette du citoyen* (Paris, 1797–8), p. 39.

[22] Diderot, *Œuvres politiques*, p. 12.

[23] *Histoire ancienne*, vol. 2, in *Œuvres de Condillac*, vol. 10 (Paris, 1798), p. 526.

[24] On 4 June 1767. *Voltaire's Correspondence*, T. Besterman ed., vol. 66 (Geneva, 1961), p. 6.

[25] Voltaire to d'Alembert, 2 Sept. 1768, *Voltaire's Correspondence*, vol. 70 (Geneva, 1962), p. 45. See also Peter Gay, *The Enlightenment, an Interpretation*, vol. 2 (London, 1969), p. 521.

[26] Lucien Goldmann, *The Philosophy of the Enlightenment* (Cambridge, Mass., 1973), p. 36.

[27] J. L. Talmon, *The Origins of Totalitarian Democracy* (New York, 1960), p. 51.

[28] Shklar, *Men and Citizens*, p. 11.

[29] Cassirer, *The Philosophy of the Enlightenment*, p. 270.

[30] See, for example, Robert Mauzi, *L'Idée du bonheur en France au dix-huitième siècle* (Paris, 1960).

[31] Pocock, *The Machiavellian Moment*, p. 498.

[32] Quoted in Emmanuel Sieyes. *Qu'est-ce que le Tiers-état?*, ed. Roberto Zapperi (Geneva, 1970), pp. 19–20.

[33] Gordon Wood, *The Creation of the American Republic 1776–1787* (New York, 1972), p. 58.

[34] Ibid., p. 61. Many points of contact, it may be added, existed between the 'Commonwealth men' theory of government, which stressed the legacy of classical Republicanism, and the contemporary French views of the good state. Indeed, the Commonwealth theory was often interpreted in the Anglo-American world through the works of French writers, many of them Huguenots and Jansenists, like Charles Rollin, for example. The ideas of the former Rector of the University of Paris met with a sympathetic response in America since Rollin was much concerned with the fact that France could no longer produce a Spartan Cleomenes or an Achean Philopoemen. The fate of her empire, he explained, would soon resemble those of Carthage and of Rome, both of which had fallen when luxury, ambition, and pride had eroded civic virtue. Abigail Adams, who inserted whole passages of Rollin's work on the Peloponesian wars in her letters to her children, was a devoted reader. So was Stendhal. Thrilled by the news of the execution of the King, which had shattered his reactionary father, the author of *Henry Brulard* hid his joy by burrowing in his book, 'probablement Rollin que mon père me faisait lire, et je fermai les yeux pour pouvoir goûter en paix ce grand évènement'. (Stendhal, *Œuvres*, Pléiade edition, vol. I, p. 128.)

[35] Gordon Wood, op. cit., p. 609.

[36] Ibid., p. 607.

[37] Ibid., p. 612. The identification of American life and economic individualism was well established in France after the Revolution. Barbé-Marbois, a minister of Napoleon who had been jailed during the Terror and had resided in the United States for some years in the 1790s, wrote in 1816 of America that 'Auparavant, toutes les choses y appartenoient indistinctement à tous, et

cette communauté jalouse ne souffrait l'exercise d'aucun droit particulier. Aujourd'hui, an contraire, il n'y a point de pays dans l'univers où la propriété individuelle soit plus respectée.' *Complôt d'Arnold et de Sir Henry Clinton contre les États-Unis d'Amérique* (Paris, 1816), p. 92.

[38] Gordon Wood, p. 610.

[39] *The Federalist Papers*, No. 10.

[40] Ibid., No. 51; quoted in Pocock, p. 565.

[41] The message of the Physiocrats was ambiguous, but it was none the less the best equivalent in France of the individualistic doctrines that prevailed in America and Britain. There is no doubt that physiocratic doctrines had a wide impact in France, as Roberto Zapperi has shown in his luminous introduction to the pamphlet of Sieyes, *Qu'est-ce que le Tiers-état?*

Thoroughly convinced, Sieyes defended not just private property, but inequalities of private property also, as had the Physiocrats. Political liberty, to which all working men were entitled, did not exclude the legitimacy of a hierarchy of wealth. For Sieyes, there was no way to avoid 'des grandes inégalités de moyens parmi les hommes. La nature fait des forts et des foibles; elle départ aux uns une intelligence qu'elle refuse aux autres. Il suit qu'il y aura entre eux inégalité de travail, inégalité de produit, inégalité de consommation ou de jouissance.' (Zapperi, p. 50.) Liberty, in fact, necessarily guaranteed such inequalities because liberty implied the guarantee of all property: 'Celui-là est libre qui a l'assurance de n'être point inquièté dans l'exercise de sa propriété personnelle et dans l'usage de sa propriété réelle.' (Zapperi, p. 52.)

[42] Quoted in Charles Rist, *Histoire des idées économiques en France depuis les physiocrates jusqu'à nos jours* (Paris, 1913), p. 12.

[43] Quoted in Talmon, *The Origins of Totalitarian Democracy*, p. 53.

[44] Ibid., p. 55.

[45] Quoted in Leroy, *Histoire des idées sociales*, p. 234. Raynal varied in the intensity of his attack on property. Minor repairs, he sometimes thought, might suffice, like the abolition of primogeniture, which disseminated the benefits of property.

[46] André Lichtenberger, *Le Socialisme au XVIIIe siècle, Études sur les idées socialistes dans les écrivains français du XVIIIe siècle avant la Révolution* (Paris, 1895), pp. 336–42. In his *Thesmographe* of 1789, Restif went on to propose another scheme. Every five years, all land would be redistributed by the relevant municipalities (see Lichtenberger, *Le Socialisme et la Révolution française* (Paris, 1899), pp. 44–5).

Similar arguments were presented in a less sophisticated way by many of the future leaders of the Revolutionary movement. Brissot's *Recherches philosophiques sur le droit de propriété et sur le vol considéré dans la nature et la société* (Berlin, 1782–6) is set within similar limits. Property is absolute, but it is also a convention. Therefore, theft is a crime, but it is not a crime against nature and must be treated accordingly: 'Jugez comme nous sommes loin de la nature. Le voleur dans l'état de nature est le riche, celui qui a du superflu; dans la société, le voleur est celui qui dérobe à ce riche.' (Lichtenberger, *Le Socialisme au XVIIIe siècle*, p. 416.) A similar hesitation on the question of property characterized Marat's *Plan de législation criminelle* of 1780 and Pétion's *Les Lois civiles et l'administration de la justice ramenées à un ordre simple et uniforme ou réflexions morales ou politiques* (London, 1783).

R. B. Rose, in his admirable biography of Gracchus Babeuf, concludes likewise that Babeuf could not have been a collectivist before 1789 as was argued by V. M. Dalin: 'To suppose that Babeuf was a doctrinaire communist from 1786 or 1787', writes Professor Rose, 'seeking to impose a preconceived utopia on mankind by revolution, reveals a misunderstanding of the contemporary function of utopian speculation in providing the moral sanction for comparatively moderate practical measures of reform. Only the repeated failure of such "palliatives" in the course of the revolution drove him finally to recognize the speculative extreme as the only truly practical policy.' (R. B. Rose, *Gracchus Babeuf* (Standord, 1978), p. 42.)

[47] Talmon, *The Origins of Totalitarian Democracy*, p. 56.

[48] Ibid. p. 56.

[49] Leroy, *Histoire des idées sociales*, p. 234.

[50] For a lucid review of the use of antiquity during the Revolution see 'La Révolution française et les Grecs', *Esprit*, Dec. 1975, pp. 825–39.

[51] Helvetius, *De l'esprit*, ed. Guy Besse (Paris, 1968), p. 154.

[52] See Paul Bastide, *Sieyès et sa pensée* (Paris, 1970), p. 387.

[53] Montesquieu, *L'Esprit des lois*, Book 3, Chapter 3.

[54] Quoted in Jean-Claude Perrot, *Caen, genèse d'une ville moderne* (Paris, 1975), p. 698.

[55] Brissot, the archetypal bourgeois Revolutionary scoundrel, was quite representative in this same respect. Like everyone, what Brissot remembered from reading Crevecœur's *Letters of an American Farmer* was that Americans had shown to 'blasé Europeans' that virtue was no fiction: 'the happiness for which they [the Europeans] have sighed does in truth exist.' Brissot's first purpose in visiting America had therefore been to study the legislation that had enabled free men to maintain their liberties. But Brissot had also come as the representative of an investment syndicate looking for good business opportunities. American virtue was imposing, but American property was not to be neglected either. Indeed, as far as Brissot was concerned, there was not enough wealth in America, much less luxury, and he was the first observer to develop the theme that the fine arts could not flourish in the United States as they did on the old Continent because the new country was 'too poor'. 'It cannot encourage the arts.' See Durand Echeverria, *Mirage in the West* (Princeton, 1957), pp. 152–8.

[56] *Dissertation sur les suites de la découverte de l'Amérique qui a obtenu en 1785 une mention honorable de l'Académie des Sciences, Arts, et Belles Lettres de Lyon* (1787), p. 51.

[57] In his introduction to Crèvecœur's *Lettres d'un cultivateur américain* (Paris, 1787), vol. I, p. xxiii. Lacretelle's introduction had first appeared in 1785 as an 'Extrait donné dans le Mercure en 1785 des Lettres d'un cultivateur américain'.

[58] Condorcet, *De l'influence de la Révolution de l'Amérique sur les opinions et la législation de l'Europe*, in *Œuvres complètes de Condorcet*, vol. 9 (Paris, 1804), p. 252.

[59] Quoted in André Maurois, *Adrienne ou la vie de Mme de La Fayette* (Paris, 1960), p. 80.

[60] R. R. Palmer, *The Age of Democratic Revolution, a Political History of Europe and America, 1760–1800* (Princeton, 1959), vol. I, p. 264.

[61] Ibid., pp. 276–7.

[62] Mably, *Observations sur le gouvernement et les loix des États Unis d'Amérique*, cited in Philip Mazzei, *Recherches historiques et politiques sur les États-Unis de l'Amérique septentrionale* (Paris, 1788), pp. 163 and 167.

[63] Louis-Sébastien Mercier, *De la littérature et des littérateurs, suivi d'un nouvel examen de la tragédie françoise* (Yverdon, 1778), p. 27 n. 11.

[64] George Rudé, *Paris and London in the Eighteenth Century* (New York, 1970), p. 69.

[65] Quoted by William Scott, *Terror and Repression in Revolutionary Marseilles* (New York, 1973), p. 224.

[66] Camille Desmoulins, *La France libre* (Paris, 1838), pp. 30–1.

[67] Quoted in Garrone, *Romme*, p. 164.

[68] Murat de Montferrand, *Qu'est-ce que la noblesse et que sont ses privilèges?* (Amsterdam, 1789), pp. 29–30.

[69] *Procès verbaux du Comité d'Instruction publique de la Convention*, ed. M. J. Guillaume (Paris, 1896), vol. I, p. 585.

[70] Jean-Yves Guiomar, *L'Idéologie nationale* (Paris, 1974).

[71] Dufourny de Villiers, *Cahiers du 4e ordre, celui des pauvres journaliers, des infirmes, des indigens, etc. . . . l'ordre des infortunés* (Paris, 1789), p. 14.

[72] Quoted in O. Hufton, 'The Poor in the Eighteenth Century', in *French Government and Society*, J. F. Bosher, ed. (London, 1973), p. 148. 'Beggary', wrote Lenoir, the royal official in charge of the police in Paris from 1774 to 1785, 'seems to be the point of transition between the laboring and the criminal classes.' Quoted in J. Kaplow, *The Names of Kings* (New York, 1972), p. 143.

[73] Quoted in B. Plongeron, 'Le Fait religieux dans l'histoire de la Révolution française', *Annales historiques de la Révolution française*, Jan.–Mar. 1975, XLVII, No. 219, p. 119.

[74] See François Furet's stimulating essay, *Penser le Révolution* (Paris, 1978).

[75] Peter Brown, *The World of Late Antiquity: From Marcus Aurelius to Muhammad* (London, 1971).

[76] Jean-Claude Perrot's massive *Caen, genèse d'une ville moderne*, the most impressive work on the social history of the *Ancien Régime* to have appeared in some years, focuses on this very problem of cultural advance in a materially backward and static setting.

[77] See Anthony Giddens, *The Structure of Advanced Societies* (London, 1973), p. 26; and Schlomo Avineri, *The Social and Political Thought of Karl Marx* (Cambridge, 1968), p. 154.

[78] Alfred Cobban, *The Social Interpretation of the French Revolution* (Cambridge, 1964), p. 67.

[79] See J. F. Bosher, *The Single-Duty Project* (London, 1964).

[80] This is, of course, a polemical point. Roberto Zapperi, in his introduction to Sieyes's *Qu'est-ce que le Tiers-état?* (p. 68) vigorously denies it. In Zapperi's view, the 'ideology of individualism' did not prepare the way for the 'birth of a new economy', and in fact took no account of new economic forms at all. The more correct view, as I see it, is developed by Guiomar in his *Idéologie nationale* (pp. 234–5), who points out that although bourgeois individualists may have been hostile to technological change, and perhaps even to the concepts of money and exchange, their individualism was none the less a critical first step to the elaboration of modern capitalism regardless of their intent. The first social implication of their individualist philosophy was the defence of private property, and out of this later arose social forms which could hardly be envisaged in pre-Revolutionary France, but which were none the less in the logical order of things.

[81] Cited in Elizabeth Fox-Genovese, *The Origins of Physiocracy. Economic Revolution and Social Order in Eighteenth Century France* (Ithaca, N.Y., 1976), p. 157.

[82] Cited by J. B. Serrer, *Histoire de la Révolution en Auvergne* (Saint-Amond, 1895), pp. 25–6.

[83] Albert Soboul, *Histoire de la Révolution française* (Paris, 1962) vol. I, p. 129.
[84] Ibid., p. 47.
[85] Cited in Albert Soboul, *La Civilisation et la Révolution française* (Paris, 1970), p. 278.
[86] The evidence on this point is presented in David Bien's 'Aristocratie et annoblissement au XVIIIe siècle', *Annales*, Mar.–Apr. 1974, p. 532. Professor Bien, a historian's historian, is not a Marxist, but some of the evidence that he presents can be used for Marxist ends.
[87] M. Gresset, *Le Monde judiciaire à Besançon de la Conquête par Louis XIV à la Revolution 1674–1789* (Lille, 1975), vol. II, p. 1195.
[88] See Vivian R. Gruder, *The Royal Provincial Intendants, a Governing Élite in Eighteenth-Century France* (Ithaca, N.Y., 1968).
[89] See Yves Durand, *Les Fermiers généraux au XVIIIe siècle* (Paris, 1971).
[90] Guy Chaussinand-Nogaret, *La Noblesse au XVIIIe siécle de la féodalité aux lumières* (Paris, 1976), pp. 157–8.
[91] See George V. Taylor, 'Types of Capitalism in Eighteenth Century—France', *English Historical Review*, July 1965, pp. 478–97.
[92] See Barrington Moore, *The Social Origins of Dictatorship and Democracy* (Boston, 1967).
[93] Guy Chaussinand-Nogaret, 'Aux origines de la Révolution: noblesse et bourgeoisie', *Annales*, vol. 30, no. 2–3, Mar.–June 1975.
[94] (Baltimore, 1960.)
[95] Cited in Marcel Reinhard, *Le Grand Carnot* (Paris, 1952), vol. II, p. 334.
[96] On 10 August 1789. Marquis de Ferrières to Mme de Médel, in *Correspondance inédite du marquis de Ferrières*, ed. Henri Carré (Paris, 1922), p. 120.
[97] Cited in Marcel Garaud, *La Révolution et l'égalité civile* (Paris, 1953), p. 6.
[98] Cited in Alessandro Galante Garrone, *Gilbert Romme, Histoire d'un révolutionnaire (1750–1795)* (Paris, 1971), p. 42.
[99] Quoted in Jean Egret, *La Pré-Révolution française, 1787–1788* (Paris, 1962), p. 322.
[100] Chaussinand-Nogaret, 'Aux origines', p. 269.
[101] Cited in Marcel Reinhard, 'Élite et Noblesse dans la seconde moitié du XVIIIe siècle', *Revue d'histoire moderne et contemporaine*, vol. III, janvier–mars 1956, p. 15.
[102] Turgot, *Œuvres*, vol. V. ed. G. Schelle (Paris, 1923), p. 188.
[103] Quoted in Betty Behrens, *The Ancien Régime* (London, 1967), p. 74.
[104] *Past and Present*, no. 60, Aug. 1973, p. 93.
[105] Lenard Berlanstein, *The Barristers of Toulouse in the Eighteenth Century (1740–1793)* (Baltimore, 1975), p. 179.
[106] Jean-Marie Goulemot, *Discours, histoire, et révolutions* (Paris, 1975), pp. 387–8.
[107] Philippe Auguste de Sainte-Foix, chevalier d'Arcq, *La Noblesse militaire, ou le Patriote françois*, in *Trois pièces sur cette question, Les Nobles doivent-ils commercer?* (London, 1758), p. 73. In this fourth edition of the *Noblesse militaire*, first published in 1756, d'Arcq appears as d'Arc.
[108] Quoted in Jean Égret, *La Pré-Révolution française*, p. 352.
[109] Cited in A. Decouflé, *L'Aristocratie française devant l'opinion publique à la veille de la Révolution française 1787–1789: Études d'histoire économique et sociale au XVIIIe siècle* (Paris, 1966), p. 15.

[110] Rabaut-Saint-Étienne, *Considérations sur les intérêts du Tiers-état, adressées au peuple des provinces. Par un propriétaire foncier* (Amsterdam, 1788), p. 67.

[111] Quoted in Marcel Reinhard, 'Élite et Noblesse', *Revue d'histoire moderne et contemporaine*, Jan.–Mar. 1965, p. 31. During the most egalitarian phase of Revolutionary Republicanism, even honorary distinctions fell into some disfavour, as Barère explained to the Convention on 28 April 1794: 'Dans un pays libre, les honneurs publics ne doivent être rendus qu'aux morts, parce qu'ils ne les corrompent pas et que la véritable gloire ne peut s'asseoir que sur des tombeaux.' *Le Moniteur*, vol. 20 (Paris, 1820), p. 333.

[112] Rivarol, *Œuvres choisies*, vol. II, *Journal politique national* (Paris, 1880), p. 83.

[113] Elinor G. Barber, *The Bourgeoisie in 18th Century France* (Princeton, 1973), p. 66.

[114] Helvétius, *Œuvres complètes*, vol. XIV, p. 61, cited in *De l'esprit*, ed. Guy Besse (Paris, 1968), p. 14.

[115] Archives Nationales (hereafter AN) F[7] 4631. Calon. The theme of the recent origin of most noble families was developed after 1789 as well, by Brossard in 1790, for example, in his *Les Métamorphoses ou Liste des noms de familles et patronymiques des ci-devant ducs, marquis, comtes, barons, & excellences, monseigneurs, grandeurs, demi-seigneurs et annoblis.*

[116] Dubois-Crancé, *Analyse de la Révolution française depuis l'ouverture des États généraux jusqu'au 6 brumaire ou IV de la République* (Paris, 1885), p. 174–5.

[117] Rabaut-Saint-Étienne, *Considérations sur les intérêts du Tiers-état*, (Paris?, 1788), p. 57.

[118] Rabaut, *Considérations sur les intérêts du Tiers-état*, Ch. XIV, in *Œuvres*, p. 290, quoted in Martin Göhring, *Rabaut-Saint-Étienne, Ein Kampfer an der Wende zweier Epochen* (Berlin, 1935), p. 78.

[119] Göhring, *Rabaut*, p. 85.

[120] Garrone, *Romme*, p. 410.

[121] Chaussinand-Nogaret, *La Noblesse*, p. 226.

[122] Reinhard, 'Élite et Noblesse', p. 30.

[123] Rivarol, *Œuvres*, vol. II, *Journal politique national*, p. 89, cited in A. Soboul 'La Révolution française et le monde contemporain. Étude comparative' in *Studien über die Revolution* (East Berlin, 1971), p. 89.

NOTES TO CHAPTER TWO

[1] Georges Lefebvre, in a review of Talmon's *Origins of Totalitarian Democracy*, in *Annales historique de la Révolution française*, XXV, no. 130 (Jan.–Mar. 1953), p. 184.

[2] The most vigorous protests were registered by the Parlementaires of Rennes who were required to make public amends on 7 January 1790.

[3] For an account of Froment's role, see James N. Hood, 'Patterns of Popular Protest in the French Revolution', *Journal of Modern History*, XLVIII, no. 2 (June 1976), p. 272.

[4] Ch. Girault, 'La Noblesse sarthoise', in *La Province du Maine*, 1954–5; quoted in Chaussinand-Nogaret, *La Noblesse*, p. 86.

[5] Quoted in Jean Bastier, *La Féodalité au siècle des lumières dans la région de Toulouse* (Paris, 1975), p. 302. In the same way, in the vicinity of Pontarlier, one of the pillars of the Revolutionary establishment was Luc Joseph de Mesmay,

an administrator of the Department of the Doubs from 1790 to 1793, a purchaser of *biens nationaux*, the father of two young men who volunteered for the army, and a noble whose branch of the family had recently 'derogated'. See Claude Brelot, *La Noblesse en Franche-Comté* (Paris, 1972), p. 93, n. 75. Many nobles felt that they had been ill-treated during the *Ancien Régime* and in 1793–4 cited this as proof of their loyalty to the Revolution, e.g. General Sorlus, who wrote to Rossignol that, yes, he was a noble (because his grandfather had bought a charge) but that this did not mean much: 'Malgré celá nous avons à nous plaindre de l'Ancien Régime.' *Correspondance de Carnot*, ed. Charavay, vol. IV, p. 448, n. 1. La Revellière, who hated nobles, was as a young man patronized by the head of the Princepré family which, he emphasizes, had been but no longer was noble. When a collateral relative urged Princepré to reclaim his birthright, the man refused in no uncertain terms: 'Dieu me garde de rien faire de ce que vous me proposez là! Qu'est-ce qui vous fait rechercher de futiles honneurs et d'injustes privilèges? L'orgueil, qui veut des distinctions, sans s'être mis en peine d'en mériter aucune; l'avarice, qui veut jouir des avantages de la société, sans contribuer aux charges communes.' (La Revellière, *Mémoires* (Paris, 1895), vol. I, p. 181).

[6] 'S'il y avoit un ordre de Citoyens victimes des abus du Despotisme ministériel,' Brissot explained in January 1790,

> . . . c'étoit la pauvre Noblesse. Cette nombreuse classe de Gentilshommes Cultivateurs, Bornée par un préjugé gothique, à-peu-près à un seul état, y existoit d'une manière si malheureuse, si pénible, si dépendante, que jamais l'Aristocratie des Grands ou des Riches ne s'étoit manifestée d'une manière plus évidente & plus injuste. Le tableau des vexations de tout genre, auxelles elle etoit exposée dans l'état militaire, est, dans la proportion, l'un des plus révoltans qu'on puisse voir, & l'esquisse que j'ai essayé d'en tracer m'a étonné moi-même lorsque j'en ai rassemblé tous les traits. (*Le Patriote français*, CLIX, p. 3.)

Dufourny in his *Cahiers du quatrième ordre* had made a similar point, if to a different end:

> Quant aux riches, les divers degrés de fortune doivent seuls servir à classer les hommes, lorsqu'il s'agit de se cotiser; il sembleroit donc que les Ordres du Clergé & de la Noblesse renfermant beaucoup d'individus très-pauvres, de même que l'Ordre du Tiers renferme beaucoup de fortunes aussi grandes que celle du Haut Clergé & de la Haute Noblesse, rien ne seroit moins relatif à toute délibération sur les contributions, que de classer les individus comme Pontifes, Gentilhommes, ou Roturiers [p. 8].

Bitter as he may have been about nobles, Sieyes in 1789, like Brissot, also saw the gentry as potential allies of the Third Estate, and he had suggested in his pamphlet that country nobles could be relied on to oppose the creation of an Upper House which would be taken over by Court nobles. (Sieyes, *Qu'est-ce que le Tiers-état?* ed. R. Zapperi, p. 168.) Optimism about the *arriviste* propensities of the *petite noblesse* did not last. Within a few months, even new émigrés like the erstwhile General Dumouriez thought that all émigrés, save himself perhaps, were drawn from this milieu: 'cette classe est purement royaliste; elle soutient et désire la monarchie absolue'. Quoted in l'abbé Grégoire, *Mémoires*, vol. II, p. 181.

Mme de Genlis liked them even less: 'Ces émigrés qui ont été persécuteurs dans les pays étrangers pour leurs compatriotes, auxquels ils supposoient des opinions *libérales*, étoient tous, sans exceptions, de petits gentilshommes de province qui n'avaient jamais été présentés à la cour, et qui n'avaient aucune connoissance du monde.' Mme de Genlis, *Mémoires* (Paris, 1825), vol. IV, pp. 196–7.

The switch is readily explicable: in 1789, country nobles, being poor, were seen as honorary members of 'le peuple' eager to improve themselves; in 1793, being backward, they were now perceived as pillars of reaction, two views that were in all likelihood equally valid.

[7] Quoted in L. Gottschalk and M. Maddox, 'From the October Days through the Federation', *Lafayette in the French Revolution* (Chicago, 1973), p. 424. It was a noble also, d'Estournel, who proposed that Protestants as well as Catholics be eligible for the Order of Saint-Louis.

[8] Jacques Menou, *A ses concitoyens* (Paris, 1792), p. 4.

[9] Marquis de Ferrières, *Correspondance inédite, 1780, 1790, 1791*, ed. H. Carré (Paris, 1932), p. 228.

[10] Thus in the *Révolutions de Paris* of 10–17 July 1789, no. 53: 'C'est du club de 1789 que nous est venu le décret sur la guerre et la paix, le décret qui a donné au roi la faculté de s'adjuger 25 millions. Beaucoup de ci-devant seigneurs de gens de lettres à pensions sous l'Ancien Régime se sont jetés dans le Club de 1789.'

[11] Thus Noailles in 1789 was a 'cadet sans fortune', A. Soboul, *Histoire de la Révolution française* (Paris, 1962), vol. I, pp. 168–9. The sincerity of liberal nobles was, however, unquestioningly accepted by conservative nobles who thoroughly detested these 'class traitors'. (See L. Hartmann, *Les Officiers de l'Armée royale et la Révolution* (Paris, 1910). Some foreign nobles also understood the need to destroy the nobility in their own countries. Inspired by the example of the French, Count Feteke renounced his titles at the Hungarian Diet of 1790–1, as did, in a different setting, the Wurtemberger Georg von Kerner. (See Godechot, *La Grande Nation* (Paris, 1956), vol. I, p. 106.)

[12] Cited in Marcel Garaud, *La Révolution et l'égalité civile* (Paris, 1953), p. 97.

[13] Ibid., n. 4.

[14] Royal approval of this act has been varyingly interpreted. In her *Mémoires* (Paris, 1969), p. 81, Mme de Tourzel suggests that the King's gesture was intended to disarm the campaign for the suppression of titles. On the other hand, one of Gouverneur Morris's correspondents, Short, wrote that the proposed suppression of titles had created consternation at the court: according to Short, the King had sanctioned the law and by the same token rejected Lafayette's sudden request for a royal veto because he was following a *politique du pire*. Lameth explained the King's passivity in much the same way: a pessimist party existed at the court, and through Mme Adélaide, succeeded in winning the King over to its views. (A. Lameth, *Histoire de l'Assemblée Constituante*, vol. II, p. 466.)

[15] Dom Leclercq, *La Fédération (janvier–juillet 1790)* (Paris, 1929), p. 93. Ferrières did not approve of this public protest: 'c'est une folie qui peut compromettre les nobles de leur province, sans aucune utilité' (Ferrières, *Correspondance*, July 1790). Ferrières's own tactic was to wait and see, as he explained in late June 1790: 'Je souhaite [que la noblesse] soit assez sage pour se soumettre aux circonstances. Ce qui m'importe, c'est que l'on n'ait aucun reproche à me faire sur la conduite que je tiendrai.' *Correspondance*, p. 213.

[16] Paul Nicolle, *Histoire de Vire pendant la Révolution 1789–1800* (Vire, 1923), pp. 200–1.

[17] Rochambeau claimed that the edict was a turning-point for many officers who had at first accepted the Revolution (*Mémoires*, vol. I (Paris, 1809), p. 411). Dom Leclercq (*La Fédération*, p. 94) feels that it was with this decree that the

provincial nobility, which until then had been uncommitted, passed into the opposition.

[18] Henri Carré, *La Noblesse en France*, p. 434.

[19] Michel Vovelle, *La Chute de la monarchie* (Paris, 1972), pp. 117, 140.

[20] *Le Point du jour*, 30 Oct. 1789, p. 488.

[21] *Archives parlementaires*, vol. 22 (Paris, 1885), p. 759, 5 Feb. 1791.

[22] Ferrières, *Correspondance*, p. 113.

[23] Ferrières, *Correspondance*, p. 227.

[24] Chateaubriand, *Mémoires d'outre tombe*; quoted in Dom Leclercq, *La Fédération*, p. 243. It is also likely that many nobles in 1789 were thoroughly confused; hence the fact that a large number of them passed rapidly from liberalism to emigration, like Cazalès, or from reaction to extreme radicalism, like le Peletier de Saint-Fargeau. Some aristocratic pirouettes were genuinely virtuoso performances. D'Antraigues, for example, moved from a denunciation of the nobility in 1788 ('La noblesse est un fléau qui dévore ma patrie'), to a neo-feudal defence of privilege in 1791, followed in April 1792 by the further suggestion of a tactical alliance with the ultra-left against the constitutional monarchists, since he much preferred 'les Jacobins aux Monarchiens, aux Monarchistes, et je le publierai toujours hautement. On peut pour l'avenir tirer quelque parti d'un bouleversement général, on n'en peut tirer aucun d'un replâtrage timide et illégal qui vous affaiblit de ce qu'il vous ôte et vous embarrasse de tout ce qu'il vous laisse.' (See Jacqueline Chaumié, *Le Réseau d'Antraigues et la Contre-Révolution, 1791–1793* (Paris, 1965), p. 160.)

[25] Taine, *Les Origines de la France contemporaine*, vol. I (Paris, 1878), p. 391. Taine's rather lofty message is borne out by more recent and concrete research. Thus, Martyn Lyons, in his admirable investigation of Revolutionary Toulouse, writes of the Parlementaires there that

> . . . for all their bombast and rhetoric, the Parlementaires were not by nature counter-revolutionary activists. They had a horror of lawlessness and public disorder, which it had always been their duty to prevent and to punish. They worked scrupulously, legalistically, in a conventional and constitutional way. The only tactics they knew were the Humble Supplications. Remonstrances, the Protestations from the *parquet* which they heaped upon the King. They could never accept responsibility for violent resistance to authority, by their closest followers. After their departure, Royalism was leaderless and timid in Toulouse, in spite of its enormous fund of latent support. It was left to the next generation to resume the struggle.

[26] Madelin, *La Révolution* (Paris, 1912), p. 114.

[27] *L'Ami du peuple*, no. 559, 25 Sept. 1791, p. 4.

[28] Robespierre, *Œuvres*, vol. X, 2 Jan. 1792, p. 83. By the summer of 1794, however, Robespierre had changed his mind. It then appeared to him that liberal nobles must have had opportunistic personal motives after all: 'Si des ambitions particulières lui ont donné le branle [to the Revolution] ou hâté son mouvement, elle n'a dû son origine et sa direction qu'à l'amour éclairé et profond de la justice et de la liberté.' (In the draft of his speech for 8 thermidor an II, *Discours*, vol. X, p. 544, n. 4.)

[29] *Archives parlementaires*, vol. 34 (Paris, 1890), p. 316, 20 Oct. 1791.

[30] In the spring of 1791, the Assembly elaborated on the suppression of titles. Henceforth, it decided, nobles who insisted on using their titles would be barred

from public life as would notaries and administrators who had acknowledged the existence of titles. A proposal to pillory for three hours those nobles who would not comply was, however, shouted down. Later, in the autumn of 1791, Lafayette among others gave serious thought to a repeal of the law on the abolition of titles as part of a planned reconciliation with the centre right.

[31] On 20 March 1791, a decree ordered that all appointments made in the next three years be assigned to employees of suppressed governmental bodies.

The complaint of the Toulouse Parlement was badly received. Robespierre on 5 October 1790 described it as 'un acte de délire, qui ne doit exciter que le mépris' (*Archives parlementaires*, vol. 19 (Paris, 1884), p. 469). Three days later, the duc de Broglie, on behalf of the Constitutional committee, presented a proposal for the arrest of the signatories (ibid., pp. 513–15): 'Chef d'œuvre, à la fois d'égarement et de perfidie, cet arrêté [of the Toulouse Parlement] est au dessus de toute qualification . . . c'est le tocsin de la rébellion sonné par ceux mêmes dont les fonctions augustes et bienfaisantes ne doivent tendre qu'à la paix et à la tranquilité (p. 514).

[32] Cited in Garrone, *Romme*, p. 198. For Talhouët see *Journal des Départements*, vol. VIII, p. 24, cited in Jean Bricart, *L'Administration du département d'Ille-et-Vilaine au début de la Révolution* (Rennes, 1965), p. 402, n. 5. In an account of Talhouët's inauguration, the ci-devant mayor was described as having risen 'au-dessus des préjugés d'une naissance chimérique et d'une fausse éducation'. Bricart, *L'Administration*, p. 402, n. 5.

[33] P. 332, Jacques-Antoine Dulaure is one of the more picaresque, minor figures of the Revolution. Like Babeuf, he was trained as a *feudiste*, which may explain his anti-nobilism. A polymath, Dulaure developed a new technique for the drafting of architectural plans, became a publicist, and would have been put in the Bastille if he had not enjoyed the protection of the King of Sweden. A ferocious anti-noble journalist, he produced in 1790 his *Histoire critique de l'aristocratie* as well as a *Liste des noms des ci-devant nobles, nobles de race, Robins, Prélats, Financiers, Intriguans, & de tous les aspirans à la noblesse ou escrocs d'icelle avec des notes sur leurs familles*, the second edition of which was 'corrigée & augmentée', a work followed shortly thereafter by a *Vie privée des ècclésiastiques qui n'ont point prêté serment.* As a journalist, Dulaure also guided the transitory fortunes of the *Evangéliste du jour*, the most interesting of whose sixteen numbers dealt precisely with nobles. In the issue of 30 June 1790, Dulaure did not mince words: 'Enfin il est tombé sous la hache de la liberté, cet arbre féodal devant lequel s'extasioit le très féodal président de Montesquieu.' Nobles had been and would forever be hateful:

> . . . nobles d'anciennes races, nobles par argent, nobles par escroquerie, nobles par cruautés, par infamies, par brigandages, nobles par héritation; & vous tous, tueurs, affronteurs, fouleurs d'hommes, proxénètes, valets, gentilshommes, pages & catins de la cour, baissez la tête & regardez votre honteuse origine: vous êtes nés de la boue de la société, & vous ne vous êtes distingués des autres hommes que par vos crimes, par l'insolence de vos prétentions & de vos actions, par votre longue ignorance, votre absurde fierté & vos brigandages. Notre histoire, souillée à chaque page par les plus horribles forfaits, n'offre par-tout que le tableau de vos forfaits.

In 1792, Dulaure was elected to the Convention. Vaguely sympathetic to the Girondins, he was attacked by Hébert and emigrated. He soon returned and, in 1795, was sent on a mission to his home department of the Puy-de-Dôme, where he once again denounced nobles but protected moderates, counter-revolutionaries, and priests. Elected to the 'Five Hundred', he did not please Bonaparte and his political career came to an end in 1800.

His numerous publications include a *Descriptions des curiosités de Paris*, as well as *Les Causes secrètes des excès de la Révolution*, which exposes the collusion of émigrés with the Paris Commune. His most durable work, however, has proved to be *Des divinités génératrices et le culte du phallus* written in 1805 and reprinted in 1905. Psycho-historians will be tempted to connect as different aspects of Dulaure's character his twin concerns for genitalian cults and his obsessive denials of the social virtues of noble birth, two interests which dovetailed nicely in an interesting *discursus* on the 'Droits du seigneurs' (pp. 232–5 of the *Divinités génératrices*). Dulaure also deserves notice as the founder of an *Académie celtique*.

Dulaure never gave up. His *Principaux évènements de la Révolution française* of 1823–1825, like his *Causes secrètes*, also developed the theme of the connection among the émigrés, the sans-culottes, the Revolutionary tribunal, and/or the Committee of Public Safety.

His case is curious. The inspiration of his thinking may well have had bizarre and personal roots. A modern historian of Paris has justly described him as 'cerveau étroit et un peu grotesque' (Héron de Villefosse, *Histoire de Paris* (Paris, 1955), p. 8), and yet the writings that Dulaure produced during the Revolution and the Restoration have often been taken to express the mood of those times, although they could be plausibly described as idiosyncratic to a degree.

[34] Quoted by Jean Égret, *La Pré-Révolution française, 1787–1788* (Paris, 1962), p. 353. In this same context, it may be added that personal relations between noble and bourgeois deputies in the National Assembly were, if not cordial, at least correct. Thibaudeau, whose father had been a deputy in 1789, was in retrospect surprised by this, and felt that this era of good feelings should be explained:

> Les porteurs de noms historiques, quoique rappelant l'oppression du peuple, en tiraient encore de grands avantages. Émancipée à peine depuis quelques mois, la nation n'avait pas secoué le joug de ses préjugés, de ses vieilles habitudes; et quand un grand seigneur daignait se rapprocher d'elle, elle en était flattée et le tenait en honneur. Je le voyais à chaque instant, dans l'Assemblée, à la manière dont les membres les plus marquants du Tiers État abordaient les principaux de la Noblesse et du Clergé.

Lameth thought much the same and remarked that individual nobles often had great weight: 'Le succès des délibérations n'était pas toujours indépendant de la considération attachée aux personnes. La position sociale, l'âge, le caractère du duc de La Rochefoucauld lui donnaient une autorité et un crédit qui pouvaient influer utilement sur l'Assemblée. (Quoted in Gaston Dodu, *Le Parlementarisme et les parlementaires sous la Révolution* (Paris, 1911), pp. 56–7, n. 5.)

In July 1791, when the temper of the Assembly had changed a good deal, and after the prominent patriot deputy, Anthoine, had spoken of a 'coalition entre les nobles et les militaires', Lameth complained; Anthoine backed off and explained:

> J'ai cru devoir faire part de mes craintes sur une coalition des ci-devant nobles. Je n'ai désigné personne. Et, s'il était besoin de donner une preuve de mon estime pour M. Lameth, je dirais que je viens de lui donner ma voix pour être président à l'Assemblée nationale; et, la Société s'en rappelle sans doute, sur les réclamations que M. Lameth fit dans la derniere séance, je me suis opposé à l'impression de mon discours.

(F. A. Aulard, ed., *La Société des Jacobins* (Paris, 1891), vol. II, p. 572. Clearly, even after Varennes, bourgeois deputies were reluctant to appear overtly anti-noble. The contrast is obvious in the tone of Marat, who did not approve of this ecumenical spirit. *L'Ami du peuple* of 5 February 1791, no. 362, p. 6, for example, took offence at a gambling party which had brought together 'Chapelier, Emmery, Target, Thouret, Tronchet, Desmeuniers, Régnier, Dandré, Riquetti, Voidel, Broglio, Desclaibes, Malouet, Montlosier, Cazalès, Bailly, Mottié.' Marat's bad manners underline the accord of his betters in 1790–1.

[35] Quoted in Zapperi, *Introduction* to Sieyes, *Qu'est-ce que le Tiers-état?*, p. 35.

[36] Sieyes, *Qu'est-ce que le Tiers-état?*, ed. Zapperi, p. 168.

[37] Cited in Castellane, *Gentilshommes démocrates* (Paris, 1960), p. 169.

[38] In his *Observations rapides sur la lettre de M. Calonne au roi* (Paris, 1789), cited in Leroy, *Histoire des indées en France*, p. 121.

[39] *Réimpression de l'Ancien Moniteur* (Paris, 1840), vol. I, 15 June 1789, p. 71.

[40] *Archives parlementaires*, vol. 27 (Paris, 1887), 14 June 1791, p. 210.

[41] Most pungently perhaps by Alfred Cobban in his *Social Interpretation of the French Revolution* (Cambridge, 1965), pp. 36–53.

[42] Quoted in Carré, *La Noblesse*, p. 499.

[43] *L'Ami du peuple*, no. 599, 25 Sept. 1791, p. 6.

[44] *Opinion de M. Necker sur le décret de l'Assemblée nationale concernant les titres, les noms, les armoiries.*

[45] Brissot, *Le Patriote français*, no. 319, 23 June 1790, p. 2 and no. 152, 7 Jan. 1790, p. 3.

[46] *Choix de rapports, opinions et discours prononcés à la Tribune nationale depuis 1789 jusqu'à nos jours* (Paris, 1818), vol. II, pp. 124, 131, 132, *et seq.*

[47] Quoted in Égret, *La Pré-Révolution française*, p. 335.

[48] Quoted in M. Garaud, *La Révolution et l'égalité civile* (Paris, 1953), p. 98.

[49] Mirabeau, *Considération sur l'ordre de Cincinnatus, ou l'imitation d'un pamphlet Anglo-Américan* (London, 1784). See also R. Saunders, *The Origins and Early History of the Society of the Cincinnati* (Ann Arbor, Mich., 1970).

[50] Durand Echeverria, *Mirage in the West* (Princeton, 1957), pp. 165–6.

[51] I am indebted for these details to my cousin, Clifford Lewis, President of the Pennsylvania Cincinnati.

[52] Condorcet, for example, was opposed to the abolition of nobility; showing a keen understanding of the revolutionary principle if not of revolutionary tactics, he supported the abolition of the practical advantages that nobles had possessed, but not of nobility itself. See Henri Carré, *La Noblesse en France et l'opinion publique au XVIIIe siècle* (Paris, 1920), p. 468.

[53] Quoted in Égret, *La Pré-Révolution française*, p. 22.

[54] Quoted in Garaud, *La Révolution et l'égalité civile*, p. 98, n. 2.

[55] The expression is Jefferson's and is cited in Charavay, *Le Général La Fayette*, p. 139.

[56] Henri Jessé, *Opinion de Henri Jessé sur la loi contre l'émigration* (Paris, 1791), pp. 5–6.

[57] Barère, *Opinion sur les mesures de Police à prendre contre les Émigrans* (Paris, 1791), p. 6.

[58] Brissot, *Discours sur les émigrations, etc. . . .* (Paris, 1791), p. 15.

[59] Condorcet, *Œuvres*, ed. M. R. Arago (Paris, 1847), vol. X, pp. 225–42.

[60] Delfau presented a similar plan. Princes of the blood would be prosecuted as would army officers who had taken actively counter-revolutionary steps.

Other émigrés would be required to take an oath of non-aggression against the state. Those who refused to comply would become *ipso facto* enemies of the fatherland and their goods might be confiscated.

[61] *Archives parlementaires*, vol. 23 (Paris, 1886), p. 566, 28 Feb. 1971.

[62] G. Walter, *Robespierre* (Paris, 1961), vol. I, p. 172.

[63] Quoted in G. E. Gwynne, *Madame de Staël et la Révolution, française, politique, philosophie, littérature* (Paris, 1969), p. 23.

[64] Georges Lefebvre took up this theme to explain Robespierre's opposition to anti-émigré legislation in the spring of 1792, and he explains that the *Incorruptible* would have found such presumptions of guilt to be 'juridiquement monstrueux' (see Lefebvre and Bouloiseau, 'L'Émigration et les milieux populaires; émigrations, panique, embauchage, 1791–1794', *Annales historiques de la Révolution française*, vol. 31, no. 156 (Apr.–June 1959), p. 125.

[65] A. Aulard, *Études et leçons sur la Révolution française* (Paris, 1910), sixième série, p. 183.

[66] Statistics from province to province have been assembled by Eberhard Weis in 'Ergebnisse eines Vergleichs der grundherrschaflichen Strukturen Deutschlands und Frankreichs vom 13. bis zum Ausgang des 18. Jahrhunderts', *Vierteljahrschrift für Sozial-und Wirtschaftsgeschichte*, 1970, vol. LVII, no. 1.

[67] See Ernst Hinrichs, '"Feudalität" und Ablösung, Bermerkungen zur Vorgeschichte des 4 August 1789', *Die Franzosiche Revolution*, ed. Eberhard Schmitt (Cologne, 1976), p. 143.

[68] Ibid., p. 144.

[69] Ibid., p. 136.

[70] In the *Cahier de doléances of Saint-Lys*, quoted by George Frêche, *Toulouse et la région Midi-Pyrénées au siècle des lumières vers 1670–1789* (Paris, 1974), p. 512. As regards the weight of feudal dues, it is suggestive that peasant revolts in 1790–2 were concentrated in areas dominated by small peasant owners whose lands were still burdened by seigneurial dues. See A. Ado, *Peasant Movement*, and Soboul, 'A propos d'une thèse récente' in *Annales historiques de la Révolution française*, vol. 45, no. 211 (Jan.–Mar. 1963), p. 90.

[71] *Archives parlementaires*, vol. 8 (Paris, 1875), p. 344. 4 Aug. 1779.

[72] Abel Poitrineau, *La Vie rurale en Basse-Auvergne au XVIIIe siècle 1726–1789* (Paris, 1965), vol. I, p. 620.

[73] P. de Saint-Jacob, *Les Paysans de la Bourgogne du Nord au dernier siècle de l'Ancien Régime* (Dijon, 1960), p. 572.

[74] Paul Bois, *Les Paysans de l'Ouest* (Le Mans, 1960), p. 654.

[75] Roland Marx, *La Révolution et les classes sociales en Basse-Alsace* (Paris, 1974), p. 175.

[76] Robert Forster, *The House of Saulx-Tavannes, Versailles and Burgundy, 1700–1830* (Baltimore, 1971), p. 208.

[77] Walter, *Robespierre*, vol. II, p. 225.

[78] Cited in Robert Lacour-Gayet, *Calonne, financier, réformateur, contre-révolutionnaire 1734–1802* (Paris, 1963), p. 327.

[79] Cited in Claude Brelot, *La Noblesse en Franche-Comté* (Paris, 1972), p. 77.

[80] Henri Sée, 'Les Troubles agraires en Haute Bretagne 1790–1791', *Bulletin d'histoire économique de la Révolution, Années 1920–1921* (Paris, 1924), pp. 231, 373. See also G. Lefebvre, *Paysans du Nord* (Bari, 1959), pp. 376–86. In 1797, Prudhomme, the author of an *Histoire générale et impartiale des erreurs, des fautes et des crimes commis pendant la Révolution française*, vol. VI, p. 522, gave out that 123

châteaux were burnt in 1789–91, and another 62 from 1 October 1791 to 20 September 1792. The precise meaning of such figures is of course moot; statistics often mean what historians want them to. Two hundred châteaux destroyed is an impressive number; but conversely, one might also say that in 1789–92, 99 per cent of French chateaux were *not* burnt.

[81] Cited in Dard, *Le Général Choderlos de Laclos* (Paris, 1936), p. 313.

[82] Olwen Hufton, *Bayeux in the Late Eighteenth Century* (Oxford, 1967), p. 152. See also H. Forneron, *Histoire générale des émigrés pendant la Révolution française*, vol. I (Paris, 1884), pp. 122–4. A. Ado, in his *The Peasant Movement During the French Revolution* (Moscow, 1971), as described by Albert Soboul in his essay 'A propos d'une thèse récente sur le mouvement paysan dans la Révolution française', in *Annales historiques de la Révolution française*, vol. 45, no. 211 (Jan.–Mar. 1973), pp. 85–101, gives instances of at least seven centres of peasant revolts in July–August 1789.

[83] Louis Ducros, *La Société française au dix-huitième siècle* (Paris, 1922), p. 238.

[84] R. B. Rose, *Gracchus Babeuf* (Stanford, 1978), p. 94.

[85] M. de Certeau, *Une politique de la langue* (Paris, 1975), pp. 212, 243.

[86] Brelot, *La Noblesse*, p. 57.

[87] The murder of an ennobled merchant near Le Mans, at Ballon, falls under a different heading, since the victim was killed *qua* merchant rather than as a noble. (See Paul Bois, *Paysans de l'Ouest*, p. 164, n. 1.)

[88] Louis Jacob, *Les Suspects pendant la Révolution 1789–1794* (Paris, 1952), pp. 13–14. See also Reinhard, *Paris*, p. 147.

[89] Beausset was massacred in Marseilles on 10 April 1790. Similar incidents took place at Valence where M. de Voisins was murdered, as was M. de Rully at Bastia. On 15 May 1790, the municipality of Brest ordered the arrest of the military commander there who was released only on order of the National Assembly. See L. Hartmann, *Les Officiers de l'Armée royale et la Révolution* (Paris, 1910), pp. 128–9.

[90] S. Lacroix, *Les Assemblées des représentants de la Commune de Paris* (Paris, 1895), pp. 358–60.

[91] Thus Prudhomme in an issue of the *Révolutions de Paris* for August 1790: 'l'insubordination des militaires est un des plus grands fléaux qui puissent nous affliger. Mais ne sont-ce pas les nobles, les privilégiés qui occupent toutes les places d'officiers? Pense-t-on qu'ils soient attachés à la Révolution? Les soldats sont patriotes, mais ils ne sont pas éclairés. Les officiers sont éclairés, mais ils ne sont pas patriotes. Voilà la source du mal.' Quoted in Hartmann, *Officiers*, p. 160.

[92] Reinhard, *Paris*, p. 183.

[93] Cited in Garaud, *Égalité civile*, p. 97, n. 8.

[94] François Louis Bruel, *Collection de Vinck, Inventaire analytique* (Paris, 1914), nos. 3613, 3634, 3637.

[95] 'L'Ami des soldats'.

[96] Reinhard, *Paris*, after p. 211.

[97] Tourzel, *Mémoires*, p. 226.

[98] Claude Brelot, *La Noblesse franc-comtoise* (Paris, 1972), p. 57.

[99] Quoted in Roger Dupuy, *La Garde nationale et les débuts de la Révolution en Ille-et-Vilaine (1789-mars 1793)* (Rennes, 1972), p. 120.

[100] R. Dupuy, 'A propos de "La Vendée" de Charles Tilly', *Annales historiques de la Révolution française*, vol. 43, no. 206 (Oct.–Dec. 1971), p. 614.

[101] Ferrières, *Correspondance*, 28 Aug. 1790, p. 275.

[102] Georges Lefebvre, *The Coming of the French Revolution* (New York, 1961), p. 45.

[103] Albert Soboul, *Histoire de la Révolution française* (Paris, 1962), vol. I, pp. 187–8.

[104] Claude Mazauric, 'Quelques voies nouvelles pour l'histoire politique de la Révolution française', *Annales historiques de la Révolution française*, vol. 47, no. 219 (Jan.–Mar. 1975).

[105] It is in this context that Mr Mazauric comments negatively on the argument presented in my 'Les Députés de la Noblesse aux États Généraux de 1789', *Revue d'histoire moderne et contemporaine*, Apr.–June 1973. The evidence presented there is not denied, but its meaning is debated.

NOTES TO CHAPTER THREE

[1] Gouverneur Morris, *A Diary of the French Revolution*, C. B. Davenport, ed. (New York, 1939), vol. II, pp. 321–2.

[2] Buchez and Roux, *Histoire parlementaire de la Révolution française* (Paris, 1834), vol. XIII, p. 178.

[3] Tourzel, *Mémoires*, p. 256.

[4] Albert Soboul, 'Le Brûlement des titres féodaux (1789–93)', in *Problèmes paysans de la Révolution (1789–1848)* (Paris, 1976), p. 136.

[5] Quoted in G. Michon, *Robespierre et la guerre révolutionnaire* (Paris, 1937), p. 68, n. 1.

[6] Cited in Marcel Reinhard, *La Révolution, 1789–1794 (Nouvelle histoire de Paris)* (Paris, 1971), p. 172.

[7] Buchez and Roux, *Histoire parlementaire*, vol. XIII, p. 88.

[8] *Archives parlementaires*, vol. 37 (Paris, 1891), pp. 492–3, 18 Jan. 1792.

[9] Buchez and Roux, *Histoire parlementaire* (Paris, 1835), vol. XVI, no. 167, 25 July 1792, p. 168.

[10] Jean Vidalenc, *Les Émigrés français 1789–1825* (Paris, 1963), p. 120.

[11] Reinhard, *Nouvelle Histoire de Paris, La Révolution*, p. 164, n. 4.

[12] Morris, *Dairy*, vol. II, p. 276.

[13] *Archives parlementaires*, vol. 56 (Paris, 1899), p. 688, 9 Jan. 1793.

[14] At the Jacobin Club on 2 January 1792. See Robespierre, *Œuvres* (Paris, 1953), vol. VIII, p. 85.

[15] Buchez and Roux, *Histoire parlementaire*, vol. XIII, p. 178. Pétion used nearly the same words in a letter to Buzot of 6 Feb. 1792.

[16] Bernardine Melchior-Bonnet, *Les Girondins* (Paris, 1969), p. 63.

[17] *Recueil de documents. La Société des Jacobins*, A. Aulard, ed. (Paris, 1892), vol. IV, p. 17.

[18] *Le Moniteur*, vol. 12 (Paris, 1842), p. 110, 12 Apr. 1792.

[19] See, for example, Georges Lefebvre, *La Révolution française* (Paris, 1951), p. 250.

[20] Cited in Leroy, *Histoire des idées sociales*, p. 312.

[21] Buchez and Roux, *Histoire parlementaire*, vol. XVI, p. 181.

[22] *Archives parlementaires*, vol. 50 (Paris, 1896), p. 87, 17 Sept. 1792.

[23] Ibid., p. 93.

[24] Adolphe Schmidt, *Tableaux de la Révolution française, publiés sur les inédits du département de la police secrète de Paris* (Leipzig, 1867), vol. I, i, p. 88.

[25] Ibid., p. 102.

[26] *Le Moniteur*, vol. 14 (Paris, 1850), p. 560, 25 Nov. 1792.

[27] Ibid., p. 153.

[28] *Archives parlementaires*, vol. 52 (Paris, 1897), p. 524, 16 Oct. 1792: and *Le Moniteur*, vol. 14 (Paris, 1840), 23 Oct. 1792, p. 179. The Girondins' deep involvement in the passing of draconian anti-émigré legislation in 1792 presented a problem during the Directory for those who would then have made common cause with them for some conservative end. Thus, in his *Défense des émigrés* published in London in 1797, Lally-Tollendal asked rhetorically if it was by 'erreur ou malice' that the Gironde had presented as conspirators those who had merely fled. On the whole, Lally prefers to let the Girondins off, and he ascribes the passing of the anti-émigré laws of August 1792 to the prevailing 'océan de licence', to a 'débordement de pouvoir, dans cette première exaltation du triomphe le plus immense peut-être que les passions ayent jamais remporté sur la terre' (p. 63). But it would make more sense to see these laws as the consequence of a very conscious and demagogic strategy.

[29] Helen Maria Williams, *Letters from France* (2nd edn., London, 1796), vol. III, p. 204.

[30] Ibid., vol. IV, pp. 49–50. On 20 November 1792, d'Antraigues wrote to one of his correspondents that many émigrés were coming back to France: 'Beaucoup y sont mis en prison. Il faut que le procès ait constaté qu'ils n'ont ni servi ni négocié, ni vu, ni parlé aux Princes, qu'ils prêtent le serment civique . . . ces gens-là deviendront de plus furieux Jacobins qu'il en ait jamais eu. Soyez-en sûr.' (Jacqueline Chaumié, *Le Réseau d'Antraigues et la contre-révolution 1791–1793* (Paris, 1965), p. 408, n. 30.)

[31] Albert Ollivier, *Saint-Just et la force des choses* (Paris, 1954), p. 158.

[32] Lidon's suggestion on 12 March 1793 of burdening 'les citoyens prétendant à la noblesse' with the cost of all litigation over common lands (*Archives parlementaires*, vol. 60 (Paris, 1901), p. 119, 12 Mar. 1793) may have been another such opportunistic manoeuvre.

[33] What the Gironde would have done with regard to nobles had it been able to get its way is hard to say. In its typically opportunistic manner it might have followed a consistent policy of no enemies to the right as it had before followed one of no enemies to the left. One clue lies in the case of a notorious noble counter-revolutionary, Thoury de la Corderie, ordered released by the Girondin administration of the Calvados in late April 1793. (See Jacob, *Suspects*, 38, and also Paul Nicolle, *Histoire de Vire pendant la Révolution* (Vire, 1923), p. 248.)

[34] Norman Hampson, *Danton* (London, 1978), p. 82.

[35] *Archives parlementaires* (Paris, 1896), vol. 47, p. 674.

[36] 22 November 1792, *Archives parlementaires*, vol. 53 (Paris, 1898), p. 548; and 27 Nov. 1792, ibid., p. 620.

[37] Kuscinski, *Dictionnaire des conventionnels*, (Paris, 1917), p. 47.

[38] Cobb, *Armée révolutionnaire*, vol. II, p. 792.

[39] *L'Ami du peuple*, no. 597, p. 8, 12 Nov. 1791.

[40] Ibid., p. 1. Marat's views were widely held on the extreme left. Thus, the *Révolutions de Paris* had also held the passport law of 31 January 1792 to be 'impolitique'. (See Buchez and Roux, vol. XIII, pp. 67–8.)

[41] *L'Ami du peuple*, no. 305, p. 7, 9 Dec. 1790.

[42] Ibid., no. 597, p. 8. The spokesmen of the popular left did not approve of the law on nobles, and neither did some of the people themselves. In his memoirs, Clermont-Gallerande reports that many Parisian workers were afraid that the law would frighten their noble customers and cause a down-turn in the economic life of the capital. Representatives of the six *corps de marchands* twice tried to petition the Assembly about the law but they were denied a hearing. See C. G. de Clermont-Gallerande, *Mémoires* (Paris, 1826), vol. II, p. 6.

[43] Buchez and Roux, vol. XIII, p. 132, 2 Jan. 1792.

[44] Cited in Walter, *Robespierre*, vol. II, p. 247.

[45] *Archives parlementaires*, vol. 52 (Paris, 1897), p. 592.

[46] At the Jacobin Club, Robespierre, *Discours*, vol. IX, p. 275.

[47] Quoted in Mathiez, *La Vie chère et le mouvement social sous la terreur* (Paris, 1927), p. 154.

[48] Ibid., p. 155.

[49] See M. J. Sydenham, *The Girondins* (London, 1961), p. 162, and Mathiez, *La Vie chère*, p. 178: 'L'attitude de la Convention [in April 1793] fit saillir au grand jour l'accord déjà réalisé entre les pétitionnaires et les Montagnards.'

[50] Robespierre, *Œuvres*, vol. 9, *Discours* (Paris, 1958), p. 492.

[51] Ibid., p. 285.

[52] *Archives parlementaires*, vol. 59 (Paris, 1901), p. 628, 5 Mar. 1793.

[53] Ibid., p. 629.

[54] Walter, *Robespierre*, vol. I, p. 85.

[55] Robespierre, *Œuvres*, vol. IX, *Discours* (Paris, 1958), p. 343, 27 Mar. 1793.

[56] Ibid, pp. 487, 489, 8 May 1793.

[57] Aulard, *La Société des Jacobins* (Paris, 1895), vol. V, p. 255, 14 June 1793.

[58] Robespierre, *Œuvres*, vol. X, *Discours*, p. 80, 25 Aug. 1793.

[59] A. Ado in 'Le Mouvement paysan et le problème de l'égalité (1789–1794)' in Soboul, *Contributions à l'histoire paysanne de la Révolution française* (Paris, 1977), pp. 119–38, gives as the dates of successive peasant 'guerre aux châteaux' movements: a first set of four waves from July–August 1789 to June–August 1791; a second and very violent convulsion from February to April 1792; and a last tremor in July–October 1792.

[60] Édouard Chapuisat, *Necker 1732–1804* (Paris, 1938), p. 210.

[61] Mme de Tourzel, *Mémoires*, p. 151. Samuel F. Scott in his essay 'Problems of Law and Order during 1790, the "Peaceful" Year of the French Revolution', *American Historical Review*, vol. LXXX, no. 4, Oct. 1975, p. 878, writes of the burning or sacking of over thirty houses and châteaux between 17 December 1789 and 18 January 1790.

[62] R. B. Rose, *The Enragés* (Melbourne, 1968), p. 36.

[63] For a description of some anti-noble acts at this and other junctures, see Henri Mazel, 'La Révolution dans le Midi; l'Incendie des châteaux du Bas Languedoc', *Revue de la Révolution*, VIII (1886), pp. 142–57, 307–19, 380–91.

[64] Marcel Reinhard, *La Chute de la royauté* (Paris, 1969), p. 87.

[65] Ibid., p. 101.

[66] Abbé Charles Jollivet, *La Révolution dans l'Ardèche (1788–1795)* (Largentière, 1930), p. 342; quoted in A. Soboul 'Le Brûlement des titres féodaux', in *Problèmes paysans de la Révolution (1789–1848)* (Paris, 1976), p. 139.

[67] Soboul, 'Le Brûlement', p. 142.

[68] Pierre Caron, *La Première Terreur, Les Missions du conseil exécutif provisoire et de la Commune de Paris* (Paris, 1950), p. 63.

[69] For an account of this encounter, see Louise Fusil, *Souvenirs d'une actrice* (Paris, 1841), vol. I, p. 277, and Garat, *Mémoires sur la Révolution* (Paris, 1862), p. 349.

[70] *Archives parlementaires*, vol. 52 (Paris, 1897), p. 524.

[71] *Archives parlementaires*, vol. 53 (Paris, 1898), p. 593, 26 Nov. 1792.

[72] *Archives parlementaires*, vol. 52 (Paris, 1897), p. 444, 10 Oct. 1792. Also, vol. 55 (Paris, 1899), p. 147, 18 Dec. 1792.

[73] *Les Comités des droits féodaux et de législation et l'abolition du régime seigneurial (1789–1793)*, Ph. Sagnac and P. Caron, eds. (Paris, 1907), pp. 777–8. See also, Richard Cobb, *Reactions to the French Revolution* (London, 1972), p. 265.

[74] For the rioting in 1789, see George Rudé, *Paris and London in the Eighteenth Century* (New York, 1970). For Grouchy, Archives nationales, W 412 946.

[75] Quoted in Charles Jollivet, *La Révolution dans l'Ardèche*, pp. 348–9.

[76] James N. Hood, 'Patterns of Popular Protest during the French Revolution', *Journal of Modern History*, vol. XLVIII, no. 2 (June 1976), p. 280.

[77] Quoted in P. de Vaissière, *Lettres d'aristocrates* (Paris, 1907), p. 204.

[78] Also at Tarbes. See Marc Bouloiseau, *Études de l'émigration et de la vente des biens des émigrés, 1792–1830* (Paris, 1953), pp. 78–9.

[79] Claude Brelot, *Besançon révolutionnaire* (Paris, 1966), p. 84. See also Henri Carré, *La Noblesse en France et l'opinion publique au XVIIIe siècle* (Paris, 1920), pp. 384–5, and Edith Bernadin, *Jean-Marie Roland et le ministère de l'intérieur 1792–1793* (Paris, 1964), p. 600.

[80] Jacob, *Suspects*, p. 27.

[81] John Sirich, *The Revolutionary Committees* (Cambridge, 1943), p. 46.

[82] Henri Carré, *La Noblesse en France et l'opinion publique au XVIIIe siècle* (Paris, 1920), pp. 494–5.

[83] 'Ainsi Paris bouscule les hiérarchies, méconnaît ce qui donne ailleurs la notabilité, rapproche les individus, tout en exagérant les écarts entre les conditions.' André-Jean Tudesq, *Les Grands Notables en France* (Paris, 1964), p. 349.

[84] In March 1794, Duquesnoy, a Montagnard Conventionnel, suggested that there were still 8,000 to 10,000 nobles in Paris (*Moniteur*, XIX, p. 670, 22 ventôse an II—12 Mar. 1794). This seems very high; earlier on, in 1789–91 it would have made sense for nobles to leave the countryside and come to Paris, which was safer for them, but the reverse was true in 1793–4.

[85] Jaurès, *Histoire socialiste de la Révolution française*, vol. I, pp. 149–50; quoted in George Rudé, *The Crowd in the French Revolution* (Oxford, 1967), p. 14. A conseiller of the Parlement of Paris likewise declared that 'There is no noble, whatever his rank, who is not accustomed to hear himself called Bourgeois of Paris, and there is none who could be offended to find himself sitting beside a member of the tiers état judged worthy of its confidence.' C. T. Chassin, *Les Élections et les cahiers de Paris en 1789* (Paris, 1888–9), vol. I, p. 360; vol. IV, p. 163; quoted in Cobban, *The Social Interpretation of the French Revolution*, pp. 31–2.

[86] *Le Moniteur*, vol. 16 (Paris, 1840), p. 550, 5 June 1793.

[87] Alexandre Tuetey, *Répertoire général des sources manuscrites de l'histoire de Paris pendant la Révolution française* (Paris, 1910), vol. IX, p. 222.

[88] Ibid., p. 651. Many Cordeliers were given posts in the administration of the War Ministry, and forwarded popular demands for a purge of the army to Bouchotte, who was not displeased to hear them. One such *commissaire aux armées*, Celliez, insisted on 16 May 1793 that the purge of the general staffs was

absolutely essential. Ci-devants were to be replaced by sans-culottes; the '*luxe asiatique*' of the general staffs would come to an end. Noble officers, he claimed, were thoroughly disliked: 'Les officiers généraux sont généralement mal vus, en ce qu'ils sont pour la plupart ou *ci-devant* ou connus pour leur incivisme. Ce qui augmente encore le mécontentement du peuple, c'est le grand nombre de femmes qui sont à l'armée, sous l'habit d'homme, et qui les accompagnent partout, soit comme militaires, soit comme suite.' (C. Rousset, *Les Volontaires 1791–1794* (Paris, 1870), pp. 199–200.)

[89] Adolphe Schmidt, *Tableaux de la Révolution française*, vol. II (Leipzig, 1867), p. 53.

[90] *Le Moniteur*, vol. 17 (Paris, 1840), p. 8.

[91] *La Société des Jacobins*, ed. F. A. Aulard (Paris, 1895), vol. V, p. 358.

[92] *Le Moniteur*, vol. 17 (Paris, 1840), p. 441.

[93] *Le Moniteur*, vol. 17 (Paris, 1840), p. 503, 26 Aug. 1793.

[94] On 10 October, Chaumette convinced the Paris Commune that it ought to refuse *certificats de civisme* not just to nobles but to those who had frequented known enemies of the Revolution, like nobles. Similar demands for the exclusion of nobles from military and civil office were made by provincial Jacobins in Dijon (*Archives parlementaires*, vol. 62, p. 106), Clermont-Ferrand (vol. 63, p. 501), Lille (vol. 70, p. 222), Chartres (vol. 72, p. 231), Toulouse (vol. 72, p. 543), Mayenne (vol. 73, p. 200), Le Puy (vol. 73, p. 238), Gray (vol. 74, p. 352), Strasbourg (vol. 72, p. 48 and vol. 74, p. 395), Chaumont (vol. 80, p. 67), as well as by a number of military units.

[95] *Le Moniteur*, vol. 17 (Paris, 1840), p. 586.

[96] *La Société des Jacobins*, ed. F. A. Aulard, (Paris, 1895), vol. V, p. 309, 21 July 1793.

[97] Prudhomme, *Histoire de Grenoble* (Grenoble, 1888), p. 216.

[98] P. Montarlot, *Les Députés de Saône-et-Loire aux assemblées de la Révolution 1789–1799*, vol. III (autun, n.d.), pp. 275–8. Names, as is well known, are rich with content, and it is worth pointing out that the return of communal names to the *status quo ante* was operated in phases. Few communes changed their names after 9 thermidor, and many of them went back to their old name after 18 brumaire. All references to explicitly Revolutionary themes was forbidden: thus, Montagne-Bon-Air reverted to Saint-Germain-en-Laye, and Marat-sur-Oise to Fontainebleau. But it was not until 1814, that Brie-sur-Hières once again became Brie-Comte-Robert. Bonaparte's regime was a denial of Revolutionary excesses, but its acceptance of nobles was conditional on their good behaviour. See A. Aulard, 'Les Noms révolutionnaires des communes', *Le Revue de Paris*, vol. 23, no. 19, 1 Oct. 1926.

[99] Richard Cobb, *Les Armées révolutionnaires*, vol. II (Paris, 1961–3), p. 593.

[100] Albert Mathiez, *The French Revolution* (New York, 1962), p. 396.

[101] Quoted in Jean Signorel, *Études historiques sur la législation révolutionnaire relative aux biens des émigrés* (Paris, 1915), p. 76.

[102] *Le Moniteur*, vol. 14 (Paris, 1850), p. 90.

[103] *Archives parlementaires*, vol. 90 (Paris, 1972), p. 103, 17 floréal an II—6 May 1794. Animosity against British prisoners soon dropped off and the decree concerning them was repealed, but the execution of captured émigrés continued as a matter of course. In a message to Conventionnels in the field, Carnot explained on 16 June 1794 how the prisoners of different nationalities were to be handled. Only émigrés, he insisted, should be shot: 'Le décret qui porte qu'on

ne fera point de prisonniers anglais ni hanovriens ne regarde pas les Hessois; il faut donc garder ceux-ci et renvoyer les autres par échange pour un nombre égal de nos soldats ou matelots; quant aux émigrés, il ne peut y avoir de grâce pour eux d'aucune manière.' (Carnot, *Correspondance*, vol. IV, p. 426.)

The fall of Robespierre did not affect this particular problem. To be sure, on 20 thermidor an II (7 Aug. 1794), Carnot had already begun to backtrack on the Convention's announced policy of no quarter for foreign prisoners of war: 'Il faut que la prudence nous mêne au but du décret sans que la fierté républicaine fléchisse en rien, mai aussi sans nous mériter le titre de barbare et sans répandre inutilement le sang des Français.' (*Correspondance générale de Carnot* (Paris, 1907), vol. IV, p. 573.) But Revolutionary policy about émigrés remained as it had been: 'Il n'est point question des émigrés; on ne peut leur faire grâce.' (Carnot, *Correspondance*, 25 Aug. 1794, vol. IV, p. 619.) So did Pichegru announce a few months later that his troops had cut some 300 émigrés to pieces; 69 of them had been captured, and were being taken to General Headquarters; 'ils ne tarderont pas à subir le sort qui leur est réservé. *Vive la République! Vive la Convention!*' (*Le Moniteur*, vol. 22 (Paris, 1847), p. 366.)

[104] *Le Moniteur*, vol. 16 (Paris, 1854), p. 34, 4 Apr. 1793.

[105] In June 1793, Marat also took up the cudgels on behalf of Ronsin and Rossignol, two notorious sans-culotte incompetents, who had quarrelled with Biron in the Vendée. The fall from favour and executions of Biron, Custine, and Beauharnais were significant landmarks in the campaign of the sans-culottes against nobles generally.

[106] Quoted in G. G. Hourteville, *Davout le terrible* (Paris, 1975), pp. 46–7. The tone of the letter is very different from that which prevailed in March 1794, when the exclusion of nobles was presented as a fundamental goal of the Revolution, in and of itself.

[107] In September 1793, Hentz had already urged this in a letter to the Committee of Public Safety. (Henri Wallon, *Les Représentants en mission* (Paris, 1880), vol. IV, p. 155.)

[108] *Le Moniteur*, vol. 19 (Paris, 1841), p. 533, 23 Feb. 1794 (5 ventôse an II). Danton's views on nobles deserve particular mention, since they are an ideal expression of uncluttered bourgeois opportunism. Danton, or d'Anton as he styled himself until 1790, was not at first hostile to nobles, and in a lawyer's brief of November 1787 he described nobility as a possession, as a 'bien'. In March 1790, he was still defending in the courts the right of a noble family to exercise its noble prerogatives. But on 21 June 1791, he did not hesitate to speak of the 'horreur que la noblesse inspire à toute la France', and he was not above comparing his stature as an athlete of liberty, with the nobility's physical inability to reproduce itself.

Danton's anti-nobilism, however, had clear limits. When on 31 July 1793, a letter from the Calais Jacobins was read in the mother house at Paris, with an eye to the expulsion of nobles from all public office, including the army, Hébert approved and Danton disapproved. Nobles, he said, were of course the enemies of the Revolution, but good nobles should not be dismissed, and Danton's idea was therefore to propose the adoption of good nobles by Revolutionary citizens. Who, he asked, would not be proud to have adopted Le Peletier as his brother?

Danton's hostility to nobles was never categorical. On 7 December 1793, he did ask for a closer examination of the loyalty of the relatives of émigrés, just as the Dantoniste Baudot had asked in the previous month that nobles be forced to disgorge the wealth that they had appropriated from the crown over the centuries. But on 21 December 1793, Danton also defended the memory of Dampierre: 'Il est notoire dans la ci-devant Champagne [where Danton came from] que Dampierre, quoiqu'il eut [eu] le malheur de naître au sein de la caste noble, fraternisait avec les cultivateurs et les paysans de ces cantons. . . . Enfin, il est mort pour la République; il est tombé en combattant pour elle: la mort a scellé sa réputation.' Then, on 23 February, came the exchange on noble officers.

Danton's initial shift on nobles from admiration to mild persecution was in the order of things, as was also his eventual inability to abominate nobles as a group: of all the leaders of the Revolution, Danton was the least ideological, the least influenced by the philosophes, whose work he knew quite well. His demagogic opportunism dictated that he should abandon nobles to their fate in 1792, and that he should refuse to exclude them from public service in late 1793–4. The evolution of his position, together with its limits, highlights by contrast the ideological motivations of his erstwhile Montagnard allies. See André Fribourg, *Discours de Danton* (Paris, 1910), pp. 10, 49, 326–7, 512, 623, and 676–7.

[109] Schmidt, *Tableaux politiques* (Leipzig, 1867), vol. II, p. 127.

[110] Helen Maria Williams, *Letters*, vol. II, p. 8.

[111] AN, W, 412, 947. Davout expressed similar feelings with less pungency in 1794: '[J'ai] abjuré ces sottises à l'âge de dix-neuf ans, dès le commencement de la Révolution sans aucun décret.' (Cited in Hartmann, *Les Officiers de l'armée royale*, p. 522, n. 1.) Once arrested, many nobles were able to defend themselves by showing that they had renounced their nobility long before it had become prudent to do so. When Talhouet, a former Parlementaire and a Revolutionary mayor of Rennes, was asked to justify his request for a *certificat de civisme*, he explained that he had long since abjured his former status:

> . . . dès les premiers instants de la Révolution sa conduite et ses actions avaient prouvé qu'il regardait comme absurdes toutes distinctions entre les hommes autres que celles que la nature avait établies, qu'il ne pouvait entendre parler de la plus barbare de toutes, celle qui attribuait une prétendue noblesse à quelques-uns d'entre eux, sans renouveler formellement le renoncement exprès qu'il fit lors de l'incendie des minutes des arrêts de noblesse déposés au greffe du ci-devant Parlement, à tous les rapports qu'il avait pu avoir eus avec une caste de laquelle il s'était séparé de fait aussitôt que l'empire de la raison et de la philosophie avait pris la place de celui des abus amoncelés qui formaient le gouvernement français avant sa régénération.

Due note was taken of this statement, but Talhouet was shortly thereafter arrested on the orders of Dubois-Crancé. He was released on 7 thermidor. (Pocquet du Haut Jusset, *Terreur et terroristes à Rennes* (Mayenne, 1974), p. 258.)

[112] Quoted in Vaissière, p. 439.

[113] Barère, *Mémoires*, vol. II, pp. 176–7.

[114] F. A. Aulard, *Recueil des actes du Comité de Salut Public* (Paris, 1900), vol. XIII, pp. 48–9. Florian, or rather the citoyen Florian, asked to be requisitioned so that he might first finish his play *Don Quichotte*, which he described as a 'satire la plus fine et la plus forte de l'esprit chevalresque'; and second write a history of Rome whose argument would supplant that of Rollin '[dont les principes] ne pouvaient convenir à l'éducation nationale'. (See G. Maréschal de Bièvre, *Les Ci-devants nobles et la Révolution* (Paris, 1914), p. 61.

[115] AN, F7 4781 (Belleville). The process of requisition was for some nobles at least problematic. To ask for such a requisition was to attract the attention of the authorities. This was the case of the writer Florian, who was doing all he could to please the new masters of the Republic, one of whom, Robespierre, he had described as a new Orpheus. Confident of securing a favourable hearing, Florian applied for an order of requisition that would allow him to leave Sceaux for Paris. His petition attracted the attention of Saint-Just, who at once ordered him to be arrested. Indeed, Florian was already under a cloud for having taken part in the deliberations of the *société populaire* at Sceaux, but he might still have stayed out of harm's way if he had been less ambitious. (See Maréschal de Bièvre, *Les Ci-devants nobles et la Révolution* (Paris, 1914), pp. 78–80.)

[116] In the Convention the Montagnard Duquesnoy likewise complained that 'les ci-devant nobles, expulsés d'une armée, rentrent aussitôt dans une autre. Il affirme qu'il existe encore dans Paris huit à dix mille de ces individus, de cette caste désastreuse; et sur sa proposition la Société arrête qu'une députation se rendra à la Convention pour lui demander l'arrestation de tous les ex-nobles, tant aux armées que dans l'intérieur'. (Séance du 18 ventôse an II (9 Mar. 1794) at the Jacobin Club, *Le Moniteur*, vol. XIX, p. 670.)

[117] William Scott, *Terror and Repression in Revolutionary Marseilles* (London, 1973), p. 328.

[118] Montgaillard, *Histoire de France* (Paris, 1814), vol. IV, p. 88; cited in Ollivier, *Saint-Just*, p. 443. See also Brelot, *La Noblesse*, p. 101.

[119] André Bernady, *Euzet, mon pays* (Uzès, 1958), pp. 145–6, and Baron de Méricourt, *Mme de Souza et sa famille* (Paris, 1907), pp. 214–15.

[120] Quoted in J. Godechot, *La Vie quotidienne en France sous le Directoire* (Paris, 1977), p. 102.

[121] William Scott, *Terror and Repression*, p. 211. Allan Forest, in his *Society and Politics in Revolutionary Bordeaux*, p. 59, also makes reference to such disavowals. Many noble officers did the same when threatened with expulsion from the army in 1793–4; Bonaparte described himself as non-noble. So did Choin de Montchoisy, who wrote to Bouchotte that since nobles might well be traitors 'un franc et loyal républicain ne doit rien négliger pour empêcher qu'on ne le confonde avec cette classe infâme'. (Cited in Hartmann, *Les Officiers de l'armée royale*, p. 522, n. 1.) One ennobled Swiss, Hennin, who had been asked to leave Paris, complied, but grudgingly, and complained to the minister of Geneva in France: 'Treize ans de noblesse ne vaillent pas la peine d'en parler. . . .' (MS Reybaz, Bibliothèque municipale de Genève, 927, fol. 323.)

[122] Raoul Rosières, *La Révolution dans une petite ville* (Paris, 1888), p. 158.

[123] Jean-Baptiste Radet, *Le Noble Roturier* (Paris, an II), p. 17. In a debate at the Convention of 17 November 1792, Ossellin alluded to the penchant of nobles to present themselves as anything but noble: 'On vous propose des exceptions de toutes espèces, [to the laws on emigration] et particulièrement pour les négociants. Si vous admettiez ces exceptions, elles serviraient de prétexte à bien des hommes coupables, car on se donne aujourd'hui des airs de marchant, comme autrefois on se donnait des airs de marquis. (Rires et applaudissements.)' *Archives parlementaires*, vol. 53 (Paris, 1896), 17 Nov. 1792, p. 457.

[124] AN, F7 4784, Villejuif.

[125] Adolphe Schmidt, *Tableaux politiques*, vol. II, p. 114.

[126] M. Bouloiseau and G. Lefebvre, 'L'Émigration et les milieux populaires: émigrations, paniques, embauchage, 1791–1794', *Annales historiques de la*

Révolution française, vol. 31, no. 156 (Apr.–June 1959), p. 21, n. 64. See also Chanoine E. Tisserand, *Histoire de la Révolution française dans les Alpes Maritimes* (Nice, 1878), pp. 118–19.

[127] AN, F7 4828.

[129] In the first days of the Vendée war, the armies of the Republic were led by the duc de Biron, the marquis de Grouchy, the baron de Menou, and at Nantes by M. de la Barollière; prominent among the leaders of the rebels were Stofflet, a gamekeeper, and Cathelineau, a carter.

[130] Brelot, *La Noblesse*, p. 103.

[131] Olwen Hufton, *Bayeux* (Oxford, 1967), p. 254.

[132] See, for example, the reports of Grigau to Merlin quoted in Harvey Mitchell's 'Resistance to Revolution in Western France', *Past and Present*, no. 63 (May 1974), p. 107. Fornier, a former deputy of the Third Estate, had a similar view of what peasants really thought in 1796; he was convinced that the chouans had no use for nobles: 'Ils veulent les livrer à la République ainsi que leurs armes, *si l'on veut leur accorder la liberté de leur religion.* Mais on leur donne une si bonne chasse qu'ils n'ont pas le temps de penser et de réfléchir.' (*Documents pour servir à l'histoire de la Révolution française*, Ch. D'Héricault and Gustave Bord, eds. (Paris, 1884), Document XXI.)

[133] Mitchell, 'Resistance to Revolution', pp. 116–17.

[134] Ibid., pp. 118–19.

[135] Michelet, *Histoire de la Révolution française*, Pléiade edition (Paris, 1962), vol. II, p. 916.

[136] Buchez and Roux, *Histoire parlementaire de la Révolution française* (Paris, 1835), vol. XX, p. 167.

[137] L. Jacob, *Les Suspects pendant la Révolution* (Paris, 1952), p. 52.

[138] Antoine de Castellane, *Gentilshommes démocrates* (Paris, 1944), p. 213.

[139] See G. Sangnier, *Les Émigrés du Pas de Calais pendant la Révolution* (Blangermont, 1959), p. 67.

[140] Louis Jacob, *Les Suspects*, pp. 59–61. When Dubois-Crancé ordered the release of some nobles imprisoned by Amar, who had preceded him in Grenoble, the local authorities refused to comply, convinced that his show of sympathy for the ci-devants was a trap laid out for them. (Dubois-Crancé, *Analyse de la Révolution française* (Paris, 1885), p. 129. See also John B. Sirich, *The Revolutionary Committees* (Cambridge, 1943), p. 185.)

[141] *Archives parlementaires*, vol. 90 (Paris, 1972), p. 484, 20 May 1794 (1 prairial an II).

[142] See, for example, Alan Forrest, *Society and Politics in Revolutionary Bordeaux* (Oxford, 1975): 'The crime for which [Monsec-Reillac *père* and *fils*] were guillotined was no more grave than that of being born of aristocratic lineage . . . (p. 240).

[143] Sometimes in a roundabout way. Rather disingenuously, for example, Marat's biographer, Jean Massin, exculpates his hero from responsibility in Lavoisier's execution as a former *fermier général*, on the grounds that Lavoisier's execution took place after Marat's death, which is obviously true. But it is also true that the *fermiers généraux* were the special prey of Maribon-Montaut, himself a noble, and one of Marat's closest disciples.

[144] Only six intendants were brought to trial before the Revolutionary Tribunal. See G. Frêche, 'Les Procès de six intendants', *Questions administratives dans la France du XVIIe siècle*, Francis Dumont, ed. (Paris, 1965), p. 208. By

contrast, the *noblesse parlementaire* was much harder hit. Though it numbered about 1 per cent of the nobility as a whole, the *parlementaires* accounted for over 7 per cent of noble casualties. (See D. Greer, *The Incidence of the Terror* (Cambridge, 1935), p. 163.) Their incidence of emigration was much greater also.

[145] AN, F7 4784.

[146] Greer, *Incidence of Emigration*, p. 96.

[147] Abraham Cahen, 'L'Émancipation des Juifs devant la société royale des sciences et des arts de Metz en 1787 et M. Roederer', *Revue des études juives*, vol. I (Paris, 1880), p. 87; report of Bonnefoy for 11 germinal an II, quoted by Ollivier, *Saint-Just*, p. 334; and, G. Lefebvre, *Études sur la Révolution française* (Paris, 1963), pp. 121–2, n. 1.

[148] Estimates of the number of officers in the royal army vary a good deal. Hartmann, in his *Les Officiers de l'armée royale*, gives 6,000 to 7,000; Sydenham, in his *The French Revolution* (New York, 1965), p. 90, 9,000; Albert Soboul, in his *Histoire de la Révolution* (Paris, 1962), vol. I, p. 284, 12,000, half of whom at least had emigrated.

[149] In January 1794, over 100 of them were left in the cavalry alone. For the artillery, and the army as a whole, the precise number, which includes 62 noble generals, is not known. See Hartmann, *Les Officiers de l'armée royale*, pp. 365, 522, 525, 529.

[150] A Blanchard, 'Les Ci-devant ingénieurs du roi', *Revue internationale d'histoire militaire*, vol. 30, 1970, *passim*.

[151] See Mathiez, 'L'Affaire Legray', in *Girondins et Montagnards* (Paris, 1930), p. 190.

[152] *Le Moniteur*, vol. 18 (Paris, 1841), p. 688, 26 brumaire an II—16 Nov. 1793.

[153] *Archives parlementaires*, vol. 88 (Paris, 1969), 26 germinal an II—15 Apr. 1794, p. 621.

[154] *Correspondance inédite du marquis de Sade* (Paris, 1929), p. 301.

[155] Ibid., p. 303.

[156] Ibid., p. 315.

[157] Antonelle, *Déclarations motivées* (Paris, n.d.), pp. 58–66, 68.

[158] Aulard, *Société des Jacobins*, vol. V, p. 640.

[159] H. Doniol, *Correspondance de Soubrany* (Clermont-Ferrand, 1867), p. 29.

[160] Garrone, *Romme*, p. 367.

[161] Hartmann, *Les Officiers de l'armée royale*, pp. 525–6, n. 1. The letter of resignation of the noble-born commander of the garrison of Cherbourg was similar in tone: the people did not want to have noble generals and the people could not be wrong: 'Je crois, citoyen président, que ceux qui sont vraiment républicains doivent quitter leurs places et ne doivent pas rester à un poste où ils sont sans confiance. La voix du peuple ne saurait être injuste.' *Archives parlementaires*, 13 Aug. 1793, vol. 72 (Paris, 1907), p. 113.

[162] Lefebvre, *Paysans du Nord*, p. 587.

NOTES TO CHAPTER FOUR

[1] Bibliothèque publique et universitaire de Genève, MS Fr. (Reybaz), 927, fol. 284.

[2] E. Dard, *Hérault de Séchelles* (Paris, 1907), pp. 307–8.

[3] Ollivier, *Saint-Just*, p. 389.

[4] *Archives parlementaires*, vol. 90 (Paris, 1972), p. 244 (item 44), 11 May 1794 (22 floréal an II).

[5] Ibid., p. 577, 23 May 1794 (4 prairial an II).

[6] Saint-Just, *Œuvres complètes*, Ch. Vellay, ed., vol. II (Paris, 1908), p. 372, on 26 germinal an II—15 Apr. 1794.

[7] A. Aulard, 'Les Noms révolutionnaires des communes', *La Revue de Paris*, vol. 23, no. 19, 1 October 1926.

[8] Robespierre, *Œuvres*, vol. 10, *Discours* (Paris, 1967), p. 259, 26 frimaire an II—16 Dec. 1794.

[9] G. Maréschal de Bièvre, *Les Ci-devant nobles et la Révolution* (Paris, 1914), pp. 150–1.

[10] *Archives parlementaires*, vol. 90 (Paris, 1972, p. 322, 14 May 1794 (25 floréal an II).

[11] Special legislation was passed to deal with such subterfuge, notably on 9 September 1792.

[12] *Le Moniteur*, vol. 20 (Paris, 1851), p. 225, 16 Apr. 1794 (27 germinal an II).

[13] D. Greer, *The Incidence of the Terror* (Cambridge, 1935), p. 96.

[14] *Le Moniteur*, vol. 19 (Paris, 1847), p. 559.

[15] Vergniaud, *Œuvres* (Paris, n.d.), p. 216; Mïchelet, *Histoire de la Révolution française*, vol. II (Paris, 1952), p. 668.

[16] Brissot, *Opinion*, p. 6.

[17] *Les Crimes de la noblesse ou le régime féodal* was in theory written by the 'Citoyenne Villeneuve', the pseudonym of an actress-impressario, Sophie Gautherot. It appears that some of her plays were in fact written either by Nicolas-Leonard Bogée, her husband, or by another playwright, Cizos-Duplessis, known before 1789 as Cizos de Duplessis.

[18] In a letter dated 22 July 1793, *Archives parlementaires*, vol. 69 (Paris, 1906), p. 485.

[19] Robespierre, *Œuvres*, vol. X, *Discours* (Paris, 1967), p. 259, 26 frimaire an II—16 Dec. 1794.

[20] *Le Moniteur*, vol. 20 (Paris, 1854), p. 243, 17 Apr. 1794 (28 germinal an II).

[21] Ibid., vol. 27 (Paris, 1854), p. 113, 10 June 1793.

[22] Ibid., vol. 19 (Paris, 1841), p. 359, in a letter dated 22 Feb. 1794 (4 ventôse an II).

[23] *The Correspondence of Edmund Burke*, vol. VI, A. Cobban and R. Smith, eds.; quoted in A. Cobban, *The Social Interpretation of the French Revolution*, p. 82.

[24] H. M. Williams, *Letters Written in France in the Summer of 1790* (London, 1796), 5th edn., vol. I, p. 74.

[25] Buonarroti, *La Conspiration pour l'égalité* (Paris, 1957).

[26] Quoted in Garaud, *La Révolution et l'égalité civile*, p. 46.

[27] E. G. Lenglet, *De la propriété et de ses rapports avec les droits et avec la dette du citoyen* (Paris, an VI), p. 111. In a similar vein, Basire on 17 September 1793 denounced the selfishness of the *aristocratie sectionnaire*. See *Le Moniteur*, vol. 17 (Paris, 1854), p. 683.

[28] F. Scott, *Terror and Repression*, p. 100.

[29] AN, AD III, 377, petition by Tharin.

[30] *Le Moniteur*, vol. 20 (Paris, 1854), p. 243.

[31] Of the 165 '*négociants*' listed in the capitation of 1777 at Rouen, 55 were noble or *annobli*. See Guy Richard, *La Noblesse d'affaires au XVIII*[e] *siècle*, vol. I

(Paris, 1974), p. 95. Not all revolutionaries, however, were as amiable as Barère, *l'Anacréon de la Révolution*. On 19 pluviôse an II, François-Abraham de Reclesne, a noble landlord in the Bourbonnais region, foolishly asked for a lower tax estimate. More foolishly yet, he also told the Comité de Surveillance at Gannat that, yes he was a noble, and that no Republic could decide that he was not. He was arrested and sent to Paris. His family tried to convince Fouquier-Tinville of his madness. Since the death of his wife and of two of his sons, they explained, Reclesne, who had always been feeble-minded, would from time to time completely lose his senses. A list of potential witnesses was produced, including a baker, a butcher, and a farmer. All to no avail. See J. Cornillon, *Le Bourbonnais sous la Révolution française* (Riom, 1891), pp. 213–14.

[32] AN, D III, 373.

[33] Banishment from Paris was very inconvenient. Thus, one Hennin, a friend of Necker's and in the 1770s a correspondent of the duc d'Aiguillon, had business in the capital and asked the Genevan minister in Paris to petition on his behalf for an exemption. After all, he had only been a noble for a short time: 'Treize ans, de noblesse ne vaillent pas la peine d'en parler. . . .' Besides, he had never made trouble: 'il n'est pas inutile que vous sachiez que j'ai eu un certificat de civisme de ma section'. Bibliothèque publique et universitaire de Genève, MS Fr. (Reybaz), 927, fol. 323.

[34] AN, D III, pp. 373–7.

[35] See *Procès verbaux de la Commission temporaire des arts*, Louis Tuetey, ed. (Paris, 1912), vol. I, p. 144, n. 4.

[36] Barère, *Mémoires*, H. Carnot, ed., (Paris, 1842), vol. II, p. 159.

[37] Lucy Davidowicz, *The War Against the Jews, 1933–1945* (New York, 1976), pp. 70–9, 84, 89–90.

[38] Saint-Just, *Œuvres* (Paris, 1946), p. 189.

[39] *Le Moniteur*, vol. 20, p. 234, 16 Apr. 1794 (27 germinal an II).

[40] Louis Jacob, *Joseph Le Bon 1765–1795*, vol. II (Paris, 1932), p. 144.

[41] *Le Moniteur*, vol. 21 (Paris, 1841), p. 705, 29 Aug. 1794, (12 fructidor an II). In a speech to the Jacobin Club.

[42] Aulard, *Recueil des actes du Comité de Salut Public*, vol. XIII, p. 225.

[43] *Le Moniteur*, vol. 18 (Paris, 1841), p. 693, 17 Dec. 1793 (27 frimaire an II).

[44] *Société des Jacobins, Recueil de documents*, A. Aulard, ed. vol. V (Paris, 1895), p. 500.

[45] On 29 July, in the wake of Custine's arrest, the Convention had indeed decreed the arrest of all suspects in the army; and in September 1793, all nobles who had not given proof of their attachment to the Republic were also declared suspects. If Destournelles's officials could be 'militarized' by virtue of their connection with army finance, and if all nobles were declared suspect, then Destournelles's conclusion was legal. But it clearly ran against the spirit of the law. (*Les Actes du gouvernement révolutionnaire*, A. Cochin and Ch. Charpentier, eds., vol. I (Paris, 1920), p. 82, 23 août 1793–27 juillet 1794.)

[46] *Le Moniteur*, vol. 21 (Paris, 1841), p. 705, 29 Aug. 1794.

[47] Ibid., p. 799.

[48] *Recueil des actes du Comité de Salut Public*, A. Aulard, ed. vol. III (Paris, 1890), p. 149, 7 Apr. 1793.

[49] Ibid., vol. XIII, p. 158.

[50] Quoted in Adolphe Schmidt, *Tableaux de la Révolution française*, vol. II, pp. 151–2.

[51] *Correspondance générale de Carnot*, E. Charavay, ed., vol. IV (Paris, 1907), pp. 364–5.

[52] *Recueil des actes du Comité de Salut Public*, F. A. Aulard, ed. (Paris, 1897), p. 85. In a marginal note Bouchotte, the Minister of War, added that 'pour entrer dans l'esprit du Comité, il ne faut rappeler ou maintenir que ceux qui sont incontestablement reconnus comme bons patriotes'. Some of them at least must have passed the test since even Saint-Just saw fit to reinstate some of the noble officers whom the uncompromising Conventionnel Duquesnoy had dismissed from the Armée du Nord. (Wallon, *Représentants* (Paris, 1880), vol. IV, p. 365.) Noble artillery officers were particularly conspicuous in the Revolutionary armies; d'Aboville, Lacombe Saint-Michel, Choderlos de Laclos, and, of course, Bonaparte himself.

[53] *Correspondance générale de Carnot*, vol. IV, p. 365.

[54] Among them, the marquis de Montalembert, the marquis de Marescot, d'Obenheim, Lacuée, Tholozé, d'Audreville, as well as a banker he had known at Calais named Pigault-Montbailla. See M. Reinhard, *Le Grand Carnot*, vol. II, p. 138.

[55] Garrone, *Romme*, p. 352, n. 1.

[56] Kuscinski, *Dictionnaire des conventionnels* (Paris, 1917), p. 340.

[57] Henri Wallon, *Les Répresentants en Mission*, vol. IV, p. 156.

[58] Aulard, *La Société des Jacobins*, vol. V, p. 674, 16 ventôse an II—6 Mar. 1794.

[59] Louis Jacob, *Lebon*, vol. II, pp. 142–3.

[60] *Documents pour servir à l'histoire de la Révolution française dans la ville d'Amiens* (Paris, 1910), vol. VII, pp. 311–12.

[61] A former priest, now a police agent, named Rousseville, was sent to the outlying suburbs of the capital to report on the exiled nobles, but he does not seem to have thought them very dangerous. Morellet writes that sans-culottes would also take walks to Neuilly to mock the exiled nobles: 'Ces b . . . là ont encore leurs parasols de l'ancien régime.' (Morellet, *Mémoires* (Paris, 1823), vol. II, p. 17. See also H. Forneron, *Histoire générale des émigrés pendant la Révolution française*, vol. I (Paris, 1884), p. 155.)

[62] AN, F 7 4781.

[63] Richard Cobb, *Paris and Its Provinces 1792–1798* (Oxford, 1975), p. 122.

[64] Adolphe Schmidt, *Tableaux politiques*, vol. II, pp. 142–3. See also p. 138.

[65] Some noble children ('enfants en bas-age') were arrested along with their parents (see Georges Sangnier, *La Terreur dans le district de Saint-Pol* (Blagermont 1938), p. 318). At the same time, this may have been thought to be a humanitarian gesture: Babeuf, for example, petitioned that his son Émile be allowed to join him in jail. Foreign children, it may be added, were also arrested in conformity with the law of 27 germinal. The release of those under twelve was ordered. (F. A. Aulard, ed., *La Société des Jacobins* (Paris, 1891), vol. V, p. 652.)

[66] F. A. Aulard, *Recueil des actes du Comité de Salut Public*, vol. XIII, p. 4.

[67] *Archives parlementaires*, vol. 48 (Paris, 1896), p. 191, 15 Aug. 1792.

[68] 'Le Comité a cru que vous ne deviez pas rappeler l'existence d'une caste détruite, en faisant des lois particulières à une classe d'hommes; il a cru que tous les gens suspects en général devaient être éloignés des armées. Les opérations qu'il faites à cet égard devaient être secrètes, pour avoir leur succès . . . Il a dû prendre des ménagements. . . .' Quoted in Hartmann, *Les Officiers de l'armée royale*, p. 523.

[69] *Archives parlementaires*, vol. 53 (Paris, 1898), p. 456, 17 Nov. 1792.

[70] *Observations d'une femme sur la loi contre les émigrés* (s.1. s.d.), pp. 3–4.

[71] On 2 August 1793. See *La Société des Jacobins*, F. A. Aulard, ed., vol. V, p. 326.

[72] *Archives parlementaires*, vol. 59 (Paris, 1901), p. 629, 5 Mar. 1793.

[73] Robespierre, *Œuvres*, vol. 10, *Discours*, p. 390. At the Jacobin Club, 18 Mar. 1794.

[74] Saint-Just, *Œuvres complètes*, Ch. Vellay, ed., vol. I (Paris, 1908), p. 319; *Esprit de la Révolution*, part 4, ch. XI.

[75] *Le Moniteur*, vol. 27 (Paris, 1840), p. 113. The theoretical undesirability of collective punishment was perceived even by terrorists, though most often when the shoe was on their own foot. Guffroy, for example, was displeased when a noble friend of his was imprisoned by Saint-Just and Lebas:

> . . . il n'y a que l'inexpérience d'une jeunesse trop bouillante . . . ou l'ignorance des hommes et de la bonne politique qui puisse excuser la démarche de Saint-Just et Lebas: quoi des hommes qui ont suivi la révolution! Quoi des enfants que la Convention a rendu à la nature seraient persécutés avant de savoir ce qu'ils sont, ce qu'ils peuvent être. . . . Amis, patience, c'est un sacrifice de plus à la Patrie, elle t'en saura gré et tu dois savoir que le patriote, comme les disciples du Christ (car je n'abjure pas sa morale, moi) sçait faire abnégation de soi, pour servir ses frères et son pays. [Quoted in Louis Jacob, *Joseph le Bon* (Paris, 1932), vol. II, p. 143.]

[76] Jean-Paul Marat, *Plan de législation criminelle*, D. Hamiche, ed. (Paris, 1974), p. 172.

[77] Buonarroti, *La Conspiration pour l'égalité*, vol. I (Paris, 1957), pp. 56–7.

[78] Georg Lukacs, *History and Class Consciousness* (Cambridge, 1971), p. 28.

[79] *Le Moniteur*, vol. 17 (Paris, 1840), p. 584–5.

[80] Pierre Caron, *Paris pendant la Terreur*, vol. VI (Paris, 1910), p. 164. In Grenoble, a theatrical performance was organized on 21 January 1794 to stimulate, *inter alia*, popular anti-nobilism: a parade wound its way from the Temple of Reason to the Place de la Liberté. There, on a scaffold, flanked by an 'Hercule française', were mannequins representing the papacy, the monarchy, and the nobility. In response to the people's cry for vengeance, Hercules 'les frappe de sa massue et leurs têtes et leurs corps tombent, sont trainés dans la boue et foulés aux pieds par les citoyens. Combien cet exemple prouve la haine que le peuple de Grenoble porte aux rois, aux nobles et aux prêtres!' *Courier patriotique*, cited in A. Prudhomme, *Histoire de Grenoble* (Grenoble, 1888), p. 640, n. 2.

[81] *Archives parlementaires*, vol. 90 (Paris, 1972), p. 368, 16 May 1794 (floréal an II).

[82] Albert Mathiez presented this idea in a review of Albert Gain's 'La Restauration et les biens des émigrés', *Annales historiques de la Révolution française*, nouvelle série, vol. 6, 1929, p. 507.

[83] Barère, *Mémoires*, vol. II, p. 169.

[84] Quoted in André Thuillier, *Économie et société nivernaises au début du XIXe siècle* (Paris, 1974), p. 38. In August 1794, the *société populaire* of Dole likewise drafted a petition in favour of the mayor, Agnus de Pouffange, who had acquired nobility in 1765, and had been expelled from office on that account. (Claude Brelot, *La Noblesse en Franche-Comté*, p. 92, n. 74.) Bouret, in the Calvados, also reported in late April 1794, that there had been local demands, which he rejected, on behalf of imprisoned nobles 'parce qu'ils en ont vu qui exerçaient

quelques fois envers eux des actes de bienfaisance dont ils sont reconnaissant'. F. A. Aulard, *Recueil des actes du Comité de Salut Public*, vol. XIII, p. 79.

[85] C. Duval, *L'Administration de la commune et du canton de Viry de l'an I à l'an VII de la république française* (Saint-Julien, 1883) vol. I, pp. 112–13.

[86] Ibid., p. 111.

[87] G. Saumade, *Une petite commune rurale du Languedoc sous l'ancien régime, Fabrègues 1650–1792* (Montpellier, 1908), p. 663, n. 1.

[88] Buonarroti, *La Conspiration pour l'égalité*, vol. II (Paris, 1957), p. 109.

[89] F. Aulard, *Paris pendant le Directoire executif*, vol. II, p. 464.

[90] Buonarroti, *La Conspiration*, vol. II, p. 199.

[91] A. Schmidt, *Tableaux politiques*, vol. III, p. 409.

NOTES TO CHAPTER FIVE

[1] Ollivier, *Saint-Just*, p. 218.

[2] Ibid., p. 385.

[3] Criticism of this view is presented, together with a reply, in Hans-Ulrich Wehler, 'Kritik und Kritische Antikritik', *Historische Zeitschrift*, Band 225, 1977, pp. 347–84.

[4] Marc Richir, in his introduction to Fichte's *Considérations sur la Révolution française* (Paris, 1974), p. 24.

[5] Ibid., p. 10.

[6] In *Annales historiques de la Révolution française*, vol. 47, no. 219 (Jan.–Mar. 1975), pp. 134–73.

[7] Georges Lefebvre, *La Révolution française* (Paris, 1930), p. 45.

[8] Jean Jaurès, *Histoire socialiste de la Révolution française* (Paris, 1927), vol. I, p. 347.

[9] Lefebvre, *The Coming of the French Revolution* (Princeton, 1961), p. 50.

[10] Crane Brinton, *A Decade of Revolution* (New York, 1963), p. 63.

[11] For a discussion of Augustin Cochin's ideological interpretation of the French Revolution, see F. Furet, *Penser la Révolution française* (Paris, 1978).

[12] Jean-Paul Sartre, *The Search for Method* (New York, 1968), pp. 41 and 173. Sartre goes on to describe the importance of ideology in these terms:

> A system is an alienated man who wants to go beyond his alienation and who gets entangled in alienated words; it is an achievement of awareness which finds itself deviated by its own instruments and which the culture transforms into a particular *Weltanschauung*. It is at the same time a struggle of thought against its social instruments, an effort to direct them, to empty them of their superfluity, to compel them to express only the thought itself. The consequence of these contradictions is the fact that an ideological system is an irreducible; since the instruments, whatever they are, alienate the one who employs them and modify the meaning of his action, the idea must be considered to be both the objectification of the concrete man and his alienation [p. 115].

Clifford Geertz has developed his illuminating interpretation of ideology in a number of books, including *The Interpretation of Culture* (New York, 1973). Geertz describes social values thus:

> Themes are outlined, of course; among the content analysts, they are even counted. But they are referred for elucidation, not to other themes nor to any sort of semantic theory, but either backward to the effect they presumably mirror or forward to the social reality

ey presumably distort. The problem of how, after all, ideologies transform sentiment to significance and so make it socially available is short-circuited by the crude device of lacing particular symbols and particular strains (or interests) side by side in such a way at the fact that the first are derivatives of the second seems mere common sense—or at ast post-Freudian, post-Marxian common sense. And so, if the analyst be deft enough, does. The connection is not thereby explained but merely educed. The nature of the lationship between the sociopsychological stresses that incite ideological attitudes and e elaborate symbolic structures through which those attitudes are given a public existence much too complicated to be comprehended in terms of a vague and unexamined notion f emotive resonance [p. 207].

[13] Keith Baker, *Condorcet* (Chicago, 1975), p. 268.

[14] Claude Mazauric, 'Quelques voies nouvelles pour l'histoire politique de la évolution française', *Annales historiques de la Révolution française*, vol. 47, no. 219 an.–Mar. 1975), p. 157.

[15] Jaurès, *La Montagne*, p. 3; quoted in Leroy, *Histoire des idées sociales*, p. 311.

[16] Georges Sorel, *Réflexions sur la violence* (Paris, 1936), p. 17.

[17] Jürgen Habermas, *Theory and Practice* (Boston, 1974), p. 105.

[18] Gordon Wood, in his *Creation of the American Republic 1776–1787* (New York, 969), implies that Hegel's interpretation applies to 1787 but not to 1776. See so Edmund S. Morgan, 'The Puritan Ethic and the American Revolution' in *he Challenge of the American Revolution* (New York, 1978), pp. 134–8.

[19] Robespierre, *Œuvres*, vol. V, *Lettres à ses commettants* (Paris, 1961), p. 16, 19 ct. 1792.

[20] Ibid., vol. 10, *Discours* (Paris, 1967), p. 445, 18 floréal an II—7 May 1794.

[21] *Esprit de la Révolution*. For Saint-Just, the nobility is a spent force:

>)n peut dire que presque toute la noblesse livrée à la molesse et aux délices n'avait ni aïeux, i postérité; elle avait ridiculisé ses maximes, il n'en existait plus qu'une ombre qui évanouit à la lumière. Si l'esclavage a été un crime dans tous les temps et dans toutes les œurs, on pourrait dire que la tyrannie eut des vertus chez nos aieux: on vit des despotes umains et magnanimes; de nos jours, on remarquait des sybarites atroces, et qui n'avaient us que les humeurs du sang de leurs aïeux. L'antique gloire était fanée. Quels secours evait attendre la patrie de cet orgueil épuisé, qui ne regretta que l'opulence et les douceurs e la domination? Que doit-on admirer le plus d'un peuple qui fit tout pour sa liberté, ou 'une aristocratie qui n'osa rien pour son orgueil? Le crime était mûr, il est tombé; disons tout noblesse fut rendue à elle-même, et l'église à son Dieu. [*Œuvres complètes*, vol. I. p. 286.]

[22] Ollivier, *Saint-Just*, p. 501.

[23] *Œuvres complètes*, vol. I. p. 389, 27 Dec. 1792.

[24] *Archives parlementaires*, vol. 88 (Paris, 1969), p. 618, 15 Apr. 1794 (28 germinal II).

[25] Quoted in Alphonse Aulard, *Études et leçons sur la Révolution française*, 9e série 'aris, 1924), p. 20.

[26] Quoted in Mathiez, *Études sur Robespierre* (Paris, 1973), pp. 166–7.

[27] Michelet, *Histoire de la Révolution française*, vol. II, Pléiade edition (Paris, 62), p. 851.

[28] Saint-Just, *Œuvres complètes*, Ch. Vellay, ed., vol. I (Paris, 1908), p. 362; at e Jacobin Club, 4 Nov. 1792.

[29] Barère, *Mémoires*, vol. II, p. 151.

[30] Maxime Leroy, *Histoire des idées sociales en France*, p. 112.

[31] Cited in L. Ducros, *La Société française au dix-huitième siècle* (Paris, 1922), p.
.

[32] R. Darnton, 'Literary Low-life in Pre-Revolutionary France', in *Frenc Society and the Revolution*, D. Johnson, ed. (Cambridge, 1976), pp. 78–9.

[33] J. A. Dulaure, *Histoire critique de la noblesse depuis le commencement de monarchie, jusqu'à nos jours; ou l'on expose ses préjugés, ses brigandages, ses crimes, l'on prouve qu'elle a été le fléau de la liberté, de la raison, des connaissances humaines, constamment l'ennemi du peuple et des rois* (Paris, 1790), p. v.

[34] *La Société des Jacobins*, F. A. Aulard, ed., vol. V, (Paris, 1895), p. 330.

[35] M. H. Abrams, *Natural Supernaturalism* (New York, 1971), p. 31.

[36] Quoted in Robert Shackleton, *Montesquieu, A Critical Biography* (Oxfor 1961), p. 317.

[37] *L'Esprit des lois*, G. Truc, ed. (Paris, 1961), Book XI, ch. 13, p. 181. See als Louis Althuser, *Politics and History* (London, 1972), ch. 3.

[38] *L'Esprit des lois*, Book VIII, ch. 12, p. 129. The 'semantic history' of th term 'corruption' is of interest also. In eighteenth-century France, as in Britai at the time, the term had come to mean not merely deterioration as in Polybi and Machiavelli, but depravation as well. See Albert O. Hirschman, *The Passio and the Interests: Political Arguments for Capitalism before its Triumph* (Princeto 1978), p. 40.

[39] Quoted in Jean Marie Goulemot, *Discours, histoire et révolutions* (Paris, 1975 pp. 371, 379. Commerce and corruption were often presented as cause and effec Even Adam Smith had reservations about the moral consequences of a moder economic life. Commerce diminished 'the courage of mankind. . . . By havir their minds constantly employed on the arts of luxury, [men involved commerce] grow effeminate and dastardly.' In summary, he concluded, 'The are the disadvantages of a commercial spirit. The minds of men are contracte and rendered incapable of elevation. Education is despised, or at least neglecte and the heroic spirit is almost utterly extinguished. To remedy these defec would be an object worthy of serious attention.' Quoted in Hirschman, op. ci pp. 106–7.

[40] Cited in M. Eude, 'La Politique de Robespierre en 1792, d'après "Défenseur de la Constitution"', *Annales historiques de la Révolution françai* vol. 28, no. 143 (Apr.–June 1956), p. 135.

[41] See, for example, Albert Mathiez, *La Corruption parlementaire sous la terre* (Paris, 1927), and A. de Lestapis, 'Un Grand Corrupteur, le duc de Châtele *Annales historiques de la Révolution française*, vol. 25, no. 133 (Oct.–Dec. 1953), 331.

[42] André Latreille, *L'Église catholique et la Révolution*, vol. I (Paris, 1970 pp. 95–96.

[43] Marcel Reinhard, *Nouvelle histoire de Paris, La Révolution, 1789–1799* (Par 1971), p. 301. The extent of popular anticlericalism has been much debate Soboul and Cobb have argued for its widespread existence. Others (Vovell Dautry, Plongeron) have insisted on its ephemeral quality and on the varieti of its manifestations. Be that as it may, it is clear that in 1792–3 popular an clericalism, especially in Paris, was far more visible than was anti-aristocratis

[44] On 6 pluviôse an II, *Déclarations motivées d'Antonnelle* (Paris, n.d.), p. 6 D'Antonnelle had an interest here but he presumably would not have made th distinction between priests and nobles if he had thought that the market wou not bear it.

[45] Abbé Grégoire, *Mémoires*, p. 161.

[46] Robespierre, *Œuvres*, vol. 10, *Discours* (Paris, 1967), pp. 259–60.

[47] Bernard Plongeron, *Conscience religieuse et révolutions* (Paris, 1969), p. 111.
[48] Quoted in A. Mathiez, *La Révolution et l'Église* (Paris, 1910), p. 143.
[49] F. A. Aulard, ed., *Les Actes du Comité de Salut Public*, vol. XIII, p. 224, 13 loréal an III—2 May 1794.
[50] E. Charavay, ed., *Correspondance générale de Carnot*, vol. IV (Paris, 1907),). 389.
[51] Michelet, *Histoire de la Révolution française*, vol. II, Pléiade edition (Paris, 962), p. 670.
[52] July 1793, quoted in Jacques Roux, *Scripta et Acta, Textes présentés par Walter Markov* (East Berlin, 1969), p. 191.
[53] Ibid., pp. 275–7.
[54] Walter Markov, *Exkurse zu Jacques Roux* (East Berlin, 1970), p. 309. In any ase, Roux was first interrogated and arrested in July, after the murder of Marat; ut in June 1793 he had already begun to suggest, rather episodically, that nerchants were worse than nobles, a thought that was echoed in late July 1793 y Leclerc in his *Ami du peuple*. See R. B. Rose, *The Enragés* (Melbourne, 1965),). 87. It is also of relevance, as has been said, that a favourable view of nobles in elation to merchants had popular echoes: On 20 ventôse an 3 (10 March 1795), or example, a police report described public feelings thusly: 'Le public disait autement: "Nous allons avoir un Roi, nous serons plus heureux, nous ne ouffrirons plus tant; les scélérats de marchands qui croient remplacer les i-devant nobles auront le nez cassé et ne seront plus si insolents; la Convention mettra ordre."' See Adolphe Schmidt, *Tableaux de la Révolution française ubliés sur les papiers inédits de la police secrète de Paris* (Leipzig, 1867), vol. II, pp. 298 nd 409. See also Chapter Four, part V.
[55] Mathiez, *La Vie chère*, p. 348.
[56] A. Mathiez, 'Un Enragé inconnu: Taboureau de Montigny', Part II, *Annales historiques de la Révolution française*, vol. 7, no. 40 (July–Aug. 1930), p. 320.
[57] Mathiez, 'Taboureau', Part I, *Annales historiques de la Révolution française*, vol. VII, no. 39 (May–June 1930), p. 215.
[58] Mathiez, 'Taboureau,' Part II, p. 308.
[59] E. G. Lenglet, *De la propriété et de ses rapports avec les droits et avec la dette du itoyen* (Paris, an VI), p. 71.
[60] Barère, *Mémoires*, vol. IV, p. 40; cited in Ollivier, *Saint-Just*, p. 547.
[61] Robespierre, *Œuvres*, vol. 10, *Discours* (Paris, 1967), p. 153.
[62] AN, F7 4437, I, plaquette 5.
[63] Hartmann, *Les Officiers de l'armée royale*, p. 495.
[64] Robespierre, *Œuvres*, vol. 9, *Discours* (Paris, 1958), p. 257, 23 Jan. 1793.
[65] Robespierre's choice of words in his speech of 25 September 1793 is in itself evealing: 'On déclame sans cesse contre les nobles; on dit qu'il faut tous les lestituer, . . .' he explained, and for him the use of the word '*on*' is revealing. The '*ons*' who are pushing him on in September 1793 are clearly not to his liking. 'or his avowed enemies, Robespierre could show brutal hostility: 'Oui, je vais onclure, et contre vous.' Indirect references and the use of '*on*' are clearly ontemptuous.
[66] The Incorruptible had no use for nobles in his private life as well. Invited by Barère to dinner, Robespierre was introduced to his fellow guests, one of them amed Loménie. Barère reports the conversation as follows:
—C'est un Brienne?—
Oui, le neveu du cardinal qui a convoqué les états généraux et établi par une

loi la liberté absolue de la presse.—C'est bon, c'est bon, mais c'est un noble —Peu d'instants après Robespierre prit son chapeau et se retira sans rien dire M. Loménie a péri ensuite dans la révolution de messidor.
See Barère, *Mémoires*, vol. II (Paris, 1842), p. 179.

[67] Saint-Just, *De la nature . . .*' p. 170, quoted in M. Abensour, 'La Pensée politique de Saint-Just, problématique et cadres sociaux', *Annales historiques de la Révolution française*, vol. 38, no. 183 (Jan.–Mar. 1966), p. 32. Or again, 'Un législateur peut exprimer la nature et ne peut exprimer la volonté générale.'

[68] Abensour, 'La Pensée politique de Saint-Just', pp. 1–32. The repeated use of the word '*petit*' in this description is symbolic: Frenchmen yearn as public persons for *Grandeur* but as private individuals prefer things small (*petits pois petite maison*, *petit jardin*, *petits plats*, *petite femme*, etc.).

[69] Lefebvre, *Études sur la Révolution française* (Paris, 1962–3), p. 147.

[70] Sade, *Français, encore un effort* (Paris, 1965), pp. 110–11.

[71] Quoted in Patrick Girard, *Les Juifs en France de 1789 à 1860* (Paris, 1976), p. 68.

NOTES TO CHAPTER SIX

[1] Albert Soboul, *Histoire de la Révolution française*, vol. I (Paris, 1962), p. 7.

[2] Ibid., vol. II, p. 201.

[3] See Jacques Godechot, *Les Commissaires aux armées sous le Directoire* (Paris 1941). The same point has also been made by J. R. Suratteau, 'Le Directoire d'après des travaux récents', *Annales historiques de la Révolution française*, vol. 48 no. 224, (Apr.–June 1976), p. 194. 'La récolte de l'été 1796 avait été excellente après celles exécrables des années précédentes. Comme l'écrit Lefebvre, cel était bon pour le maintien de l'ordre, en permettant aux pauvres de manage un peu plus, mais ce fut catastrophique pour les producteurs.'

[4] Soboul, *Histoire de la Révolution*, vol. II, p. 298.

[5] Ibid., p. 298.

[6] Ibid., p. 363.

[7] Thus: 'Sur *l'affaire Chabot* se greffèrent sucessivement le procès de Hébertistes, le procès des dantonnistes, la Conspiration de l'Étranger, etc. . . Tous ces procès en apparence distincts les uns des autres se tiennent étroitement par un lien logique et nécessaire. Ils ne forment qu'une seule et même affaire qu'une unique conspiration.' (Quoted in A. de Lestapis, *La Conspiration de Bat* (Paris, 1969), p. 7.)

[8] Lefebvre, *Histoire de la Révolution française* (Paris, 1963), p. 418. Or again:

> La notion généralisée de complot aristocratique, étendue à tous ceux qu'on inculpa d'hostilité à l'égard du régime, explique la pratique croissante de l'«amalgame», qui au déni de toute procédure vraiment judiciaire, rassemblait dans la même sentence d accusés qui s'ignoraient et dont les actes ou les paroles n'offraient rien de commun que le solidarité préjugée dans la «conspiration contre le peuple français». Finalement, cet ét d'esprit s'exaspérant parce que des attentats menacèrent la sécurité personnelle des che révolutionnaires, la procédure terroriste se transforma en effet, mais pour se simplifi davantage encore.

(Lefebvre, *Révolution française*, p. 421.) Albert Soboul is more cautious: 'La terreur fut donc essentiellement un instrument de défense nationale et révolutionnair contre les rebelles et les traîtres' (*Histoire de la Révolution française*, vol. II, p. 98

an interpretation that more closely follows Mathiez's rather chauvinistic view of 1916: 'La Terreur était essentiellement un instrument de défense patriotique.' (A. Mathiez, *La Victoire an l'an II* (Paris, 1916), p. 223.) In the same vein, Soboul's introduction to Lestapis's fanciful *Le Conspiration de Batz* is also very cool. None the less, it must also be said that Soboul does not do very much to substitute some other causal factor for the plot theory, of which he is rightly suspicious. Jacqueline Chaumié, by contrast, is an enthusiastic supporter of the plot theory: 'La grandeur de Robespierre et de Saint-Just est d'avoir sans cesse dénoncé le danger et vu la continuité du complot à travers la Révolution.' ('Saint-Just et le procès des Girondins', *Annales historiques de la Révolution française*, vol. 40, no. 191 (Jan.–Mar. 1968), p. 21.)

[9] The French were particularly prone to conspiratorial explanations and, as a nation, had been riveted by the affair of the Queen's necklace, Mesmerism, Cagliostro, and the like. One can indeed argue that the reverse would have been strange: the disintegration in France of traditional social links had created in that society an atmosphere of suspicion of which conspiracies and denunciations were perhaps the most conspicuous political manifestation during the Revolution. The extraordinarily stilted quality of social forms in eighteenth-century France can similarly be interpreted as a barrier made necessary by a pessimistic view of individual motivations. It is striking in this regard that Revolutionary discourse, in theory a conscious alternative to the stiff conventions of noble mores, was itself highly ritualized.

[10] See M. J. Sydenham, *The First French Republic* (Berkeley, 1973), p. 142. Also, M. Reinhard, *Le Grand Carnot*, vol. II, p. 229.

[11] Quoted in A. Meynier, *Les Coups d'état du Directoire, le 18 fructidor* (Paris, 1927), p. 204. In the same vein, Directorial officials saw the proof of the complicity of royalist notables in their non-appearance; this was the explanation of a municipal officer who observed that the leading royalists in his district were not 'des individus bien recommandables': The reason was, he thought, that 'Le royalisme a sans doute pensé que s'il se montrait lui-même, ses menées seraient bientôt connues. Il s'est servi pour cela de personnes qui ne fussent pas capables de donner aucun soupçon. Ceux qui ont le plus figuré sont: un nommé Dupoux, faiseur de cribles; Fréchou fils, instituteur particulier, et Courtade, dit Galot, habitants de la commune de Muret.' Cited in l'abbé Joseph Lacouture, *Le Mouvement royaliste dans le sud-ouest—1797–1800* (Hossegor, 1932), pp. 61–2.

[12] Mallet du Pan, *Correspondance*, cited in Sydenham, *First French Republic* (Berkeley, 1973), p. 80.

[13] Although the fact is played down by many historians (see Lefebvre, *Napoleon* (Paris, 1953), p. 90, or Mathiez, *Contributions à l'histoire religieuse de la Révolution française* (Paris, 1907), pp. 201–5), a great many overtures were made to the Directorial regime by the non-juring clergy, which scandalized adamant royalists. See Marcel Reinhard, *La France du Directoire* (Paris, 1956), 2ème partie, p. 130; Ernest Daudet, 'L'Église et le roi pendant l'émigration', *Le Correspondant* (10 May 1905), vol. LXXVII, p. 419; Bernard Plongeron, *Les Ecclésiologies* (Paris, 1963), p. 191; and C. Ledré, *Le Culte caché sous la Révolution* (Paris, 1949), p. 247.

[14] Ernest Daudet, 'L'Église et le roi pendant l'émigration', p. 419.

[15] J. R. Suratteau, 'Le Directoire d'après des travaux récents', *Annales historiques de la Révolution française*, vol. 48, no. 224 (Apr.–June 1976), p. 204.

[16] M. Reinhard, *Le Grand Carnot*, p. 229. Quite understandably, Lefebvre in

his unenthusiastic review of Reinhard's *Carnot*, chides both the author and his subject for their inability to see that no middle course was to be found there: 'il [Carnot] s'aveuglait volontairement sur les conséquences qu'entrainerait le triomphe de la faction anglo-royaliste; il en eut mené tout droit à la réaction et comme régicide, il eût souffert'. *Annales historiques de la Révolution française*, vol. 26, no. 134 (Jan.–Mar. 1954), pp. 87–8.

[17] Kuscinski, *Dictionnaire*, p. 243.

[18] As is well known, the work of the Directory in this field was very considerable: Biot, in his *Essai sur l'histoire générale des sciences pendant la Révolution française*, remarked that 'les savants jouissent d'un crédit sans bornes. On n'ignorait pas que la République leur devait son salut et son existence' (quoted in Reinhard, *Nouvelle histoire de Paris*, p. 386). This was a view of things that was perhaps even more true than Biot thought. Primary and secondary education were of course thoroughly disrupted, but much was done at the highest level where 'les hommes à talent' were to be found. The Institutes were re-created with, among their most prominent members, La Révellière and Sieyes. Also created or newly refunded were the École Normale, the Ponts et Chausées, the Langues Orientales, the Conservatoire des Arts et Métiers, the École des Géographes, with last and least the École d'Aérostatique.

[19] J. Ehrard, 'Les Lumières et la fête', *Annales historiques de la Révolution française*, vol. 47, no. 221 (July–Sept. 1965), p. 373.

[20] Michel Vovelle, 'Sociologie et idéologie des fêtes de la Révolution', *Annales historiques de la Révolution française*, vol. 47, no. 221 (July–Sept. 1975), p. 413.

[21] Sydenham, *First French Republic*, p. 169.

[22] Vidalenc, *Émigrés*, p. 427.

[23] Greer, *Emigration*, p. 101.

[24] Georges Belloni, *Le Comité de Sureté Générale de la Convention Nationale* (Paris, 1924), p. 248.

[25] *Le Moniteur*, vol. 27 (Paris, 1843), p. 411, 6 Feb. 1796 (17 pluviôse an IV).

[26] AN, BB[1] Plaquette 11.

[27] *Le Moniteur*, vol. 21 (Paris, 1851), p. 384.

[28] Plusieurs des hommes dont il s'agit dans ce moment ont rendu de grands services à la patrie. Pourquoi cette opiniâtreté à nous ramener sans cesse sur deux castes dont il ne devrait plus être question depuis longtemps; pourquoi ramener sans cesse notre attention sur des individus proscrits par les brigands de la Vendée et tous les tyrans? Je ne connais que deux espèces d'hommes dans la république, les bons et les méchants; punissez les derniers, rendez les autres heureux. Il est aussi une classe d'hommes qui a fait autant de mal à la révolution que les deux castes dont il s'agit, ce sont les hommes de la loi. A Dieu ne plaise que je veuille jeter de la défiance sur ceux de ces citoyens qui ont rendu, qui rendent encore de grands services à la révolution; mais j'ai voulu faire sentire à la Convention jusqu'où on pourrait la mener, si une fois on la faisait dévier.

Le Moniteur, vol. 21 (Paris, 1841), p. 384.

[29] Kuscinski, *Dictionnaire des Conventionnels*, p. 117.

[30] *Recueil des actes du Comité de Salut Public, Les Representants en mission*, F. A. Aulard, ed., vol. XVI (Paris, 1904), p. 665, 27 fructidor an II—13 Sept. 1794.

[31] Ibid., p. 498, 17 fructidor an II—3 Sept. 1794.

[32] John B. Sirich, *The Revolutionary Committees* (Cambridge, 1943), p. 195.

[33] Pocquet du Haut Jussé, *Terreur et terroristes à Rennes* (Mayenne, 1974), p. 373. The law of 21 messidor, which ostensibly ordered the release of agricultural

workers for harvest time, was sometimes invoked to justify the release of nobles. See Martyn Lyons, *Revolution in Toulouse* (Berne, 1978), p. 66.

[34] Louis Hugueney, *Les Clubs dijonnais sous la Révolution* (Dijon, 1905), p. 199.

[35] *Le Moniteur*, vol. 21 (Paris, 1841), p. 706, 10 Sept. 1794 (24 fructidor an II).

[36] Bentabole's 'ups and downs' on nobles are revealing. A weak man, he espoused different opinions in rapid succession, as the times demanded. On 1 April 1793, Bentabole successfully refuted Albitte, who had moved that nobles be excluded from the Jacobin Club, in June 1793. However, he joined the chorus which was denouncing General de Beauharnais. Then, in October 1793, he married a noble lady, and in November 1793 (*Le Moniteur*, vol. 18, p. 688), he publicly objected to an anti-noble measure on the grounds that it might be 'injuste a l'égard de quelques prêtres ou nobles qui ont rendu des services à la république'. Bentabole died in 1798 penniless, his wife having gambled away what money he had been able to put aside.

[37] *Le Moniteur*, vol. 22 (Paris, 1853), p. 180, 10 Oct. 1794 (19 vendémiaire an III).

[38] Hartmann, *Les Officiers de l'armée royale*, p. 527.

[39] Ludovic Sciout, *Le Directoire*, vol. III (Paris, 1896), seconde partie, p. 164.

[40] Victor Pierre, *La Terreur sous le Directoire* (Paris, 1887), p. 164.

[41] *Le Moniteur*, vol. 29 (Paris, 1843), p. 19, 1 Oct. 1797 (8 vendémiaire an VI).

[42] Ibid., vol. 28 (Paris, 1843), p. 819, 9 Sept. 1797 (23 fructidor an V).

[43] Maugenest, *Opinion* (Paris, 6 vendémiaire an VI), p. 4.

[44] Cornudet, see *Le Moniteur*, vol. XXIX (Paris, 1853), p. 79, 6 Frimaire an VI—26 Nov. 1797.

[45] Laussat, ibid., p. 78.

[46] J. G. Beyts, *Opinion de Beyts, député de la Lys, contre le projet de résolution tendant à exclure les ci-devants nobles des fonctions publiques* (Paris, 1797), p. 7.

[47] Duchesne, *Opinion*, pp. 4, 7.

[48] A. C. Thibaudeau, *Mémoires sur la Convention et le Directoire*, vol. II (Paris, 1824), p. 319.

[49] *Paris pendant la réaction thermidorienne et sous le Directoire,* F. A. Aulard, ed., vol. IV (Paris, 1900).

[50] Barras, *Mémoires of Barras*, vol. III (London, 1896).

[51] Aulard, *Directoire exécutif*, vol. IV, p. 401.

[52] Duvergier, *Décret du 6e jour complémentaire de l'an III*, vol. VIII, p. 285, 22 Sept. 1795.

[53] Barante, *Histoire du Directoire*, vol. II (Paris, 1855), p. 445.

[54] AN, C 428 123, 8 nivôse an VI.

[55] Decency and 'la pitié individuelle' would forever incite non-nobles to help nobles. 'Il fallut toujours recourir à la terreur pour y soumettre.' Benjamin Constant crossed out this last sentence when he revised Mme de Staël's manuscript, but he allowed the rest of the passage to stand: 'Il faut le consentement de la majorité non seulement pour la formation métaphysique de la loi, mais aussi pour son exécution. . . . Si vous faites une loi assez barbare pour avoir nécessairement beaucoup d'adversaires, vous constituez votre état en dictature perpetuel, c'est à dire que vous ne l'amènerez jamais à l'accord social. . . . (Mme de Staël, *Des Circonstances actuelles qui peuvent terminer la Révolution française et des principes qui peuvent fonder la République en France* (Paris, 1906), p. 155.)

[56] Henri Carré, *La Noblesse en France et l'opinion publique au XVIIIe siècle* (Paris, 1920), p. 546.

[57] Barante, *Directoire*, vol. IV, p. 401.

[58] Morellet, *Mémoires* (Paris, 1823), vol. II, p. 504.

[59] Dufort de Cheverny, *Mémoires*, p. 432.

[60] Mme de Staël, *Des circonstances*, p. 157.

[61] Ibid, pp. 157, 159.

[62] Cited in Maurois, *Adrienne* (Paris, 1960), p. 28.

[63] *Archives parlementaires*, vol. 88 (Paris, 1969), p. 616, 15 Apr. 1794 (26 germinal an II).

[64] Ollivier, *Saint-Just*, p. 564.

[65] 'Un Singulier Ouvrage de philosophie historique en l'an II', in *La Révolution dans les Vosges*, *Revue d'histoire moderne*, 1911, pp. 125–6.

[66] A. Aulard, 'Les Noms révolutionnaires des communes', *La Revue de Paris*, vol. XXIII, no. 19 (1 Oct. 1926), p. 559. Conversely, Saint Amour, in the Jura, became Franc-Amour, but '*franc*' was taken here in the sense of '*franchise*' rather than of '*Franc*'.

[67] Quoted in M. Reinhard, *Le Grand Carnot*, vol. II, p. 85.

[68] Décembre-Alonnier, *Dictionnaire de la Révolution française*, vol. II (Paris, 1868), p. 82.

[69] R. B. Rose, *Babeuf*, p. 393, n. 1.

[70] For Barère, see F. Brunot, *Histoire de la langue française* vol. IX (Paris, 1927), part 1, p. 181.

[71] In a short note, entitled 'Noblesse et lutte de classes', *Annales historique de la Révolution française*, vol. 30, no. 150 (Jan.–Mar. 1958), p. 67, Marc Bouloiseau presents an excerpt from a counter-revolutionary pamphlet and points to its international and aristocratic tone:

> Elle [la noblesse française] était là [à Coblentz] où son devoir l'appelait: elle avait fui une terre où Louis la vouait à la mort, sans utilité pour le trône, où il lui défendait de se rassembler pour accourir à sa défense; elle croyait revenir victorieuse auprès de son Roi, elle espérait trouver partout des compagnons d'armes. Quelle croisade eût été si pure, si légitime! Elle ne pouvait se croire étrangère à la Noblesse de tous les pays. Les peuples peuvent être divisés par nations, être vraiment étrangers l'un à l'autre; mais la Noblesse est une: nulle nuance de climat, de langage, de mœurs, ne peut la diviser: elle existe par-tout sur les mêmes bases, sur le même pivot, par les mêmes privileges, et quand ses bases sont attaquées dans un païs elles le sont également dans un autre. Ce n'était pas ici une guerre de commerce, de frontières, de pré-éminence: c'était une guerre déclarée à tous les éléments de la domination, de la royauté, de la religion, de la morale, de la hiérarchie des rangs, des privilèges, et de la propriété; tous les Souverains, tous les Nobles, tous les Propriétaires ont le même intérêt de l'étouffer.

But another reading of the passage might be to suggest that its noble author was in fact quite confused since his appeal was pitched not just to foreign nobles but to French property-owners also.

[72] The assumption of citra-ultra conspiracy had never lapsed completely. In 1795, Sergent, an ex-Septembriseur, had raised it on the floor of the convention:

> Ce n'est pas dans la Convention qu'il faut chercher les auteurs de ces troubles, ils sont hors de son sein. C'est cette minorité de la noblesse dans l'Assemblée constituante (on murmure), cette minorité si habile dans l'art de l'insurrection, qui avait combiné avec Lafayette le massacre du Champ-de-Mars; c'est cette portion de l'Assemblée législative qui a fui lorsque le trône s'est écroulé; c'est le comité secret des Feuillants, qui fut établi par un ministre contre lequel l'Assemblée nationale avait sévi, parce qu'il avait fait un acte législatif.

Dussaulx: Il ne faut point divaguer, il faut nommer les gens.
Sergent: C'est Adrien Duport, ce sont les Lameth. (*Plusieurs voix*: Ils sont en Angleterre.) Sieyès peut vous dire qu'il connaît comme moi les auteurs de ces insurrections; il sait qu'ils demeurent ou derrière les boulevards ou au Palais-Égalité.

Le Moniteur, vol. 24, p. 117 (15 germinal an III).
The *Courrier républicain* of 24 ventôse an IV had an interesting variant on this same theme:

Qu'on y prenne garde: pendant tout le cours de la Révolution, c'est particulièrement sur les nobles et les prêtres qu'on a frappé, et c'est presque toujours des nobles et des prêtres qui ont excité les mouvements qui ont donné le signal du massacre. Par quelle fatalité ont-ils toujours été à la tête de toutes les séditions? Pourquoi? Craignant d'être tués, ils se sont faits tueurs.

F. A. Aulard, ed., *Paris pendant la réaction thermidorienne et sous le Directoire* (Paris, 1899), vol. II, p. 54.
[73] Quoted in Barante, *Histoire du Directoire*, vol. II, p. 443.
[74] Charles-Gaspard Toustain Richebourg, *Sur le Projet* (Paris, 1797), pp. 6, 7, 10, 11.
[75] Cited by Benjamin Constant in his *Fragments des mémoires de Madame Récamier*, *Œuvres*, Pléiade edition (Paris, 1957), p. 965. Though written in 1805, these 'memoirs' were published only in 1832. The lines quoted here were then 'appropriated' by Barante in his *Histoire du Directoire* (see vol. II, p. 443). Most of Constant's sketch of Sieyes deals with the former priest's detestation of nobles:

Siéyès avait environ trente-cinq ans quand la révolution commença. Il embrassa le parti de la liberté, parce que ce parti était l'ennemi de la noblesse, et que la noblesse était ce qu'il détestait le plus. Depuis son enfance, cette haine l'avait dominé; et comme il avait plus d'esprit que les autres révolutionnaires, sa haine s'augmentait du sentiment qu'on ne parviendrait pas à la détruire. Quand il avait bien déclamé contre elle, il finissait par dire en soupirant: «Et après tout cela, je ne serais jamais un Montmorency!» Quand il fut question de chasser tous les nobles de France, il n'y eut aucun raisonnement qui pût faire impression sur lui.

[76] J. A. Dulaure, *Esquisses historiques des principaux évènements de la Révolution française*, vol. IV (Paris, 1824), p. 480. Hébert, Ronsin, Vincent, and Momoro had been accused at their trial of being covert royalists, since royalism was served by their exaggerated radicalism. But what was already fanciful in a court of 'law' in 1794 was in 1797 very bizarre indeed.
[77] Oudot, *Opinion*, 6 vendémiaire an VI. Prudhomme, the author of an *Histoire générale et impartiale des erreurs, des fautes, et des crimes commis pendant la révolution française*, published in Paris in 1797, presumably after the coup of fructidor, also blamed the nobility for having abandonned the monarchy, leaving the way open for the terrorists, who had then attacked the innocent bourgeoisie:

Ce n'est pas le Peuple français qui abolit la royauté et conduisit Louis XVI d l'échafaud Nobles et Prêtres! le renversement de la monarchie en France, et la destruction de la dynastie régnante furent votre fait. Royalistes ingrats et sanguinaires, c'est vous-mêmes qui poussâtes le Français à la république! Nous vous devons ce bienfait, contre votre gré, sans doute. Vous n'étiez point attachés au Roi, vous ne formiez sa Cour qui pour en pomper des faveurs. Sitôt que la source en fut tarie, vous abandonnâtes lâchement la main qui s'était appauvrie pour vous enrichir. Bas flatteurs! vous cachâtes au Roi l'abîme au bord duquel vous le conduisîtes par une route de fleurs. C'est vous qui l'empêchiez de se populariser. Son crime est d'avoir sacrifié à vos intérêts de préférence aux siens et à ceux du Peuple. Qu'avez-vous fait pour lui? Lâches ingrats, vous avez émigrés. . . . [P. 317.

[78] *La Gazette de France*, 2 vendémiaire an IV.

[79] Albert Soboul, 'La Révolution française dans l'histoire du monde contemporain. Étude Comparative', in *Studien über die Revolution* (East Berlin, 1971), p. 70.

[80] François Furet, 'Le Catéchisme révolutionnaire', *Annales, Économies, Sociétés, Civilisations*, no. 2 (Mar.–Apr. 1971), p. 288.

[81] Quoted in Reinhard, *Carnot*, vol. II, pp. 184–5.

[82] (Paris, 1974), p. 24.

[83] Marcel Reinhard, *La France du Directoire* (Paris, 1956), deuxième partie, p. 143.

[84] Richard Cobb, *Reactions to the French Revolution*, p. 115.

[85] Cited by Godechot in his review of A. Ollivier's 'Dix-huit brumaire', in *Annales historiques de la Révolution française*, vol. 33, no. 163 (Jan.–Mar. 1961), p. 132.

[86] Stein, *History of the Social Movement in France*, p. 189.

[87] Quoted in Zapperi, introduction to *Qu'est-ce que le Tiers-état?*, pp. 78–9.

[88] Quoted in Leroy, *Histoire des idées*, p. 356.

[89] Mme de Staël, *Des circonstances*, p. 170. Constant concurred in his *Des réactions politiques* of 1797: 'Dans le XIVe siècle, les paysans égorgeaient la noblesse, dans le XVIIIe les philosophes l'ont abolie.' Cited in H. Grange, *Les Idées de Necker* (Paris, 1974), p. 468, n. 197.

[90] Ibid., pp. 44, 45.

[91] Ibid., p. 149.

[92] Ibid., pp. 74 and 75.

[93] Ibid., p. 128.

[94] In 1793–4, Marc-Antoine Baudot had also thought of making Protestantism the official religion of the French Republic. See Marc-Antoine Baudot, *Notes historiques sur la Convention Nationale, le Directoire, l'Empire et l'exil des votants* (Paris, 1893), pp. xiv–xv.

[95] To emphasize the exemplary nature of Revolutionary politics in France is not to make a statement about the nature of politics in all climes and times. The non-appearance of social class during the American Revolution can be seen as equally exemplary of American politics in the nineteenth and twentieth centuries. The lessons of class politics during the French Revolution have an applicability that is limited to those societies (mainly European) and those times (mainly the late nineteenth and early twentieth centuries) when class was discernibly the fulcrum of social and political life.

[96] A. Mathiez, *La Vie chère*, p. 107.

[97] Quoted in M. Reinhard, *Le Grand Carnot*, vol. II, p. 87.

[98] Mme de Staël, *Des circonstances*, p. 47.

[99] Quoted in R. Zapperi, 'Sieyès et l'abolition de la féodalité', *Annales historiques de la Révolution française*, vol. 44, no. 209 (July–Sept. 1972), p. 348. Or again, 'la philosophie de Sieyès . . . est la philosophie même de la Révolution française, . . .' Paul Bastide, *Sieyès et sa pensée* (Paris, 1970), p. 633.

[100] Bastide, *Sieyès et sa pensée*, p. 380.

[101] 'Je me figure la loi au centre d'un globe immense; tous les citoyens sans exception sont à la même distance sur la circonférence et n'y occupent que des places égales; tous dépendent également de la loi, tous lui offrent leur liberté et leur propriété à protéger: et c'est ce que j'appelle les *droits communs* de citoyens, par où ils se ressemblent tous.' (*Qu'est-ce-que le Tiers-état*, Zapperi, ed. (Geneva, 1970), p. 209.)

[102] Quoted in Zapperi, Introduction to *Qu'est-ce que le Tiers-état?*, p. 63.

[103] Quoted in Albert Ollivier, *Saint-Just et la force des choses* (Paris, 1954), p. 570. For a discussion of the similarities between the world views of Robespierre and Sieyes, see Bastide, *Sieyès et sa pensée*, p. 150.

[104] Barante, *Histoire du Directoire* (Paris, 1855), vol. II, pp. 449–50.

[105] It need not be emphasized that what might be called an ideological explanation of politics during either the Revolution or the Directory runs against the grain of established thinking on the issue. By and large, most historians, as Richard Cobb has satirically pointed out, see the Revolution as the alternation of a 'pas de deux' (bourgeois and nobles) with an occasional 'pas de trois' (bourgeois, nobles, and sans-culottes). Supposed and inexorable social need sets the tune here. Ideology is a cypher. Where rivalries of class are opaque, conspiracy is then presented as the missing link.

This method has been taken up even by those historians who have an interest in rejecting it. In their history of the Revolution, Furet and Richet, for example, describe a Directory that is neither fish nor fowl. The new élite, they explain, did try in 1795 to forge an alliance among all owners of property in order to give meaning to Barnave's premature verdict of 1791, 'La Révolution est finie'. But, they go on to say that no one in France really wanted such an agreement: 'It was rejected by refractory and constitutional priests, by royalists and the Directory, by La Reveilliere-Lepeaus, Reubell, Barras,' and, it seems, by everyone else as well. 'At the Beginning of 1797, a policy of conciliation has failed.' (F. Furet and D. Richet, *La Révolution française* (Paris, 1973), pp. 351–52.) Moreover, Furet and Richet also work from the importance of conspiracy and assert that one of the achievements of the Directory was, in fact, to extirpate the Anglo-royalist plotting 'by the roots'. (P. 480.)

This interpretation of the Directory, though plausible of course, is out of step with their over-all view of the *dérapage* of a French Revolution engineered by a cross-class élite, and the reader may well ask of these two authors why it was that bourgeois and nobles, who agreed in 1789 when they did not fear the poor, should have been in such dramatic disagreement in 1797 when the threat of subversion from below was on everyone's mind.

Some modern authors, it is true, are more sympathetic to the idea that there did exist in 1797 the social prerequisites of a unified moderate government. Even they, however, hesitate to deny the importance of conspiracy or to point to the bourgeoisie's ideological stance as the causes of Directorial failure. Relying on Meynier's work, M. J. Sydenham, for example, has argued that the use of force by the Directory in the late summer of 1797, 'was certainly unnecessary'. As d'André had anticipated, he explains, 'The recklessness of the extreme Right had soon alarmed the more moderate deputies, and by July, the number of potential supporters of cooperation between the Directory and the Councils was obviously increasing rapidly.' (*The First French Republic, 1792–1804*, p. 136.)

But Sydenham does not take the next, logical step. For, if what he argues is correct, some other explanation of Directorial intransigence must then be found:

if fear did not cause the Directorials to destroy the legitimacy of their regime, what did?

Here again, contemporary views are of use to us. Just as Marx and Hegel's description of Robespierre's terrorism provides the kernel of an ideological interpretation of the Revolution as a whole, so can one find in Buonarroti's *Conspiration de l'égalité* a partial explanation of Directorial politics in September 1797.

For Buonarroti, the Directory's avowed fear of plots was a fraud which was consciously used to rally moderates who feared the royalists: 'D'hypocrites apostats se répandaient dans les lieux publics pour exagérer le nombre et les tentatives des conspirateurs royalistes, détourner l'attention du peuple des crimes des faux amis de l'égalité, et les remettre en possession de sa confiance.' (Vol. I (Paris, 1957), p. 117.)

The essence of politics as Buonarroti saw it was elsewhere, not in the debate between royalists and Republicans, but in the contrast between rich and poor. Rumours of royalist plots were fabrications designed to fool the moderates and the popular left. The argument has a flaw. In Buonarroti's terms, it is difficult to see why the *faux amis de la liberté* did not themselves become avowed monarchists. Buonarroti's explanation was a condescending one: the Directorials were inside the fort and did not wish to share. This is unfair: the Republicans, in my view, did not compromise with the right because they were genuinely committed to a decaying universalism. It was ideology rather than greed that stood between them and their class allies. But Buonarroti's explanation, though lacking in some respects, has much to commend it.

NOTES TO CHAPTER SEVEN

[1] One can add here also that executions of priests and nobles had already tapered off dramatically in the first half of 1799 (see Victor Pierre, *La Terreur sous le Directoire* (Paris, 1887), p. 164), some months, therefore, before the rise to power of Bonaparte as First Consul. Like many of the most significant administrative aspects of his regime, the readmission of émigrés to the body social can be said to have had practical antecedents in the Directorial period itself.

[2] M. Bloch, 'Sur le passé de la noblesse française', *Annales*, vol. VIII, no. 40, 1936, p. 377. The varying conclusions of studies on the extent of noble property have been admirably presented by Robert Foster in his essay, 'The Survival of the Nobility during the French Revolution', *Past and Present*, no. 37, July 1967. Foster concludes that a survey of the various components of noble income leaves the reader with a rather ambiguous, imprecise picture. In short, nobles were neither ruined nor unscathed.

[3] Mme de Staël, *Considérations sur la Révolution française* (London, 1818), vol. II, p. 6.

[4] G. Lefebvre, *Histoire de la Révolution française*, p. 418.

[5] Morellet, *Mémoires*, vol. I (Paris, 1825), pp. 360–1.

[6] Roberto Unger, *Knowledge and Politics* (New York, 1975), p. 289.

[7] Quoted in Marcel Reinhard, *Nouvelle histoire de Paris: La Révolution, 1789–1799* (Paris, 1971), p. 224.

[8] Quoted in Werner Weiland, *Der Junge Friedrich Schlegel oder die Revolution in der Frühromantik* (Mayence, 1968), pp. 18–19.

[9] Quoted by l'abbé Grégoire, *Mémoires*, vol. 2 (Paris, 1837), p. 181.

[10] Castries, *La Vie quotidienne des émigrés* (Paris, 1966), p. 203.

[11] Richard Cobb, *Reactions to the French Revolution* (London, 1972), p. 133. It should also be said that some of the noblewomen who committed suicide in 1794 had more than canaries on their mind: 'Après la loi qui chassait sous trois jours tous les nobles de Paris', wrote one prisoner,

> j'ai vu arriver avec beaucoup d'autres, une jeune femme qui, depuis plusieurs jours, n'avait pris aucune nourriture; sa raison était égarée: née dans l'opulence, elle avait à peine trouvé depuis un ans dans l'ouvrage de ses mains de quoi fournir à son existence; cette loi lui ôtait tous les moyens de vivre, et n'ayant plus de ressource que la mort, elle était venue la demander en se dénonçant elle-même. Sa pâleur extrême causée par le chagrin et l'inanition, n'empêchait pas de trouver sur son visage avec un air de décence les traces de la jeunesse et de la beauté. Ses malheurs n'étaient pas encore au comble, elle devait apprendre qu'un époux adoré dont elle ignorait le sort avait péri peu de jours auparavant. Sur son acte d'accusation elle lut qu'elle était veuve . . . elle fut rejoindre son époux.

Quoted in A. des Étangs, *Du suicide politique en France depuis 1789 à nos jours* (Paris, 1860), p. 192.

[12] A. Soboul, *Histoire de la Révolution française*, vol. II, p. 168. There is an additional irony in the greater concern that some historians show for the six conventionnels, *martyrs de prairial*, than for the victims of Directorial courts. For the Montagnards, death in the name of justice had genuine grandeur: 'Les martyrs de Prairial se sont conçus comme chargés du devoir ultime et néo-stoïcien d'incarner exemplairement cet idéal républicain d'un amour de soi qui s'achève dans le dévouement total au bonheur de la cité. Cette conscience de soi politique exigeait le suicide des martyrs de Prairial. (J. Dautry, 'Nouveau Christianisme ou nouvelle théophilanthropie?' in *Archives sociales des religions*, no. 20, (July–Dec. 1965), pp. 7–29.)

In the same line, the Revolutionary speeches, and especially those of Saint-Just and Robespierre contain numerous allusions to suicide and to the metaphor of '*la ciguë*'. Death for the convinced Revolutionary had a genuinely metaphysical dimension. So did it also for convinced Catholics and royalists. But for politically indifferent and agnostic émigrés, execution made no moral sense at all.

[13] Richard Cobb, *The Police and the People* (Oxford, 1970), p. 207.

[14] Included in the 748 were 361 nobles, 104 non-nobles, 108 *chouans*, 18 priests, 5 doctors, 54 servants of émigrés, and 98 men who had previously been enrolled in the Republican army. About 5,500 other prisoners (including children who had left France before their fourteenth birthday) were spared. See G. Maréschal de Bièvre, *Les Ci-devant nobles et la Révolution* (Paris, 1914), pp. 312–13.

[15] A. Soboul, 'Georges Lefebvre, historien de la Révolution française, 1874–1959', *Annales historiques de la Révolution française*, vol. 32, no. 159 (Jan.–Mar. 1960), p. 20.

[16] Georges Lefebvre, *Études sur la Révolution française* (Paris, 1954), p. 405.

[17] Cited in M. A. Baudot, *Notes historiques sur la Convention nationale* (Paris, 1893), p. 128.

[18] In a review of Greer's book in *Annales historiques de la Révolution française*, vol. 24, no. 127 (July–Aug. 1952), p. 332.

[19] Philippe Paul de Ségur, *Histoire et mémoires* (Paris, 1873), vol. I, p. 12.

[20] Mme de Staël, *Des circonstances*, p. 37.

[21] Albert Mathiez, *Études sur Robespierre* (Paris, 1973), p. 80.

[22] Richard Cobb, *Reactions to the French Revolution* (Oxford, 1972), p. 36.

[23] B. Plongeron, *Conscience religieuse en révolution* (Paris, 1964), p. 48.

Thematic Index

Index of Names and Places

Legislators of the period are identified by the following abbreviations: C.A. = Constituent Assembly; L.A. = Legislative Assembly; Conv. = Convention; *500* = Conseil des 500; A. = Anciens; D. = Director